"The essence of Government is power; and power, lodged as it must be in human hands, will ever be liable to abuse."

— James Madison

"Sometimes it is said that man cannot be trusted with the government of himself. Can he, then, be trusted with the government of others? Or have we found angels in the forms of kings to govern him? Let history answer this question."

— Thomas Jefferson

"What is history but the story of how politicians have squandered the blood and treasure of the human race?"

— Thomas Sowell

"Is it conceivable that a newly emancipated people can soar to the heights of liberty, and, unlike Icarus, neither have its wings melt nor fall into an abyss? Such a marvel is inconceivable and without precedent. There is no reasonable probability to bolster our hopes."

— Simon Bolivar

"Money is preferable to politics. It is the difference between being free to be anybody you want and to vote for anybody you want. And money is more effective than politics both in solving problems and in providing individual independence. To rid ourselves of all the trouble in the world, we need to make money. And to make money, we need to be free."

— P.J. O'Rourke

"In this present crisis, government is not the solution to our problem; government is the problem."

— Ronald Reagan

iii

Acknowledgments

I wish to acknowledge my gratitude and debt to my colleagues at George Mason University. These friends and associates assisted me by acquiring and sending many necessary resources and materials for this book that were not available to me in Chile. I would like to thank Fred Foldvary, Eugenio Guzmán, Jerry Ellig, Tracy Harms, Randall Holcombe, Ray Harbaugh, and N. Stephan Kinsella for their review of the first edition and helpful comments on drafts or ideas pertaining to it, as well as Universidad Finis Terrae in Santiago, Chile for financing it. Finally, I would like to thank Universidad Andrés Bello for financing the second edition (Spanish translation) and for giving me leave to write it, as well as Universal Publishers for publishing the English version.

Contents

Preface

Free market economics has made many advances during the past thirty years. These advances are due to the maturing of public choice theory and empirical studies, along with a resurgence of interest in Austrian economic themes like free banking, market process entrepreneurship, and the critique of socialism and interventionism. In addition, new avenues have opened in law and economics and regulatory studies which favor free market ideas.

The purpose of this book is to introduce and summarize some of the important advances in contemporary free market economics and policy. It is written as a document to be translated, primarily for my Chilean and Latin American students who do not read well in English, but who would like to read about free market ideas from the original sources. For that reason, the English version seems a bit rough at points. And my academic colleagues will notice the oddity of having so many long quotations in the text. Having these quotations makes sense once one understands that the main purpose of the book is to provide access to translations of original sources for non-English speakers.

But the English version should nonetheless prove useful for students in *ad hoc* seminars, such as the ones I regularly conduct in Europe, Belgrade and Prague in particular, just as it would for students in classic liberal summer programs such as those offered by the Institute for Humane Studies in Fairfax, Virginia, etc. Accordingly, many free market thinkers have been cited which will help acquaint the reader with many key contributors and their contributions. The book is designed for a variety of uses:

- as a textbook in an upper-division or graduate economics elective course,
- as a textbook in an economics-based social science elective for advanced undergraduates in political science, public administration, legal studies, or public policy,
- for academics, free market advocates, policy analysts, or serious intellectual readers (with some knowledge of economics or political science) who want to gain a broad understanding of free market motifs,
- as a textbook to facilitate discussion in an MBA or law school elective course in regulation, and
- in some cases, the text could be the basis for an upper-division required trampoline course in economics or business programs, especially in universities which offer electives in public choice, Austrian economics, law and economics, regulation, and public policy.

In the latter case, a course following this book would serve as a springboard to more in-depth studies, especially when the general focus is on regulation and policy. The book is purposefully eclectic, in that it does not favor any single branch of free market theory. There are five public choice chapters (1, 2, 3, 4 and 6), five Austrian economics chapters (7, 8, 9, 10, and 11), three chapters on public policy themes (5, 12, and 15), and two chapters on law and economics (13 and 14).

There are many long quotations in some parts of the book so that students (or even a casual reader) may have some direct exposure to the theorists behind the ideas. This format should prove to be an effective teaching device, and hopefully encourage classroom discussion of the statements by the various free market theorists. Indeed, the quotations should be exploited for their full pedagogical value given that they will likely represent the lion's share of many students' direct exposure to key free market theorists—especially for student whose first language is not English. As an additional exercise, I typically require students to memorize the definitions of rent seeking, free banking, public goods, and the Coase Theorem because I think they will be useful during other courses and their academic and professional careers. I also require students to write a paper on environmental policy, using the sources brought up in chapter six as a basis, and applying their knowledge of public choice, Austrian economics, and law and economics theory.

When I teach a semester-long course covering all the topics in the text, I follow this arrangement of the material.

Chapter	Number of 90 minute classes
1	2
2	1½
3	2½
4	2
5	1½
6	1½
7	1
8	2
9	1½
10	1½
11	2
12	2
13	2
14	3
15	2

Given this system, the weights for each area of analysis are (roughly):

Public choice	34%
Austrian economics	29%
Law and economics	18%
Public policy	19%

However, there is always considerable overlap between the topics and students will usually spend more time studying outside class for the relatively copious law and economics and public policy portions.

My course also requires some outside readings, including (1) selections from newspapers and magazines which report relevant cases that can be applied to the class, I have used for example: Hillary E. MacGregor (1997), "City Process for Granting Permits Due for Overhaul Development: Many Say Winning the Right to Build Houses in Ventura Is Based On Politics and Deal-Making Rather than Good Planning," *Los Angeles Times*, Ventura County Edition, Tuesday, January 21, p. B1 (Metro), (2) <u>Highly recommended:</u> William H. McNeill (1976), *Plagues and Peoples*, Doubleday (Anchor Books): New York, pp. 1-13, 33, 40, 48, 56, 59-68, 75-76, 164-165, 196, 206-207, 216, 256-257, (3) Ludwig von Mises (1996/1949), *Human Action: A Treatise on Economics*, Fourth Revised Edition, The Foundation for Economic Education: Irvington-on-Hudson, New York, (4) George Selgin (1990), "Short-Changed in Chile: The Truth about Free-Banking Episode," *Austrian Economics Newsletter*, Winter/Spring, pp. 5-7, (5) Fred Foldvary (1994), *Public Goods and Private Communities: The Market Provision of Social Services*, Edward Elgar Publishing Co. [The Locke Institute]: Brookfield, Vermont, chapters 1 and 2, (6) Randall Holcombe (1997), "A Theory of the Theory of Public Goods," *Review of Austrian Economics*, vol. 10, no. 1, January, pp. 1-22, (7) Robert Cooter and

Thomas Ulen (1997), *Law and Economics*, second edition, Reading, Mass.: Addison-Wesley, chapters 1, 3 and 4, (8) John Robson and Owen Lippert, "Introduction: Law and Markets," chapter 1 in John Robson and Owen Lippert, eds., *Law and Markets: Is Canada Inheriting America's Litigious Legacy?*, Vancouver, B.C.: The Fraser Institute, 1998, pp. 3-10, and (9) any other material I find of interest.

1 Ideas and interest groups in public choice economics and public policy

What is public choice economics?

Consider a market negotiation, including a political decision which has economic implications, between a buyer and a seller. When a deal is concluded, there is manifested an agreed upon choice for person 1 and person 2. However, when this choice also affects person 3, or persons 4, 5, 6, 7...x, then the choice is said to be a *public* choice.

Public policy generally involves public choices. Politicians, bureaucrats, judges, lobbyists, special interest groups, and similar political actors make choices and deals, compromises and arrangements. These arrangements are distilled into legislations, rulings, and executive orders which allocate scarce resources, imposing costs on certain people and conferring benefits on others. In general, all of these choices are public choices. And public choice economics seeks to study choice and maximizing behavior found within the political process. As a concept, public choice has been absorbed into the mainstream of economic thought to some extent. But it is still considered by many to be a bit of an outcast on account of its perceived nexus with classic liberalism. Nevertheless, its logic and conclusions are both simple and powerful, and can hardly be ignored.

The hard-wrought influence of free market ideas

Never underestimate the power of ideas. An idea despised in one generation can rule the world in subsequent generations. Marxism is a good example. There has been no one since Jesus Christ and the Apostles who have had more influence on the world than Karl Marx. Even Mohammad, Einstein, Jefferson, Luther, Calvin, Beethoven, Ford and Gates have failed to penetrate every corner of the world as Marxism has done. Obviously, Marxism was embellished and spread considerably by future generations of Marxian thinkers and activists such that the twentieth century and current versions are considerably different than from what Marx himself taught.

Yet Marx was basically derided and despised in his day. He was a Jew who disdained Jews. He was an odd-looking, bushy-bearded German academic who lived off of the kindness his comrade Friedrich Engels' wealthy father in London. Who would have thought in the late nineteenth century that such a man would engender disciples that would so dramatically impact the world? And yet his ideas did influence the world. Marxian doctrine applied to twentieth century public policy resulted in the deaths of some 272 million non-combatants and the greatest destruction of the environment and private property ever known to man. Thus, one should never underestimate the power of an idea, no matter how absurd or ludicrous it may appear.

Public choice economics, along with Austrian economics, tend to be aligned with classic liberalism: small government and free markets. While their influence continues to grow, the ideas generated in these schools still tend to be disdained or ignored by mainstream neoclassical economists and policymakers. There have been several Nobel Laureates in economics from these research programs in the last 40 years: Friedrich von Hayek (1973), James Buchanan (1986), and Vernon Smith (2002). These achievements have made it harder to ignore free market theories from public choice and Austrian economics. They also add to the strong University of Chicago derived line up of Nobel laureates, whose methodology is neoclassical but whose policy conclusions tend to be similar: Milton Friedman (1976), George Stigler (1982), Robert Solow (1987), Ronald Coase (1991), Gary Becker (1992), Robert Fogel (1993), and Robert Lucas (1995). Then there is a notable line up of influential free market thinkers who did not receive a Nobel Prize, such as Ludwig von Mises, Murray Rothbard, Israel Kirzner, Gordon Tullock, Armen Alchian, Paul Heyne, Julian Simon, and many others. Obviously free market economists are not monolithic in their thought and there is often considerable, healthy disagreement between them.

Free market thought has several branches, each with distinctive methodologies and research programs. Public choice has perhaps the widest appeal, given the dissemination of ideas through the University of Chicago and George Mason University in Fairfax, Virginia, that have led to the generation of interest in other major research universities, such as University of California at Los Angeles, Rochester, Minnesota, Washington University, University of California at Santa Barbara, and numerous liberal arts colleges. Law and economics has likewise enjoyed a growing appreciation in the academy, having a particularly free market thrust in recent years, which has also impacted regulation studies. Moreover, there has been a revitalization of "Austrian" economics (named for the nationality of the school's founder and chief proponents). There are now Austrian economics programs at New York University and George Mason University, plus leading Austrian thinkers at Auburn University, the University of Georgia, University of Missouri, and Florida State University, in addition to numerous liberal arts colleges and smaller schools like Pace University, Grove City College, Hillsdale College, Universidad

Francisco Marroquín in Guatemala, Universidad San Pablo in Guatemala, and Universidad Andrés Bello in Santiago, Chile. Thus, there has been growing interest in these free market perspectives. Despite the resistance encountered by free market factions from the neoclassical mainstream, the potency of their ideas has made it impossible to ignore them. Indeed, a growing number of their ideas have been and continue to be incorporated into the mainstream of economic thought. However, they have not always been welcomed with open arms. Despite the fact that several members from these traditions won Nobel prizes during the 1970s and 1980s, those thinkers hardly enjoyed widespread repute during those decades. Nevertheless, winning Nobel prizes requires considerable scholarship. And there are a number of other widely-respected economists with substantial publication records in these schools, including Ludwig von Mises, Israel Kirzner, Murray Rothbard, Charles Rowley, Richard Wagner, Robert Tollison, Larry White, Jack High, George Selgin, Roger Garrison, and Gordon Tullock. Yet it is not always easy to be a leader of a new idea. Consider Buchanan's frustration in a statement cited by Peter Boettke.

If I am not an economist, what am I? An outdated freak, whose functional role in the general scheme of things has passed into history? Perhaps I should accept such an assessment, retire gracefully, and, with alcoholic breath, hoe my cabbages? Perhaps I could do so if the modern technicians had indeed produced "better" economic mousetraps. Instead of evidence of progress, however, I see a continuing erosion of the intellectual (and social) capital that was accumulated by "political economy" in its finest hours (Buchanan 1979, p. 279).

Boettke discusses the fate of such "brave individuals who buck the intellectual trends of their time" (Boettke

4

1997, p. 1). They pursue truth usually at great professional cost, although their contributions are often admired eventually. Indeed, perhaps the ideas contained in this book will finally achieve the full recognition they deserve in public policy and the academy—in both North and South America, as well as the rest of the world. Boettke has a favorite tale by which he warns economists and other scholars not to ignore public choice ideas.

> There is an ancient legend that has it that a Roman Emperor was asked to judge a singing contest between two participants. On hearing the first contestant, the Emperor simply gave the prize to the second under the assumption that the second could be no worse than the first. Of course, the Emperor's assumption could in fact be wrong. The second singer could have indeed been worse. The theory of market failure as developed in the 1950s committed the same mistake as the Emperor. Demonstrating that the market economy failed to live up to the ideas of a general competitive equilibrium was one thing, but to gleefully assert that public provision could costlessly correct the failure was quite another matter (Boettke 1997, p. 9-10).

Nevertheless, the worldwide Financial Crisis beginning in 2009 brought yet another attempt at using government policy to correct a perceived market failure. People's faith in the state is striking, in spite of the fact that the state has so often failed to further the so-called "public interest." Public choice attempts to explain why public policies often fail to yield the expected outcome of their designers, or why such policies were never really intended to further the public interest at all but rather some private interest.

The public choice insight of Buchanan and Tullock must be credited for changing the focus on market failure. Public choice applies economic theory to collective action, primarily government and public policy. That is because public choices are made when one person's decision is also a decision for another person. Moreover, public choice theory suggests that people are self-interested in all choices, including public choices. Accordingly, Boettke's tale reminds us about the basic symmetry between politics and the market, and the importance of letting both sides tell their story.

Public choice theory (and other free market theories) needs to be heard. Moreover, ideas are not without consequences—they can have a significant impact in directing the course of a field of study like economics, public policy, history, or political science. Watching the gradual advances of public choice theory manifests the paramount importance of ideas.[1]

The influence of ideas in academia, politics, and society

In his paper, "Economic Education and Social Change," Boettke argues that ideas still reign. He describes an "intellectual pyramid of society," in which scholars produce ideas that are distributed by policy think tanks and teachers, which are in turn passed on to the government, media, students, and businesses. Boettke's sentiment parallels that of the famous Austrian economist Ludwig von Mises, who said that most people do not have their own ideas but parrot them from others.

> Most people are common men. They do not have thoughts of their own; they are only receptive. They do

---

[1] Boettke is a leader in a younger generation of scholars and an archetype of the eclectic free market thinker. He received his graduate training at George Mason University under his mentors Buchanan and some Austrian economists. While Boettke is a distinctively Austrian theorist in terms of methodology, he also has a substantial appreciation for public choice and other free market spheres. Thus, Boettke's work is a good starting point for a compendium of free market themes like this book.

not create new ideas; they repeat what they have heard and imitate what they have seen. If the world were peopled only by such as these, there would not be any change and any history. What produces change [are] new ideas and actions guided by them. What distinguishes one group from another is the effect of such innovations. These innovations are not accomplished by a group mind; they are always the achievements of individuals. What makes the American people different from any other people is the joint effect produced by the thoughts and actions of innumerable uncommon Americans (Mises 1969/1957, pp. 191-192).

Building on Mises, Boettke suggests that while scholars are often an under-appreciated class of producers (which is especially true in places like Latin America and Africa), their contribution is the most significant of any other segment of the pyramid. Certainly both the producers and distributors of ideas are necessary, and Boettke is arguing for recognition of the integrated capital structure of ideas more than the relative importance of each branch. However, like the goose and the golden eggs, there is a cardinal value difference in some sense between the relatively scarce producers of ideas and the multitude of more easily replaced distributors of ideas. This fact holds true in spite of the existence of extraordinary distributors (creating some cardinal value distinction between them as well). And the public, which relies almost exclusively on the ideas they hear from the media, receives ideas perhaps without realizing that they ultimately come from the academy (Boettke 1992, pp. 64-65). Correspondingly, Boettke cites Keynes's famous statement about the power of ideas.

The ideas of economists and political philosophers, both when they are right and when they are wrong, are more powerful than is commonly understood. Indeed, the world is ruled by little else. Practical men, who believe themselves to be quite exempt from any intellectual influences, are usually the slaves of some defunct economist. Madmen in authority, who hear voices in the air, are distilling their frenzy from some academic scribbler of a few years back. *I am sure that the power of vested interests is vastly exaggerated compared with the gradual encroachment of ideas* [emphasis added by Boettke] (Boettke 1992, p. 66—quotation from Keynes, *The General Theory*, p. 383).

This statement serves as an excellent prologue for public choice theory, and interest group theory in particular, as we begin to consider just how powerful special interest groups (SIGs) can be. Is the power of SIGs *paramount*, even exceeding the power of ideas and those who generate them? Does SIG influence exceed the influence of the entrepreneur? According to Keynes and Boettke, interest groups are ultimately driven by ideas. It is as if a voice from the past is continually reminding the progenitors of interest groups about the ideology that drives them. Thus, it may seem that ideas are dwarfed by special interests but in reality ideas still reign.

Table 1.1 Intellectual Pyramid of Society

The intellectual pyramid of society is composed of:
(1) Generators of ideas (scarce).
↓
(2) Distributors of ideas.
↓
(3) The masses: "common men," "practical men."

Ideas vs. special interests

An extreme application of public choice economics would conclude the victory of special interests over ideas, such that SIGs now rule the world. As Boettke summarizes:

Politicians are vote seekers and most voters are rationally ignorant of the vast majority of issues—concentrating instead on those that are of special interest to them...the logic of the political process is to concentrate benefits on well-informed and well-organized interest groups, and to disperse the costs among the ill-informed and unorganized mass of voters (Boettke 1992, p. 67).

Indeed, this insight is a key implication of public choice theory. However, Boettke contends that this insight does not negate the preeminent role of ideas. Alternatively, Boettke shows that ideas produce a "climate of opinion" wherein policy activists and interest groups make decisions. Academics also retain an important role in developing appropriate rules to organize society, as well as explaining human behavior.

Boettke contends that free market ideas like public choice and constitutional economics have enjoyed considerable success in recent years, especially since the fall of the Soviet Union in 1989 and the vindication of the Austrian School. Public choice theorists have found strong empirical support for public choice theory in Western democracies too. Boettke notes that, "In many ways, free market ideas are now an acceptable part of intellectual conversation (Boettke 1992, p. 70)."

Nevertheless, special interest pressures still serve to stall reform movements and the dissemination of ideas. Boettke isolates the problem succinctly.

"The main objective of praxeology and economics," Ludwig von Mises wrote, "is to substitute consistent correct ideologies for the contradictory tenets of popular eclecticism." But such a substitution does not occur just by winning the battle of ideas. Ideas are intertwined with interests, and for the substitution of correct ideologies for false beliefs, ideas must not only be developed but must be utilized to reconstruct the basic rules of social inter-action when opportunities arise (Boettke 1992, p. 73—citing Mises, *Human Action*, p. 185).

Pariahs of economics

Boettke identifies the major "Virginia School" economic contributions of Buchanan that previously led some to con-sider his work wayward. These include a retreat from ma-thematical methods and a revitalization of moral philoso-phy that reopened a nexus for Austrian economics and modern political economy. The Austrian School has em-phasized case study and apodictic methodologies for policy and economics, rather than the static and statistical tech-niques used by mainstream theorists (see chapters 7 and 8). Austrian School and Virginia School public choice foun-ders share a common disdain for the overuse of physical science methods in economics, on account of the subjective nature of the data available to analyze human action.

For instance, Hayek emphasizes the "essentially subjec-tive character of all economic theory," where "social phe-nomena can be recognized by us and have meaning to us only as they are reflected in the minds of men" (Hayek 1979, pp. 54, 58; cf. 44, 46, 48-49, 51). Buchanan split with the more quantified Chicago tradition and adopted a similar methodology as Mises and Hayek. According to Buchanan, the goal of economics is to show "how choices are made in non-equilibrium settings will generate shifts toward equi-librium." He especially points to the subjective nature of opportunity costs and sunk costs, since "objectively-meas-ured marginal outlay is not a veritable expression of genu-ine opportunity cost" due to the subjective nature of choice, which is "a purely mental event" (Buchanan 1969, pp. 49, 50, 46, cf. 47-48).

Mises had earlier decried the trend toward mathematical economics. Traditional market-clearing equilibrium models, beyond their proper use in simple abstraction and classroom exercises for "undergraduates," are characterized by Mises as "inconceivable, self-contradictory, or unrealizable," easily resulting in "fallacious syllogisms" which spawn "sterile" diversions and distortions (Mises 1966, pp. 236, 237, 333, 350).[2] Mathematical economics, with its "constant relations," cannot describe reality, but "only a hypothetical and unrealizable state of affairs" and, consequently, it is "a useless piece of mental gymnastics" (Mises 1966, pp. 353, 354). As Boettke notes, many public choice theorists in the Virginia tradition have a similar view, although much less vituperative or extensive (mathematical methods are still used by many public choice theorists). Boettke states:

> Standard economics is trapped within a static framework that cannot deal with the important issues of political economy. As a result, modern economics seems to be losing its ability to shed light on economic problems and in the process losing the meaning of its mission (Boettke 1994, p. 245).

Economics is a philosophical science, not a physical science. Thus, equilibrium models may have some usefulness but only when one recognizes their limits. The focus should be on the process of exchange rather than maximization (Boettke 1997, p. 8). Boettke points out the major outcomes of this metamorphosis.

---

[2] Mises (1966) further contends, "What they are doing is vain playing with mathematical symbols, a pastime not suited to convey any knowledge" (p. 250). Moreover, "The mathematical method must be rejected not only on account of its barrenness. It is an entirely vicious method, starting from false assumptions and leading to fallacious inferences" (p. 350). And, "Statistics is a method for the presentation of historical facts concerning prices and other relevant data of human action. It is not economics and cannot produce economic theorems and theories" (p. 351).

Before Public Choice it was commonplace in economic theory to postulate an objective welfare function which "society" sought to maximize, and to assume that political actors were motivated to pursue that objective welfare function. The Buchanan/Tullock critique amounted to simply pointing out that (1) no objective welfare function exists, (2) that even if one existed "societies" do not choose, only individuals do, and (3) that individuals within the political sector, just as in the private sector, base their choices on their private assessment of costs and benefits. Many major insights of modern political economy flow from these three elementary propositions, including the vote motive; the logic of dispersed costs and concentrated benefits; the shortsightedness bias in policy; and the constitutional perspective in policy evaluation. Politics must be endogenous in any reasonable model of economic policy-making, and reasonable political processes are not something to be romanticized (Boettke 1997, p. 10).

The end of the romantic vision of government

Buchanan and Tullock led the way into developing public choice economics and thus dramatically undermined traditional conceptions in public policy theory and political science. As Boettke summarizes, "Buchanan burst the romantic vision of politics that dominated political science and was reflected in the mainstream economics treatment of market failure theory and public economics in general during the 1950s to 1970s" (Boettke 1997, p. 2). Concurring, Tullock, the other leading public choice thinker, describes the public choice theory of economics as the "invasion of political science by the economists" (Tullock 1988, p. 1). Public choice says that politicians and bureaucrats, far from being altruists, act as any other economic agent in the marketplace or society. As Jerry Ellig, another eclectic Austrian–public choice scholar notes:

> Government leaders respond to political pressures, regardless of the consequences for the "public interest." Government officials do so, not because they are inherently corrupt or evil, but because of the political incentives they face (Ellig 1994, p. 8).

Boettke applies the same reasoning to economic policy.

> Economic policy, therefore, can not be modeled with the assumption that government is operated by a benevolent despot. Recognition must be made of the fact that politicians, like the rest of us, are purposive actors pursuing their own self interest (Boettke 1994, p. 246).

Buchanan has also given a synopsis of the affect of public choice on economics, politics, and political science.

> What are the rewards and penalties facing a bureaucrat located in a hierarchy and what sorts of behaviour would describe his efforts to maximise his own utility? The analysis of bureaucracy fell readily into place once this question was raised. The mythology of the faceless bureaucrat following orders from above, executing but not making policy choices, and motivated only to forward the 'public interest', was not able to survive the logical onslaught [from public choice thinking]. Bureaucrats could no longer be conceived as 'economic eunuchs'. It became obligatory for analysts to look at bureaucratic structure and at individual behaviour within that structure (Buchanan 1991, p. 37).

In sum, the nature of man does not change on account of passing through the test of the ballot box or by receiving a political appointment. For years scholars in disciplines like political science and history presumed that most men who succeeded in being elected to office would reasonably be the "cream of the crop"—able to govern his fellow man with virtue—and subordinating his own self-interest motives for publicly-spirited ideals. Paradoxically, the mass of self-interested and often selfish voters would evidently elect such a virtuous man from their own dissolute ranks. Democratic processes and majority voting may thus bring about optimal social results, especially when "the voice of the people" has been heard through large voter turnouts.

Public choice economists have dispelled this romantic notion. They promote a simple but radical idea. They extended the work of Adam Smith in *The Wealth of Nations* (1776) and other economists to conclude that being elected or appointed to office does not affect man's nature. Men still pursue their own self-interest in the political arena just as men in the private sector would.

Table 1.2 Principal themes of public choice

The two fundamental ideas of public choice are:
(1) All people, including politicians, bureaucrats, and regulators, serve their own self-interest (that does *not* mean that they are selfish necessarily). The errant romantic or quixotic vision of the state is devastated by applying the fundamental self-interest doctrine of Adam Smith.
(2) The logic of *concentrating* benefits on well-informed and well-organized interest groups, and *dispersing* the costs among the ill-informed and unorganized mass of voters.

Furthermore, public choice scholars discovered a simple phenomenon of political life that can be explained with economic tools. Self-interested actors, whether they are in the private or public sector, will maximize profits by working to concentrate benefits from public revenues or beneficial regulation. The costs of these benefits are widely dispersed over millions of uninformed taxpayers and voters in society, each of which bear an insignificant part of the overall cost.

The large sums or regulatory benefits will be carefully guarded by the relatively small group on which they are bestowed, while largely ignored by the masses who stand so little to gain (in term of tax savings, for instance) by taking the time and effort to protest. The former are like flies and mosquitoes, bothersome to the latter but not worth taking too much time to stop. In other words, they impose a relatively small cost that is not worth expending a lot of effort to eliminate.

Political scientists William Mitchell and Randy Simmons have noted that economic analysis of politics has been handicapped by a popular romanticized view of government. "The problem is that few economists have applied their powerful tools for analyzing market processes to an analysis of government processes" (Mitchell and Simmons 1994, p. 35). Consequently, as Tullock summarizes, public choice analysis begins with a fundamentally different approach that is superior to traditional analyses.

For this approach, the government is not a romanticized generator of public goods or a protector of virtue but simply a prosaic [mundane] set of instruments for providing certain types of goods and services that may be hard to provide. Instead of thinking of the government as something that stands above the market, public choice theorists regard the government and the market as parallel organizations sharing a basic objective: filling the demands of the citizens (Tullock 1994, p. xiii).

Indeed, the recent "flourishing state of the field [of public choice]" (Tullock 1994, p. xiv) is testimony to the power of its conclusions. This flourishing has produced seven important research programs or ideas that comprise modern public choice theory. Each of these ideas will be considered in the following chapters of this book:

1. Intensified interest group activity (chapter 1)
2. Demosclerosis (chapter 1), related to interest group activity and vote seeking
3. Regulatory capture (chapter 2)
4. Rent seeking (chapter 3)
5. The transitional gains trap (chapter 3), related to rent seeking, perverse incentives, and vote seeking
6. Vote seeking (chapter 4)
7. Perverse incentives (chapter 6)

Interest groups and gridlock

Interest group theory

Public choice theory focuses on the impact of SIGs. Rowley, citing Wagner, suggests that, "constitutional parchment, however unanimously it was ever once endorsed, cannot be sustained if the guns of special interests are targeted uniformly against it. Property rights that define thine and mine are not easily maintained even by the minimal state" (Rowley 1993, pp. 52, 88).[3] Constitutional parchment may not be very stalwart when it must contend with the guns of special interests. As Mitchell and Simmons potently summarize:

---

[3] Rowley is citing Richard E. Wagner (1987), "Parchment, Guns and the Maintenance of Constitutional Contract," in C. K. Rowley, ed., *Democracy and Public Choice: Essays in Honor of Gordon Tullock*, Basil Blackwell: Oxford, pp. 105-21; Richard E. Wagner (1988), "Agency, Economic Calculation and Constitutional Construction," in C. K. Rowley, R. D. Tollison and G. Tullock, eds., *The Political Economy of Rent-Seeking*, Kluwer Academic Publishers: Boston, pp. 423-446; and Richard E. Wagner (1993), *Parchment, Guns and Constitutional Order*, Shaftesbury Paper Number 3, Edward Elgar Publishing: Aldershot and Brookfield, Vermont.

Public choice scholars have shown that governments do not easily fix market failures; they usually make things worse. The fundamental reason is that the information and incentives that allow markets to coordinate human activities and wants are not available to government. Thus, voters, politicians, bureaucrats, and activists who believe themselves to be promoting the public interest are led by an invisible hand to promote other kinds of interests (Mitchell and Simmons 1994, p. 39).

They describe these other kinds of interests as the "small groups who benefit from government expenditures [who] have more incentives and cheaper means of organizing than do the diffused taxpayers" (Mitchell and Simmons 1994, p. 49). So voters prefer to contribute to powerful interest groups who then do a more efficient and effective job of influencing politicians. Mitchell and Simmons have summed up the situation circumspectly.

Rational citizens in pursuit of private desires quickly learn the superiority of organized groups over individual pursuit of welfare through the ballot box. By organizing into an interest group, voters can pursue their goals with great efficiency. The interest group provides a division of labor, specialization, and the power of concentrated passion and incentives. Surely, by coordinated effort, two people can lift more than the sum of what each might lift independently (Mitchell and Simmons 1994, p. 62).

Interest groups do not...seek public goods for the nation but more private goods for themselves that could not be gained in the private economy. [They] seek to have income and wealth distributed to themselves. And because hundreds of billions of dollars can be redistributed, interest groups are only too willing to make political investments of a substantial magnitude (Mitchell and Simmons 1994, p. 63).

The political process not only promotes inefficiency but is skewed to advance the interests of those who are better off (Mitchell and Simmons 1994, p. 81).

William Shughart adds the following synopsis of the basic tenets of interest group theory.

Public policymakers are not benevolent maximizers of social welfare, as assumed by the market failure model, but are instead motivated by their own self-interests...Thus, the interest-group theory is not a theory about how government should work, but rather it is a theory about how government does work, based upon the application of the tools of positive economic science to the analysis of political choices (Shughart 1990, p. 37).

It [interest-group theory] applies to any situation in which the monopoly power of the state can be mobilized selectively to benefit one group at the expense of others (Shughart 1990, p. 38).

Moreover, the private gains realized by those who receive transfer payments from the government are far less than the cost incurred by society. But this fact is of no great concern to any economic actor who subordinates collective interests to his own interests. Thus, individuals and firms find it profitable to form SIGs that can make "good" use of the political process machinery for its members' benefit.

Furthermore, there is a benefit available for "brokers" of wealth transfers in the process; that is, the lobbyists, politicians, bureaucrats, and suppliers who profit, by pecuniary or other means, from interest group activity. In this sense, regulation and antitrust policies can be viewed as benefiting their own constituencies by securing direct wealth transfers or indirect gains by erecting barriers to entry. In addition, a firm may be able benefit handsomely if the services of a public law enforcement agency can be used against competitors or potential entrants, and the firm is thus able to transfer the cost of litigation to taxpayers (see Shughart 1990, pp. 41, 43, 46, 48). As Tollison argues, this brokering is done through legislative and regulatory processes.

In the interest-group theory, the supply of legislation is an inverse demand curve. Those who "supply" wealth transfers are individuals who do not find it cost effective to resist having their wealth taken away. In other words, it costs them more than one dollar to resist having one dollar taken away. This concept of a supply curve of legislation or regulation suggests that costs of political activity to some individuals exceed the potential gains (or avoided losses). The supply of legislation is, therefore, grounded in the unorganized or relatively less-organized members of society. Who runs this supply-demand process? The individuals who monitor the supply-demand process are politicians, bureaucrats, and other political actors. These individuals may be conceived of as brokers of legislation, and they essentially act like brokers in a private context—they pair demanders and suppliers of legislation (Tollison 1988, p. 343).

Interest group theory can be examined from the perspective of both capture theory (with antitrust applications) and rent seeking. The former theory considers the benefits firms obtain by capturing the vehicles of regulation, while the latter theory considers opportunities for individuals or firms to use the political process to create artificial scarcity (and thus demand for their services or products). The next two chapters consider each of these perspectives in succession.

Demosclerosis

The flurry of interest group activity leads to other public choice phenomena. Jonathan Rauch has written extensively about *demosclerosis*: the mistaken perception that the political process is gradually collapsing into apparent gridlock as a result of special interest group pressures, when in fact political actors respond so quickly to competing pressures that the movement from one policy to another is not perceived. The idea was first promoted by Mancur Olson to explain what Rauch calls "government's gradual collapse into manic [uncontrolled] maladaptation" (Rauch 1996, p. 18). The apparent gridlock in the political process caused by interest group pressures is a misperception. Actually, Rauch thinks that American politics and government are anything but in a condition of gridlock. "American politics has never been more responsive, indeed more capricious, than it is now. Washington has never been more eager to react to every passing electoral mood" (Rauch 1996, p. 17).

Rauch's idea of demosclerosis is simply an extension and application of the public choice theory of concentrated benefits and dispersed costs. SIGs work very hard to retain antiquated programs and as a result they never get cut. The fact that reform is popular will not likely cause a change. This stagnation is especially true when vote-seeking politicians prefer not to cut programs that will upset a block of voters represented by special interests.

As the economist Mancur Olson has shown, society inherently generates goody-hunting, demand-making interest groups (lobbies basically) much faster than it gets rid of them. The lobbies stream to Washington seeking to win and then defend some subsidy, regulation, or tax break. The more eagerly government scrambles to keep everybody happy, the less able it is to pluck these barnacles from its sides. So it succumbs to a kind of living rot...Stuck with all of its first tries [at various regulations or programs] virtually forever, government loses the ability to end unsuccessful programs and try new ones. It fails to adapt and, as maladaptive things do, becomes too clumsy and incoherent to solve real-world problems (Rauch 1996, p. 18, cf. Mitchell and Simmons 1994, pp. 53, 76).

One important implication of Rauch is that special interest groups tend to become permanent fixtures; entrenched in their objective capacity to influence government. The solution is to (1) put pressure on entrenched lobbies by exposing them to competition via trade and deregulation and (2) get rid of many government programs, thereby freeing captured resources and also defunding the lobbies that capture them (Rauch 1996, p. 18).

Summary of main public choice insights

In sum, basic public choice insights challenge the naive view of government, and question the veracity of the popular notion that "markets can row but government must steer" (Mitchell and Simmons 1994, p. 34). These insights include the vote-seeking motive, the rational ignorance of voters, demosclerosis, the role of SIGs (with rent seeking and capture theory), perverse incentives, and the constitutional imperative.[4] Each of these insights provides theoretical and/or empirical support for the theory of public choice. Shughart provides this synopsis:

> As James Buchanan artfully defined it, public choice is "politics without romance." The wishful thinking it displaced presumes that participants in the political sphere aspire to promote the common good. In the conventional

---

[4] That is, the distinction between policy within politics or policy as examination of the rules, where policy within politics is analogous to post-constitutional analysis and its concern is with self-interested strategies.

"public interest" view, public officials are portrayed as benevolent "public servants" who faithfully carry out the "will of the people." In tending to the public's business, voters, politicians, and policymakers are supposed somehow to rise above their own parochial concerns.

In modeling the behavior of individuals as driven by the goal of utility maximization—economics jargon for a personal sense of well-being—economists do not deny that people care about their families, friends, and community. But public choice, like the economic model of rational behavior on which it rests, assumes that people are guided chiefly by their own self-interests and, more important, that the motivations of people in the political process are no different from those of people in the steak, housing, or car market. They are the same human beings, after all. As such, voters "vote their pocketbooks," supporting candidates and ballot propositions they think will make them personally better off; bureaucrats strive to advance their own careers; and politicians seek election or reelection to office. Public choice, in other words, simply transfers the rational actor model of economic theory to the realm of politics.

Two insights follow immediately from economists' study of collective choice processes. First, the individual becomes the fundamental unit of analysis. Public choice rejects the construction of organic decision-making units, such as "the people," "the community," or "society." Groups do not make choices; only individuals do. The problem then becomes how to model the ways in which the diverse and often conflicting preferences of self-interested individuals get expressed and collated when decisions are made collectively.

Second, public and private choice processes differ, not because the motivations of actors are different, but because of stark differences in the incentives and constraints that channel the pursuit of self-interest in the two settings. A prospective home buyer, for example, chooses among the available alternatives in light of his personal circumstances and fully captures the benefits and bears the costs of his own choice. The purchase decision is voluntary, and a bargain will be struck only if both buyer and seller are made better off. If, on the other hand, a politician proposes a project that promises to protect the new homeowner's community from flooding, action depends on at least some of his neighbors voting for a tax on themselves and others. Because the project's benefits and costs will be shared, there is no guarantee that everyone's welfare will be improved. Support for the project will likely be forthcoming from the owners of houses located on the floodplain, who expect to benefit the most. Their support will be strengthened if taxes are assessed uniformly on the community as a whole. Homeowners far from the floodplain, for whom the costs of the project exceed expected benefits, rationally will vote against the proposal; if they find themselves in the minority, they will be coerced into paying for it. Unless the voting rule requires unanimous consent, which allows any individual to veto a proposal that would harm him, or unless those harmed can relocate easily to another political jurisdiction, collective decision-making processes allow the majority to impose its preferences on the minority. Public choice scholars have identified even deeper problems with democratic decision-making processes, however (Shughart 2008).

An example supporting public choice: Arrow's theorem

Perhaps one of the most fundamental examples of theoretical support for public choice is provided in the following application of Arrow's Impossibility Theorem. Three people are to vote on how to allocate a scarce piece of land.

They are asked, "Should the land be used as a school, a park, or a garage?" Let S = school, P = park, G = garage.[5] The three voters have the following preference scales:

Person 1: S > P > G
Person 2: P > G > S
Person 3: G > S > P

So if there is pair wise voting, then

S vs. P → S wins 2 to 1
P vs. G → P wins 2 to 1

Following the law of transitivity (if A > B and B > C then A > C) we would expect that if we run S vs. G that S would win. However, in this case G wins 2 to 1, meaning that the law of transitivity is violated (because S > P and P > G *but* G > S). Moreover, the rationality of the political process is brought into question and, consequently, the theory of public choice is vitalized. As Shughart explains:

It has been recognized at least since the time of the Marquis de Condorcet (1785) that voting among three or more candidates or alternatives may fail to select the majority's most preferred outcome or may be prone to vote "cycles" producing no clear winner. Indeed, Kenneth Arrow's "impossibility theorem" shows that there is no mechanism for making collective choices, other than dictatorship, that translates the preferences of diverse individuals into a well-behaved social utility function. Nor has any electoral rule been found whose results cannot be manipulated either by individuals voting insincerely—that is, casting their ballots strategically for less-

---

[5] Adapted from Boettke's overview lecture on public choice at *Liberty & Society— Academic*, a seminar sponsored by the Institute for Humane Studies, Belmont, California, 1995. Also cf. Mitchell and Simmons 1994, pp. 77-78.

preferred candidates or issues in order to block even worse outcomes—or by an agenda setter who controls the order in which votes are taken (Shughart 2008).

Indeed, through his impossibility theorem (developed in 1950), Arrow had shown that the idea of optimizing social welfare could only work by authoritarian imposition.

If we exclude the possibility of interpersonal comparisons of utility, then the only methods of passing from individual tastes to social preferences which will be satisfactory and which will be defined for wide range of sets of individual orderings are either imposed or dictatorial (Rowley 1993, p. 8).[6]

However, Rowley points out that this fact has hardly deflected "leading contributors to social choice theory from social engineering ventures which Hayek has termed 'synoptic delusion'" (Rowley 1993, p. 9, cf. pp. 18, 19).[7] Rowley traces the history of attempts to deflect the strong implication of Arrow: "Scientists as well as moral philosophers not infrequently will clutch at straws to protect their own programmes from logical devastation" (Rowley 1993, p. 14). Thus, there remains much work to do in public choice and in other free market research programs if the errant trends within a rather ossified social science paradigm and its resulting interventionist policies are to be curtailed.

---

[6] Quoting Kenneth J. Arrow (1950), "A Difficulty in the Concept of Social Welfare," *Journal of Political Economy*, Vol. 58, p. 342.

[7] Rowley sees the intrusion of constructivist rationalism, part of what Sowell calls the "unconstrained vision," as the key problem of modern welfare economics and the implications drawn from it. Conversely, the "constrained vision," which champions methodological individualism, can be traced through the writings of scholars such as David Hume, John Locke, Adam Smith, Alexander Hamilton, Edmund Burke, Carl Menger, Ayn Rand, Mises, Hayek, and Buchanan. Man can be expected to behave well not because he is perfected but because of the egocentric constraints of his nature.

For class discussion

With their theories of self-interest and SIGs, economists not only broke with traditional political science theories, they have also challenged received views of history. (1) Were the black slaves in antebellum America generally treated as badly as depicted in Harriet Beecher Stowe's *Uncle Tom's Cabin* (1853)? What were the views of economists Robert Fogel and Stanley Engerman in *Time on the Cross: The Economics of American Negro Slavery* (1995/1974) regarding the efficiency of slavery? (2) The pre-Railroad United States relied largely on canals across the Appalachian range to connect the eastern seaboard with the Mississippi and Tennessee valleys. Who provided the manual labor to build the canals in the South? (3) What can we learn from public choice insights regarding SIGs and self-interest with regard to these institutions and events?

References

Boettke, Peter J. (1992), "Economic Education and Social Change," in John W. Robbins and Mark Spangler, eds., *A Man of Principle: Essays in Honor of Hans F. Sennholz*, Grove City College Press: Grove City, Pennsylvania, pp. 63-74.

Boettke, Peter J. (1997), "James M. Buchanan and the Rebirth of Political Economy," in Steve Pressman, and Ric Holt, eds., *Against the Grain: Economic Dissent in the 20th Century*, Edward Elgar: Brookfield, Vermont. (Note: the quotations were taken from the manuscript version, New York University, 1996).

Boettke, Peter J. (1994), "Virginia Political Economy: A View from Vienna," in Peter J. Boettke and David L. Prychitko, eds., *The Market Process: Essays in Contemporary Austrian Economics*, Edgar Elgar: Brookfield, Vermont.

Buchanan, James M. (1969), *Cost and Choice: An Inquiry in Economic Theory*, University of Chicago Press: Chicago.

Buchanan, James M. (1991), "Private Preferences to Public Philosophy: The Development of Public Choice," in James M. Buchanan, *Constitutional Economics*, Basil Blackwell: Cambridge, Massachusetts.

Buchanan, James M. (1979), *What Should Economists Do?*, Liberty Press: Indianapolis, Indiana.

Ellig, Jerry (1994), "The Economics of Regulatory Takings," in Roger Clegg, ed., *Regulatory Takings*, National Legal Center for the Public Interest: Washington, D.C.

Gunning, J. Patrick (2003), *Understanding Democracy: An Introduction to Public Choice*, Nomad Press: Taiwan, details available from http://www.nomadpress.com/public_choice/.

Hayek, Friedrich A. von (1979), *The Counter-Revolution of Science: Studies in the Abuse of Reason*, Liberty Press: Indianapolis, Indiana.

Mises, Ludwig von (1966/1949), *Human Action: A Treatise on Economics*, Third Revised Edition, Contemporary Books, Inc. (Henry Regnery Co.): Chicago.

Mises, Ludwig von (1969/1957), *Theory and History: An Interpretation of Social and Economic Evolution*, Arlington House: New Rochelle [first edition by Yale University Press: New Haven, Connecticut].

Mitchell, William C., and Simmons, Randy T. (1994), *Beyond Politics: Markets, Welfare, and the Failure of Bureaucracy*, Westview Press: San Francisco, California.

Rauch, Jonathan (1996), "Eternal Life: Why Government Programs Won't Die," *Reason*, vol. 28, no. 4 August–September, pp. 17-21.

Rowley, Charles K. (1993), *Liberty and the State*, The Shaftesbury Papers, 4, Edward Elgar Publishing Co.: Brookfield, Vermont.

Shughart, William F. II (1990), *Antitrust Policy and Interest-Group Politics*, Quorum Books: New York.

Shughart, William F. II (2008), "Public Choice," *The Concise Encyclopedia of Economics* (Library of Economics and Liberty), retrieved on March 4, 2009 from http://www.econlib.org/library/Enc/PublicChoice.html.

Tollison, Robert D. (1988), "Public Choice and Legislation," *Virginia Law Review*, vol. 74, no. 2, March, pp. 339-71.

Tullock, Gordon (1994), "Foreword," in William C. Mitchell, and Randy T. Simmons, *Beyond Politics: Markets, Welfare, and the Failure of Bureaucracy*, Westview Press: San Francisco, California.

Tullock, Gordon (1988), *Wealth, Poverty, and Politics*, Basil Blackwell: New York.

2 Capture theory and antitrust

The essential research implications of public choice

Public choice theory contributes to social science research and policy analysis with some straightforward, profound tenets. First, public choice applies economic theory to collective action, primarily government and politics. Second, public choices are made when A's decision is also a decision for B, and/or vice versa. Third, as is typical in economics in general, public choice theorists argue that people are self-interested in all choices, including public choices. Fourth, while retaining neoclassical economic tenets of individual welfare maximization in the analysis of public choices, public choice derives far different hypotheses than otherwise. Public choice begins with the neoclassical axiom of subjective individual wealth maximization, but it departs from the neoclassical tradition by endogenizing government or, more generally, collective action, as a means to increase or decrease wealth. Hence, what remains is a rivalrous or even a dichotomous means for achieving well-being.[8]

---

[8] Summary from email messages by Ed Lopez (August 28th and September 4th 1996).

Building on these tenets, one of the major public choice insights became *the logic of concentrated benefits and dispersed costs*, which effectively demonstrates the conflict between good politics and good economics. Thus, the myopic bias in policy making is highlighted. Policymakers prefer short term and easily identifiable benefits at the expense of long term and largely hidden benefits. They also prefer costs that are long term and/or not easy to identify, e.g., deficit finance, inflation, "takings,"[9] etc.).

Mitchell and Simmons point out that government regulation is not all that it is cracked up to be by mainstream social scientists, planners, and policy analysts. They contend that allowing free markets is the best means to attain socially-beneficial ends.

[W]elfare economists see government as merely a means to achieving the normal ends of consumption and utility maximization. That is, it facilitates the allocation of resources desired by consumers...The solution to these perceived ills [caused by corporate manipulations and "incorrect" values generated by the market against the common interest]...is the expansion of government... [However], government is not the frictionless plug welfare economists blindly propose as a means of stopping the losses caused by markets...Instead of being "government by the people," politics is often an intense competition for power to benefit particularized interests at the cost of wider society. Instead of politics ennobling participants, it promotes myth making, suppression and distortion of information, stimulation of hatred, and legitimation of envy...The solution from the Left and the Right is straightforward—elect, appoint, or hire honest, well-trained people and government will function

---

[9] Regulatory "takings" are the noncompensated reduction in a real property's value (up to 90%) due to a proactive policy or a judicial ruling which restricts the land's use.

smoothly, efficiently, and fairly. Our analysis is entirely different. It exposes the problems of government as being far greater than those that might be caused by incompetent or grasping political actors. A government and polity composed entirely of saints would produce results approximating those we currently get from admittedly imperfect political participants. These problems will continue unless the rules of the game are changed...Recognizing the failures of government to promote widely shared values must be accompanied by a renewed acceptance of markets, property rights, and prices (Mitchell and Simmons 1994, pp. 211, 212, 213).

Public choice analysis of monopoly and antitrust

Public choice insights naturally led to a new understanding of monopoly creation. Tollison and Wagner argue that monopoly can be either "accidental" or "intentional," although they mainly use the former as a heuristic contrivance. They suggest that most (if not all) monopoly is "something that people seek intentionally, as through investing in legislative favors" (Tollison and Wagner 1991, p. 58). Indeed, beginning with Tullock, economists have treated monopoly as intentional, "in that it results from people trying to acquire monopoly positions" (Tollison and Wagner 1991, p. 61) via *rent seeking* (see chapter 3). Rent seeking is a term coined by public choice economists which describes the practice of seeking private benefits (e.g., favorable legislation, subsidies, or government funding) from democratically elected governments through legal and politically viable avenues such as lobbying or bidding on (and competing for) concessions. These activities result in a net loss of social welfare.

Tollison argues that antitrust theory has a weak foundation because it "rests on the public interest theory of government" where "judges and antitrust bureaucrats are assumed to operate in the public interest" (Tollison 1985, p. 905). In order to correct this deficiency, Tollison tries to "achieve a positive understanding about how antitrust decision makers behave" (Tollison 1985, p. 906). In the end, he embraces a very different perspective than policy scholars and planning models traditionally provided. Tollison describes the impact of public choice in policy research.

"Public choice" refers to a revolution in the way government is analyzed. Before public choice, government was treated as exogenous to the economy, a benign corrector of the market economy when it faltered. After public choice, the role of government in the economy became something to be explained, not assumed. As a result of the public choice revolution, economists now place government failure alongside market failure as a useful category of analysis. What is public choice? I advance my own particular answer to the question. Public choice is an expansion of the explanatory domain of economic theory. Traditional economic analysis uses the apparatus of economic theory to explain the behavior of individuals in private settings. Public choice represents the use of standard economic tools (demand and supply) to explain behavior in nonmarket environments, such as government. This expansion of economic theory is based on a simple idea. Individuals are the same people whether they are behaving in a market or nonmarket context (Tollison 1985, p. 906).

The hypothesis is simply that individuals promote their self-interest in all environments or circumstances. Thus, the idea that markets are guided by private interest while government is guided by public interest is merely a fantasy (Tollison 1985, p. 907). All government action, or public policy, is guided by private interests and utility-maximizing individuals who use the notion of public interest to cover the real interests involved. Hence, pursuing the so-called public interest, no matter how well-intentioned, is merely a ruse to mislead the public or voters into accepting legislation, executive orders, and judicial rulings that further well-disguised private interests. Monopoly power grants and the supposed means to break it—antitrust regulation—are prime examples of this phenomenon.

Table 2.1 Monopoly problems

Monopoly power arises by two means:
(a) *accidentally* or from market failures, and/or
(b) *intentionally* or from government failures.
Monopoly can be either short term (normal and beneficial) or long term (abnormal and damaging)

With respect to antitrust cases, Tollison wondered why antitrust bureaucrats repeatedly prosecute the same firms (about 25% of all antitrust action is for repeat offenses). Perhaps the bureaucrats are minimizing costs, or maybe offenders find it worthwhile to violate repeatedly. He noted that in studying the organizational behavior of antitrust branches of the U.S. government, Katzman found "that the desire to gain trial experience biases FTC lawyers toward shorter and less complicated initiatives as opposed to the FTC economists" who want longer and more complex ones (Tollison 1985, p. 909).[10] Thus an incentive existed to prefer repeat prosecution. Tollison went on to cite other evidence that antitrust enforcement has little nexus with the traditional economic conception of social welfare. In fact, there is evidence "that antitrust is at least partly a veil over a wealth-transfer process fueled by certain relevant interest groups" (Tollison 1985, p. 910, 911).

---

[10] Citing R. A. Katzman (1980), *Regulatory Bureaucracy: The Federal Trade Commission and Antitrust Policy*, MIT Press: Cambridge, Massachusetts.

Antitrust policy is usually rational from a public choice perspective, inasmuch as it can purposefully provide a buffer against losses when demand for a firm's products falls. Indeed, it is rational since it can be used as a means for interest groups to benefit. Given that the apparatus of the political process makes benefits available, it is rational that cost minimizing economic actors will seek to use those means to enhance profit maximization. Quite often, doing so is best facilitated by directing regulation with the organizational efficacy and efficiency of SIGs.

Capture theory

Given the economic incentives available to producers, it is likely that they will form interest group coalitions to "use the apparatus of public regulation for their own gain" (Shughart 1990, p. 38). They can "capture" their regulators and procure benefits derived from regulation. By concentrating benefits into special interest groups that seek beneficial regulation, while dispersing the costs of the regulation over a wide range of consumers or taxpayers, they are able to direct the regulatory process. Such analysis falls under the public choice classification known as "capture theory." Shughart summarizes some of the benefits available.

As a result of its lobbying advantage, industry can therefore often successfully use the political process to secure for itself such regulatory favors as direct cash subsidies, control over the entry of new rivals, restrictions on the outputs and prices of complimentary and substitute goods, and the legitimization of price-fixing schemes (Shughart 1990, p. 38).

With the romanticized view of the state destroyed by Buchanan and Tullock, economists in the Chicago School, notably George Stigler and Sam Peltzman, began to develop congruent theories of regulation that matched the new view of political actors. As Stigler argued, policies can be recognized as originating to benefit private interest groups, perverting any public interest origins since the policy-makers have been captured by politically proficient groups. At its origins, it is plausible that economic regulation was sought by firms in order to use the political process to increase profits, while passing the costs to taxpayers and consumers. But in contemporary society, policy-makers are aware of the advantages of managing, selling, and distributing political favors. Thus, they too can use regulation for political gains. Moreover, Mitchell and Simmons point out that professed legislative or regulatory reform movements may simply be means for legislatures to reload discharged favors, and thus benefit politicians who are able to provide more goodies and so attract industrial customers.

The enactment of [tax] rate reductions, elimination of loopholes, and simplification of rate schedules in fact support our analysis. Congressional politicians have in effect wiped the slate clean so that they may once more "auction" off tax exemptions and other privileges. (Mitchell and Simmons 1994, p.58)

A simple capture is costless to political actors in the sense that it merely requires a policy maker to grant political favors, as if with a stroke of his magic wand. Peltzman improved capture theory by modeling the tradeoffs legislators face between gains in political support (from granting favors) and losses in political support (from explicitly or implicitly taxing other groups). A crucial implication is that the losing groups are not taxed as much as the winning groups would like (i.e., as would maximize their political profits)." Regulators can be captured by a firm or industry exercising undue influence on the policies of the regulators, even by selecting or controlling the regulators themselves.[11]

Table 2.2 Means of regulatory capture

Two means of capturing regulators:
(1) Suggest and create a *new* committee which favors a firm or industry, or
(2) Influence or buy (even bribe) a current committee in order to achieve the same thing.

Chicago School work in regulatory theory

Although generally supportive of regulation and antitrust policies, Chicago school economists actually pioneered what would become the essential criticism of such regulation. Stigler argued that "regulation is acquired by the industry and is designed and operated primarily for its benefit" (Stigler 1971, p. 1). In fact, regulation may be viewed as either a resource or a threat to any industry. It may provide *defense* against both market forces and harmful rent seeking activities by other actors, or *offense* against a firm's present or potential competitors. Stigler noted four particular policies which are sought by industries or firms.

- Cash subsidies for firms or complimentary industries.
- The erection of barriers to entry against rivals.
- The suppression of substitutes for its own products.
- Price fixing—e.g., preventing payments for special services or price controls in order to foster higher than competitive returns.

However, Stigler also noted three elements of the political process which limit the effectiveness of industries or firms in seeking these things.

---

[11] Some of these ideas adapted from Edward Lopez, supra.

- Dispersion of political power in the market, notably small firms in regulated industries have more political power than they otherwise would.
- Bureaucratic red tape makes such actions costly and time consuming.
- Powerful outside interests add to the policy process.

Stigler states: "The industry which seeks political power must go to the appropriate seller, the political party... [which] has costs of operation...The industry which seeks regulation must be prepared to pay with the two things a party needs: votes and resources" (Stigler 1971, p. 12). Stigler later considered the political benefits available from industrial interest groups, as Tollison summarizes:

> Stigler suggested that an asymmetry of firm sizes, products, and interests in an "industry" tends to promote more effective collective action by the industry (e.g., a larger association budget). He argued that participation is mandated by the desire to protect specialized industry interests (Tollison 1988, p. 342).[12]

Peltzman built on Stigler's premise, noting that his theory may be used to determine broadly "the optimum size of political coalitions" and highlighting the fact that a small group with a large per capita stake will dominate large groups with diffused interests (Peltzman 1976, p. 212). He concludes:

> The central question for the theory then becomes to explain this regularity of small group dominance in the regulatory process (and indeed in the political process generally). The way the question is posed already fore-

---

[12] Citing George J. Stigler (1974), "Free Riders and Collective Action: An Appendix to Theories of Economic Regulation," *Bell Journal of Economics and Management Science*, vol. 5, p. 359.

shadows one of the results of the theory. For in Stigler's model, unlike most market models, there are many bidders, but only one is successful. There is essentially a political auction in which the high bidder receives the right to tax the wealth of everyone else, and the theory seeks to discover why the successful bidder is a numerically compact group. The answer lies essentially in the relationship of group size to the costs of using the political process (Peltzman 1976, p. 213).

Peltzman went on to create a formal mathematical model of regulation (building on Stigler's basic model), in which he shows that the "supply-demand apparatus can be converted into a constraint on regulatory behavior" (Peltzman 1976, p. 240). Some of his more significant implications include: (1) regulation being weighted toward consumers during expansions and producers during depressions, (2) that producer protection will lead to consumer protection over time, (3) that profitable regulated firms will tend to have the lowest prices, (4) that regulation reduces systematic and diversifiable risk, and (5) that regulators have an incentive to limit entry by restricting new firms who would cater to low-cost customers but to be more tolerant of new firms who will tend to suppress differences in the elasticity of demand (Peltzman 1976, pp. 226-232, 235-239).

Such earlier work provided theoretical support for public choice tenets that would be developed in the late twentieth century. They presented a new way of looking at regulation.

Antitrust origins

Stigler argues that a political market exists for regulatory action (Stigler 1975, pp. x, xi). According to public choice theory, firms have an incentive to capture their regulators, which is in fact what occurs.

Indeed, historically, regulation has its roots in private industry rather than the efforts of shrewd legislators (High 1991, p. 1). Hence, it is plausible that rent seeking produces regulation in order to promote private interests at taxpayer expense (High 1991, p. 2). There is evidence that certain businesses benefited from regulation in the nineteenth century, strategically using public policy to capture regulators and thus retain considerable control over the regulatory process (High 1991, pp. 6-8). As Tollison notes, the costs of regulation become a mechanism for driving out marginal competitors (High 1991, pp. 10, 17—quoting Tollison).

Subsequently, economists began to analyze the origins of antitrust theory apart from the romanticized, public interest theory of government. In the United States, federal antitrust began with the Sherman Act in 1890. In an important historical survey, Thomas DiLorenzo provides evidence that the Sherman Act may not have been in the public interest. The antitrust laws served private interests and were antithetical to competition and economic efficiency. In fact, these laws were a major source of monopoly power (DiLorenzo 1985, pp. 73-74). The business conglomerates allegedly receiving monopoly power were known as *trusts*.

However, the trusts, which were subjected to considerable political scrutiny resulting in the imposition of the Sherman Act, were from industries that "were expanding much faster than the economy as a whole, a phenomenon that has been overlooked by those who adhere to the standard account of the origins of antitrust" (DiLorenzo 1985, p. 80). It seems that some pertinent data had been missed or ignored. Some congressmen knew that the Sherman Act was not in the public interest. But they supported it anyway out of fear of "political backlash." The public interest angle was merely a ruse of public policy.

Actually, businesses seem to have benefited from antitrust legislation over time, which has served to protect them from competition more than curtailing monopoly power (DiLorenzo 1985, p. 81). Indeed, "it was government regulation itself that was the source of monopoly power" but "the average voter has little or no financial incentive to discover the true costs of protectionism" given the logic of concentrated benefits and dispersed costs (DiLorenzo 1985, p. 82). Even the *New York Times*, which had been a supporter of antitrust legislation initially, changed its mind after considering the Sherman bill's proponents. "It is not unlikely that the Sherman Act was passed to help draw public attention away from the actual process of monopolization in the economy [via government privilege], among the major beneficiaries of which have always been the legislators themselves" (DiLorenzo 1985, p. 83). In summarizing his study, DiLorenzo notes:

It is held as an article of faith by most economists that the Sherman Antitrust Act is a guarantor of competitive markets. Even though it is now widely held that the enforcement of the Sherman Act over the past 95 years has probably reduced industrial competitiveness, there is faith that the original intent of the Sherman Act was to promote competition in an increasingly monopolized economy. The evidence, however, indicates otherwise. The trusts of the late nineteenth century caused output to expand even faster than the rest of the economy—in some cases more than ten times faster for decades at a time. As a result, prices in the allegedly monopolized industries were *falling*. This was even acknowledged by the critics of the trusts in Congress, who complained that falling prices drove less efficient "honest men" out of business. There was relatively little enforcement of the Sherman Act for at least ten years after it was passed, but it did serve to immediately divert attention from a more certain source of monopoly, tariffs, which were sharply increased just three months after passage of the Sherman Act by a bill sponsored by Senator Sherman himself. Interestingly, the great majority of economists of the day viewed competition as a dynamic process and thought that mergers (formal or informal) facilitated social coordination. There was no substantial support among economists for the Sherman Act, even from the most severe critics of *laissez-faire* such as Richard T. Ely...Even though modern economics embodies an "efficiency" rationale for the Sherman Act, that rationale was never used to make a case for the original enactment of the law. Rather, it was constructed, *ex post*, as a rationalization for a law that already existed. Moreover, it appears that the efficiency rationale for antitrust has often been used by legislators as a justification for protectionist policies. Legislators have always had incentives to enact protectionist legislation, and the economics of antitrust has sometimes provided intellectual support for these objectives (DiLorenzo 1985, p. 87).

While the historical evidence of falling prices and rising output does not necessarily conclude (on account of the possibility of strong positive demand and supply shifts) that there was no monopoly power among the trusts prior to the Sherman Act, it is surely strong corroborating evidence. Classifying the Act as a public choice phenomena enacted to benefit private interests at public expense must certainly be a credible judgment.

DiLorenzo and High further extended this thesis by suggesting that acceptance of the perfect competition model actually drove acceptance of Sherman by twentieth century economists. Most economists around the time of the Act were opposed to it. They believed that the existence of profits would automatically limit monopoly durability and so legislation was unnecessary. However, those economists held a view of rivalrous competition, similar to the Austrian School's conception of rivalry, rather than the form found in static competitive models. Using such perfect competition models, standard monopoly power can be found in most industries.

Austrian economists have long been keen to repeal the Sherman Act, especially in light of their view of analyzing competition as dynamic rivalry rather than pinpointing properties of equilibrium in a static model (DiLorenzo and High 1988, pp. 424, 425). As noted in chapter one, ideas have a powerful influence over economists and policymakers, as well as social phenomenon, over time. Thus, the widespread acceptance of modern antitrust legislation has much to do with the acceptance of static ideas about competition. This change in economic theory has caused a dramatic change in policy analysis in the last century.

The judgment of professional economists regarding intervention to promote competition has changed dramatically in the last two centuries. Economists at the time of Sherman were "doubtful of the necessity of antitrust laws" and "objected to trust-busting," recognizing the efficiency value of the process of competition (DiLorenzo and High 1988, pp. 428, 429). But this thinking was abandoned later in the twentieth century as the model of perfect competition grew to hold preeminence in microeconomic theory.

Once perfect competition was accepted as the idea benchmark, economists concluded that most markets were inherently monopolistic. It was not that markets themselves had become less competitive; it was that the *idea* of competition had changed. This logically led to endorsement of antitrust law as a cure (DiLorenzo and High 1988, p. 431).

DiLorenzo and High conclude that the perfectly competitive model has misled the economics profession, at least in terms of antitrust policy. They suggest that competition as rivalry, held by both nineteenth century economists and modern Austrian economists, provides a better understanding of competition (DiLorenzo and High 1988, pp. 433, 432).

Shughart also investigated the antitrust statutes and disputes the notion that they were "a public-spirited effort on the part of their framers to limit the extent of monopoly power in the economy" (Shughart 1990, p. 11). The first antitrust legislation occurred in Maryland (1867). The policy expanded to other states, and eventually to the federal level. Both Shughart and Stigler argue that popular conceptions of the Sherman Act are seriously incomplete. However, Shughart criticizes Stigler's assumptions.

Stigler's analysis of the origins of the Sherman Act is flawed by the fact that he assumes throughout that the statute was intended to promote competition. This presumption leads him to use the term "potential monopoly" as a synonym of "large" and perhaps more efficient enterprises rather than in the proper sense of firms having the power to restrict output and raise prices (Shughart 1990, p. 15).

Furthermore, Stigler went so far as to say, "I like the Sherman Act." He deemed it a veritable public interest law.[13]

Shughart goes on to discuss the development of key cases which apply the Sherman Act. He shows that it was more of an act of social policy than of economic efficiency—sort of an economic engineering endeavor. Courts have rarely been concerned with whether firms have actually restricted competition, as evidenced especially in *Addyston Pipe & Steel*, *Standard Oil*, and *Brown Shoe* (see

---

[13] See DiLorenzo 1985, p. 74, citing T. Hazlett (1984), "Interview with George Stigler," *Reason*, vol. 46, January.

chapters 13 and 14). Indeed, economic variables seem to have had little influence on the Antitrust Division of the United States government in recent decades (Shughart 1990, pp. 18-30).[14]

Overall, then, antitrust enforcement does not appear to be predictable on the basis of social welfare criteria. The empirical evidence indicates that the antitrust agencies do not select cases to prosecute on grounds of their potential net benefit to consumers...Likewise, various studies have found that the mergers challenged by government are generally not anticompetitive...In short, there is little or no credible evidence suggesting that the actual effects of antitrust comport with the effects implied by the model of the "public interest." Scholars and policymakers have typically responded to such findings in the past by calling for closer adherence to economic principles in the future, but it is time to abandon this tired rhetoric. The absence of systematic support for the idea that the consumers are the beneficiaries of antitrust provides firm ground for rejecting the hypothesis that they were the intended beneficiaries. Indeed, because it requires that all failures of policy be explained by error or ignorance, the consumer interest theory of antirust is no theory at all. A rethinking of antitrust is clearly in order, but not with the conventional tools of welfare economics (Shughart 1990, p. 30).

Furthermore, McChesney concludes that private interests are mainly served by antitrust regulation:

In a series of studies done in the early 1970s, economists assumed that important losses to consumers from limits

---

[14] The case citations are *U.S. v. Addyston Pipe & Steel Co.*, 85 F. 271 (6th Cir. 1898); *Standard Oil Co. v. U.S.*, 221 U.S. 1 (1911), and *Brown Shoe Co. v. U.S.*, 370 U.S. 294 (1962). Shughart provides a lucid critique of antitrust via these cases.

on competition existed, and constructed models to identify the markets where these losses would be greatest. Then they compared the markets where government was enforcing antitrust laws with the markets where governments *should* enforce the laws if consumer well-being was the government's paramount concern. The studies concluded unanimously that the size of consumer losses from monopoly played little or no role in government enforcement of the law. Economists have also examined particular kinds of antitrust cases brought by the government to see whether anticompetitive acts in these cases were likely. The empirical answer usually is *no*. This is true even in price-fixing cases, where the evidence indicates that the companies targeted by the government either were not fixing prices or were doing so unsuccessfully. Similar conclusions arise from studies of merger cases and of various antitrust remedies obtained by government; in both instances, results are inconsistent with antitrust's supposed goal of consumer well-being.

If public-interest rationales do not explain antitrust, what does? A final set of studies has shown empirically that patterns of antitrust enforcement are motivated at least in part by political pressures unrelated to aggregate economic welfare. For example, antitrust is useful to politicians in stopping mergers that would result in plant closings or job transfers in their home districts. As Paul Rubin documented, economists do not see antitrust cases as driven by a search for economic improvement. Rubin reviewed all articles written by economists that were cited in a leading industrial organization textbook (Scherer and Ross 1990) generally favorable to antitrust law. Per economists' evaluations, more bad than good cases were brought. "In other words," wrote Rubin, "it is highly unlikely that the net effect of actual antitrust policy is to deter inefficient behavior...Factors other than a search for efficiency must be driving antitrust policy"

(Rubin 1995, p. 61). What might those factors be? Pursuing a point suggested by Nobel laureate Ronald Coase (1972, 1988), William Shughart argued that economists' support for antitrust derives considerably from their ability to profit personally, in the form of full-time jobs and lucrative part-time work as experts in antitrust matters: "Far from contributing to improved antitrust enforcement, economists have for reasons of self-interest actively aided and abetted the public law enforcement bureaus and private plaintiffs in using the Sherman, Clayton and FTC Acts to subvert competitive market forces" (Shughart 1998, p. 151) (McChesney 2008).

Other social losses from milking and damage abatement

All long term monopoly power is a function of sustained benefits accrued from public policy. Some groups have been especially proficient in maintaining legislative favors. For instance, Mitchell and Simmons point out the fact that labor unions are an example of government-mandated monopoly.

For decades, they [labor unions] have been awarded a special status in the law permitting them to benefit in ways not permitted other organizations, especially private firms...although monopoly tendencies exist in the free market, the chief form of monopoly is found in government-mandated labor unions. If there is a role for antitrust laws, perhaps they ought to be applied to labor organizations (Mitchell and Simmons 1994, p. 200).

Milking

However, there are also back-door or indirect profits possible in the political process, and political actors can avail themselves of these benefits. Fred McChesney notes that when political actors are placed in power, they also gain the curious *right* to impose (or threaten) costs on economic actors, and thus extract booty from them. Public choice economists are not surprised that such phenomena occur.

> Because political action can redistribute wealth generally, it is now seen that private interest groups other than producers also have an incentive to organize, both to obtain the gains and to avoid the losses from a whole menu of government actions…Political office confers a property right, not just to legislate rents, but to impose costs (McChesney 1987, pp. 101, 102).

Most academics understand that McChesney is simply using a euphemism for theft with his rhetoric about rights to impose costs. He contends that "existing estimates of the welfare costs of government regulation overlook the costs of inducing government *not* to regulate" (McChesney 1987, p. 103). He also notes euphemisms for threats of robbery, such as *milking*. "Milked victims describe the process simply as blackmail and extortion" (McChesney 1987, p. 108). The desire by victims to avoid being milked (or violated) by political actors often leads to economic distortions and game playing. McChesney explains:

> With any given firm or industry, producers and politicians may be locked in a "chicken" game: since legislators seemingly gain nothing if they actually destroy private capital, capital owners may be tempted to call politicians' bluff by refusing to pay. But a politician's demonstrated willingness actually to expropriate private rents in one situation provides a lesson for other firms or industries that will induce them to pay in their turn. To make credible expected later threats to destroy others' capital, politicians may sometimes have to enact legisla-

tion extracting private rents whose owners do not pay. (And... legislators can always enact statutes now and sell repeal later.) (McChesney 1987, p. 109).

The social costs of games like capturing regulators, avoiding being milked, and rent seeking are not always recognized as substantial, especially by those who cling to the naïve view of government. Yet these activities impose considerable social losses as political favors are sought by firms or industries.

If expected political rents net of the costs of organizing and procuring favorable legislation are positive, then producers will demand—pay for—regulation. Deadweight consumer loss is measured by the welfare triangle. Producers stand to gain the rent rectangle, but political competition for it produces additional social loss from rent seeking (McChesney 1987, p. 109).

Compensating legislators not to intervene

However, seeking rents is costly, and rents can be reduced or destroyed by government intervention. For instance, politicians can mandate minimum quality or information standards and then send agents to police the market for quality and truth (McChesney 1987, p. 113).

By requiring and policing seller disclosure of warranty and defect information, government would have substituted for sellers' investments in quality-assuring reputation. Rather than suffer the capital losses that regulation would entail, firms predictably would—and did [in the American used car industry]—compensate legislators not to intervene (McChesney 1987, p. 115).

In this case, an industry sought damage abatement, distorting private investment decisions. Political actors benefited merely by threatening costs, rather than by offering a favor or goody (McChesney 1987, pp. 116-117). McChesney notes that this often overlooked aspect of political action is an integral part of the theory of public choice. Indeed, "the problems of political opportunism and the imperfections of private-capital protection create disincentives or capital owners to buy off legislators. Yet several instances have been presented here in which private actors in fact have paid significant sums to induce government not to impose costs." These costs must be added to the costs of deadweight loss, rent seeking, compliance with regulation, and "diversion of resources to less valuable but unregulated uses." Thus, he concludes, "There is no such thing as a free market" (McChesney 1987, p. 118).

For class discussion

Many institutions and things are sacred in Western culture. One example is nationality (citizenship) and passports—at least in advanced societies in North America and Western Europe. They are said to belong to a person but he is not permitted to sell them. (1) What regulation prohibits a person from selling them? Does it create monopoly power? (2) Who benefits from the restriction? (3) What would happen if selling them were made legal? Would it have efficient results? Might a stereotypical poor Negro woman living in the slums of Washington, D.C. be better off selling her citizenship to a wealthy (but hated) white South African man (for $1 million) who wants to live in America, and then taking her proceeds and retiring in Guatemala? (4) Might the restriction be lifted if governments were paid a commission to allow the transfer of citizenship? Does one government fear competition from another government for its citizens? (6) What can we learn from public choice insights regarding these things? (7) Would you be willing to sell your citizenship and passport if it were legal? If so, what would your minimum price be?

References

DiLorenzo, Thomas J. (1985), "The Origins of Antitrust: An Interest-Group Perspective," *International Review of Law and Economics*, vol. 5, pp. 73-90.

DiLorenzo, Thomas J. and High, Jack C. (1988), "Antitrust and Competition, Historically Considered," *Economic Inquiry*, vol. 36, July, pp. 423-435.

Higgins, Richard S., and Tollison, Robert D. (1988), "Life Among the Triangles and Trapezoids: Notes on the Theory of Rent-Seeking," in Charles Rowley, Robert Tollison, and Gordon Tullock, eds., *The Political Economy of Rent-Seeking*, Kluwer Academic Publishers: Boston, pp. 147-157.

High, Jack C., ed. (1991), *Regulation: Economic Theory and History*, University of Michigan Press: Ann Arbor, Michigan.

McChesney, Fred S. (2008), "Antitrust," *The Concise Encyclopedia of Economics* (Library of Economics and Liberty), retrieved on March 5, 2009 from http://www.econlib.org/library/Enc/Antitrust.html.

McChesney, Fred S. (1987), "Rent Extraction and Rent Creation in the Economic Theory of Regulation," *Journal of Legal Studies*, vol. 16, January, pp. 101-118.

Mitchell, William C., and Simmons, Randy T. (1994), *Beyond Politics: Markets, Welfare, and the Failure of Bureaucracy*, Westview Press: San Francisco, California.

Peltzman, Sam (1976), "Toward a More General Theory of Regulation," *The Journal of Law and Economics*, vol. 19, no. 2, August, pp. 211-240.

Shughart, William F. (1990), *Antitrust Policy and Interest-Group Politics*, Quorum Books: New York.

Stigler, George J. (1975), *The Citizen and the State: Essays on Regulation*, University of Chicago Press: Chicago.

Stigler, George J. (1971), "The Theory of Economic Regulation," *The Bell Journal of Economics and Management Science*, vol. 2, no. 1, spring, pp. 1-21.

Tollison, Robert D. (1985), "Public Choice and Antitrust," *Cato Journal*, vol. 4, no. 3, winter, pp. 905-916.

Tollison, Robert D. (1988), "Public Choice and Legislation," *Virginia Law Review*, vol. 74, no. 2, March, pp. 339-371.

Tollison, Robert D., and Wagner, Richard E. (1991), "Romance, Realism, and Economic Reform," *Kyklos*, vol. 44, no. 1, pp. 57-70.

3 Rent seeking

The theory of rent seeking

Up to this point, Tullock's contribution to public choice has only been lightly touched upon. However, he is clearly one of the leading public choice theorists. In addition to his early work with Buchanan, he is probably best known for his seminal insights into the theory of *rent seeking*, which David Henderson points out would be more accurately labeled *privilege seeking* (Henderson 2008). Indeed, rent seeking is perhaps one of the foremost advances in economics over the last fifty years.

Tullock defines rent seeking as "the manipulation of democratic [or other types of] governments to obtain special privileges under circumstances where the people injured by the privileges are hurt more than the beneficiary gains" (Tullock 1993, p. 24, cf. p. 51). Rent seeking is a natural outcome of the political process, especially in democratic nations. Special interest groups seek political favors and politicians seek reelection primarily (although cash seeking does play some smaller role) (Tullock 1993, p. 31). As Arnold Harberger elaborates:

Rent seeking also occurs when something of value (like import licenses or radio/TV franchises) is being given away or sold below its true value. In such cases potential buyers often spend large amounts "lobbying" to improve their chances of getting the prize. Indeed, a broad view of rent seeking easily covers most cases of lobbying (using real resources in efforts to gain legislative or executive "favors") (Harberger 2008).

Table 3.1 Rent seeking

Definitions of rent seeking from Tullock and Buchanan:
(1) Tullock defines rent seeking as "the manipulation of democratic [or other types of] governments to obtain special privileges under circumstances where the people injured by the privileges are hurt more than the beneficiary gains."
(2) Buchanan says that "the term *rent seeking* is designed to describe behavior in institutional settings where individual efforts to maximize value generate social waste rather than social surplus."

As Boettke points out, "The problem, as Mancur Olson argued in his *Rise and Decline of Nations*, is that as political stability occurs, entrenched interests form which, eventually, through their rent-seeking activity, retard the further economic development of a country" (Boettke 1992, p. 71). Then as the condition of demosclerosis becomes more pervasive and critical, rent seeking develops into part of the normal course of business. Firms begin to see various taxes, both explicit and implicit (i.e., via regulation, liability rulings, takings, inflation, etc.) as normal expenses, along with the increased expense of hiring professionals to minimize these implicit taxes. Thus, they seek means to secure rents from the political process that either offset or exceed the tax expense. Once an economy is inundated by rent seeking, the level of distortion in the economy and the level of resource misallocation will be so high that it will be hardly possible to measure the social costs of rent seeking.

Some evidence of the historical tenacity of rent seeking

Rent seeking effectively grants monopoly power to the successful seeker. Wealth is transferred from consumers to these firms or special interests, with the legislator, bureaucrat, or third party broker receiving a commission from the boodle. Remarkably, while rent seeking has reached unprecedented levels today, it has been a problem previously, especially among democratic societies. Consider the comments of French politician Frederic Bastiat in 1850, which might be considered a forerunner to public choice theorists.

The law has been used to destroy its own objective [to serve as a defense of life, liberty, and property]: It has been applied to annihilating the justice that it was supposed to maintain; to limiting and destroying rights to which its real purpose was to respect.

This fact [that force is entrusted to those who make the law], combined with the fatal tendency that exists in the heart of man to satisfy his wants with the least possible effort, explains the almost universal perversion of the law...instead of checking injustice [it] becomes the invincible weapon of injustice...This is done for the benefit of the person who makes the law, and in proportion to the power he holds...the few practice legal plunder on the many...

It is impossible to introduce into society a greater change and a greater evil than this: the conversion of the law into an instrument of plunder.

As long as it is admitted that the law may be diverted from its true purpose—that it may violate property instead of protecting it—then everyone will want to participate in making the law, either to protect himself against plunder or to use it for plunder.

The person who profits from this law will complain bitterly, defending his *acquired rights*. He will claim that the state is obligated to protect and encourage his particular industry; that this procedure enriches the state because the protected industry is thus able to spend more and to pay higher wages to the poor workingmen. Do not listen to this sophistry by vested interests. The acceptance of these arguments will build legal plunder into a whole system. In fact, this has already occurred (Bastiat 1990/1850, pp. 9, 11, 12, 18).

Hence, public choice problems are not new. Those whose consciences normally would not permit them to steal from their neighbors are pacified when a law sanctions the plunder.

Moreover, since some people are using the law for their profit at the expense of others, many others are determined to do likewise. "Thus, the beneficiaries are spared the shame, danger, and scruple which their acts would otherwise involve...the law benefits one citizen at the expense of another by doing what the citizen himself cannot do without committing a crime" (Bastiat 1990/1850, pp. 13, 17, 20-21). Sometimes the plunder is purely a matter of the profit motive and other times its true motivation is disguised by a layer of false philanthropy. Furthermore, Bastiat argues that as "government failure" becomes wide-spread as a result of government fostering legal plunder (i.e., rent seeking), the inevitable result will be revolution, just as there have been relatively frequent revolutions in France. Therefore, politics must receive an education from economics. As Bastiat said, "A science of economics must be developed before a science of politics can be logically formulated" (Bastiat 1990/1850, pp. 66, 67, 71).

Table 3.2 Objectives of a rent seeker

Two goals of a rent seeker:
(1) To create monopoly power, or
(2) To create artificial scarcity.

Rent seeking as positive science: three levels

Public choice theory is positive science, and as such it is not interested in accusing rent seekers of committing crimes. However, what Bastiat argues is compelling, and is congruent with public choice theory in the sense that he recognizes the natural tendency of men to use the political process for their own gain. It is not that some men are particularly evil and thus they seek rents, but because the natural course for any person, either in business or in politics, is to avail himself of profitable opportunities. The fact that Bastiat points out this very thing over a century prior to the advent of public choice theory demonstrates both his insightfulness and the fact that rent seeking problems have been pervasive and onerous. As Buchanan notes, the existence of rent seeking today should come as no surprise to economists.

Rent is that part of the payment to an owner of resources over and above that which those resources could command in any alternative use. Rent is a receipt above opportunity cost...So long as owners of resources prefer more to less, they are likely to be engaged in rent seeking, which is simply another word for profit seeking...The term *rent seeking* is designed to describe behavior in institutional settings where individual efforts to maximize value generate social waste rather than social surplus...As institutions have moved away from ordered markets toward the near chaos of direct political allocation, rent seeking has emerged as a significant social phenomenon (Buchanan 1980, pp. 46, 47).

Buchanan goes on to explain his understanding of rent seeking. While entrepreneurs and innovators can secure short-lived monopoly benefits in the market, they are quickly dissipated in the absence of barriers to entry as others rush to capture the potential profits. In other words, competition is a natural check against long term monopoly. However, the one who obtains monopoly power via rent seeking causes a long term and socially distortive loss in consumer welfare.

Suppose that, instead of discovering a new commodity or service or production process, an innovating entrepreneur discovers a way to convince the government that he "deserves" to be granted a monopoly right, and that government will enforce such a right by keeping out all potential entrants. No value is created in the process; indeed, the monopolization involves a net destruction of value. The rents secured reflect a diversion of value from consumers generally to the favored rent seeker, with a net loss of value in the process...*Rent seeking*...refers to...the activity motivated by rent but leading to socially undesirable consequences (Buchanan 1980, pp. 50, 51).

A larger public sector will produce greater amounts of rent seeking and vice versa. When rent seeking occurs, it serves to create artificial scarcity—that is, demand for products that would not otherwise exist at such levels (Buchanan 1980, pp. 52, 53). Yet rent seeking can take different forms. Buchanan identifies three levels of rent seeking (Buchanan 1980, pp. 56, 57).

- Lobbying for government-sanctioned privileges.

- Excessive waste of resources for training and for campaigns to advance bureaucrats and politicians to positions with better salaries or more power.
- Attempts by special interests to secure political favors or abatement of threatened costs by regulation.

Normative vs. positive rent seeking analysis

Tollison adds that monopoly rights may be given to rent seekers by (1) venality, e.g., bribery, (2) selling the monopoly right to the highest bidder and giving government officials control over them, likely leading to higher wages for them as a result, or (3) selling it the same way but then dispersing the booty to increase expenditures or cut taxes (Tollison 1982, pp. 578-579). However, Tollison argues that rent seeking is not always analogous to profit seeking, and that rent seeking has both positive and normative elements.

The theory of rent seeking involves the study of how people compete for artificially contrived transfers. Like the rest of economic theory, rent seeking has normative and positive elements. Normative rent-seeking theory refers to the specification and estimation of the costs of rent-seeking activities to the economy…The positive side of rent-seeking is directed to the question of what explains the sources of contrived rents in society (Tollison 1982, p. 576).

Table 3.3 Levels of rent seeking

Three levels of rent seeking (Buchanan):
(1) lobbying for government-sanctioned privileges,
(2) excessive waste of resources for training and for campaigns to advance bureaucrats and politicians to positions with better salaries or more power, and
(3) attempts by special interests to secure political favors or abatement of threatened costs by regulation.

Normative analysis focuses on competition for rents, consumer reactions, the types of government (if any) necessary to foster rent seeking, and imperfections that might exist to cause efforts to capture monopoly positions to "exceed or fall short of the rents that inhere [occupy] them." Positive analysis focuses on the effects of monopoly power gained from rent seeking, and "goes behind the facade of microeconomic theory and attempts to explain why some sectors of the economy are sheltered and some not" (Tollison 1982, p. 576).

Rent seeking may be distinguished from profit seeking because the rent seeking operation creates "artificial scarcity" by the state and thus monopoly profits are available to be captured. Yet, "aspiring monopolists employ no real resources to compete for the monopoly rents...these expenditures create no value for a social point of view. It is this activity of wasting resources in competing for artificially contrived transfers that is called rent seeking" (Tollison 1982, p. 577). Accordingly, a link is made with the Austrian idea of competition as rivalry and the dynamic market process driven by entrepreneurship. As Tollison remarks:

> When competition is viewed as a dynamic, value-creating, evolutionary process, the role of economic rents in stimulating entrepreneurial decisions and in prompting an efficient allocation of resources is crucial [Kirzner 1973]. 'Rent seeking' or 'profit seeking' in a competitive market order is a normal feature of economic life (Tollison 1982, p. 577).[15]

For instance, the desire to obtain rents will deflect lawyers from otherwise normal pursuits, and thus create disequilibrium in the supply of lawyers that will subsequently lead to

---

[15] Also congruent with Austrian thinking, Tollison notes that "advances in economics do not naturally have to flow from a highly mathematical or statistical approach to the subject." pp. 597-598.

"excessive entry into the legal profession." Therefore, "such rent-seeking costs must be added to the standard welfare-triangle loss associated with monopoly to obtain an estimate of the total social costs of monopoly and regulation" (Tollison 1982, p. 578). Consequently, "rent-seeking analysis tends to magnify the problem of monopoly power over and beyond the traditional measurements made by Harberger..." (Tollison 1982, p. 582).

Tollison, concurring with Peltzman's implication, contends that the costs to consumers from rent seeking are not inconsequential, as "a vote-maximizing regulator trades-off industry price and profits between consumer and producer forces" (Tollison 1982, p. 582). The cost of rent seeking monopolization is thus increased by "the cost of rent-seeking by producers *as well as* any blocking investment made by consumers" (Tollison 1982, p. 583). Since consumers face an upward sloping supply curve, they will have an interest in "forming a buyers' cartel in order to monopsonize against producers" (Tollison 1982, p. 584).

The social cost of monopoly and regulation in this formulation is a variable which is related to the behavior of regulators who set political prices. Past behavior of the regulatory agency is important since it influences the formation of expectations by those affected by the regulatory process. These expectations determine the optimal level of resources that the parties will devote to the 'monopolization-demonopolization' process. It stands to reason that attempts to extract rents will be fought by affected parties unless such a contest is deemed futile. Thus, while the conventional result that rent-seeking expenditures are socially wasteful stands, the extent of such welfare losses is related to the nature of the institutional environment in which rent-seeking takes place (Tollison 1982, p. 584).

Tollison adds that most rent seeking is imperfectly competitive, an idea best developed in Tullock's work on efficient rent seeking which "shows the potential complexity of rent-seeking games" (Tollison 1982, p. 585, 586). Tullock also addresses such games in his book *Rent Seeking* (Tullock 1993, pp. 62-65).

Rent seeking costs or problems and rent dissipation

There are a number of costs and problems which complicate rent seeking. The principal-agent problem is an important consideration once both political actors and voters are viewed as wealth maximizers. It is not easy to control the behavior of the agent and thus it is not likely to "always comport with the interest of the principal." Indeed, "political agents face different constraints than private agents because their principals (e.g., voters and stock-holders) face different incentives to control the behavior of their agents" (Tollison 1982, p. 589). Not only is complaining about rent seeking behavior inefficient for the typical, rationally ignorant voter, it is further complicated by the misalignment of values implicit in the principal-agent problem.

Table 3.4 Social losses from rent seeking and monopoly

Three social losses from rent seeking besides the deadweight monopoly loss (i.e., the Harberger triangle), that do not represent a mere utilitarian transfer include: (1) "paperwork contests" that dissipate the Tullock rectangle, (2) the displacement of workers from the productive sector to the public sector, and (3) the rise in consumer prices due to monopoly power, complicated by the principal-agent problem.

Compounding this problem, Gary Becker suggests that as pressure groups actively try to raise their political influence which in turn leads to considerable competition between groups on account of the scarcity of obtainable rent.

The political budget equation between the total amount raised in taxes and the total amount available for subsidies implies that the sum of all influences is zero, which has a significant effect on the competition among pressure groups (Becker 1983, p. 395).

Producing pressure efficiently involves controlling free riding among members, and thus increasing the optimal subsidy or tax reduction available to the rent seeker. "Policies that raise efficiency [that is, lower deadweight costs] are likely to win out in the competition for influence because they produce gains rather than deadweight costs, so that groups benefited have the intrinsic advantage to groups harmed" (Becker 1983, p. 396). Subsequently, government favors to pressure groups are determined by a competitive process. The separation of ownership and control in the principal-agent problem gives government "significant political power" (Becker 1983, p. 396). However, Tullock contends that Becker's analysis is partly defective.

Becker, who wrote a very good article on interest group competition (Becker 1983) in which he pointed out that the result of certain groups pushing for special privileges and other groups counter-pressuring to avoid being victimized should lead to a balance which is at least arguably some kind of political equilibrium, failed to emphasize the rent-seeking cost of this exercise (Tullock 1993, p. 31).

As previously noted by Tollison, public choice extends the traditional or utilitarian conception of social deadweight costs as proposed by Harberger. Tollison and Wagner suggest that, from a utilitarian perspective, the transfer of benefit from consumers to a monopolist poses no social cost beyond the normal deadweight losses. But Tullock contends that the rent seeker will spend up to that additional portion of benefit in his quest to acquire a monopoly position. Thus, while consumers still pay the higher price, a portion of the captured benefit has been dissipated in the process of seeking the monopoly position. As shown in Figure 3.1, the costs of the intentional monopoly sought via rent seeking equal the deadweight costs *plus* the entire amount of potential monopoly benefit spent by interest groups that compete for it (Tollison/Wagner 1991, pp. 60-61).

Figure 3.1: Rent seeking and deadweight social losses

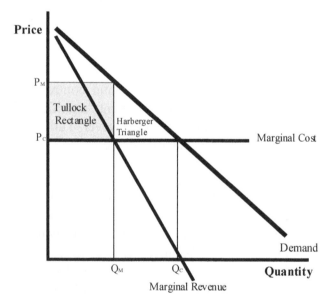

Likewise, reforming active monopolies that result from rent seeking are costly. The gains from making them competitive will be partly offset by the costs associated with the resistance by the monopolist, and Tollison and Wagner conclude that in some cases it may be best for utilitarian reformers to "leave existing deformities alone" (Tollison and

Wagner 1991, pp. 63-64). Conversely, they find that there is some consumer surplus available to successful consumer-oriented reformers after monopoly price and output are set. Thus, there may be some effective counter-rent seeking to capture back a portion of which was taken by the rent seeking monopolist and, as a result, the size of the dead-weight loss triangle will be diminished. Accordingly, Tollison and Wagner argue that seeking to reform monopolies (which are usually intentional results of rent seeking rather than accidental) "may be justified from a factional or private-interest perspective, but not from a utilitarian or general interest perspective" (Tollison and Wagner 1991, p. 66). In addition:

> [R]eform itself is, at least for the most part, an activity *within* the rent-seeking society. Reformist activity is profitable to those who undertake it, but this is only because reformers do not have to take into account the costs that their activities impose on monopolists, who must step up their defensive activities as the reformers increase the intensity of their agitation. There would be little investment in reform, at least of the backward-looking sort, in a utilitarian or general-interest world (Tollison and Wagner 1991, p. 67).

Richard Higgins and Tollison suggest that rents may not always be dissipated, especially in the case of venality or in wining-and-dining political actors where the rents are merely transferred to them. But rents can be dissipated by other things like "paperwork contests" whereby rent seekers expend all the potential gains trying to demonstrate that they are the most worthy recipient of the rent (Higgins and Tollison 1988, p. 150-151). Moreover, from the point of view of a politician:

> [T]o the extent that the method of assigning monopoly rights by politicians resembles exchange, rents are *not*

dissipated. Moreover, the value of holding office is, in general, proportional to the efficiency of the assignment mechanism in controlling rent dissipation (Higgins and Tollison 1988, p. 151).

Thus, politicians have an interest in minimizing dissipation and thus maximizing potential gain. To the extent that dissipation occurs there is a social loss, which Higgins and Tollison say is understated by simply looking at welfare triangles.

In the extreme, when all rent is dissipated, the social cost of monopoly is the Harberger triangle plus the Tullock rectangle. Thus, for a given average degree of rent dissipation, the overall social cost of monopoly rises as the amount of government monopoly rises in society. Moreover, as the degree of dissipation rises, the social cost of a given amount of monopoly will rise (Higgins and Tollison 1988, p. 152).

Concurring, Tullock offers this comment about the welfare loss from monopoly.

Even when a monopoly is established, continual efforts to break it up or to muscle into it would be predictable, once again involving a considerable investment of scarce resources. Such attacks would induce the monopolist to invest resources in defense of its monopoly powers. The welfare triangle method of measurement ignores these important costs and hence greatly underestimates the welfare loss of monopoly. Evidently, the 'Tullock rectangle' must be added, in whole or in part, to the 'Harberger triangle' when calculating the potential loss of welfare associated with monopoly (Tullock 1993, p. 10).[16]

---

[16] Also see a similar explanation of welfare losses from cartels due to rent seeking in Mitchell and Simmons 1994, p. 103.

Transitional gains and permanent losses

Tullock says that there are "transitional gains" made available to a favored interest group when government establishes special privileges. Obtaining this rent is quite a feat, since manipulating the government is difficult—even the most potent organized pressure group cannot completely control it. Worse yet, the transitional gains obtained by the initial rent seekers are similar to bait in a trap. New entrants into an affected market only receive normal profits, but "surviving original owners have opportunity costs equivalent to the price of the entry barrier and consumers are worse off" (Tullock 1975, pp. 671-675).[17] After the transitional gains have been dissipated, there is both a deadweight social loss and many people who will lose considerably by ending the program originally established through rent seeking. (They have invested capital in the privilege.) Thus, reform is costly since it may well require compensating those who would be harmed. As Tullock describes:

> It is certainly true that this type of institution [fostered by rent seeking] is very widely found in our society and the social cost is great. It is also true that, in general, the benefits are now long in the past. They were transitional benefits at the time the institution was first founded. As of now, there is no one who is positively benefiting from the organization and there is a large dead-weight loss. However, there is [*sic*] a large number of people who would suffer large transitional costs if the institution were terminated. These transitional costs in many cases are large enough so that compensation of the losers would impose upon society an excess burden which

---

[17] Noting that the medallions required to drive New York City taxis, former blue laws (prohibiting commerce on Sunday), and labor unions are examples of the trap.

would be of the same order of magnitude as the cost of the present institution. (Tullock 1975, p. 677)

In a recent restatement of the trap, and implying the relationship between rent seeking and demosclerosis (without mentioning it specifically), Tullock remarks:

> The problem posed by the transitional gains trap is the ratchet-like nature of rent seeking. Once a rent has been successfully sought out through government lobbying, it is very difficult to remove even after it has ceased to produce positive profits for its rent-seeking beneficiaries. Its elimination almost always implies losses for those who now exercise the privilege. To avoid such losses, they will rent seek yet again to retain the privileges. Politicians are rightly reluctant to inflict direct losses on specific sections of the electorate—inevitably a vote-losing strategy (Tullock 1993, p. 68).

Accordingly, vote seeking politicians have little incentive to eliminate the residual costs from transitional gains acquired by prior rent seeking. The average voter or citizen likewise has little incentive to work to remove the relatively small dispersed cost, and the prior rent winners (or successive owners) have a considerable incentive to maintain the *status quo*. Tullock suggests that the best solution to this problem is to simply simultaneously abolish all the privileges to everyone, but he admits that action would be politically unlikely. Thus, perhaps with dour conciliation, he offers this advice.

> The moral of this, on the whole, depressing tale is that we should try to avoid getting into this kind of trap in the future. Our predecessors have made bad mistakes and we are stuck with them, but we can at least make efforts to prevent our descendants from having even more such dead-weight losses inflicted upon them (Tullock 1975, p. 678).

Rent seeking's effect in economic development and social cost

Tullock suggests that the expropriation from consumers and taxpayers, and subsequent redistribution of the money, obtained from rent seeking is considerable. He states that perhaps 90% of government transfers are *involuntary charity*. "They are the result of lobbying activities on the part of recipients, combined with ignorance and/or political weakness on the part of those individuals who supply the transfers" (Tullock 1993, p. 15).[18]

Rent seeking can take either legal or illegal routes, as Krueger has pointed out, (Tullock 1993, p. 19) and in some countries it has had a devastating effect. Tullock observes:

> The *émigré* Chinese of Southeast Asia and the United States perform extremely well, as do the *émigré* Indians of Africa. Only in their own homelands do they fail to perform well. The phenomenon is not peculiar to Chinese, Indian, or Islamic cultures, but rather is located in the traditional government institutions of these various backward societies. Rent seeking offers a powerful general explanation of this apparent paradox. It is not surprising that our common exposure to economic failure in culturally-advanced societies led Krueger, Bhagwati and myself [*sic*] to the rent-seeking explanation (Tullock 1993, pp. 20-21).

Accordingly, rent seeking has now taken a prominent place in economic thought as an explanation for why certain areas of the world are less developed than others. Traditional economic explanations for underdevelopment include climate and religious culture. Economists have suggested that people in colder climates tend to work harder and save

---

[18] Citing as examples farm subsidies and import protection for steel firms or automakers.

more than those in other climates, tending to produce greater development. There are exceptions, of course, such as tropical Hong Kong. Following Max Weber, some economists have suggested that historically Protestant countries tend to be more developed on account of the religious requirement to work hard in order to please God (see chapter thirteen, appendix). Thus, there are notable differences between New Zealand or Australia and Papua New Guinea, between Spain or Italy and Germany, and between the United States or Canada and Mexico. Now, rent seeking has become a strong economic explanation for underdevelopment. Rent seeking might actually explain why the size of government in general has grown so much in recent decades, although the empirical evidence is not compelling (Tullock 2008).

Table 3.5 Possible causes of underdevelopment

The three possible causes of being underdeveloped are:
(1) the climate of a country,
(2) the culture or religion of a country, especially considering the thesis of Max Weber in *The Protestant Ethic*,
(3) the amount of rent seeking that exists in a country.

Perhaps all of these factors contribute to underdevelopment—each to a greater or lesser degree depending on the country in question. Tullock's idea can also be melded to Austrian School theorist Mises's view that "predatory militarism," as with all government failure, retards economic development.

Maybe the Mises-Tullock view of economic success is right, or at least right in some or most cases, but the Altiplano region makes us at least stop and take notice of Weber's theory again. Predatory militarism and exorbitant rent seeking just do not seem like plausible explanations, and vote seeking distortions seem unlikely as well...

The detractions from Weber by DeLong, Brenner, and even Tullock are not very compelling given the Altiplano [Peruvian Indian] case. Instead, I would suggest that a more eclectic view be adopted. This view would generally accept the Mises-Tullock perspective, while leaving room for a Weberian explanation at times, especially when there is no clear-cut case of government failure. The result view would seem to be more robust, with more explanatory power. Indeed, by leaving room for Weber, at least now and then, we attain a more comprehensive theory of development. Otherwise, the Mises-Tullock thesis alone simply does not well explain Altiplano underdevelopment, where cultural and religious values seem to be the main culprits.

Furthermore, the resulting fusion of Mises-Tullock and Weber would be knit together by a common thread. There may indeed be different *proximate* reasons for underdevelopment: predatory militarism, rent seeking, or lack of a Protestant ethic. But there is only one *ultimate* cause of underdevelopment: the generation of bad ideas among intellectuals that are transmitted into adverse public policies. (Cobin 2000)

Any sort of public policy which leads to *legal involuntary transfers* is rent seeking, or is a public policy that in some way involves rent seeking activity (see Table 3.1). Moreover, since rent seeking produces negative sum games for society, it may be deduced that rent seeking tends to retard economic development too. Alternatively, it would seem less likely that policies encouraging voluntary exchange would retard development, since all voluntary market or *catallactic* activity results in positive sum games for both the game players and society. Consider the taxonomy in Table 3.6:

Table 3.6: Taxonomy of economic exchange

Economic Exchange	Legal	Illegal
Voluntary	Market	Black Market
Involuntary	Rent Seeking	Theft

For Tullock, both the climatic and cultural (i.e., religious) explanations of development must be discarded when one considers the industrious, non-Protestant Chinese and certain Africans. Instead, he argues that development depends on how free a society is from rent seeking and other institutional distortions. Tullock explains:

"The *émigré* Chinese of southeast Asia and the United States perform extremely well, as do the *émigré* Indians of Africa. Only in their own homelands do they fail to perform well. The phenomenon is not peculiar to Chinese, Indian, or Islamic cultures, but rather is located in the traditional government institutions of these various backward societies. Rent seeking offers a powerful general explanation of this apparent paradox. It is not surprising that our common exposure to economic failure in culturally-advanced societies led Krueger, Bhagwati and myself [*sic*] to the rent-seeking explanation" (Tullock 1993, pp. 20-21).

Considerable rent seeking in a society harms economic development and forces it to remain "backwards" (to use the term employed by Mises). It is not only militarism which causes underdevelopment, but rather the state institutions which retard growth, foster corruption, and promote privilege seeking.

Paul Craig Roberts and Karen Araujo imply that underdevelopment in Latin American countries has been due to rent seeking activities and bad public policies (Roberts and Araujo 1997). Moreover, public policy that compromises property rights is harmful and will magnify underdevelopment problems. Richard Pipes notes that there is a "symbiotic relationship between property and freedom" (Pipes 1999, p. 287). Realized leftist movements during the twentieth century, antithetical to private property rights and political freedom, have left a legacy of underdevelopment around the world (Pipes 1999, pp. 209-225). Alternatively, public policy which encourages strong property rights, along with a consistent and fair rule of law, leads to greater economic development. Accordingly, a comprehensive taxonomy of economic development may be derived, as noted in Table 3.7.

Table 3.7: Taxonomy of economic development

Development Criteria	Weak Rent Seeking	Strong Rent Seeking
Strong Property Rights	Strong Development	Underperformance
Weak Property Rights	Despotism / Paucity	Backwardness

Although Mises' work predated the formal inauguration of rent seeking theory, he seems to have understood the concept and that it had a substantial economic effect on development. Accordingly, without using the precise term, Mises describes the fundamental problem of rent seeking:

In an unhampered market economy the capitalists and entrepreneurs cannot expect an advantage from bribing officeholders and politicians. On the other hand, the officeholders and politicians are not in a position to blackmail businessmen and to extort graft from them. In an interventionist country powerful pressure groups are intent upon securing for their members privileges at the expense of weaker groups and individuals. Then the businessmen may deem it expedient to protect themselves against discriminatory acts on the part of the executive officers and the legislature by bribery; once used to such methods, they may try to employ them in order to secure privileges for themselves. At any rate the fact that businessmen bribe politicians and officeholders and are blackmailed by such people does not indicate that they are supreme and rule the countries. It is those ruled—and not the rulers—who bribe and are paying tribute. (Mises 1996, pp. 272-273)

Accordingly, both Mises and Tullock alike viewed underdevelopment and "backwardness" as a function of government failure. Some of the most important failures have been proactive policies of predatory militarism. Mises rejected the climactic or environmental explanations for underdevelopment, in favor of a paradigm which is remarkably similar to Tullock's. However, Mises emphasized the lack of respect for individual rights in China and Africa rather than institutional problems leading to increased rent seeking activity. But he did point out institutional problems that led to the diminution of capital accumulation in those areas on account of predatory militarism.

[T]he temporal head start gained by the Western nations was conditioned by ideological factors which cannot be reduced simply to the operation of environment. What is called human civilization has up to now been a progress from cooperation by virtue of hegemonic bonds to cooperation by virtue of contractual bonds. But while many races and peoples were arrested at an early stage of this movement, others kept on advancing. The eminence of the Western nations consisted in the fact that they succeeded better in checking the spirit of predatory militarism than the rest of mankind and that they thus brought forth the social institutions required for saving and investment on a broader scale. Even Marx did not contest the fact that private initiative and private ownership of the means of production were indispensable stages in the progress from primitive man's penury to the more satisfactory conditions of nineteenth-century Western Europe and North America. What the East Indies, China, Japan, and the Mohammedan countries lacked were institutions for safeguarding the individual's rights. The arbitrary administration of pashas, kadis, rajahs, mandarins, and daimios was not conducive to large-scale accumulation of capital. The legal guarantees effectively protecting the individual against expropriation and confiscation were the foundations upon which the unprecedented economic progress of the West came into flower. These laws were not an outgrowth of chance, historical accidents, and geographical environment. They were the product of reason. (Mises 1996, pp. 497-501)

Like Tullock, Mises saw that bad or distortive ideas mainly stem from the academics, which find their way into public policies that produce widespread rent seeking and theft in backwards countries. Therefore, the Mises-Tullock nexus is manifest. Both scholars would consider that extensive rent seeking is the key culprit causing underdevelopment, Moreover, general political and economic views that produce and develop a rent seeking society are ultimately responsible. In short, backwardness is a function of *government failure*, seen in both its predatory militarism and rent seeking forms. And all government failures are ultimately the result of bad intellectual ideas that find their way into public policy. Hence, Mises and Tullock together provide the *complete* government failure view of underdevelopment, as noted in Table 3.8.

Table 3.8: Comprehensive (Mises-Tullock) taxonomy of economic development

Development Criteria	Little Government Failure	Much Government Failure
Strong Property Rights	Strong Development	Underperformance
Weak Property Rights	Despotism / Paucity	Backwardness

A rent seeking society ends up being harmful to virtually everyone. By and large, voters must be responsible for the leaders they choose. However, there is no guarantee that politicians will abide by the will of the electorate. Capturing rents through special interests is also problematic. Tullock notes that while voters are pleased with the rents their favorite special interest groups are able to secure, they also have reason to be unhappy.

> Thus, the voter is a rather shaky reed on which to depend if the object is to achieve good government and a government which in particular only spends money on things that are generally worth purchasing. The average voter benefits from the activities of those pressure groups of which he is a member although the benefit may be much smaller than he thinks it is. On the other hand he is injured by all the other pressure groups and the net effect is that he is actually worse off than without any of them. The limits of information, however, mean that he is actually only able to function effectively by promoting pressure groups. In consequence, the outcome is that there is a good deal more wasteful rent-seeking that there would be if somehow or other people were able to vote in terms of their long term interests (Tullock 1993, p. 38).

Table 3.9 Social costs of regulation caused by rent seeking

The five social costs of regulation caused by rent seeking are (per McChesney 1987, p. 118):
(1) the deadweight monopoly loss or Harberger triangle,
(2) rent seeking, represented by the Tullock rectangle,
(3) costs of complying with regulations,
(4) the diversion of resources to less valuable but unregulated uses, and
(5) the costs of protecting private capital even when politicians do not have any real inclination to regulate or change a regulation, but simply *threaten* to do so (a process called "milking").

Tullock admits that, due to empirical and theoretical reasons, "good measures of rent seeking cost" are not available yet. However, he believes that there are good reasons to suspect the costs are high and hidden within:

> ...failed bids, aborted enterprise, uncharted waste and threatened but never activated public policies. We also know that most senior executives of large companies and trade associates now spend a fair amount of time in Washington. In 1890, they never went there at all (Tullock 1993, p. 78).

Some evidence of rent seeking

There is evidence that regulation of business emanating from the political process is actually the result of rent seeking activity, especially with respect to legislation in the United States. In many cases, private interests seem to dominate the public interest at the expense of consumers and taxpayers. Stigler concludes that the Sherman Act was a result of rent seeking, specifically "from small business interests or that opposition came from areas with potential monopolizable industries or both" (Stigler 1985, p. 7). Business interests have given strong support to antitrust legislation.

Rent seeking visible in public policy

High and Clayton Coppin have shown that rent seeking was a force behind the passage of the Pure Food Act (High and Coppin 1988, pp. 286-309). Donald Boudreaux and Robert Ekelund argue that gains to municipalities and others by rent seeking were the driving force behind the Cable Television Consumer Protection and Competition Act of 1992 (Boudreaux and Ekelund 1993, pp. 356, 390). Extending this notion of municipalities seeking rents from state or federal political processes, Tullock showed how rent seeking has been rationally used by local governments.

In 'Competing for Aid' (Tullock 1975), I illustrated my thesis by reference to public road building programmes. I discussed a situation, common in the United States, in which a higher level of government programme provided assistance to lower-level government organizations in accordance with their 'need'. I showed how lower-level organizations would respond to such a set of incentives by deliberately neglecting road repairs in order to qualify for higher-level subsidies. My arguments were not hypothetical. I showed how the city of Blacksburg had deliberately skewed road repair contracts away from its most damaged roads in order to be targeted for repair by the Commonwealth of Virginia. I showed how the development of divided centre, limited access toll highways during the early 1950s was almost completely self-aborted once President Eisenhower introduced the federally-subsidized interstate system. The local community that allows its road system to deteriorate in order to qualify for state subsidies or that runs down its hospital system in the expectation that the federal government will replace it is in exactly the same situation as the Chinese beggar who mutilates himself to obtain [more] charity from passers-by. In both cases, the action is rational. In both cases, the effect is to lower the welfare of those involved (Tullock 1993, pp. 17-18).

Tullock also cites the post office in the United States as a prime example of successful rent seeking to maintain a monopoly privilege, although a private postal service, *ceteris paribus*, might actually generate more rent seeking (Tullock 1993, pp. 53, 64). So rent seeking is not limited to outside special interests or to politicians. Bureaucrats also seek rents, as Tullock remarks:

[B]ureaucrats themselves actively rent-seek through the political process, often conspiring with powerful interest groups and relevant congressional committees. In some cases, this rent seeking results in excessive rates of output, in others in bloated budgets and in yet others in manifest laziness and ineptitude. It should be kept in mind, however, that bureaucrats are often manipulated by other rent seekers, and that they certainly could not rent-seek as effectively as they do without the widespread compliance of politicians and the rational ignorance of much of the electorate (Tullock 1993, p. 58).

Accounting costs of rent seeking activity

Mitchell and Simmons have documented several interesting and "disturbing" outcomes of rent seeking behavior. For instance, the social losses due to protectionism (via tariffs) are astounding. "The deadweight loss to society of protectionism has been estimated to range from 1 to 6 percent of the GNP, translating into tens of billions of dollars each year" (Mitchell and Simmons 1994, p. 104). Subsidies have likewise been enormous in the United States, as Mitchell and Simmons remark:

Congress is reluctant, for understandable reasons, to sponsor inquiries into subsidies, but on two occasions it has done so and the results are flattering neither to Congress nor to the subsidized organizations. During the late 1970s and early 1980s the federal government spent more than $250 billion annually on subsidies and subsidy-like programs. In the maritime industry, for example, the income gains were substantial: Every employee in the industry was made better off annually by about $16,000. The automobile industry negotiate a wage settlement with the United Auto Workers that increased wages by more than twice the average negotiated amount in all other industries. The settlement was on top of employment costs that were already 60 percent higher than those operating in other manufacturing industries (Mitchell and Simmons 1994, p. 104).

Social waste from the rent seeking of lobbyists has also been substantial. Regarding state-level lobbying in the United States, Mitchell and Simmons note:

> For example, more than 500 lobbyists spent more than $12.5 million to influence Washington's state legislature. With 147 legislators, that amounts to $85,000 per member. In the state of Oregon, which has a population of only 2.9 million citizens, lobbyists spent more than $1.6 million in 1989 on workers' compensation legislation alone. These examples illustrate that vast sums are spent on the political process because it is now an unavoidable cost of doing business, just as purchasing raw materials, paying employees, and so on are regular costs of running an enterprise. We believe it is regrettable that so many scarce resources are devoted to this process, but it is understandable, once the rent game begins. Those who do not participate fail to reduce the scope of the game but pay the costs of not protecting themselves. Instead of hearing applause, they are deemed suckers because they must pay for the gains of those who do not play. In any event, tens of thousands of lawyers and others devote their time to shifting money from one pocket to another and make good money doing so (Mitchell and Simmons 1994, p. 107).

Rent seeking academics

The academy is also prone to rent seeking behavior, particularly in public universities that offer tenure. "The professor-monopolist decides what to teach, how to teach it, when, and under what conditions. Although dedicated, student-oriented, humane, and so on, the professor remains a monopolist and a potential free-rider (Mitchell and Simmons 1994, p. 122-123). While they complain that their salaries are low, in fact their opportunity cost is usually not that high (except perhaps in a few disciplines like business, law, and engineering) and the number of days they work each year is far less, perhaps one-twelfth, of their typical professional counterparts in the private sector. Accordingly, Mitchell and Simmons propose some analysis.

Our age-old depiction of the university as a hallowed, disinterested searcher for truth and exemplar of altruistic values must be subject to the same careful analysis we accord business firms, political parties, interest groups, and other organizations (Mitchell and Simmons 1994, p. 123).

Regulation as cartel management

Mitchell and Simmons agree with other public choice theorists that most monopoly power today is derived from political favors. They describe regulation as nothing more than "cartel management" (Mitchell and Simmons 1994, pp. 129-130). Successfully gaining a political favor may be pleasant but, like brass that must be polished, the costs of maintaining it will continue. "Eternal vigilance is the price of rent seeking" (Mitchell and Simmons 1994, p. 132). In the final analysis, everyone must be on their guard against potential predators in a rent seeking society.

We must, therefore, be suspicious of and opposed to claims for safety nets and other protectionist policies that reduce efficient market competition but necessarily increase inefficient political competition (Mitchell and Simmons 1994, p. 128).

Consumer action groups as rent seekers

Sometimes consumer action groups can be effective proxies to watch special interests on the behalf of consumers (Mitchell and Simmons 1994, p. 136).[19] It is plausible that such "reformers" (as Tollison and Wagner call them) are likewise pursuing a rent seeking agenda and must, therefore, be scrutinized like other participants in the political process. Government does not consist of publicly-interested people, so "consumers ought to be wary of their benefactor" (Mitchell and Simmons 1994, p. 139). The state is not necessarily their ally. Instead, Mitchell and Simmons contend that the consumer ought to be concerned over the "real monopolists,[20] our 80,000 governments that simultaneously oversupply some services and fail to provide for many other important daily wants" (Mitchell and Simmons 1994, p. 139).

Solving the ugly, insidious problem

Perhaps ironically, Mitchell and Simmons point out an insidious element of rent seeking by political actors. "Those who benefit most from any specific policy are rarely those who have fought for it, and those injured are rarely those who opposed it or even know that they have been injured. And of course the unborn cannot possibly oppose their masters" (Mitchell and Simmons 1994, p. 112). Indeed, when looking at a rent seeking society, we do not see a pretty picture. Alternatively, we see a picture of venality, economic distortions and misallocations of colossal proportions caused by government failure.

---

[19] However, Mitchell and Simmons find it odd that "consumers of private goods are assumed by Naderites to be incapable of assessing their own risks but highly capable of voting for public officials who can assess those risks for others" (p. 136).

[20] Mitchell and Simmons note the inefficient or ineffective provision of roadways, mail delivery, public schools, poorly maintained parks and other facilities, national defense and social security (p. 139).

Nevertheless, Tullock suggests that there is a potential partial solution to the problem of rent seeking.

[C]onstitutional constraints and institutional reforms can mitigate the extent of rent seeking on the part of interest groups (Buchanan 1980a and b). However, as Wagner (1987, 1988) has argued, the parchment of the Constitution itself is vulnerable to the guns of special interests unless the Constitution itself can be protected by those general interests that find it so difficult to engage in democratic politics (Tullock 1993, p. 51).

While recognizing that government is an instrument of force and compulsion—and is thus evil—Tullock is hopeful that some good will, paradoxically, come out of it (Tullock 1993, p. 78).

For class discussion

Tragically, thousands of people die in automobile or trucking accidents every year. Thus, proactive public policy is often enacted to make cars, trucks, and driving safer, especially in developed countries. (1) From an economics perspective, what is one policy that could be enacted that we *know* would reduce traffic fatalities to zero? Why is such policy not enacted? (2) Do we put a value on human life? (3) Thinking like an economist, does making cars safer during accidents lead to fewer or more accidents? How would you drive if you knew with 100% certainty that you would not die or be injured in a traffic accident—no matter how serious? (4) What incentives are changed by installing airbags? (5) Following Tullock's famous story, would people drive more safely, and thus have fewer fatalities, if a latent lance were installed on steering wheels instead of an airbag? How would you drive then? (6) Who benefitted by using public policy to force cars and trucks to come equipped with airbags? (7) Was airbag policy really enacted in the "public interest" or were private interests being served? (8) When would it make sense for airbag companies or any other firm struggling to sell its products to invest in rent seeking activities to buy favorable legislation?

References

Bastiat, Fredric (1990/1850), *The Law*, Foundation for Economic Education: Irvington-on-Hudson, New York.

Becker, Gary (1983), "A Theory of Competition among Pressure Groups for Political Influence," *Quarterly Journal of Economics*, vol. 98, no. 3, pp. 371-400.

Boettke, Peter J. (1992), "Economic Education and Social Change," in John W. Robbins and Mark Spangler, eds., *A Man of Principle: Essays in Honor of Hans F. Sennholz*, Grove City College Press: Grove City, Pennsylvania, pp. 63-74.

Boudreaux, Donald J. and Ekelund, Robert B., Jr. (1993), "The Cable Television Consumer Protection and Competition Act of 1992: The Triumph of Private Over Public Interest," *Alabama Law Review*, vol. 44, no. 2, winter, pp. 355-391.

Buchanan, James M. (1980), "Rent Seeking and Profit Seeking," in James Buchanan, Robert Tollison, and Gordon Tullock, eds., *Toward a Theory of The Rent-Seeking Society*, Texas A&M University Press: College Station, Texas, pp. 3-15.

Cobin, John M. (2000), "The Andean Altiplano: Lessons for the Mises-Tullock View of Development," manuscript retrieved on March 6, 2009 from http://www.policyofliberty.net/AndeanAltiplano.html.

Harberger, Arnold C. (2008), "Microeconomics," *The Concise Encyclopedia of Economics* (Library of Economics and Liberty), retrieved on March 6, 2009 from http://www.econlib.org/library/Enc/Microeconomics.html.

Henderson, David R. (2008), "Rent Seeking," *The Concise Encyclopedia of Economics* (Library of Economics and Liberty), retrieved on March 6, 2009 from http://www.econlib.org/library/Enc/RentSeeking.html.

Higgins, Richard S., and Tollison, Robert D. (1988), "Life Among the Triangles and Trapezoids: Notes on the Theory of Rent-Seeking," in Charles Rowley, Robert Tollison, and Gordon Tullock, eds., *The Political Economy of Rent-Seeking*, Kluwer Academic Publishers: Boston, pp. 147-157.

High, Jack C., and Coppin, Clayton A. (1988), "Wiley and the Whiskey Industry: Strategic Behavior in the Passage of the Pure Food Act," *Business History Review*, vol. 62, pp. 286-309.

McChesney, Fred S. (1987), "Rent Extraction and Rent Creation in the Economic Theory of Regulation," *Journal of Legal Studies*, vol. 16, January, pp. 101-118.

Mises, Ludwig von (1996/1949), *Human Action: A Treatise on Economics*, Bettina Bien Greaves, ed., Fourth Revised Edition, The Foundation for Economic Education: Irvington-on-Hudson, New York.

Mitchell, William C., and Simmons, Randy T. (1994), *Beyond Politics: Markets, Welfare, and the Failure of Bureaucracy*, Westview Press: San Francisco, California.

Pipes, Richard (1999), *Property and Freedom*, Alfred A. Knopf: New York.

Roberts, Paul Craig and Karen Araujo (1997), *The Capitalist Revolution in Latin America,* Oxford University Press, New York.

Stigler, George J. (1985), "The Origin of the Sherman Act," *Journal of Legal Studies*, vol. 14, January, pp. 1-12.

Tollison, Robert D. (1982), "Rent Seeking: a Survey," *Kyklos*, vol. 35, fasc. 4, pp. 575-602.

Tollison, Robert D., and Wagner, Richard E. (1991), "Romance, Realism, and Economic Reform," *Kyklos*, vol. 44, no. 1, pp. 57-70.

Tullock, Gordon (2008), "Government Spending," *The Concise Encyclopedia of Economics* (Library of Economics and Liberty), retrieved on March 6, 2009 from http://www.econlib.org/library/Enc1/GovernmentSpendi ng.html.

Tullock, Gordon (1993), *Rent Seeking*, The Shaftesbury Papers, 2, Edward Elgar Publishers Co.: Brookfield, Vermont.

Tullock, Gordon (1975), "The Transitional Gains Trap," *The Bell Journal of Economics*, autumn, pp. 671-678.

4 The calculus of consent and vote-seeking

The *Calculus* and logrolling

While this book is about modern and recent themes in free market economics, some appreciation for the beginnings of public choice is in order. The public choice revolution took off in 1962 with Buchanan and Tullock's *The Calculus of Consent*. They wrote, "our purpose in this book is to derive a preliminary theory of collective choice that is in some respects analogous to the orthodox theory of markets" (Buchanan and Tullock 1962, p. 17). They developed what they termed the "costs" approach to collective action, in which utility maximizing individuals seek to use the political process in order to eliminate external costs and to secure external benefits. "The individual's utility derived from any single human activity is maximized when his share of the 'net costs' of organizing the activity is minimized" (Buchanan and Tullock 1962, pp. 43, 45).

Just how are public choices concluded? Collective actions are the result of individuals employing this calculus, assuming that a man "confronted with constitutional choice, will act so as to minimize his expected costs of social interdependence" (Buchanan and Tullock 1962, p. 49). Their analysis justified an "older and more traditional role of the state," noting that interdependence costs and externalities in collective action scenarios have not been properly understood in their use as a basis for proactive public policy.

The collectivization of an activity will be supported by the utility-maximizing individual when he suspects the interdependence costs of this collectively organized activity (interdependence benefits), as he perceives them, to lie below (to lie above) those involved in the private voluntary organization of the activity. Collective action may, in certain cases, lower expected costs because it removes externalities; in other cases, collective organization may introduce externalities. The costs of interdependence include both external costs and decision-making costs, and it is the sum of these two elements that is decisive in the individual constitutional calculus (Buchanan and Tullock 1962, p. 62).

Logrolling

One problem in taking collective action through the legislative process is that the incentives and interests of each political actor (as he represents his voting district) tend to produce inefficient or socially undesirable outcomes. Buchanan and Tullock argued that majority voting could lead to economic distortions or misallocations. "There is nothing in the operation of majority rule to insure that public investment is more 'productive' than alternative employments of resources, that is, nothing that insures that the games will be positive sum" (Buchanan and Tullock 1962, p. 169). Often, the hopeful politician has to "offer a 'package' program sufficiently attractive to encourage the support of a majority of his constituents," which take the form of implicit logrolling actions (Buchanan and Tullock 1962, p. 218). Tollison, citing Tullock, notes:

Logrolling is the trading of votes on one issue for desired votes on other issues. It usually occurs in situations where individual votes represent a significant percentage of the total electorate and where compliance with trading arrangements can be observed easily (Tollison 1988, p. 340, footnote 8, citing Tullock 1959, p. 571).

The existence of implicit and explicit logrolling is now recognized as having more than trivial consequences. Mitchell and Simmons remark that logrolling leads to distortions in policymaking. "Vote trading will therefore favor projects in which total costs exceed total benefits. In other words, bad projects that would normally be defeated can be enacted into law when votes are traded, making all concerned worse off" (Mitchell and Simmons 1994, p. 71).

Buchanan and Tullock created an extensive logical depiction of "the calculus of the rational utility-maximizing individual as he confronts…constitutional choices" using methodological individualism as a basis. In the political process, "when an opportunity for mutual gains exists, 'trade' will take place" (Buchanan and Tullock 1962, pp. 265, 267). Therefore, logrolling is a predictable outcome of modern democratic institutions.

They also anticipated imperfections in the voting process, whereby individuals would vote to impose external costs on others, and vote brokers via permanent interest groups would form (Buchanan and Tullock 1962, pp. 272-273). Then, when problems arise, policymakers who hold the public interest view of government will make misguided determinations. Nevertheless, most academics and people in general have failed to appreciate the institutions and perverse incentives that lead to problematic public policies. "Breakdowns and failures in the operation of the system are attributed to 'bad' men, not to the rules that constrain them" (Buchanan and Tullock 1962, p. 281).

The impetus of constitutional analysis

In *The Calculus of Consent*, Buchanan and Tullock develop what would become the public choice theory of interest groups, and the logic of dispersed costs and concentrated benefits—which have been discussed in the preceding chapters (Buchanan and Tullock 1962, pp. 283-291). They considered that by identifying these tenets and applying them in their analytical models, they would be better able to advance the good society.

> In our more rigorous analytical models we have adopted the extreme assumption that each participant in the political process tries, single-mindedly, to further his own interest, at the expense of others if this is necessary. We were able to show that, even under such an extreme behavioral assumption, something closely akin to a constitutional democracy as we know it would tend to emerge from rational individual calculus. We believe that this in itself is an important proof that should assist in the construction of a genuine theory of constitutional democracy (Buchanan and Tullock 1962, p. 305).

Going beyond a seminal understanding of what "constitutional democracy as we know it" would become, and aiding in the development of constitutional economics, Buchanan and Tullock led the way into public choice theory: a sweeping research program that has provided a powerful means of analyzing public choices. In addition, it gave life to the field of constitutional economics. As Tollison notes:

> Different rules of the game (read legislative production functions) lead to different outcomes in the supply of legislation, both in the aggregate and with respect to what kind of legislation is passed. The relevant supply curve of laws, then, is a function of how the political

process is governed by explicit and implicit constitutional constraints (Tollison 1988, p. 344).

Voting and vote seeking

Tullock notes that even the smallest information costs swamp the expected benefits from voting. Because individual votes have such a minuscule influence on an election it is rational for them not to vote (see Tullock 1993, pp. 34-35).[21] Indeed, for a public choice economist, voting is generally an inefficient or time-wasting activity, unless the voter has some sentimental or other special benefit from voting (e.g., he is a staffer employed by the Congressman and he wants to please his boss). Stigler notes some problems associated with democratic political processes that are absent in the market.

This compelled universality of political decisions makes for two differences between democratic political decision processes and market processes...[(1)] The condition of [decisions being made in] simultaneity imposes a major burden upon the political decision process. It makes voting on specific issues prohibitively expensive...To cope with the condition of simultaneity, the voters must employ representatives with wide discretion and must eschew direct expressions of marginal changes in preferences...(2) The democratic political process must involve all the community, not simply those who are directly concerned with a decision (Stigler 1971, p. 218).

---

[21] Tullock says the payoff from a voter in any election is $BD_pA - C - C_p = P$, where B is the expected benefit from one's candidate winning, D_p is the probability that the individual's vote will be decisive given the likely effect of the candidate's persuasion on the casually informed voter, A is the probability that the voter's political information is accurate, C is the cost of voting, C_p is the cost of effort invested in persuasion, and P is the pay-off. (See Tullock 1993, pp. 39, 42.)

Thus, democratic processes, in particular the quest to optimize individual voting or find more optimal substitutes for voting, lead to public choice distortions and resource misallocations caused by SIG activities. Mitchell and Simmons argue that since government has a monopoly on power people want to control it. But governments, unlike firms, do not seek profits for owners. Thus, they face different incentives and must be controlled by political rather than market mechanisms. "That most voters choose to remain rationally ignorant is hardly surprising. And only in politics can a person make ethical comparisons of logical contradictions." For instance, they might favor more national defense or social program spending while simultaneously supporting lower taxes or less regulation, creating a logical contradiction (Mitchell and Simmons 1994, pp. 45, 47).

As a result, many voters will find it more profitable to support favored interest groups rather than voting themselves. Thus, the role of lobbying becomes a central feature of democratic politics. Simply stated: voters learn that they can get more done with special interest groups or lobbies than they can at the ballot box (Mitchell and Simmons 1994, p. 62). Humorist P.J. O'Rourke quips, "The worst offsloughings of the planet are the ingredients of sovereignty. Every government is a parliament of whores. The trouble is, in a democracy the whores are us" (O'Rourke 1991, p. 233). Accordingly, Tullock notes that the democratic political process causes voters to become ardent rent seekers.

The result of all this is that voters are, to a considerable extent, a major source of rent seeking. It should be pointed out, however, that for some types of policy determination a system of direct popular votes or referenda is superior to logrolling within the legislature. Well-organized pressure groups can frequently manoeuvre the legislature into enacting legislation that would never get through a popular vote" (Tullock 1993, p. 37).

The median voter theory

Another significant challenge to voting, especially for those with principled positions on the left or the right sides of the political spectrum, is the *median voter theory*. This theory implies that outcomes in the political process will tend to be inefficient in terms of any supposed public interest criteria. As Shughart explains:

> Studying collective decision-making by committees, Duncan Black deduced what has since been called the median-voter theorem. If voters are fully informed, if their preferred outcomes can be arrayed along one dimension (e.g., left to right), if each voter has a single most-preferred outcome, and if decisions are made by simple majority rule, then the median voter will be decisive. Any proposal to the left or right of that point will be defeated by one that is closer to the median voter's preferred outcome. Because extreme proposals lose to centrist proposals, candidates and parties in a two-party system will move to the center, and, as a result, their platforms and campaign promises will differ only slightly. Reversing 1964 presidential hopeful Barry Goldwater's catchphrase, majority-rule elections will present voters with an echo, not a choice. If the foregoing assumptions hold, the median voter's preferences also will determine the results of popular referenda. As a matter of fact, anticipating that immoderate proposals will be defeated, the designers of ballot initiatives will strive to adopt centrist language, in theory moving policy outcomes closer to the median voter's ideal point than might be expected if decisions are instead made by politically self-interested representatives.

> Modeling the decision to vote in a rational choice context, Anthony Downs pointed out that the act of voting itself is irrational. That conclusion follows because the

probability of an individual's vote determining an election's outcome is vanishingly small. One person's vote will tip the scales in favor of the preferred candidate or issue only if the votes of all other voters are evenly split. As the number of voters becomes large, the chances of that happening quickly approach zero, and hence the benefits of voting are likely to be less than the costs. Public choice reasoning thus predicts low rates of voter participation if voters are rational. Indeed, if there is an unsolved puzzle, it is not why turnout in U.S. elections is so low, but why it is so high.

Downs and other public choice scholars also conclude that voters in democratic elections will tend to be poorly informed about the candidates and issues on the ballot. Voter ignorance is rational because the cost of gathering information about an upcoming election is high relative to the benefits of voting. Why should a voter bother to become informed if his vote has a very small chance of being decisive? Geoffrey Brennan and Loren Lomasky, among others, have suggested that people vote because it is a low-cost way to express their preferences. In this view, voting is no more irrational than cheering for one's favorite sports team (Shughart 2008).

Investing in lobbyists and pressure groups

With respect to lobbying costs in the political process, Tollison comments that a free rider problem develops.

Politicians will have incentives to search for the issues on which well-organized groups gain transfers at the expense of the diffuse general polity [nation]. Another point about organization costs is that these costs are like start-up costs. Once they are borne, they do not affect marginal costs...In addition to organization and information costs there are costs which are due to the potential for others to 'free ride' on the lobbying efforts of others" (Tollison 1982, p. 590).

Consequently, political actors have a tendency to support interest group activities which have the greatest expected return at the margin. The marginal gain from directly supporting bloated interest groups which already have substantial support and power may be less than the political gains to be made from nurturing other activities. Thus, political actors may free ride on the support given by other people for some lobbying efforts they like or admire, while contributing resources to other interest groups that offer the prospect for greater political gains. In other words, they invest their political contributions where they expect to get the biggest bang for the buck.

Alternatively, some political actors will choose to free ride completely. Perhaps interest group activity in areas which are of concern to them is already strong and successful. The monopoly privileges and benefits accrued from regulatory capture or rent seeking might already be at desirable levels—or at least at a level where expected benefits at the margin are less than the costs of making additional political investments, and thus they refrain from contributing more resources. Or perhaps they prefer to assume the risk that others will see deficiencies in political support and thus make greater contributions, creating a free riding opportunity for gain.

Vote-seeking

Public choice theory suggests that politicians are self-interested actors who are driven by an overriding objective to be reelected. Successful politicians will master the art of producing political benefits in excess of political costs. Mitchell and Simmons summarize the process of vote optimization:

In short, a politician asks two questions: (1) How many additional votes will I receive for an additional dollar spent? (2) How many additional votes will I lose for advancing the welfare of some groups at the expense of others? In choosing among alternative spending projects, politicians attempt to compare the added votes from each dollar of spending per project and determine the mix that guarantees the maximization of votes (Mitchell and Simmons 1994, p. 52).

Politicians practice vote-seeking because they want to gain or retain political power, money, and other benefits that accrue to them as a result of their office. The most astute and successful politicians will employ thoughtful strategies based on their knowledge of public choice (even if they are unaware of the rubric) and other political phenomenon. They also choose to be ambiguous and emotive in their public remarks in order to perfect their overall vote-seeking strategy. As Mitchell and Simmons comment:

Because voters are rationally ignorant (the costs of gaining particular kinds of information are greater than the benefits since one vote is essentially meaningless), politicians must employ a language designed to evoke emotion—enough emotion to motivate the right people to turn out and vote…Understanding the politician is therefore extremely frustrating for those who value precise statements. But note that this problem is not the fault of the politician; it is rooted in the rational ignorance of voters, the distribution of conflicting sentiment among voters, and the nature of collective endeavor (Mitchell and Simmons 1994, p. 73).

Emotional appeals are most effective to the least principled voters. In other words, considering again the median voter theory, emotional appeals will tend to sway voters who lack a principled position (whether left-wing or right-wing). Such appeals will tend to move marginal voters who reside near the political center from one side of the median to the other. Astute politicians and their consultants will know this fact and exploit it. The fact that most people who actually vote are women—at least in the United States—means that the emotional appeals will be skewed towards a feminine perspective (e.g., a candidate will make a big show of kissing his wife on national television). Vote-seeking influences the revealed disposition of politicians. O'Rourke candidly remarks on their duplicitous nature.

Government is boring because political careers are based on the most tepid [lukewarm] kind of lie: "I'll balance the budget, sort of." "I won't raise taxes, if I can help it." Of course politicians don't tell the truth: "I am running for the U.S. Senate in order to even the score with those grade-school classmates of mine who, thirty-five years ago, gave me the nickname Fish Face," or, "Please elect me to Congress so that I can get out of the Midwest and meet bigwigs and cute babes." But neither do politicians tell huge, entertaining whoppers: "Why, send yours truly to Capitol Hill and I'll ship the swag home in boxcar lots. You'll be paving the roads with bacon around here when I get done shoveling out the pork barrel. There'll be government jobs for your dog. Leave your garden hose running for fifteen minutes, and I'll have the Department of Transportation build an eight-lane suspension bridge across the puddle. Show me a wet basement, and I'll get you a naval base and make your Roto-Rooter man an admiral of the fleet. There'll be farm subsidies for every geranium you've got in a pot, defense contracts for Junior's spitballs and free day care for Sister's dolls. You'll get unemployment for sixteen hours every day when you're not at your job, full disability benefits if you have to get up at night to take a leak, and Social Security checks will come in the mail not just when you retire at age sixty-five but when you retire each night to bed. Taxes? Hell, I'll have the government go around every week putting money *back* into your paycheck, and I'll make the IRS hire chimpanzees from the zoo to audit your returns. Vote for me, folks, and you'll be farting through silk (O'Rourke 1991, pp. 4-5).

Legislative voting influenced by macroeconomic variables

Politicians also pay close attention to the macroeconomic variables (e.g., inflation and unemployment) that tend to generate the greatest concerns among voters in their states or districts. The right-center party members tend to show greater enthusiasm in voting during periods of rising inflation, ostensibly because their constituents tend to have more exposure to various interest rate risks. Left-center party members tend to react more to higher unemployment rates, perhaps because their constituencies tend to be comprised of union and labor interests. As Edward Lopez and Carlos Ramirez found regarding legislators in the United States:

> The career voting of individual legislators exhibits cyclical sensitivity to contemporaneous and lagged economic conditions, although more strongly in the House than in the Senate. In response to higher inflation, individual Democrats vote more conservatively and individual Republicans more liberally, such that inflation leads to convergence. Meanwhile, unemployment leads to greater polarization between the typical Democrat and her Republican counterpart. Thus, previously reported economic cycles in *party* polarization can be attributed at least partly to movements in legislator specific ideal points, net of turnover effects and of movements in the policy space across time and chamber. This implies that

congressional bodies (parties and chambers) can shift policy positions even in the absence of member turnover, so long as the relevant economic conditions in the economy change sufficiently. Individual voting also exhibits trends over tenure in office: members of both parties become more conservative on the broad-issue index (ADA scores) but more liberal on fiscal issues (the NTU index) as tenure accumulates. However, our tenure results do not support polarization between the typical Democrat and her Republican counterpart over time, even though many researchers have reported polarization of party means/medians.

Researchers have become accustomed to interpreting vote indexes—such as ADA and NTU scores—as measures of legislator ideology. To the extent that the indexes do measure ideology, our results would suggest that there is an empirical relationship between legislator ideology and the business cycle. Perhaps legislators are not strictly ideologues but use ideological voting as a means of investing in reputation (Dougan and Munger 1989). It is well known that political parties value reputation because it signals party platform positions to rationally ignorant voters (Downs 1957). Voters, too, value reputation because it economizes on their information costs by reducing the number of issues on which candidates are evaluated. Individual legislators value their own reputations for additional reasons: reputational capital allows legislators to deviate from immediate constituent interests in order to seek support from interest groups (campaign donations) and party leaders (committee seats), and this support, in turn, situates legislators to better serve constituents over a longer term. As a seminal paper in this vein points out, "What each [legislator] needs is a way to commit himself credibly to the voters' preferred positions" (Dougan and Munger 1989: 125). A Republican responds more to inflation, a Democrat more to unemployment. Both are using economic conditions as a way of committing to their respective constituencies' preferences. Thus, ideological voting can itself be a rational tendency. So we should not be surprised to observe legislators voting in response to the economy according to their parties' historical positions on economic issues (e.g., Coates and Munger 1995). Observed vote scores—if understood as the outcomes of vote maximizing agents responding dynamically to electoral constraints and reputational investment incentives—would be better interpreted as revealed preferences rather than ideology per se (Lopez and Ramirez 2008, p. 17).

Therefore, legislators vote rationally, in order to maximize their reputations and enhance the probability of being re-elected. And ideological voting too can be rational behavior within the vote seeking model.

Budget chicanery

Political charades by legislative candidates do not cease after the election is over. Re-election is always on the horizon and successful politicians must be on their guard. They must optimize votes while simultaneously catering to special interests, along with attempting to optimize the personal gains available from their office. Tollison notes that one way politicians minimize the negative vote impact of costly policies is by keeping them off budget.

[M]any of the government's intrusions into economic life (e.g., minimum wage laws, nonprice trade barriers, antitrust exemptions, and price-entry regulations, to name a few) are off budget. That is, taxing and spending activities are just the tip of the government iceberg (Tollison 1988, p. 365).

99

Mitchell and Simmons summarize the politician's calculus in seeking the proper tax policy to optimize votes, personal gain, and favors to special interests.

Again, the most powerful concern for a politician wishing to remain in office is how many votes he or she will lose for each dollar of taxation. In making choices among revenue instruments their idea is to balance these vote losses among the different taxes so that the total vote loss is minimized...When legislatures assemble to levy taxes, the first thing they do is denounce taxation, huge budgets, and deficits. Once this charade is over, tax bills are designed in such a way as to distract attention from the proceedings. Since old taxes are usually considered more palatable than new ones, the goal is to increase either the tax base or and/or the rates of the familiar taxes and to do so in minute ways that escape immediate attention (Mitchell and Simmons 1994, p. 55).

Tax reform chicanery

Tullock argues that interest group activities which seek tax loopholes and pork barrel benefits will be very difficult to reform without dramatic or extreme changes, such as simultaneously abolishing all such benefits. However, the rent seeker has an incentive to resist any reform which reduces the potential rents available to them (Tullock 1988a, pp. 37-38, 40-41, 43, 47). Mitchell and Simmons suggest that rent seekers and politicians have a big advantage over taxpayers in promoting their goals for tax policy and, in particular, loopholes for the wealthy or special interests.

[T]he taxpayer has only the vaguest notion of how loopholes affect others and appears at least partially satisfied that the rich must be paying much more; how much more remains a mystery to all but the rich. Because they are hidden, these tax breaks are politically more acceptable than outright subsidies of the same amount. Note too that government forces the employer to collect the income tax and collect it not once a year but at every pay period, thus assuring or stabilizing the continuous flow of revenues (Mitchell and Simmons 1994, p. 56).

Indirect or hidden subsidies are typically most beneficial in the vote maximization calculus. In addition, any real reduction in taxes may serve as a cover for some ulterior agenda. As Mitchell and Simmons note, real tax reform is often an inverted means for political actors to revitalize their product line—i.e., the political favors they have available to offer to rent seekers.

The enactment of rate reductions, elimination of loopholes, and simplification of rate schedules in fact support our analysis. Congressional politicians have in effect wiped the slate clean so that they may once more "auction" off tax exemptions and other privileges (Mitchell and Simmons 1994, p. 58).

The self-interest motive is always paramount for political actors. In order to ensure their continued power and profits, political actors must extend the role of government. To do otherwise would be harmful. Mitchell and Simmons argue that all political actors work together to ensure growth in government spending and taxes, and "…bureaus, at least in the short run, protect their budgets by decreasing consumer satisfaction" (Mitchell and Simmons 1994, pp. 61, 59). A real tax reduction and subsequent budget cut means that many bureaucrats will lose their jobs.

Thus, when threatened with cutbacks, bureaus choose to reduce essential or most important services first, rather than less desirable ones, a defensive action which has been termed the "Washington Monument strategy" (Mitchell and

Simmons 1994, pp. 61-62). By threatening its most popular aspects first, such as the Washington Monument, a bureau may garner an emotive response from voters or special interests and thus successfully rent-seek to protect their political benefits. Self-interested and appointed (rather than elected) bureaucrats, who must obey the orders of vote-seeking politicians, want to maximize their budgets. A larger budget implies greater power and prestige. When faced with a mandated budget cut, by cutting out the most well-known or loved attractions, the bureau chief can tell the press that he had no choice. He was merely following orders. The outraged public—voters—will put pressure on legislators until the budget of the bureau is restored. In this way, bureaucrats have a measure of control over politicians

There are different ways to interpret the behavior of political actors. Public choice theorists have not been in accord with respect to how to view interest group activity, logrolling, and vote-seeking practices by politicians. In addition, there have been divergent views on the activity, effectiveness, and efficiency of other political actors like judges and bureaucrats. Although both the Virginia and Chicago Schools of public choice have the same basic core and methodology, they come up with very different conclusions about the efficiency of political wealth transfers. Some differences between these school are addressed in the appendix.

The state as predator

Nevertheless, most public choice theorists, and even some theorists in other fields, believe that large and growing states are harmful on account of public choice problems. Historian William McNeill in his famous work *Plagues and Peoples* describes the process by which the state becomes a consuming parasite. By and large, government is transformed into something harmful, just as a parasite injures its host.

The state becomes a macro-predator which consumes part of a country's capital assets, human capital, and human lives (at least in the case of its soldiers in war), much like a lion or a wolf does a herd of herbivores. Not being involved in productive activity itself, the state and political actors feed off of the labors of others. The most successful states are those which learn *not* to consume too much of the host by taxes, military conscription (and war deaths), regulations, and so forth. Less astute states die off by consuming too much of the host and thus bring on their own demise (McNeill 1976, pp. 1-13, 33, 40, 48, 56, 59-68, 75-76, 164-165, 196, 206-207, 216, 256-257).

Appendix: Virginia vs. Chicago political economy

In previous chapters, we have sampled some of the friction in public choice thinking between Chicago School theorists like Becker, Wittman, Peltzman, and Stigler, and Virginia School theorists like DiLorenzo, High, Shughart, Tollison, and Tullock. Indeed, public choice theorists have disagreements. They are not an entirely homogeneous group in terms of methodology, selection of criteria or constraints, and conclusions. While it is clear that the Virginia tradition was derived from the Chicago School (particularly from the influence of Professor Frank Knight), and thus disagreements may be seen as healthy disagreements among friends with more or less common agendas, it is important to note some of the distinctions between the schools at this point.

The Chicago brand of public choice is basically neoclassical microeconomics applied to politics. The Virginia brand of public choice is the quasi-philosophical, sometimes normative, application of microeconomic theory to politics. The former often takes a rigid mathematical approach based on the typical Chicago equilibrium modeling constraints and assumptions, while the latter does the same at times but permit other elements to be added to the composition— e.g., from philosophy, legal studies, cliometric (i.e., econometrics applied to the field of history) and non-econometric historical studies, etc. Consequently, the Chicago School pays less attention to things like institutions and perverse incentives than the Virginia School.[22]

Akin to the Austrian School, the Virginia School is open to non-quantitative methods and case studies (alike to, perhaps ironically, the outstanding contribution of Chicago's Ronald Coase). In addition, the Virginia School is open to incorporating aspects of ethics and moral philosophy, even to the point of abandoning the utilitarian paradigm for one based on a Hobbesian understanding of nature or Lockean natural rights theory. In this sense, the Virginia School is far less constrained than the Chicago School.

While some Virginia School theorists use quantitative methods full time (i.e., in every publication), most of them use them only part time, and some hardly ever use them (favoring logical methods instead). While it is also true that some Chicago theorists, notably Stigler and Coase, have at times employed non-quantitative approaches, the Chicago School seems to have an incessant urge to formalize public choice theory with mathematics via a static or competitive equilibrium framework. As a result of their openness, Virginia School theorists have been more willing to use logical methods to analyze other issues pertaining to public choice, such as social theory and constitutional economics.

In addition, there is somewhat of a rift between Chicago and Virginia created by Virginia's partial or occasional nexus with the Austrians. Since the Austrians proffer a non-mathematical methodology, they may be viewed as sub-

---

[22] The Austrian School has also been keen to analyze the role institutions have in affecting economic behavior. Institutions are regular patterns of life that have evolved over time that permit greater predictability in human action.

standard or even as a threat to traditional Chicago models. But the Austrians pose no intolerable threat to the Virginia School. Some of the best examples of the more or less eclectic approach that has resulted may be seen in the work of scholars like Boettke, DiLorenzo, Ellig, High, Rowley, and Wagner, as well as Randall Holcombe, Fred Foldvary, and many other emerging scholars. In some respect, there has been a merging of Austrian and public choice themes, to the chagrin of purists on both sides. Yet this merger is not new, but had its impetus in the beginning of the Virginia tradition. Tullock claims that he was influenced greatly by Austrian economist Mises (Tullock 1988b, pp. 1-2), and one may see the Austrian influence on Buchanan by reading his early work *Cost and Choice*.

Furthermore, there is a non-utilitarian thrust in many Virginia School theorists, notably Rowley, Tollison, and Wagner. This also leads to different emphases on rent seeking costs, as is evident in Tullock's comments about Becker's work in the previous chapter. Chicago School theorists say that political markets transfer wealth efficiently with low rent seeking costs (with the possible late exception of Harberger), while Virginia School theorists say rent seeking costs are very high and wealth transfers are inefficient due to low quality information (rational ignorance).

Given this synopsis of differences between the Virginia and Chicago Schools of public choice, we are ready to consider five serious criticisms of the Chicago School by Virginia School adherents: (1) Chicago is theoretically linked with left-wing rationale, (2) Chicago underestimates the problem of rent seeking, (3) Chicago has an unhealthy optimism regarding interest groups, (4) Chicago's view of judicial and antitrust action is dubious, and (5) Chicago (from Posnerian analysis and its west-coast outpost, UCLA) permits interpersonal utility comparisons. In the ensuing paragraphs, long quotations from the original sources will be used to facilitate a robust discussion of the issues.

Chicago is theoretically linked with left-wing rationale

The debate between Chicago and Virginia has drawn considerable attention, notably from the Virginia School, the Austrians, and some scholars in other disciplines. Mitchell and Simmons, who are not economists *per se*, but rather political scientists who are enthusiastic about public choice theory, link the Chicago School's perspective of public choice to left-wing social theory (and they have thus implied some allegiance to the Virginia School by way of exclusion).

In language familiar to economists, liberal [left-wing] welfare analysts assume that the political process is an efficient one in which all actors possess more or less complete information, transactions are almost costless, and there is an absence of externalities. Such a view of the polity is strikingly similar to the notion of a perfectly competitive market. In a perfect market there are no unexploited opportunities for gain; Pareto optimality has been achieved. All plans of the participants have been realized through the perfect coordination of activities. Under this scenario, the political process, like the perfect market, is assumed to be efficient. [Theodore] Lowi, in fact, wrote [in 1969] that the assumptions underlying [the model of government he called] interest group liberalism "constitute the Adam Smith 'hidden hand' model applied to groups." The pluralist position is supported, surprisingly enough, by two prominent members of the Chicago School of political economy. Gary Becker (1983) and George Stigler (1975) have each argued at length and in detail that present policies are politically efficient, that is, nothing better can be done under existing rules. Protectionist policies are the rational outcome of the current political process. Politicians and voters adopt the more efficient or less efficient policies—a rather startling claim in view of all the rent seeking evidence. In any event, although the pluralists surely would not employ the same reasoning as the Chicago analysts, it is clear that these groups share an essentially benign view of politics" (Mitchell and Simmons 1994, p. 26).

Chicago underestimates the problem of rent seeking

Tullock has likewise been critical of the deficiencies of the Chicago School's public choice program, the lack of applying rent seeking theory in particular.

Peltzman's work has been directly connected with income transfers and he has argued that politically powerful people, essentially in the middle class, have used the government structure to transfer funds from the wealthy to the poor. Actually, to say that they transfer resources from [to *sic*] the poor is not literally true. What happens is that the poor do not get very much of the largesse of the welfare state, indeed, probably less than their votes would normally entitle them to (Tullock 1989). It is unfortunately true that both Stigler and Peltzman, prominent economists to say the least, made a fundamental mistake. They talked about the whole process in terms of its welfare transfer outcomes and did not discuss at all the rent-seeking cost of the process. This is a particularly impressive lacuna in the case of Stigler, who talked about regulatory bodies as being set up for the specific purpose of benefiting the interests that had arranged them, but never discussed the cost of this process. Recognition that such costs exist is of course the heart of rent seeking. Becker, who wrote a very good article on interest group competition (Becker 1983) in which he pointed out that the result of certain groups pushing for special privileges and other groups counter-pressuring to avoid being victimized should lead to a balance which is at least arguably some kind of political optimum, failed to emphasize the rent-seeking cost of this exercise (Tullock 1988b, pp. 30-31).

Tullock continues:

Becker (1983, 1985) more or less explicitly plays down the cost of rent seeking in his theory of pressure group competition. His 1983 article incorporates the normal costs of organization into the theory of pressure group organization. Except for this, however, the paper centres attention exclusively on Harberger triangles as a source of social loss and ignores Tullock rectangles. His 1985 paper notes that aggregate efficiency 'should be defined not only net of dead weight costs and benefits of taxes and subsidies, but also net of expenditures on the production of political pressure...since these expenditures are only rent-seeking inputs into the determination of policies'. Becker does not follow through on this insight, but lamely concludes that 'little is known about the success of different kinds of political systems in reducing the waste from competition among pressure groups' (Becker 1985, p. 335) (Tullock 1988b, p. 51).

Chicago has an unhealthy optimism regarding SIGs

In the following passage, Tullock provides some analysis of the problems of the Chicago School's approach to interest group theory.

Becker places considerable emphasis on the deadweight costs of taxes and subsidies and the fact that such costs generally rise at an increasing rate as taxes and subsidies increase. He suggests that an increase in the deadweight cost of a subsidy discourages pressure by the subsidized group while an increase in the deadweight cost of a tax encourages pressure by taxpayers. Consequently, deadweight costs give taxpayers an intrinsic advantage in the competition for influence. Groups that receive large subsidies presumably manage to offset their intrinsic disadvantage by efficiency, optimal size or easy access to political influence. In Becker's analysis, all groups favour and lobby for efficient taxes, whereas efficient methods of subsidization raise subsidies and benefit recipients, but harm taxpayers unless recipients are induced to produce less pressure by a sufficiently rapid increase in their deadweight costs as their subsidy increases. He claims relevance for his theory not only to taxes and subsidies that redistribute income, but also to regulations and quotas, as well as to policies that raise efficiency by the production of public goods and the curtailment of other market failures. In his view, policies that raise efficiency are likely to win out in the competition for influence because they produce gains rather than deadweight costs, so that groups benefited have an intrinsic advantage compared to groups harmed. In Becker's world, where there is open competition between interest groups, together with free entry and exit, inefficient transfer mechanisms will not be widespread in political market equilibrium. For a number of reasons, I do not share Becker's optimism regarding the impact of interest groups in democratic politics, at least in the absence of important constitutional constraints. Let me start with the free-rider problem emphasized by Mancur Olson in his seminal discussion of the logic of a collective action (Olson 1965). The free-rider proposition asserts that in a wide range of situations, individuals will fail to participate in collectively profitable activities in the absence of coercion or of individually appropriable inducements (Stigler 1974). This proposition is easily illustrated. Let the gain to an individual be equal to G if a collective activity is undertaken. For instance, G may be the individual's gain from the tariff which might be obtained by an effective interest group lobby. The cost of the collective action is C, and there are n identical self-seeking individuals. By hypothesis, the joint action is collectively profitable, so $nG > C$. However, the individual will refrain from joining the collective action if n is of some appreciable size, given his judgement that the viability of the action does not depend on his participation. If enough individuals free ride in this manner, the collective action will not be taken. Even though rides, like lunches, are never completely free, if n is large the free-rider problem is widely believed to be endemic [communicable/dangerous]. Mancur Olson (1965) set out to prove logically that free-riding was not a universal problem for collective action but rather that it struck differentially at particular types of interest groups, thereby providing unequal or asymmetric access to the political process. The paradox that he presented is that (in the absence of special arrangements or circumstances) large groups, at least if they are composed of rational individuals, will *not* act in their group interest. The reason for this is to be found in the publicness characteristics of the benefits that flow from successful collective action (Olson 1965, 1982). In such circumstances, interest groups will not exist unless individuals support them for some reason *other* than for the collective goods that they may provide (Tullock 1988b, pp. 44-46).

Tullock concludes that the Virginia School follows the better logic of collective action than the Chicago School.

Olson's logic of collective action, which I essentially endorse, is sharply different from that of Gary Becker. It focuses attention on the problem of asymmetric access to political markets, whereas Becker tends to emphasize equal access. It emphasizes problems of free-riding whereas Becker emphasizes deadweight social losses as the principal reason for collective action failures. It stresses, much more than Becker, the importance of small size as a determinant of lobbying impact. It highlights the cost of organizing interest groups and the difficulty of holding them together, whereas Becker tends to emphasize the ease of organization and the attraction of the gross returns to collective action (Crew and Rowley 1988a). In my view, the preponderance of the evidence is in favour of Olson, though further testing of both theories is desirable (see Mitchell and Munger 1991 for an excellent survey) (Tullock 1988b, pp. 49-50).

Chicago's view of judicial and antitrust action is dubious

Recall DiLorenzo and High's contention (in chapter two) that the Chicago School's marriage to the perfect competition model has caused it to make faulty judgments about the persistence of monopoly power and the need for antitrust to correct this supposed market failure. Tullock, Rowley, and other Virginia School scholars have also been critical of the Chicago School view of antitrust, the judiciary, and law and economics ideas of prominent judges/scholars Richard Posner (see Tullock 1988b, p. 60) and Robert Bork. For example, Ellig points out the "arbitrary" nature of Bork's antitrust opinions based on the Chicago model of "Tight-Prior Equilibrium" (Ellig 1992, p. 875).[23]

The problem with this approach is that most of the phenomena that Bork and other Chicago theorists seek to explain are the result of imperfect information. But imperfect information prevents attainment of a Pareto-optimal general equilibrium (Ellig 1992, p. 876).

---

[23] In the application of the Tight-Prior Equilibrium model, observed prices are often presumed to approximate their long term competitive equilibrium values.

Continuing his argument, Ellig reveals a logical contradiction in the Chicago School analysis of public choice problems, antitrust analysis problems in particular.

The Chicago toolkit seeks to combine two conflicting notions of competition. Perfect information is a prerequisite for perfect competition; imperfect information is a prerequisite for rivalrous competition. Bork's analysis of business practices in an imperfect information world is compatible with market rivalry analysis, while his attempt to combine allocative and productive efficiency is not...Since the Chicago view tries to blend contradictory notions of competition, it should come as no surprise that it has failed to produce a logically consistent theory of economic efficiency (Ellig 1992, p. 877).

Rowley has been particularly critical of the Benthamite utilitarian stance which Posner has adopted. Judges simply cannot use economic tools from Chicago to provide welfare state resource allocation in violation of subjectivism.

In many ways, perhaps the most aggressive attempt to apply the utilitarian calculus, and in its narrowest, wealth-maximizing mode, to a major area of policy importance is the research programme launched by Richard Posner over a decade starting in the early 1970s to transform jurisprudence in favour of the efficiency criterion. In this view, judge-made law, most particularly the common law of property, contract and tort, together with parts of statutory law where it is shaped by judicial interpretation, is and should be designed to maximize the wealth of society. Posner clearly recognizes that wealth maximization and utilitarianism are closely related...and he claims that 'most economists, like most judges and most practical people, are still utilitarians despite the forceful challenges to utilitarianism that have been mounted in the contemporary literature' (ibid., p. 133). He may well be correct with respect to both assertions. However, in so far as wealth maximization is analytically equivalent to the Kaldor-Hicks criterion in its potential form at least as applied by the courts, it is open to all the criticisms outlined above. In essence, judges and juries assume the role of omniscient and impartial social welfare maximizers (in place of economists and public officials). One set of undisciplined bureaucrats simply replaces another, and probably judges are less-well versed in the complexities of cost-benefit analysis than are most economists, though no less disposed to imposing their preferences on the hapless individuals who plead their cases before them (Rowley 1989a and b). At least, Posner sees little prospect for courts attempting to apply social welfare functionals as a mechanism for pursuing wealth-enhancing income-redistribution (but see Rowley 1992) and argues, indeed that courts might be justified in refusing to allow such considerations to influence the determination of liability: "Courts can do very little to affect the distribution of wealth in society, so it may be sensible for them to concentrate on what they can do, which is to establish rules that maximize the size of the economic pie, and let the problem of slicing it up be handled by the legislature with its greater taxing and spending powers" (Posner 1984, p. 132) (Rowley 1993, pp. 42-43).[24]

Rowley states his view as concurring with Buchanan with respect to constitutional views regarding welfare maximization by bureaucrats or judges.

---

[24] Rowley notes (p. 34) the justification for the wide application of Chicago theory: "Indeed, in vigorously competitive markets individuals who do not take care of themselves economically may not survive to indulge their other self-interested or altruistic passions, or may be too impoverished to do so. Fundamentally, this is the Chicagoan defence of the wide deployment of narrow self-interest as the projected core of the positive economic research programme" (Stigler 1958).

The answer surely is that of transferring, again voluntarily, at least at some ultimate constitutional level, activities with some publicness characteristics to the community as a collective unit. In this sense, a political constitution emerges as part of a voluntaristic exchange process...For Buchanan, economics is the study of the whole system of exchange relationships and politics is the study of the whole system of coercive relationships. There is no role whatsoever for social engineering within economics or for providing would-be social engineers with the economic tools of their trade. Rather, economists should concentrate on the institutions, the relationships among individuals as they participate in voluntary organized activity, in trade or exchange, broadly considered (Rowley 1993, p. 30).[25]

Chicago (UCLA) permits interpersonal utility comparisons

The Posnerian approach is not the only Chicago theme to violate the subjectivism axiom prohibiting interpersonal utility comparisons via Kaldor-Hicks-Scitovsky. The Virginia School's criticism has also extended to UCLA's Arnold Harberger for much of the same reasons. Harberger opened himself up to criticism with a bold public statement, as Rowley summarizes:

In September 1971, Arnold Harberger published a remarkable 'open letter' to the economics profession, in one of its leading and most widely-read journals, pleading that three basic postulates should be accepted as pro-

---

[25] Rowley later noted: "Although Buchanan relies upon his supposed intuition of individuals in the state of nature concerning positive public choice to predict that the constitutional contract will endorse a state empowered beyond anarchy but constrained short of Leviathan, he can only guess at such an outcome. His own subjectivist methodology denies him any ability either to read their minds or to pass judgement upon their actions." (p. 54)

viding a 'conventional framework' for all applied welfare economics, namely:

1. The competitive demand price for a given unit measures the value of that unit to the demander;

2. The competitive supply price for a given unit measures the value of the unit to the supplier; and

3. When evaluating the net benefits or costs of a given action (project, programme or policy) the costs and benefits accruing to each member of the relevant group should normally be added without regard to the individual(s) to whom they accrue.

In essence, Harberger's plea is for the general acceptance by economists working in the field of welfare economics of a Bergson social welfare function that maximizes the sum of consumers' and producers' surplus over competitive cost and which is neutral with respect to income distribution. Such a social welfare function essentially replicates a narrow form of the utilitarian ethic as understood prior to the attack launched by Lionel Robbins in 1932 on the notion that utility is comparable across individuals. There is no evidence in Harberger's paper that he recognizes that he is advancing an ethical judgement based on a set of value judgements. Rather, he rests his case for such a proposal on the alleged simplicity, robustness and long tradition of his three postulates. If Harberger's plea is banal and opportunistic, it appears to have fallen on fertile soil, accepted by the vast majority of neoclassical economists as the unexceptional foundation for their policy analyses (Rowley 1993, p. 32).

Virginia is the more robust free market research program

In the final analysis, the Virginia School appears to have more congruence with basic economic principles like subjectivism, and to be more conducive to free market tenets generally, than its institutional counterpart in the Chicago

School. That is not to say that the Chicago School is generally anti-market. But some applications of the Chicago methodology and models have led to conflicting and irreconcilable judgments, as well as ideas that open the door for resource allocation by political actors rather than by markets. Thus, some Chicago School applications have been more of a justification for continued intervention by the state than for advances in free market economics. Surely, a Chicago School response to this charge would simply be to agree while noting that the Chicago School is much less normative, and when it is normative it maintains a strong utilitarian posture which might be better.

Without doubt, this dichotomy of research programs is the result of strict methods and modeling assumptions. Yet the Virginia School's rejection of such rigidities and willingness to entertain other paradigms in analysis has permitted it to take the lead in advancing modern themes in free market economics. At least it seems that of the two approaches, the Virginia School arguably provides a more accurate understanding of reality and is thus more useful in guiding policy decisions.

For class discussion

Another sacred institution in the world, Western societies in particular, is the right to vote. (1) Should a person be allowed to sell his vote? (2) What would happen to elections if rich people could buy a sufficient number of votes to win an election? (3) What would the market for buying votes look like? Would prices per vote be bid up or down? Would many entrants appear in the market looking to buy votes? (4) Who would have the greatest interest in buying votes? In making sure that votes could not be bought or sold? (5) Would your country be better or worse off if it were governed by a rich person or group that was able to pay the most for votes instead of a popularly elected politician? (6) What happens to incentives and outcomes when people are forced to vote? (7) How would being able to sell one's vote change his incentive to vote? (8) Would vote selling create political rulers which are more or less inclined to listen to, and provide for, the needs of the people? (9) Would you be willing to sell your vote if it were legal? (10) At what price would you be willing to vote for a man who has a detestable ideology?

References

Buchanan, James M. and Tullock, Gordon (1962), *The Calculus of Consent: The Logical Foundations of Constitutional Democracy*, University of Michigan Press: Ann Arbor, Michigan.

DiLorenzo, Thomas J. and High, Jack C. (1988), "Antitrust and Competition, Historically Considered," *Economic Inquiry*, vol. 36, July, pp. 423-435.

Ellig, Jerome (1992), "Untwisting the Strands of Chicago Antitrust," *The Antitrust Bulletin*, Winter, pp. 863-879.

Lopez, Edward and Carlos Ramirez (2008), "The Influence of Economic Conditions on Individual Legislator Voting," *Public Choice*, vol. 136, pp. 1-17.

McNeill, William Hardy (1976), *Plagues and Peoples*, Doubleday (Anchor Books): New York.

Mitchell, William C., and Simmons, Randy T. (1994), *Beyond Politics: Markets, Welfare, and the Failure of Bureaucracy*, Westview Press: San Francisco, California

O'Rourke, P.J. (1991), *Parliament of Whores: A Lone Humorist Attempts to Explain the Entire U.S. Government*, Vintage Books [Random House]: New York.

Rowley, Charles K. (1993), *Liberty and the State*, The Shaftesbury Papers, 4, Edward Elgar Publishing Co.: Brookfield, Vermont.

Shughart, William F. II (2008), "Public Choice," *The Concise Encyclopedia of Economics* (Library of Economics and Liberty), retrieved on March 4, 2009 from http://www.econlib.org/library/Enc/PublicChoice.html.

Stigler, George J. (1971), "The Theory of Economic Regulation," *The Bell Journal of Economics and Management Science*, vol. 2, no. 1, spring, pp. 1-21.

Tollison, Robert D. (1988), "Public Choice and Legislation," *Virginia Law Review*, vol. 74, no. 2, March, pp. 339-371.

Tollison, Robert D. (1982), "Rent Seeking: a Survey," *Kyklos*, vol. 35, fasc. 4, pp. 575-602.

Tullock, Gordon (1959), "Problems of Majority Voting," *Journal of Political Economy*, vol. 67, pp. 571-579.

Tullock, Gordon (1993), *Rent Seeking*, The Shaftesbury Papers, no. 2, Edward Elgar Publishing Co.: Brookfield, Vermont.

Tullock, Gordon (1988a), "Rent Seeking and Tax Reform," *Contemporary Policy Issues*, vol. 6, October, pp. 37-47.

Tullock, Gordon (1988b), *Wealth, Poverty, and Politics*, Basil Blackwell: New York.

Wittman, Donald A. (1995), *The Myth of Democratic Failure: Why Political Institutions Are Efficient*, American Politics and Political Economy series, University of Chicago Press: Chicago and London.

5 Public policy and public choice

Self-interested action vs. selfishness

Economic theory tells us a lot about what behavior to expect from political actors, along with the inadequacy of their knowledge in regulating society to bring about the common good (see chapter 8). All rational men—including political actors who enact public policies—act purposefully to remove uneasiness from their lives. They try to maximize those things in life that give them the greatest satisfaction (e.g., money, love, power, influence, charity, altruism, holiness, etc.).

Thus, as Mises postulates, acting men aim purposefully at ends and goals, constantly adjusting their actions to meet their needs (Mises 1966, p. 11). Sane people do not act without reason, and they do not act unless they believe that their action will remove some uneasiness.

Outside of the political process, men act in such a way that engenders cooperation with others. They facilitate and exploit mutually beneficial gains from trade. Peaceful cooperation is the result of the operation of the market economy. People pursuing their self-interest voluntarily cooperate to provide the needs or wants demanded in society.

We must be careful to not equate self-interested motives with selfish ones. The former describes one's economic motivation while the latter deals with one's character. A selfish person is one who is absorbed in himself to the exclusion of others. He is self-interested too but his motivation is hamstrung by a character flaw. Nonetheless, not all of the self-interested purposes of men are bad or selfish.

For example, a person might have altruism as his highest goal. He would thus pursue the self-interested agenda that he believes has the highest probability of attaining his altruistic goals. He might also pursue other things along with this objective, such as owning his home debt-free, raising seven children, and taking his nephew on an annual fishing trip. But all such elements combine together into concerted, purposeful, self-interested action used to attain the conglomerate goal which maximizes his utility.

We are left to marvel that men of such character, pursuing their own self-interests, can produce peaceful social cooperation. Capitalism and private property (DiLorenzo 2004), especially when coupled with thrift, industry, and entrepreneurship, allow civilizations to rise and survive within an imperfect world. Accordingly, the self-interest motivation is helpful and good, and wrongly demonized by some journalists and academics that have confused self-interest with selfishness.

However, the political process, like theft, does not necessarily involve mutually beneficial gains from trade. Its public policies usually involve public choices that do not necessarily benefit all parties involved. Political actors certainly aim at ends and seek to maximize their personal utility according to what serves their own self-interest. But their actions, with the possible exception of national defense and criminal justice policies, tend to merely shift wealth, power or other benefits from one party to another rather than benefit all members of a society.

What is public policy?

Public policy generally means action by government. Public policy is designed to accomplish national defense and secure justice, or to facilitate various social, political, or economic ends. Public policy includes regulation of all areas of life by the state: family, religion, education, culture, trade, international relations, etc. and the philosophy which supports the various "public interest" rationales upon which such regulation is based. As such, public choice phenomena are mingled with public policy. Political actors and judges make choices for individuals that have little or no say in the process but who must absorb the costs of such choices by paying taxes for it or by altering their lifestyles to conform to its requirements.

A simple taxonomy may be used to distinguish policies and facilitate more robust policy analysis. The resulting policy categories are (1) reactive policy, (2) the inefficient provision of genuine goods and services, and (3) proactive policy. Proactive policy takes three forms: (a) policy that is aimed at changing people's behavior, (b) policy that seeks to change the way people think and (c) policy that is dedicated mostly or wholly to redistribution. These categories are useful for normative analysis, which is what public policy often tends to be, but are also useful for positive inquiry. They permit us to classify policies according to the philosophical sources that drive them and thus we can make explanations or predictions using different assumptions.

Although often obscured by the common use of highly mathematical models, economics is firmly based in philosophy. It is hardly accidental that the highest academic degree in economics and public policy is the Ph.D. (i.e., Doctor of Philosophy), which reveals the historical basis of all the social sciences in philosophy. As a prelude, consider the following philosophical synopsis of positive and negative rights, and the related discussion of reactive and proactive public policies (adapted from Cobin 2006).

Positive and negative rights

Many public policies have to do with the implementation of some *positive right*: viz. a right granted to people by the state, a right that people do not have naturally, and a right that other people must pay to sustain. Sometimes positive rights are couched in terms of "social justice" or sublime "public interest" planning objectives. Many economists have been critical of public policies based on positive rights. For example, Eric Schansberg divides the major subcategories of public policies based on positive rights theory by using the terms "legislating morality" (LM) and "legislating justice" (LJ). He eloquently explains why people should avoid promoting LM policies and only with great caution (and guided by strong principles) encourage LJ policies (Schansberg 2003).

Examples of positive rights include rights to minimum standards of health care, food or nutrition, income, and a "decent" education. These rights may be found in statements like the United Nations *Declaration of Rights* (1945), as well as in Marxian writings and elsewhere. These rights can also include things like a "livable" wage (a minimum wage or greater), a crime-free and unpolluted environment, and even "reasonable air conditioning" in a rental unit.[26] Thus, positive rights obligate one class of people to provide benefits for another. Consequently, they are *artificial* in nature.

Conversely, *negative rights* are fundamentally construed to be "natural" or "fundamental" rights that people have to life, liberty, and property. Such rights-bearing has been ex-

---

[26] For instance, the Virginia Residential Landlord and Tenant Act, amended in 1987, provides for "reasonable air conditioning" if air conditioning is provided in the unit. Va. Code 55-248.13(a)(6).

tolled by political philosophers such as John Locke and Thomas Jefferson. Public policy based on negative rights rests upon the notion of *self-defense*. Indeed, in its most basic form, civil government exists as the collective means of self-defense. If self-defense cannot be justified then neither can civil government itself be justified. If a government did not defend its citizens, what would it do? Would it merely redistribute wealth, run public enterprises, certify products, and issue edicts for politically correct conduct? If that were the case, one might be able to argue in favor of preferring tax-free and regulation-free political anarchy? If the civil authority cannot or will not defend its citizens then it is not worth having around. So the doctrine of negative rights has paramount importance in public policy theory.

Reactive policy

Negative rights theory mandates that people restrain themselves from acting against the natural rights of others in society. Yet unlike positive rights they are costless; no person has to pay to maintain the negative rights of other people. That is why they are often said to exist *naturally*.

Reactive policy is action by government designed to provide collective self-defense against predators: a social service that the market cannot provide well. There are only three "pure" reactive policy categories: national defense, the establishment and enforcement of legal rules to facilitate social certainty and commerce (based on the common law of property, contract, and tort), and criminal justice. Domestic defense against any predator—even infectious microorganisms—would qualify as well. These policies are reactive in the sense that they react to, or become effectual when there is, a violation of someone's negative rights by a clearly nonconsensual act (e.g., murder, rape, or robbery). These kinds of policies are also termed *defensive* policies

(Bastiat 1990, p. 28), since they are designed to defend people from those who would harm life, liberty or property. In their pure form, such policies are devoid of behavior modification objectives or schemes, but instead provide safeguards that are perceived to be collective boons or "public goods." Of course, there is a "proactive" by-product in these policies, namely that predators are *deterred* from bad behavior. But only through such an abstraction (i.e., where the policy inadvertently ends up changing bad behavior) may they be considered proactive. Nevertheless, since the operation of such policies only becomes effective after a rights violation occurs, they may reasonably be maintained as having an essentially reactive character.

The government is called upon to provide these collective goods either because the market "fails" to provide them well or, perhaps, because such collective action is itself the result of market provision. Accordingly, minimal state libertarians or "minarchists" and political conservatives (or constitutionalists) typically argue that reactive policies are the *only* necessary and just forms of government action. Many of them would restrict policy to defense from predators, together with lethal or noxious microorganisms perhaps, and criminal justice. Markets could provide civil procedure services and courtrooms, as well as local rules or laws to facilitate commerce (Benson 1990, 1998).

Policies of inefficient public provision

Governments can provide genuine goods or services that are normally provided by the market. However, following economic theory, such provision will likely be inefficient since (1) bureaucrats face different incentives than managers or entrepreneurs in competing firms who seek to maximize profits and (2) bureaucrats are protected from the discipline of the market by having enhanced job security. Thus, public enterprises tend to focus less on quality improvement and cost cutting, and often are over-staffed with over-paid employees (especially at higher levels of government). This predicament ends up driving up prices that consumers must pay for those goods and services, which in turn lowers social welfare. Such policies are usually neither proactive nor reactive, nor do they necessarily have a basis in positive or negative rights, but they might be species of either proactive or reactive policies in some instances.

Most tariffs, quotas, and "dumping" laws probably fall under this policy category, since the protectionism they foster promotes inefficient provision in a country's private sector (Bovard 1991). However, such "hidden taxes" on consumption are complicated, and must be judged on a case-by-case basis as to what category they belong. Examples of professions that clearly fall within this policy group include the county recorder, postal service workers, mechanics who repair city vehicles, building safety inspectors, workers in dams and public utilities, road construction crews, public defenders, and the staff of a country's central bank. (Note that when taken generally, the actions of a central bank, along with legal tender laws, deposit insurance, and currency monopolization may comprise proactive policy during its course of facilitating indirect taxation by inflation.)

Proactive policies aimed at changing behavior or thinking

The first two divisions of proactive policy are action by the state designed to alter people's behavior or way of thinking. These policies are not usually implemented because the targeted behavior is harmful to other people as much as it is antithetical to some lofty philosophical meta-goal. Proactive policy seeks to alter behavior that would otherwise be commonplace, normal, typical, and not harmful to others. The targeted behavior is simply designated as something naughty by a legislature or by a bureau, usually upon the expert advice of academics, policy pundits, or pressure groups (lobbyists). Conversely, curtailing most recidivistic or criminal behavior (e.g., murder, assault, etc.) would more likely be a function of reactive policy rather than this species of proactive policy.

Sometimes such proactive policies are derided as "big brother" actions. They are so-called because people are compelled to behave in a manner not of their own choosing (as if an older and wiser person were providing direction for a child). In this sense, someone in government and/or academia has determined that certain behavior is detrimental to the individual, society, or both.

Accordingly, proactive policies can be actions that aim at changing social institutions based on the suggestion of some academic theory (e.g., Marxism) or the wrangling of some activists (e.g., protesters from the Sierra Club, the Audubon Society, Greenpeace, the National Organization for Women, etc., or corporate and government "watchdogs" like Ralph Nader and Noam Chomsky). Examples of proactive policies include hate crimes and marriage legislation, family courts, narcotics or vice legislation, seat belt legislation, smuggling and gambling restrictions, "sin" taxes on cigarettes and alcohol, regulation requiring "fairly" priced and decent housing, environmental "protection" (e.g., for certain species or the ozone layer), prohibition of alcohol or illicit drug use, compulsory attendance in government schools—which Bruce Shortt colorfully calls "pagan seminaries" designed to manipulate the way citizens think about the state and its favored policies (Shortt 2004)—and constabulary or offensive (aggressive) military operations.

Note that a proactive policy may also include minor reactive elements. For instance, protecting others from "second-hand smoke," shielding society from ozone depletion, and defending potentially innocent victims from intoxicated drivers all have (arguably) reactive qualities. Nevertheless, the central tenets of such policies remain proactive, aiming at coercing change in behavior or thinking.

Also included in this proactive category are policy projects and institutions designed to serve higher social goals or "the public interest." Items that are deemed to be "public goods" or that result from the occurrence of "negative externalities" (see chapter twelve) are used to rationalize public interest policies.[27] A negative externality occurs when a person who is not involved with the beneficial market exchange of others ends up bearing some of the costs of that bargain without receiving any of the benefits. A negative externality is a public choice that arises in the market process, usually as a result of a poorly-defined property right. The classic example is a woman who bears the cost of having her laundry soiled by the smokestack of a nearby factory but gets no benefit from the factory's production.

Another example, although it is not usually recognized as such, would be a person who pays taxes for the education of children when he has no school-age children. He pays for the costs of "production" without *directly* receiving any of its benefits. He probably does receive *indirect* benefits from the production, such as being able to live among a literate population, but that does not disqualify the policy from being a negative externality in theory.

The woman with the laundry might also have indirect benefits from the smokestack because it creates jobs for others, including her husband or children. Yet the smokestack is still considered in theory to be a negative externality. If the smokestack would cease production, there would

---

[27] "A 'public good' is a good or service which is characterized as non-excludable and non-rival in consumption. That is, if a public good is provided to one person, it may be provided to all at no additional cost, such that people who do not pay for it cannot be prevented from consuming it (i.e., a positive externality). Examples of public goods often include national defense, law and order, pollution abatement, flood control, and perhaps building safety and quality. It is common for government to either provide (or at least regulate) such goods, based on the rationale that markets do not make adequate provision of them, and that it is not fair or efficient that some people should be free riders (leading to underproduction of the public good). Thus, some scholars contend that such market 'failure' obliges government intervention" (Cobin 1997, pp. 81-82).

be more jobless (and poorer) men, which might increase robberies. Instead, men working at the factory improve her community as their spending bolsters the quality of local commerce. Accordingly, some public policies can be considered, at least abstractly, to be negative externalities too. Hence, the specious idea of market failure (see chapter twelve) stemming from pervasive negative externalities in turn provides a specious rationale for proactive policy.

Proactive policy aimed at redistribution

The third major division of proactive policy is redistributive policy. It entails proactive action by government designed to coercively transfer the wealth of one or more individuals (or segments of society) to others in conjunction with a higher or meta-social goal. In other words, government uses its power to extort money from (typically) "the haves" against their will and to give it to "the have-nots" in a sort of modern Robin Hood role. Moreover, a socially detrimental payoff is also often available to quasi-government agencies, politicians, bureaucrats, regressive entrepreneurs (see chapters six and nine), or private suppliers who participate in rent seeking (see chapter three)

Such legal extortion policies (for which Bastiat coined the term "legal plunder") are typically based on a positive rights theory, if not an outright socialist ideology. These proactive policies are popularly described as "welfare state" policies. They have an overarching societal or moral meta-goal, rather than just a goal of improving lifestyle risks, ensuring "fair" prices and information, providing public goods, or alleviating negative externalities. Like all proactive policies, this species is accomplished by direct taxation, indirect or hidden taxation (e.g., inflation), or by regulation (e.g., restricting the use of private property and thus lowering its value—also known as "takings" , or by taking away private property in order to remove urban blight, spur new development, and increase local tax revenue as in the infamous 2005 U.S. Supreme Court decision *Kelo v. City of New London*).

Examples of redistributive policy programs include food stamps, Aid to Families with Dependent Children (welfare), Social Security, most child support and alimony payments, subsidies to farmers or other groups, most unemployment "insurance", subsidized housing, public (state) education, university-level grants, and many student loan programs. Some proactive policies of redistribution are frequently mistaken as simply being policies of inefficient provision, in particular Social Security (or old-age) benefits, unemployment insurance, and university student loans—at least those varieties found in the United States. Yet they are clearly proactive because they involve the direct plunder of one group in society in order to benefit another group.[28]

Table 5.1: Policy types and their philosophical bases

Type of public policy	Rights basis
1. Reactive (defensive)	Negative
2. Inefficient public provision	Negative, positive, or neither
3. Proactive	
(a) to change behavior	Positive (typically)
(b) to alter ways of thinking	Positive (typically)
(c) to foster redistribution	Positive

Social Security and unemployment tax contributions are used to create a savings or insurance fund that an individual can draw upon when in need. Thus, they feel justified when accepting Social Security and unemployment benefits since

---

[28] For instance, in passing legislation for the collection of Social Security (and unemployment) "contributions" or taxes, government may mandate that the employee and the employer *each* pay one-half. However, the reality is that the employee pays the tax in its entirety. When employers hire their employees they evaluate the labor services they expect to receive against the *total* cost they expect to have to pay for those services. By implication, an employee's wages would likely be higher if the firm did not pay his Social Security and unemployment "contributions" (Schansberg 1996, p. 74).

they think that they have "paid-in" to the program for many years.[29]

In reality, they have not paid-in anything. They were forced to participate in a state-run Ponzi scheme[30] that facilitates income redistribution. Recipients are not *getting back* any of their own money; they are getting money from other people who are currently working.

University student *grants* work the same way and their character as welfare is more evident than Social Security. But educational *loans* for university study are frequently misunderstood by principled people to be justified because money is paid back to the state with interest. However, upon closer analysis, it is clear that many (but not all) student loans are forms of welfare for two principal reasons.

First, "the government"—viz. taxpayers—is forced to pay the interest on most student loans while the student is at the university. Second, student loans offer a lower rate of interest than a typical student would be able to acquire in the marketplace. Notwithstanding this fact, if an educational loan were taken out by a parent for his child, based on the parent's credit rating, and the interest was paid back by the parent from the outset; such a loan (if offered or backed by the state) would be inefficient provision rather than proactive policy since it is not a form of welfare.

Mixed policies

Some policies are not easy to classify based on their leading characteristics. They are comprised of a mixture of re-

---

[29] There may be some unemployment policies that actually are savings or true insurance plans—just as in Chile the national social security plan and associated disability insurance is privatized (albeit regulated). But these are exceptions rather than the rule.

[30] Charles Ponzi (1882-1949), a short (5 ft., 2 in.) Italian immigrant to the United States, was one of the greatest swindlers in American history. He was an incurable liar and possessed boundless self-confidence. Although there was a huge discrepancy between Ponzi's grand opinion of himself and his actual talents, he was an extraordinary con artist. He had a big smile and a fast line of talk. Ponzi's sales pitch for his pyramid postal coupon scam (offering huge returns on investment) was smooth and low-key, suckering many Americans and later became known as the original "Ponzi scheme."

active, inefficient provision and/or proactive policy objectives. Yet useful classification is still possible.

For instance, public health policy might have a reactive component, such as staving off infectious disease, while the rest of public health policy is proactive. Thus, when classifying the policy, one can split it into two parts: (1) public health for infectious disease control—reactive and (2) public health for behavior modification—proactive.

The tendency toward corruption in public policies

We must also never overlook or discount the possibility of corruption or inefficiencies being incorporated into modern public policy within a rent seeking society. Edmund Opitz reminds us of the inevitable legacy of corruption and privilege peddling by political leaders.

As long as the state, the agency of coercion, stands over society offering to dispense economic privilege to those who pay it homage, conferring an advantage on some men at the expense of other men, the misuse of political power should be the first line of attack for the moralist. It is inevitable that political privilege will be used in this way if it is available and begging to be used. No people has [*sic*] ever resisted it who have been led into this temptation. (Opitz 1999, p. 84)

Consequently, public choice theory leads us to conclude that there are rarely any true "statesmen." Rarely, if ever, is a man so publicly-spirited that he is able to subordinate his self-interest in favor of the "public interest." Public policy is always questionable, no matter how benign or useful it may appear to the public eye. Public choice suggests that men desire public office primarily on account of their self-interested motivations (e.g., money, power, or prestige). Not surprisingly, therefore, it is widely recognized that few

131

men today come close to exhibiting the public servant ideals. As Steven Yates notes:

> [W]hile politicians have never been our noblest or most honest, I do not believe most people today even expect much in the way of honesty or personal integrity from those seeking or holding high public office. They see politicians as pragmatists and judge them accordingly...Both dominant parties became repositories of pragmatism and expediency instead of principle and honorability long ago. Both see massive government [state] actions as the solution to problems, disagreeing only on the details—and again never looking beneath the surface of events or questioning premises. (Yates 2005, pp. 51-52)

The practical part: Why do public policy research?

Public policy is fraught with many problems, and public choice theory, along with other free market programs, has been providing ample empirical and theoretical studies to demonstrate these failures. But along with these studies, public choice is a research program that has sought to explain social phenomena in order to find solutions to policy problems and perhaps improve the quality of life for everyone. For that reason, public policy research is an important pursuit of public choice theorists.

All modern themes in free market economics: public choice, Austrian economics, law and economics, and regulatory studies, have application to public policy. Essentially, public policy is at odds with the normative side of free market thinking.[31] Thus, recommendations against most (non-reactive) public policy would become predictable.

---

[31] In a related remark, High has said that strictly speaking, there is no such thing as Austrian public policy. See High 1984, p. 40. Also see further remarks in chapter eight.

However, there is much that disciplines with free market themes can contribute to positive public policy analysis. Accordingly, free market theorists undertake policy research in order to enhance the selection of public policies. Public policy analysis opens additional means to apply public choice and Austrian economics (cf. chapters seven to eleven) theories in new ways. Congruent with the openness in the Virginia School to other fields (as well as the Austrian School's), important work in social theory, culture,[32] moral philosophy, and politics can be made by free market economists. In addition, practical analysis can be facilitated by using tools from regulation studies and law and economics. In many situations, quantitative methods will be useful but, perhaps more often, case studies (utilizing the "close-up" research method of gathering archival data) will prove to be the most effective means of policy analysis.

There is considerable room for mixing public choice and Austrian ideas in policy research, which can serve as a very powerful combination. Instead of simply shouting "foul" at public policies when a normative tenet of liberty-enhancing institutions is violated, free market theorists can be more productive by making their views known gradually. Indeed, the gradual encroachment of ideas is of paramount significance in changing public policy (see chapter one). For this reason, the underlying tenets of market failure theory must be a primary research focus, since that theory provides the rationale or reason for most regulation and public policy.

Free market policy theorists create or apply the theoretical tenets of public choice and Austrian economics—from rent seeking to the knowledge problem[33]—by injecting them

---

[32] For example, Seymour Martin Lipset's renowned American exceptionalism thesis. See *American Exceptionalism: A Double-Edged Sword* (1995) and *First New Nation* (1979), both published by W. W. Norton & Company, Inc.: New York.

[33] The "knowledge problem" is a central feature of Austrian economic theory. See chapter eight.

into the mainstream of the policy thought. Many policy theorists, as well as bureaucrats and politicians, are unaware of the powerful insights of modern themes in free market economics. Many of them may have yet to see an effective critique of commonly favored notions pertaining to negative externalities, judicial activism for ameliorating resource allocation, and the extent of the public goods problem. There is also room to raise issues common to many economists but novel to those in other disciplines (e.g., inflation and other meddling are just disguised taxation, that "takings" are also taxes that violate the basic premises of property rights). Moreover, free market theorists can avoid canned criticisms by discussing these issues without resorting to Chicago static equilibrium models, and their corresponding unrealistic assumptions about perfect information, or their use of esoteric mathematics.

Policy-relevant research: A note for graduate students

There is an important distinction between kinds of policy research. Academic social scientists should strive for what he calls *policy-relevant* research, but should avoid public policy analysis in academic discussions.[34] Policy-relevant research is *not* advocacy. This distinction may be used to determine the function of the various public policy think tanks today, most of which seem to primarily do public policy analysis. Hence, policy-relevant research by free market theorists is not advocacy; it is not free market propaganda undertaken to persuade others of preconceived "answers" to social problems. It is research intended to answer real questions by doing theoretical and empirical investigation with openness.

---

[34] I am grateful to Peter Boettke for mentioning Russel Hardin's ideas on this matter. Hardin is a leading rational choice theorist and Chair in political science at New York University.

Policy-relevant research can be very effective and influential in the political process, developing both new ideas and what Boettke called the climate of opinion (see chapter one). Policy-relevant research is usually not, of course, pure theory.[35] Perhaps the purely theoretical aspects of free market economics are, ultimately, most important. However, policy-relevant research plays an important and necessary role. Its goal is often just as theoretical as the goal of economics proper, the key difference being that it is always applied to some area of perceived market failure. Therefore, policy-relevant researchers belong in the first tier of the intellectual pyramid of society, along with other academics, described in chapter one. Since ideas have consequences, the writing of both living and dead policy-relevant theorists may have a tremendous impact on society.

Many problems in government can be explained by public choice insights into rent seeking and interest group theory. Public choice has done us a great service in unmasking the faceless and altruistic bureaucrat who serves the public interest, and has thus provided an excellent starting point for policy-relevant research by free market theorists. There are many policy issues to analyze and plenty of people who can benefit from knowing about free market contributions. Yet idea battles will not be won by simply writing-off opposing views by glibly listing a priori reasons why free market is best. A case must be made with policy-relevant research, not just public policy analysis, using logic bolstered by empirical work related to the theory of market failure and guided by public choice and Austrian economic theories. As in other disciplines, policy-relevant theorists must command the literature in the field, giving credit where it is due, and engage in scholarly debate. Accord-

---

[35] In some sense, one might consider the relationship between free market theory and applied policy-relevant research as being analogous to the $1,000 serum and the necessary $10 syringe to apply it.

ingly, the following sections summarize several examples of policy-relevant research.

Successful policy failures

By endogenizing government action in economic models, public choice theorists establish distinct hypotheses. A traditional economic approach might view public policy failure as a product of bad governance, with the solution being to simply incorporate better analysis, more talented people, or more stringent congressional oversight. The primary purpose of most public policy is to correct market failures.

Alternatively, public choice analysis endogenizes public policy into market outcomes simply by applying the same behavioral postulate to individuals in government as in markets (i.e., self-interest). Hence, the apparent failure of public policy may not be a failure at all. It might rather be an accurate manifestation of how the policy was designed to work in the first place.

For example, Eric Schansberg uses public choice premises to demonstrate why labor unions support minimum wage legislation.

It would seem that unions would be mostly unaffected by a higher minimum wage, but a numerical example illustrates how this works [to the benefit of union workers by restricting competition for their labor]. If the minimum wage is $4 and three less skilled workers can together do the work of a union worker, then the more skilled union workers will be hired only if their wage is below $12. An increase in the minimum wage to $5 allows union workers to demand up to $15 from the firm. By artificially increasing the wage of the less skilled workers, union workers can gain a higher income (Schansberg 1996, p. 59).

Most economists have been citing the failure of minimum wage policy since it has the adverse side effect of decreasing employment. But the reality is that minimum wage policy has been marvelously successful in achieving the ends of labor union interests. Eventually, Tullock's transitional gains trap capitalizes benefits to unions into the total compensation packages of higher-skilled and lower-skilled workers. Moreover, increases in the minimum wage then become necessary to sustain benefits to unions. As a result, those in unions gain tremendously from such rent seeking while poor people and consumers lose.

Public choice input into public policy

The incursion of public choice into policy research has resulted in the recognition of many problems which had been previously overlooked. As Mitchell and Simmons note, "Those who hope for pervasive market imperfections and failures to be properly handled and improved by government are apt to be disappointed." Rules do not guarantee the attainment of fair and efficient policies and political actors "cannot afford disinterest" but are prone to manipulating the rules that supposedly constrain them (Mitchell and Simmons 1994, p. 80). In fact, politicians use proactive public policy to influence elections and thus create a political business cycle (Mitchell and Simmons 1994, p. 178). In pursuing their self-interest, political actors will naturally tend to ravish the long term for the benefit of the short term. Thus, Mitchell and Simmons correctly point out that the assumption is mistaken that firm leaders are more myopic than government leaders, even with issues pertaining to the environment or natural resources (e.g., timber harvesting, global warming) (Mitchell and Simmons 1994, p. 74).

One important implication of public choice is that institutions matter. As Dennis Mueller notes, "The outcomes of a democratic process vary with the types of issues decided, the methods of representation, and the voting rules employed" (Mueller 1990, p. 6). Institutional rules affect the way politicians, legislatures, and bureaucrats operate and manipulate the rules. Just as with these branches of government, the judiciary is also prone to manipulate rules for ostensibly sublime social goals. Tullock has expressed concern that the courts have taken the liberty to unscrupulously (but judiciously) change the Constitution on occasion (Tullock 1980, p. 186). This behavior is referred to as *judicial activism*.

There are other social distortions are derived from the political process, including a propensity toward vote-seeking chicanery by politicians motivated by public choice incentives. Gary Anderson and Tollison found evidence that President Abraham Lincoln drafted troops at disproportionately higher rates from states where he had a wider probability of being reelected. In states where the election was going to be close, Lincoln evidently chose to reduce his political cost by drafting fewer soldiers from them and thus avoided political backlash (see Anderson and Tollison 1991).

Schansberg has analyzed government policy toward the poor and found that it actually harms them. The available evidence about poverty has been misapplied, inappropriately favoring proactive policies to "combat" poverty. Proactive policies for education and jobs training, of minimum wages and welfare, and against drugs that were designed to help the poor have had the opposite effect (see Schansberg 1996, p. 59). Therefore, one area in which free market theorists may provide policy-relevant research is to do empirical studies in economic history. These studies may be used to extend public choice theory and defend its application to modern public policy issues.

Another area in which free market theorists can make a valuable contribution to policy relevant research is to demonstrate the advantages of using market-based alternatives.

There is considerable evidence from free market theorists that markets are able to provide goods and services which have traditionally been thought to be subject to market failure. Much of the policy-relevant research on market alternatives has relied on public choice tenets. For instance, Mitchell and Simmons observe that in Hong Kong traffic jams have been lessened by a market innovation. By using computer chips and computer cables across city streets, the authorities have been able to effectively price the streets. People pay according to their usage and so automatically economize on their scarce resources, alleviating traffic problems substantially (Mitchell and Simmons 1994, p. 94). I have shown that grading and certification services can be effectively and efficiently provided by the market, indicated by government-free grading and certification providers in the rare coin and gemstone industries. Thus, there is less reason left for policy to demand that similar government provision be maintained in other industries (see Cobin 1997, chapter 3).

Foldvary provides a criticism of market failure theory and then examines evidence from private communities—market-based institutions—to show that markets successfully provide social services which are commonly assumed to fall under the realm of government action (see Foldvary 1994). Ellig and High found that the market's provision of education was adequate in America and Great Britain. Education has often been considered to be a public good because of the external benefits it generates to non-recipients, but their results called this premise into question (see High and Ellig 1988). Ellig, Jeff Kaufman, and Tom Rustici studied attempts by a Texas–Arizona pipeline firm to supply natural gas in California. The firm entered the market, despite high sunk costs of capital construction. It had to pay the high initial costs of laying new pipe, in addition to having to dodge the attempted legal blockade by its rent seeking competitor. Thus, by implication, natural monopoly regulation is frequently illegitimate.[36] Holcombe has shown the need to reevaluate policies of public provision. Market incentives are more effective providers of quality than the perverse incentives faced under government provision. He argues that planners cannot be as effective or efficient as markets in preserving the environment, protecting natural resources, and providing things such as health care and housing. He also suggests that many quality of life problems are the result of poorly defined property rights. Thus government failure is the root of many problems proactive policies seek to fix.[37]

Public choice problems in proactive anti-drug policy

Holcombe also provides policy-relevant research and theory in support of legalizing drugs. He concludes that the negative social costs from maintaining drug criminalization are far higher than the benefits, due in large part to the perverse incentives faced by law enforcement agencies. While some corruption may be found in these agencies, the main problem has been in other areas. As Holcombe comments:

> Corruption may not be the major problem related to the legal enforcement of drug crimes. Incentives in the legal system may lead law enforcement officers to pursue drug crimes at the expense of other types of crime, with the result that other crimes increase. The most obvious incentive is that often property confiscated by law enforcement officers through drug arrests remains with the law enforcement agency (Holcombe 1995, p. 149).

---

[36] See Ellig, Kaufman, and Rustici 1995. Persistent public choice problems caused the firm to withdraw later but its successful entrance indicates that genuine natural monopoly is rare; it is the result of high contracting sunk costs rather than high capital construction sunk costs.

[37] See Holcombe 1995. The need to define property rights is covered on pp. 169-171.

Victimless crimes, whether they involve drugs, prostitution, gambling, or anything else, distinguish themselves because the participants have no incentive to reveal the crimes. Rather, the participants take measures to conceal the activities from law enforcement officers. If a burglary occurs, the victim will summon law enforcement officers, but without a victim none of the participants to a drug deal will notify the police. Therefore, law enforcement officers must actively seek out the activities that participants are trying to conceal. The privacy of individuals must be invaded for law enforcement officers to investigate drug crimes, so the rights of individuals are bound to suffer...Because of the war on drugs, the rights of individuals are being systematically narrowed, and the power of the government law enforcement agency is being consistently broadened. The constitutional rights of the citizens of the United States, which have been jealously guarded for two centuries, are now being sacrificed to fight a war on drugs. Law enforcement officers are seizing vehicles—cars, boats, airplanes—if they have found drugs on them, regardless of whether the owner is found responsible (Holcombe 1995, p. 157).

Schansberg concurs with this evidence and further suggests that proactive drug policy in the United States has actually harmed poor people on account of economic incentives influenced by public choice problems.

Probably the biggest problem with prohibition of drugs is that it dramatically increases violent crime. Drug *laws* are directly responsible because they create extremely high profits. As a result, gangs engage in turf wars to protect and enlarge their share of this highly profitable market (Schansberg 1996, p. 97).

The biggest problem with implementing a "war on drugs" is that sale and purchase of drugs are mutually beneficial—both parties perceive that they benefit. Most crimes involve one party harming another. In those cases, there is always an incentive for someone to provide evidence against the party causing harm. In drug transactions and other "crimes" of this sort (prostitution, gambling, and so on), both parties believe they benefit. Why would they want to talk to the police? For this reason, drug laws are especially difficult to enforce. In addition, high profits lead to corruption. Bribes are mutually beneficial as well. And they are especially tempting for those in the criminal justice system whose incomes are not especially high. Evidence of this is seen in the rampant drug use of our prison population and the occasional "bust" of police officers themselves. If drug use can't be stopped in the prison, how can law enforcement stop drugs in the community? Moreover, because the illegal drug market is tax-free in both product and labor markets, it is mutually beneficial to remain outside the law in black markets. Finally, even if the government is successful in reducing supply, it makes all of these problems worse…[Modern drug prohibition] causes high profits and wages. These opportunities are a great temptation to young unskilled laborers, especially given the low-quality education that they often receive from the public school (Schansberg 1996, p. 99).

[The origins of prohibiting consumption of alcohol earlier this century] were not based on concerns about morality. The Harrison Act of 1914 was designed to allow pharmacists and physicians monopoly power in prescribing medication. What began as using government to restrict competition quickly evolved into a total restriction on the purchase and sale of currently illegal drugs. I understand this is an extremely difficult issue. As an Evangelical Christian, I often receive incredulous looks whenever I say ending prohibition is the third most important issue facing the poor (behind education and welfare).

Prohibition might be best for middle class America, but the costs to the inner-city poor are tremendous: gangs and gang violence, a seductive enticement to low-skilled inner-city young people, and the creation of improper role models. The suburbs may benefit, but the inner cities suffer greatly (Schansberg 1996, p. 103).

O'Rourke observes: "Who wouldn't rather have a couple of plump, flaky lines on a mirror and half a disco biscuit than lead the lives these [poor] people are leading" (O'Rourke 1991, p. 118). In addition, he observes that politicians face difficult public choice constraints that inhibit drug policy's effectiveness.

While the government is waiting for everyone to die [from crack in order to automatically solve the drug problem], it can create government agencies and organizations, such as the drug czar's office to combat the sale and use of illegal drugs. There are now a total of forty-one federal government organizations and agencies combating the sale and use of illegal drugs. The drug czar's Office of National Drug Control Policy is typical. The drug czar was given the responsibility for curing the entire nation's drug ills and was also given the same approximate civil authority as Ann Landers. The drug czar is a general without soldiers. But the hell with metaphors, in the war against drugs we've got real generals without soldiers. We could send the marines to Latin America and put some holes in the blow lords. But we won't. It would upset our foreign policy. You know how it is when you've got a well-thought-out and carefully crafted foreign policy that consists of cuddling up to Pol Pot, apologizing for everything Israel does, abandoning the democratic opposition in China and congratulating Hafez Assad on his human rights record—you don't want to do anything to upset that. Former Customs

Commissioner William Von Raab, calls the State Department "conscientious objectors in the war against drugs." Von Raab instituted the "zero tolerance" customs policy, which means you can kiss your yacht good-bye if customs agents find so much as a roach clip in your scuppers [an opening to let water run off the deck of a ship]. He advocated shooting drug-smuggling planes on sight and putting a price on the heads of drug traffickers. Von Raab is serious about drugs. He is also looking for work...What the federal government really ends up doing about drugs is palming the problem off on local police departments (O'Rourke 1991, p. 113-114).

Table 5.2 Costs of drug prohibition

Summary of the various costs of drug prohibition:
(1) increases in crime,
(2) there are no victims, since the activity is consensual, and thus people are punished when they harm no one,
(3) creation of monopoly rents,
(4) following Eric Schansberg in *Poor Policy*, poor people are harmed more than others,
(5) some regulations originated from problematic public choice phenomena, e.g., the Harrison Act dealing with oil from the marijuana plant and its relation to makers of hemp rope,
(6) violation of individual rights and privacy,
(7) confiscation of property,
(8) destruction of "suspicious" goods by customs officials in the United States,
(9) activities of government employees at times to take advantage of available gains,
(10) perverse incentives, especially with the police departments, and
(11) conflicts of interests in international relations and policy.

Holcombe, Schansberg and O'Rourke provide a strong argument for decriminalizing drug use based on public choice and microeconomic theory. The costs of drug prohibition, summarized in Table 5.2, almost certainly exceed the social benefits from the policy. Indeed, the poor are harmed in order to fulfill the righteous desires of the relatively wealthy.

An example of usable public policy analysis

Free market theorists must engage in policy-relevant work. However, there is often much empirical evidence and many interesting analogies to be gleaned by reading advocacy and public policy analysis. This data may be used in developing policy-relevant research. Much public policy analysis is quite scholarly, in the sense that it is well-researched, documented, and cogently written. In recent years, there have been lucid, high quality achievements in this normative endeavor. Perhaps an example of such work is in order at this point, to illustrate its features and to contrast it with the policy-relevant work of free market theorists like Holcombe and Schansberg.

One of the foremost public policy analysts today is James Bovard. In his book *The Fair Trade Fraud*, he provides a stinging account of so-called "fair trade" in the U.S.A., describing plainly the costs to consumers from rent seeking.

Fair trade often consists of some politician or bureaucrat picking a number out of thin air and imposing it on foreign businesses and American consumers. Fair trade means that Jamaica is allowed to sell the U.S. only 970 gallons of ice cream a year, that Mexico is allowed to sell Americans only 35,292 bras a year, that Poland is allowed to ship us only 350 tons of alloy tool steel, that Haiti is allowed to sell the US only 8,030 tons of sugar.

Fair trade means permitting each American citizen to consume the equivalent of only one teaspoon of foreign ice cream per year, two foreign peanuts per year, and one pound of imported cheese per year. Fair trade means the U.S. government imposing import quotas on tampons, typing ribbons, tents, twine, table linen, tapestries, and ties. Fair trade means that the U.S. Congress can dictate over 8,000 different taxes on imports, with tariffs as high as 458% (Bovard 1991, p. 2).

In practice, fair trade means protectionism. Yet, every trade barrier undermines the productivity of capital and labor throughout the economy. A 1979 Treasury Department study estimated that trade barriers routinely cost American consumers eight to ten times as much as they benefit American producers. A 1984 Federal Trade Commission study estimated that tariffs cost the American economy $81.00 for every $1.00 of adjustments cost saved. Restrictions on clothing and textile imports cost consumers $1.00 for each 1 cent of increased earnings of American textile and clothing workers. According to the Institute for International Economics, trade barriers are costing American consumers $80 billion a year—equal to over $1,200 per family…The myth of fair trade is that politicians and bureaucrats are fairer than markets—that government coercion and restriction can create a fairer result than voluntary agreement—and that prosperity is best achieved by arbitrary political manipulation, rather than allowing each individual and company to pursue their own interest. Government cannot make trade more fair by making it less free (Bovard 1991, p. 5).

Bovard has done an excellent job of thoroughly researching his topic, digging up data and evidence from archives and other applicable sources. He finds that promoting fair trade along with other political agendas leads to dolorous inspections and seizures, as he comments:

When Customs Commissioner William von Raab was asked why his agency was using its new seizure authority so frequently, he replied, "Because it's easier." In 1987, the Fingerhut Corporation imported a large shipment of sewing kits, including needles and spools of thread; the kits were seized by Customs, which claimed the sewing kits were actually luggage, which carried a tariff three times higher and required a quota import license. Fingerhut lost hundreds of orders as a result (Bovard 1991, p. 25).

Some Customs inspectors appear to have been heavily influenced by the 1970s cult film classic, "The Texas Chainsaw Massacre." In Seattle, Customs inspectors chainsawed an imported cigar store wooden Indian to prove beyond a shadow of a doubt that the Indian did not contain any narcotics. Customs agents used chainsaws to "inspect" a large container tightly packed with paper products. Congressman J.J. Pickle berated Customs Commission William von Raab: "We have had instances where you brought antique [teakwood] elephants in or articles like that and you chain-sawed it. That doesn't leave that elephant with a heck-of-a-lot of value." Chainsaws are an attractive, efficient means of inspecting imports in part because the Customs Service never compensates property owners for damage it does during inspections. The House Ways and Means Committee investigation concluded, "The U.S. Customs Service has little or no incentive to avoid damaging cargo during examinations." Customs officials take apart airplanes during inspections—and then the aircraft owner has to pay to put the plane back together (Bovard 1991, p. 26).

Quotas are also part of contemporary fair trade, yet they too are riddled with public choice problems. Bovard notes:

> Quotas are the epitome of fair trade—trade based on political negotiation rather than consumer sovereignty. Quotas allow politicians and bureaucrats to pick individual winners and losers, to distribute economic advantages according to political clout, and to dictate how Americans may spend their paycheck. Quotas are an affirmative action program that operate not by strengthening the protected industry, but by crippling its foreign competition and sacrificing its American dependents (Bovard 1991, pp. 98-99).

Bovard reports that the notion of "dumping," which began earlier in the twentieth century, was a product of special interest group activities. While many Americans think dumping is bad for them, in reality just the opposite it true.

> If foreigners are selling below cost, that means that they are transferring wealth to the Americans—they are giving Americans a handout. Should the U.S. be so paranoid of foreigners bearing gifts? How can a foreign company give Americans money and at the same time weaken the American economy? If the net amount of capital and goods in the U.S. increases, this means more economic opportunity. The economic argument against dumping is justified solely on the grounds that dumping is predatory behavior that means cheap prices in the short run and extortionary prices in the long run. Dumping margins often have little or no relation to the actual prices charged by foreign companies. Most dumping margins are statistical delusions created by putting thousands or millions of largely irrelevant bits of data through the Commerce Department's blenders (Bovard 1991, p. 153).

Dumping law encourages American companies to gamble on high legal fees to get a federal license to levy surcharges on their American customers (Bovard 1991, pp. 154-155).

Indeed, rent seeking by pressure groups for government favors is the nature of the game. Bovard suggests that it is in the interest of consumers that the game comes to an end.

Wendy Hansen concluded in a 1990 *American Political Science Review* analysis of the ITC that the likelihood of industries being granted protection "seems to depend less on economic need and more on their ability to apply political pressure and influence the decision makers" (Bovard 1991, p. 220).

After 200 years of protection for sugar and textiles, and over a century for steel, maybe it is time to stop giving America's laggards the benefit of the doubt (Bovard 1991, p. 264).

"Power corrupts" summarizes congressional trade policy. In general, politicians have as much natural affection for fairness as they do for honesty. Advocates of fair trade and managed trade tend to imply that America must choose between free trade or of benevolent protection. But in reality, the choices are free trade and mindless protection—a protection that shoots blindly at people's living standards—a protection that is simply a political auction—a political spoils system consisting of the entire national economy. Congressmen have perpetually sought to seize power over something that they did not understand. The history of American trade policy vivifies the perennial economic illiteracy and moral irresponsibility of the U.S. Congress (Bovard 1991, p. 300).

"Fair trade" is a misnomer for modern protectionist poli-cies. Bovard contends that Americans should be free to buy what they want, despite the trend favoring government re-strictions that result from granting political favors.

Trade barriers come down to a question of political le-gitimacy. What gives one person a right to arbitrarily and forcibly reduce another person's living standard? Should election into office automatically give a person the right to dictate the food other people eat, the clothes they wear, and the cars they drive? Does winning a seat in Congress mean that a person—or group of people—can rightfully dictate that each American will be allowed on-ly one teaspoon of foreign ice cream a year, one pound of foreign cheese per year, and that only one American out of 10,000 will be allowed to buy a Czech wool sweater each year? Fair trade is nothing but politically controlled trade—which means political control of the life of the average citizen…The U.S. government cannot be paternalistic to American companies without being sadistic toward American consumers (Bovard 1991, p. 318).

Bovard's information, questions and conclusions all pro-vide useful leads for new policy-relevant research.

Public policy writing based on concerns about liberty

Especially in the Virginia School, a clear normative bias has developed as a result of the application of public choice principles to public policy. Accordingly, free market theo-rists have been concerned that public choice problems will lead to more proactive public policies that in turn foster greater erosion of individual liberty. Bruno Leoni notes:

Even those economists who have most brilliantly defended the free market against the interference of the authorities have usually neglected the parallel consideration that no free market is really compatible with a lawmaking process centralized by the authorities (Leoni 1991, p. 89).

If we admit that the general trend of present-day society has been more against individual freedom than in favor of it, how could the said honoratories *escape the trend?*
...How could judges any better than legislators, escape the contemporary trend against individual freedom (Leoni 1991, p. 183)?

The negative impact from overused rhetoric in public policy has also been significant. Both Mises and Hayek believed that the debasement of language by the socialists would lead to social problems. Mises complained: "The socialists have engineered a semantic revolution in converting the meaning of terms into their opposite" (Mises 1988, p. 28). And Hayek suggested, for instance, that the word "social" has lost most of its meaning since it is now used to make many compound words that often are used in support of proactive policy goals (see Hayek 1988).

As far as Mises was concerned, the best public policy was minimal public policy and then only dedicated to reactive functions. Other policies merely curtail individual liberty.

Government is essentially the negation of liberty. It is the recourse to violence or threat of violence in order to make all people obey the orders of the government, whether they like it or not. As far as the government's jurisdiction extends, there is coercion, not freedom... government is repression not freedom. Freedom is to be found only in the sphere in which government does not interfere. Liberty is always freedom from the government (Mises 1988, p. 33).

The ultimate end that men aim at by establishing government is to make possible the operation of a definite system of social cooperation under the principle of the division of labor (Mises 1988, p. 34).

Government means always coercion and compulsion and is by necessity the opposite of liberty. Government is a guarantor of liberty and is compatible with liberty only if its range is adequately restricted to the preservation of what is called economic freedom. Where there is no market economy, the best-intentioned provisions of constitutions and laws remain a dead letter (Mises 1966, p. 285).

Advocacy writing is also popular among professional economists and scholars. For instance, Walter Williams has made substantial contributions in labor and race economics. He shows how proactive government policy harms black people and the poor (Williams 1982), echoing the concerns of Mises while extolling the benefits of reactive policy.

The benefit of the free enterprise system is that private ownership and control of property minimize the capacity of one person to coerce another. Additionally, the coercive powers of the state are minimized...Through numerous successful attacks, private property and free enterprise are mere skeletons of their past. Jefferson anticipated this when he said, "The natural progress of things is for government to gain ground and for liberty to yield" (Williams 1993, p. 4).

George Washington, not our most radical Founder, said "Government is not reason, it is not eloquence. It is force. Like fire, it is a dangerous servant, and a fearsome master" (Williams 1993, p. 19).

Free market theorists are generally concerned with the same policy problems that Bastiat was concerned with in the nineteenth century. Bastiat wanted government action to be restricted to reactive or "defensive" policy and was concerned by the dominance of policy to enhance special interests at the expense of other people. Commenting on Hayek's famous criticism of what might be deemed proactive policy, Williams laments the degeneration of individual liberties in the United States.

The federal government has become destructive of the ends it was created to serve. Rule of law is an alien value in today's America. As Friedrich Hayek warned, "The important point is that all coercive action of government must be unambiguously determined by a permanent legal framework which enables the individual to plan with a degree of confidence and which reduces human uncertainty [and, thus, individual economic insecurity] as much as possible." We have made a mockery of the inscription carved into the wall at the U.S. Department of Justice, "Where the law ends tyranny begins." Federal and state agencies have used Nazi-style justice where people are declared to be criminals, not on the basis of their act but on the consequences of their actions (Williams 1993, p. 17).

[*The Road to Serfdom*] is the most powerful yet to be refuted argument that fascism, communism and socialism are kindred forms of collectivism whose survival critically depends upon the undermining of private property rights, rule of law, limited government and other institutions that make liberty possible...We Americans must stop asking and allowing Congress to trash the Constitution and our liberty-enhancing institutions. If we don't, we will travel farther down the road to serfdom and meet with the same disasters of other collectivist nations (Williams 1994, p. 24).

And, from a free market perspective, just look at how much further advanced the world has gone down the road to serfdom in the fifteen years after Williams wrote those prophetic words! Perhaps there are further grounds for pessimism. O'Rourke reminds us that democracy contains the public choice-affiliated seeds of its own destruction.

Selfishness consumes our body politic. The eighteenth century Scottish historian Alexander Tyler said: "A democracy cannot exist as a permanent form of government. It can only exist until a majority of voters discover that they can vote themselves largess out of the public treasury" (O'Rourke 1996, p. 105).

James Dorn suggests that the problems created by public policy in a rent seeking society also adversely affect social morality. Government's role is not to "instill values" but to protect rights in a society of free and responsible individuals. Unless public policy is limited, majoritarian politics will decay further into a crass game where the winners get to impose their vision, and costs, on the losers; in short, to transform itself into an immoral society.

During the past 50 years, the welfare state has divorced freedom from responsibility and created a false sense of morality. Good intentions have led to bad policy. The moral state of the union can be improved by following two simple rules: "Do no harm" and "do good at your own expense." Those rules are perfectly consistent in the private moral universe. It is only when the second rule is replaced by "Do good at the expense of others" that social harmony turns into chaos as interest groups compete at the public trough for society's scarce resources (Dorn 1996, p. 140, cf. p. 138).

If Dorn's assessment is correct, then free market theorists have added reason for pursuing policy-relevant research: to make a positive impact on public policy by the application of the insights from public choice theory. In addition, public policy may be similarly analyzed and enriched by the insights of Austrian economic theory, to which our attention will turn in chapters seven through eleven.

Appendix: the anecdotal policy analysis of P.J. O'Rourke

As we have already seen, O'Rourke adds flair to policy work, and his efforts can even be useful in augmenting policy-relevant research. Of course, he is a humorist and does not intend to provide scholarly discourse on theoretical problems in public policy. Yet his work leads both to some insightful quips and, occasionally, to some evidence usable in more serious inquiries. In addition to the earlier quotations from him in this book, the following long quotations about policy issues provide examples of O'Rourke's work that might, if used sparingly, have such an auxiliary use in more serious studies. Consider his comments on poverty policy:

I went to a federal low-income housing project in Newark, New Jersey, and just going inside and climbing the stairs was more exposure to questions of poverty policy than most people can stand and not pass out. The stairwell was a cascade of filth, a spillway of human urine and unidentifiable putrefying matter. There was nothing on these steps wholesome enough to call trash. It would have cheered me up to see anything as vibrant as a rat. The housing project was one of those War on Poverty, a-Hand-Not-a-Handout, Great Society, Give-a-Damn edifices that they tore down a perfectly good slum to build in the 1960s. The stairwell was lighted by dim bagel-shaped, twenty-two-watt fluorescent tubes—"landlord halos"—each protected by a steel cage lag-bolted to the reinforced-concrete ceiling. Only the strongest and most purposeful vandals could destroy light fixtures like these, but that's the kind of vandals this housing project has, and dangling electric wires and foot-wide craters in the cement marked the former location of each lamp. There was some illumination, however, from a large puddle of lighter fluid blazing away on the third-story landing, and phlegm-colored sun shone through a befouled skylight seven stories above. I don't know what, or if, the stairwell walls had once been painted. I couldn't even tell what they were made of. Smoke, dirt, spray paint and marker-pen scribbling were caked on every surface in a cover-all hue of defeat and exasperation, the same shade small children achieve with their first set of watercolors. Graffitied names and sign overlapped, layered in a density of senselessness to do a Yale semiotics [the study of signs and symbols] professor proud (O'Rourke 1996, pp. 123-124).

So O'Rourke gives us some reason to doubt the effectiveness of proactive policies against poverty via subsidized housing. He also describes the tenacity of rent seeking farmers.

Farming has always carried emotional freight. Thomas Jefferson, caught in a moment of rare idiocy arguing against the industrialization of the United States, said, "Those who labor in the earth are the chosen people of God . . . whose breasts He has made a peculiar deposit for substantial and genuine virtue." This, is by the way, from a gentleman farmer who owned two hundred slaves and kept at least one of them as his mistress. The farm lobby makes good use of such lofty forms of nonsense and, also, of less lofty forms of nonsense, such as congressmen. For instance, sugar growers donate about half a million dollars a year to congressional election campaigns, and the dairy industry donates $2 million. Even though only 46 out of 435 congressional districts are controlled by farm votes, farmers have gained heavy leverage on Capitol Hill by combining rhetoric, ready money and a talent for political logrolling that dates back to the Constitutional Convention, when southern farmers managed to get slaves counted as three fifths of a voter without letting any slaves do three fifths of the voting. As a result of this disproportionate influence, 25 percent of the net income U.S. farmers receive is in the form of direct cash payments from the government. The only other businessmen who put this kind of lip clamp on the public teat are defense contractors. And at least when we give billions to defense contractors, we get something back for it, Star Wars or something. Maybe we don't need Star Wars, maybe it doesn't work, but at least the defense contractors were thinking of us. They made, you know, a gesture. But we give billions to farmers and don't even get a basket of zucchini on the front porch (O'Rourke 1996, pp. 150-151).

O'Rourke also gives us some reason to doubt the veracity of emotion-laden proactive policies against homelessness.

The big, resentful woman I mentioned earlier went on to extol a group of what appeared to be just plain street bums called the New Exodus Marchers who had walked to DC from New York. When the New Exodus people arrived in Washington, they promptly got into a fistfight at the Center for Creative Non-Violence. The fight had to do with the disposition of royalty proceeds from the sale of HOMELESS T-shirts. (I am not making this up.) Ms. Big Resentful said, "Five babies died on the walk from New York City! The mothers miscarried but they kept on walking! This was amazing! This was super-natural!" This was grounds for arrest. Over on the other side of the crowd I heard somebody shouting through a bullhorn that they were from Alliance, Ohio. "And you may not believe this," they shouted, "but even in little Alliance, Ohio, we have two hundred people in our shelter." I didn't believe this. I'm from Ohio. Alliance is a pleasant, semirural town in the northeast of the state. On Monday I called the Alliance town office and was put right through to Mayor Carr, who sounded puzzled. "The figure is new to me," he said. "I'd never heard the two-hundred figure. Our shelter was put up for people whose houses burn down, things like that. We haven't thought of it in terms of the homeless" (O'Rourke 1996, pp. 188-189).

Finally, O'Rourke also makes some anecdotal remarks pertaining to proactive environmental policy.

The environmental movement has, I'm afraid, discovered a unifying agent, a devil, a . . . (I can't say "scapegoat." Scapegoats are probably an endangered species. Besides, all animals are innocent, noble, upright, honest, fair in their dealings and have a great sense of humor.) The environmental movement has found its enemy in the form of that ubiquitous evil—already so familiar to Hollywood scriptwriters, pulp paperback authors, and all the dim-bulb Democrats in Congress—big business…This is why it's rarely an identifiable person (and, of course, never you or me) who pollutes. It's a vague, sinister, faceless thing called industry. The National Wildlife Federation's booklet on toxic chemical releases says, "industry dumped more that 2.3 billion pounds of toxic chemicals into or onto the land," and, "industry pumped more than 1.5 billion pounds of toxic chemicals into the land via deep-well injection." What will "industry" do next? Visit us with a plague of boils? Make off with our first born?..." Once durable products like furniture are made to fall apart quickly, requiring more frequent replacement," claims the press kit of Inform, a New York-based environmental group that seems to be missing a few sunflower seeds from its trail mix...Business and industry and "their friends in the Reagan administration and Congress" make easy and even appropriate targets. Nobody squirts sulfur dioxide into the air for a hobby, after all, or tosses PCBs into rivers as an act of charity. Pollution occurs in the course of human enterprise. It is a by-product of people making things, things like a living. But whatever is required to clean up the environment people are going to have to make that, too. If we desire, for ourselves and our progeny, a world that's not too stinky and carcinogenic, we're going to need the technical expertise, entrepreneurial vigor and marketing genius of every business and industry. And if the Perennially Indignant think pollution is the fault only of Reaganites wallowing in capitalist greed, then they should go take a deep breath in Smolensk or a long drink from the River Volga. Business and industry—trade and manufacture—are inherent in civilization. Every human society, no matter how wholesomely primitive, practices as much trade and manufacture as it can figure out. For good reason. It is the fruits of trade and manufacture that raise us from the wearying muck of subsistence and give us the health, wealth, education, leisure and warm, dry rooms and Xerox machines that allow us to be the ecology-conscious, selfless committed, splendid individuals we are...Worship of nature may be ancient, but seeing nature as cuddlesome, hug-a-bear and too cute for words is strictly a modern fashion (O'Rourke 1996, pp. 195-196).

References

Anderson, Gary and Tollison, Robert and Halcoussis, D. (1996), "Drafting the Competition: Labor Unions and Military Conscription," *Defence and Peace Economics*, vol. 7, pp. 189-202.

Anderson, Gary and Tollison, Robert (1991), "Political Influence on Civil War Mortality Rates: The Electoral College as a Battlefield," *Defence Economics*, vol. 2, pp. 219-233.

Bastiat, Fredric (1990/1850), *The Law*, Foundation for Economic Education: Irvington-on-Hudson, New York.

Benson, Bruce L. (1990), *The Enterprise of Law: Justice Without the State*, Pacific Research Institute: San Francisco.

Benson, Bruce L. (1998), *To Serve and Protect: Privatization and Community in Criminal Justice* (Political Economy of the Austrian School Series), New York University Press, New York.

Bovard, James (1991), *The Fair Trade Fraud: How Congress Pillages the Consumer and Decimates America's Competitiveness*, St. Martin's Press: New York.

Cobin, John M. (2006), *Christian Theology of Public Policy: Highlighting the American Experience*, Alertness Books: Greenville, South Carolina.

Cobin, John M. (1997), *Building Regulation, Market Alternatives, and Allodial Policy*, Avebury Press: London.

DiLorenzo, Thomas J. (2004), *How Capitalism Saved America*, New York: Crown Forum.

Dorn, James A. (1996), "The Rise of Government and the Decline of Morality," *The Freeman*, vol. 46, no. 3, March, 136-140.

Ellig, Jerry; Kaufman, Jeff; and Rustici, Tom (1995), "When Do Sunk Costs Prevent Entry: The Case of Gas Pipelines," unpublished manuscript dated March 17, 1995, George Mason University: Fairfax, Virginia.

Foldvary, Fred (1994), *Public Goods and Private Communities: The Market Provision of Social Services*, Edward Elgar Publishing Co. [The Locke Institute]: Brookfield, Vermont.

Hayek, Friedrich A. von (1988), *The Fatal Conceit: The Errors of Socialism*, University of Chicago Press: Chicago.

Hayek, Friedrich A. von (1944), *The Road to Serfdom*, University of Chicago Press: Chicago.

High, Jack C. (1984), "The Case for Austrian Economics," *Intercollegiate Review*, winter, pp. 37-42.

High, Jack C., and Ellig, Jerome (1988), "The Private Supply of Education: Some Historical Evidence," in Tyler Cowen, ed., *The Theory of Market Failure: A Critical Examination*, George Mason University Press/Cato Institute book: Fairfax, Virginia, pp. 361-382.

Holcombe, Randall G. (1995), *Public Policy and the Quality of Life: Market Incentives versus Government Planning*, Greenwood Press: Westport, Connecticut.

Leoni, Bruno (1991), *Freedom and the Law*, expanded Third Edition, Liberty Press/Liberty Fund: Indianapolis, Indiana.

Mises, Ludwig von (1966/1949), *Human Action: A Treatise on Economics*, Third Revised Edition, Contemporary Books, Inc. (Henry Regnery Co.): Chicago.

Mises, Ludwig von (1988), "Liberty and Property," in *Two Essays by Ludwig von Mises*, The Ludwig von Mises Institute: Auburn, Alabama.

Mitchell, William C., and Simmons, Randy T. (1994), *Beyond Politics: Markets, Welfare, and the Failure of Bureaucracy*, Westview Press: San Francisco, California

Mueller, Dennis (1990), *Public Choice II*, Cambridge University Press: New York.

Opitz, Edmund (1999), *The Libertarian Theology of Freedom*, Tampa, Florida: Hallberg Publishing Company.

O'Rourke, P.J. (1991), *Parliament of Whores: A Lone Humorist Attempts to Explain the Entire U.S. Government*, Vintage Books [Random House]: New York.

Schansberg, Eric (1996), *Poor Policy: How Government Harms the Poor*, Westview Press: Boulder, Colorado.

Schansberg, Eric (2003), *Turn Neither to the Right nor to the Left*, Alertness Books: Greenville, South Carolina.

Shortt, Bruce N. (2004), *The Harsh Truth About Public Schools*, Chalcedon Foundation: Vallecito, California.

Tullock, Gordon (1980), *Trials on Trial: The Pure Theory of Legal Procedure*, Columbia University Press: New York.

Williams, Walter E. (1994), "Liberals care only about results," *Conservative Chronicle*, vol. 9, no. 6, February 9, p. 24.

Williams, Walter E. (1993), *The Legitimate Role of Government in a Free Economy*, The American University: Bryn Mawr, Pennsylvania.

Williams, Walter E. (1982), *The State Against Blacks*, McGraw-Hill Publishing Company: New York.

Yates, Steven (2005), *Worldviews: Christian Theism versus Modern Materialism*, The Worldviews Project: Greenville, South Carolina.

6 Perverse incentives and public choice issues for regulation

Seven major tenets of public choice theory

The first four chapters of this book provided an overview of public choice theory, citing many original sources. Before embarking on the application of public choice to some regulatory concerns, and subsequently leaving the theory in order to undertake an overview of Austrian economics in the next five chapters, it will be useful to consider again a summary of seven of the principal tenets of public choice theory. This review is, of course, repetitive, albeit far more concise. But the motifs will recur so often in the analysis of regulation and legislation, that it will be valuable for the reader and the student. In addition, the ensuing summary is clearer and more condensed—without long quotations.

Intensified interest group activity

A single vote is virtually meaningless and commands infinitesimal political influence. Thus, choosing not to vote is rational, especially when citizens are not obligated to vote by legislation (as they are, for example, in countries like Chile—where, barring extreme circumstances, once they initially register to vote they must continue to do so for the rest of their lives). Instead, the most effective use of time and resources under democratic processes will be for citizens to support special interest groups (SIGs) that advance the issue(s) of greatest importance to them. Since SIGs represent large blocks of votes, they command considerable political influence. Thus, mature democratic processes tend to proliferate SIG activity, especially when coupled with an expanding regulatory environment. The self-interest motive and the logic of concentrated benefits and dispersed costs will naturally continue to spawn SIGs. Accordingly, SIG proliferation is a result of rational behavior rather than social degeneration. A government composed only of saints would produce similar results.

The market process is led by an invisible hand to coordinate human affairs among millions of self-interested economic actors. However, the political process is "led by an invisible hand to promote other kinds of interests" (Mitchell and Simmons 1994, p. 39). The political process lacks the market information and incentives which lead to catallactic coordination of human action, and SIG activity distorts political outcomes in favor of private interests.

Likewise, public choice theory suggests that government action cannot cure market failures (and often makes things worse). It has exploded the idea that government is a "frictionless plug" which, as welfare economists often propose, can be used to alleviate market failures. On the contrary, instead of facilitating democratic majority rule and genuine social benefits, the political process often entails "intense competition for power to benefit particularized interests at the cost of wider society" (Mitchell and Simmons 1994, pp. 211, 212, 213). SIGs distort the democratic process, making public policy a battle between special interests rather than rule by the people. The proliferation of SIG activity lessens individual control of government and, perhaps more importantly, permits the use government power to embellish private interests at public expense (although often under the guise of the public interest).

Correspondingly, such government failure can only be mitigated by limiting government, rather than by electing or appointing the most honest or well-trained planners. Public choice theorists regard SIGs as being one of the most potent influences in a democratic process, second only to perhaps the innate self-interest motive itself and the influence of academic ideas on the climate of public opinion. Even the strongest, most widely endorsed political constitution is vulnerable to the onslaught of what Wagner calls the "guns" of SIGs.

Public choice theory indicates that political action does not occur in a vacuum. Congruently, Austrian theory suggests that all human action (including political action) is purposeful and aims at ends that remove uneasiness (Mises 1996/1966, pp. 10, 13). Therefore, whether blatantly or incognito, SIGs must be active participants backing the implementation of regulation or legislation.

Rent seeking

In the market process, entrepreneurs normally gain short-lived monopoly benefits, which are quickly dissipated (in the absence of barriers to entry) as others rush to enter the market. In the political process, however, competition is not a natural check against the long-lived monopoly privileges attained by government sanction. The government enforces the monopoly privileges by barring all potential entrants. Thus, government-sanctioned monopoly is very attractive, and public choice theorists call attempts to attain it a form of rent seeking.

Tullock defines rent seeking, probably better termed "privilege-seeking," as "the manipulation of democratic [or other types of] governments to obtain special privileges under circumstances where the people injured by the privileges are hurt more than the beneficiary gains" (Tullock 1993, p. 24, cf. p. 51). Buchanan says, "The term *rent seeking* is designed to describe behavior in institutional settings where individual efforts to maximize value generate social waste rather than social surplus" (Buchanan 1980, pp. 46, 47). There are mutually beneficial gains from all voluntary market exchange (i.e., it is akin to a positive-sum game). However, no social gains are created by rent seeking. Instead, there is likely to be a net destruction of value on account of the monopoly privileges granted. Thus, rent seeking is *at best* a zero-sum game.

According to public choice theory, the social loss from rent seeking is not just the "Harberger Triangle" in the typical monopoly diagram, but that area *plus* the "Tullock Rectangle" (the area to the left of the Harberger Triangle). Social losses are exacerbated by "paperwork contests," as the Tullock Rectangle is dissipated by competing rent seekers and counter rent-seekers (also called "reformers") try to attain the monopoly benefits (Higgins and Tollison 1988, pp. 150-151). A successful rent seeking monopolist may lose all or a portion of his rent seeking gains to reformers, or by the expenditures he makes to retain his privileges (Tollison and Wagner 1991, 60-64). Consumers lose because they have to pay higher prices for the duration of the government-enforced monopoly privilege, and on account of other distortions in labor markets. Moreover, at least a portion of the rent seeking costs will likely be born by taxpayers.

Rent seeking is not limited to attempts to obtain monopoly power. Rent seeking may take many forms. Broadly speaking, it is any attempt to gain concentrated benefits by way of the political process while dispersing the costs widely in society (resulting in social losses). For instance, a rent seeker might try to petition government to create artificial demand for his product. Maybe he would like to create artificial demand for some costly but environmentally friendly processes, innovation, or service that would have little market demand apart from regulation. Or perhaps he desires to secure an exclusive license over some production method. It is possible to obtain these favors by successfully petitioning legislators or regulators.

However, successful rent seeking might entail compensating political actors—or favor brokers—directly or indirectly. Thus, rent seekers can be expected to hire consultants that help them to both identify rent seeking opportunities and to minimize the commission paid to favor brokers. Rent seeking costs can also be reduced by wisely manipulating the media. For instance, a firm might profit by developing an environmentally friendly and socially conscious image for itself. With this asset, reelection minded politicians might find it more difficult to constrain the rent seeking demands of the firm with attempts to extract higher compensation through "milking" the company.

The successful rent seeker will be masterful at discovering ways to convince government that he deserves to be granted a monopoly right or other special privilege. Those who are eminently *alert* to discovering rent seeking opportunities might be called *regressive* entrepreneurs (as opposed to the *progressive* entrepreneurs found in the market). They are regressive because their activity creates social losses, in spite of the fact that they profit personally (also see chapter nine).

Any kind of regulation, especially new regulation, creates opportunities for rent seeking and propagates *regressive* entrepreneurship (i.e., activities of entrepreneurs who have extraordinary capacities to reap profits via the political process). There are rarely, if ever, exceptions. There will be many self-interested individuals, firms, and industries that are willing to seek rents. Moral scruples might prevent many economic actors from pursuing some or all rent seeking activity, in the same way that their moral scruples prevent them from running objectionable businesses in the marketplace (e.g., prostitution rings, drug dealing, etc.).

However, there will be plenty of economic actors who will avail themselves of rent seeking opportunities without hesitance, just as there are plenty of people willing to operate objectionable enterprises. The self-interest motive tells us nothing about individual morals or ethics. Some people will likely be persuaded, for better or for worse, that there is nothing wrong with rent seeking.

Therefore, sustaining regulation free of rent seeking is hardly plausible. Economic actors have a natural inclination to secure benefits or rents from the political process to at least offset the tax expense they bear. Favor brokers have an incentive to permit rent seeking since they can gain from it directly by payoffs (e.g., corruption) or by auctioning off a monopoly right or other privilege and thus gaining indirect benefits (e.g., augmenting their budget, likely leading to higher personal wages and power). In sum, regulation will create many opportunities for rent seeking that lead to economic distortions and social losses. As a result, consumers can expect to pay higher prices for many goods and services and face economic distortions and social welfare losses.

Regulatory capture

Producers are likely to form SIGs to use public regulation for their benefit. They might thus be able to obtain beneficial regulation by rent seeking that:
- creates or sustains artificial demand for their products,
- assails their competitors,
- generates direct cash subsidies,
- restricts the output and prices of compliments and substitutes,
- legitimizes price-fixing schemes, or
- erects barriers to entry against potential competitors.

Moreover, the firm or industry that successfully captures its regulators will likely be able to disperse most (if not all) of the costs of the regulation to rationally ignorant voters, consumers or taxpayers over time.

When a regulator is captured, private interests will be able to dominate the public interest, at the expense of consumers and taxpayers. Studies of business regulation in the United States suggest that calls to legislate regulation did not originally emerge from the political process but from rent seeking activity. For instance, work by DiLorenzo, Shughart, and Stigler imply that the Sherman Act of 1890 —the initial federal antitrust legislation in the United States—came about to benefit private interests rather than the public interest. Indeed, business interests have been strong supporters of antitrust legislation, and it is not clear that antitrust legislation has actually curtailed monopoly power as it was supposedly intended to do.

Likewise, Jack High and Clayton Coppin found that rent seeking prompted passage of the Pure Food Act (High and Coppin 1988). Donald Boudreaux and Robert Ekelund contend that rent seeking by municipal governments and others led to the Cable Television Consumer Protection and Competition Act of 1992 (Boudreaux and Ekelund 1993, pp. 356, 390). Tullock has provided an example in which state or local governments also practice rent seeking to obtain federal funding for road repairs (Tullock 1993, pp. 17-18). Mitchell and Simmons go so far as to say that the "real monopolists" that consumers should be wary of are the "80,000 governments that simultaneously oversupply some services and fail to provide for many other important daily wants" (Mitchell and Simmons 1994, p. 139).

The rent seeking society is not glamorous, except perhaps to rent seekers and favor brokers. It is characterized by venality and ongoing social losses, resource misallocations, and economic distortions. Nevertheless, rent seeking and regulatory capture are natural outcomes of self-interested participants in democratic processes. All democratic societies are susceptible to rent seeking distortions evinced by regulatory capture. Even if a country's constitution is strong, and relatively resilient to rent seeking, it provides no perfect repellent to regulatory capture seeking to secure the benefits of rent seeking.

Vote-seeking

From a public choice perspective, self-interested politicians are driven by a dominant objective to be reelected. To be successful, they must find a way to produce political benefits in excess of political costs. When they spend public money they calculate how many votes they will receive per dollar spent. Likewise, they calculate how many votes they will lose from favoring one group at the expense of another. In the end, they attempt to determine the policy mix that optimizes the votes they receive (Mitchell and Simmons 1994, p. 52). Astute vote-seekers will be expert strategists in finding the optimal policy mix and seek consultants that will assist them in the art of producing ambiguous and emotive statements that simultaneously minimize voter animosity and maximize sympathetic voter motivation and total votes earned (Mitchell and Simmons 1994, p. 73). The median voter theory, coupled with the fact that most people who actually vote are women, instructs vote seekers regarding the optimal methods of securing more votes. Accordingly, the target their emotional appeals to the relatively unprincipled and usually female voters near the center of the distribution. Subsequently, vote-seeking politicians will be able to retain political power, perks, money, favor-broker benefits, and even opportunities for venality that proceed from their office. Conformably, Austrian theorist Mises notes:

> The politician is…always selfish no matter whether he supports a popular program in order to get an office or whether he firmly clings to his own—unpopular—

convictions and thus deprives himself of the benefits he could reap by betraying them...Unfortunately the office-holders and their staffs are not angelic. They learn very soon that their decisions mean for the businessmen either considerable losses or—sometimes—considerable gains. Certainly there are also bureaucrats who do not take bribes; but there are others who are anxious to take advantage of any "safe" opportunity of "sharing" with those whom their decisions favor. (Mises 1996/1949, pp. 734-735, cf. p. 852, also see chapter 10)

The politicians who decree and oversee regulation will practice vote-seeking. Their first objective will be to get re-elected, *not* to serve the public interest. They can be expected to prefer using ambiguous statements, for instance, about a zoning policy that maximizes total votes gained by it. For example, they might say the social costs have been enlarged by the "indiscriminate expansion of the metropolitan area." They will tell people that "society" has expressed its "preference for modernizing the regional urban system" and to stop "violating the natural environment" by preserving the "heavily compromised natural balances of the urban basin," while at the same time finding "equilibrium between the city and its surroundings." Planners might hope to enable society "to cope with the estimated population in the year 2020, in conditions and quality of life compatible with human dignity." These ambiguous, emotive sentiments are not fiction. They were excerpted from Santiago, Chile's Metropolitan Regulatory Plan of 1996.

Although the Santiago plan does contain some specific details, its major tenets are ambiguous, just as all regulatory language will tend to be, and vote-seeking politicians will be sure to stick to that portion of the plan in their public comments (lest they offend more voters than they gain). Since the meanings of words or phrases such as: "indiscriminate expansion," "modernizing," "violation," "natural balances," "equilibrium," "cope," "dignity" and others in the plan will differ dramatically across the wide range of Chilean voters, they have no specific meaning in the context of the goals of zoning policy, other than perhaps the private definitions given to them by politicians and planners. Vote-seeking politicians will avoid talking about the precise details and costs of regulation, preferring to focus attention on the ambiguous benefits. Over time, political actors often succumb to pressures from rent seeking SIGs that control large blocks of votes. Consequently, regulatory policy tends to promote the triumph of private interests over the public interest.

Demosclerosis

Public choice theorists contend that the apparent gridlock in the political process caused by SIG pressures is a misperception. According to Jonathan Rauch, political actors are becoming ever more responsive and willing to change, especially in the United States (Rauch 1996, pp. 18, 17). The concept of demosclerosis is simply that SIGs work hard to retain the benefits (government programs) that they were granted in the past and, as a result, these benefits never get cut—no matter how popular reform movements become. Democratic societies generate SIGs (or lobbies) faster than they eliminate them, and these SIGs seek to win (and then defend) some government subsidy, regulation, or tax break. Vote-seeking politicians exacerbate the problem when they choose to retain programs rather than upset a substantial block of voters represented by the affected SIG. They will eagerly try to keep everyone happy, making it increasingly difficult to remove benefits once they have been granted. Hence, Rauch concludes that government "succumbs to a kind of living rot...Stuck with all of its first tries [at various regulations or programs] virtually forever, government loses the ability to end unsuccessful programs and try new ones. It fails to adapt and, as maladaptive things do, becomes too clumsy and incoherent to solve real-world problems" (Rauch 1996, p. 18 and also see Mitchell and Simmons 1994, pp. 53, 76).

The transitional gains trap

Tullock identifies what he calls "transitional gains" for favored SIGs that win special privileges from government, specifically monopoly privileges through licensing requirements and so forth. Such rent seeking gains are difficult to secure and even the most effective and efficient SIGs often have to expend considerable resources to get them. However, the monopoly privileges won by initial rent seekers are transitional. New entrants into an affected market will be "trapped" into paying an entrance fee, effectively transferring the monopoly profits they might have received to government.

Tullock contends that "surviving original owners have opportunity costs equivalent to the price of the entry barrier and consumers are worse off" (Tullock 1975, pp. 671-675). Accordingly, the original rent seekers will have transitional gains but afterwards there is a permanent deadweight social loss and consumers will have to pay perpetually higher prices. Reform is difficult since removing the restriction will likely require compensating those who would suffer the loss of the fee paid to enter the market. Moreover, reform requires convincing government to give up a source of tax revenue. Consequently, firms who have paid for such privileges will rent seek to retain them, even if they received none of the transitional gains. Maintaining restrictions will likely be easier than obtaining the original transitional gains, since political actors have a natural incentive to retain the current level of fees received and, as Tullock notes, vote-seeking politicians will be "reluctant to inflict direct losses on specific sections of the electorate" (Tullock

1993, p. 68). The best way to avoid the transitional gains trap is, of course, to not make any transitional gains available to rent seekers.

The implementation of any new regulation creates new opportunities for rent seekers to obtain monopoly or artificial demand privileges. Self-interested rent seekers will garner transitional gains without regard to the long term social losses they will inflict on others. For instance, zoning policy will augment rent seeking opportunities as prohibitions and restrictions are enacted against potential competitors who want to do business in affected sectors of a city (while existing firms in those sectors are, of course, "grandfathered").

The only way to avoid the transitional gains trap from regulation is to abolish the policy. But this is difficult and costly. Even if some people oppose a regulation on ideological grounds, there are bound to be many who support it because they benefit by it. Thus, along with demosclerosis, the transitional gains trap will make it increasingly unlikely that a regulation, once enacted, will ever be repealed.

Perverse incentives

The final public choice theme covered in this book is *perverse incentives*. Public choice theory does not impugn the motives or character of planners and others who create public choice problems. These difficulties are simply the predictable result of the human self-interest motive. Accordingly, public choice theory suggests that self-interested political actors will be subject to perverse incentives, i.e., incentives that provide individual benefits but create social losses or government failure in public policies.

For instance, Holcombe remarks that planners have a perverse incentive to be ineffective. "The government will never lose profits from being a poor regulator; in fact, the opposite is likely to be true" (Holcombe 1995, p. 103). If regulation were completely effective at eliminating a negative externality then there would no longer be a need for regulation. A regulator or planner who wants to maintain his employment (and we may assume that virtually all of them do) will have an incentive to maintain some minimum levels of negative externalities in order to preserve his job. In addition, planners have a perverse incentive to encourage adverse public information which suggests that current regulation is failing. The typical response to this information will be increased calls for government to augment regulation, likely leading to larger budgets and salaries for planners. Thus, from a public choice perspective, regulatory failures may actually be successes, depending on one's perspective. Rent seekers and regulators will, plausibly, be pleased by a non-catastrophic regulatory failure, while consumers and tax-payers will not.

The perverse incentives problem can be illustrated by Figure 6.1—a hypothetical example of air pollution levels (and regulatory constraints) for a major city. Let us suppose that (1) clean air is a normal good, (2) people's earnings rise over time, (3) all production produces some smog, either directly or indirectly, and (4) that the urban area is growing (along with its production) over time. As the city develops, people will enjoy rising incomes and will be willing to accept higher amounts of air pollution to sustain that income—up to a certain point of *contentment* C. However, as the level of smog rises above point C, people start becoming *concerned*, and a few will even become *preoccupied*, about the smog problem. But most are still willing to tolerate the dirtier air because of the other benefits they have from urban life, at least up to point P. At that smog level they become critically preoccupied, although intense complaining might not begin right away. Accordingly, as the smog level surpasses point P, people might not complain or change their smog producing behavior in the short run if they believe that the rise above point P is only temporary. However, once people realize that the preoccupant level of smog is permanent they will take steps to alleviate the problem. Two options are feasible.

Figure 6.1: Clean air levels constrained by public policy

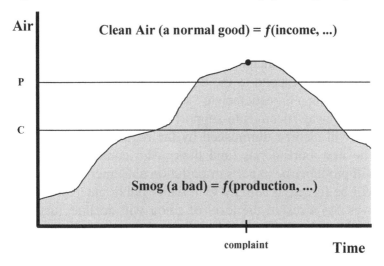

The first option is to simply let entrepreneurs and market institutions develop spontaneously to solve the pollution problem. Since clean air is a normal good, people will prefer to buy more of it as their incomes rise. Above point P, people will tend to trade some of their relatively high incomes for cleaner air. Consequently, pollution control experts and entrepreneurs will emerge to meet the demands of consumers, and competition will cause improvements in technology that make pollution abatement increasingly cheaper. Over time, the lower price will mean that more clean air can be acquired by trading the same percentage of income, and the result will be a smog level that continually declines, probably at a decreasing rate. The level of smog might be reduced to zero someday, but it is unlikely because the opportunity cost of doing so will be rising at an increasing rate. Thus, the costs of purity are often sufficiently high to deter people from achieving it. However, it is likely that the level of smog will remain somewhere below point C over the long run, where there would be little uneasiness from smog.

The second option is for voters to demand that public policies be initiated to deal with the smog problem. The "public interest" would be invoked citing both positive rights to clean air and negative rights to protection from the pollution and its negative external costs. Vote seeking politicians will respond to the demands of voters and SIGs (1) by creating a bureaucracy to "solve" the problem and (2) by taxing away incomes to support it. Personal freedom (utility) will also be diminished by the regulation it generates. The new bureaucrats (and those who consult with them) will probably be experts in pollution abatement, and people will be forced to comply with their "public interest" objectives. As a result, the level of smog will decline, just as it would under the first option. Once people perceive that the long run level of smog has fallen below point P, they will stop complaining. Hence, bureaucrats will have an incentive, either directly or through the pressure of vote seeking politicians, to reach that point as soon as possible. When they succeed, voters will be happy with the regulatory effectiveness and will in turn laud the politicians who initiated it.

However, with the level of smog below point P, the bureaucrats are faced with a perverse incentive. If the smog level should drop below point C, social uneasiness would diminish sufficiently far that people would begin to complain more about the taxes and regulation pertaining to the bureaucracy than the smog. People would prefer to have more disposable income and freedom from regulations. The bureaucrats, who want to keep their jobs and maximize their departmental budgets, will thus realize the importance of maintaining the smog level above point C, and will choose policies and favor technologies that do so.

Therefore, smog problems *will* likely be alleviated by public policy. Evidence of urban regulation often confirms this fact. But the *key insight* from public choice theory is that smog will *never* be eliminated or brought to a level below point C in the long run. *Political intervention to eliminate smog problems will simply tend to make an uncomfortable yet tolerable amount of smog a permanent part of social life. The same is true for **any** policy aimed at improving the quality of life or alleviating negative externalities.*

Table 6.1 The dawning of costly regulation

Three reasons why regulations arise and cause social costs (McChesney 1987, pp. 103-104):
(1) in Stigler's view, when net political benefits of a regulation (i.e., benefits less the costs of organizing and seeking it) are positive, producers will demand and pay for it; the social cost will end up being the trapezoid of the Harberger triangle plus the Tullock rectangle,
(2) when a regulation creates Ricardian or inframarginal rents (i.e., rents due to having better productive power), it will raise the costs of some firms more than others, and generate strategies of "cost-predation,"
(3) when politicians trade with private firms by offering them the Tullock rectangle in exchange for votes or money, or by threatening to impose costs (i.e., political blackmail).

There is no compelling reason to believe that self-interested planners and regulatory enforcers will be free from perverse incentives. Therefore, reports of at least some minimum level of negative externalities concerning population densities, transportation, drought, energy consumption, environment and surroundings, land, the "natural heritage," and many similar meta-terminologies will certainly circulate in order to provide a basis for continued regulation (as noted in the remarks of Mises and Hayek in chapter five).

At the same time, studies that find the present level of regulation to be inefficient can be expected to be heralded (at least to some level) by planners, who in turn can be expected to make strategic appeals to the public for larger budgets by blaming regulatory problems on being underfunded and under-staffed. Chicago School economists, famous for their criticisms of regulation on the grounds of its inefficiencies, will likely find (to their chagrin) that their studies are being used to augment regulation.

Environmental regulation failures

The failure to appreciate the role of private property rights has led to regulatory blunders in environmental policy. These mistakes have been the focus of important works by Chicago School economist Julian Simon in *The Ultimate Resource 2* (1996), Joseph Bast, P.J. Hill, Richard Rue, and Sandra Bast in *Eco-Sanity: A Commonsense Guide to Environmentalism* (1994), and Ronald Bailey, who edited *Global Warming and other Eco Myths: How the Environmental Movement Uses False Science to Scare us to Death* (2002). These works show that most environmental policy demonstrates the triumph of sentiment over data and reason. Evidence shows a world which is not out of control or threatened by humans. Indeed, there is much room for optimism as technology continues to make natural resources more accessible, to the point that they are effectively infinite. Energy supplies are bountiful and growing, and pollution continues to be mitigated over time. Global warming and ozone depletion are not grave problems caused by humans, and there is no need to rush to develop alternative energy programs. Human population, far from being a problem, represents the world's ultimate and most scarce resource. Only minds can create new ideas and therefore we need more of them. Other resources can be synthesized or found with new or better technology. Thus, greater population and quality immigration should be encouraged. Consequently, environmental policy has been a failure in that it often seeks to solve problems that do not warrant fixing or do not exist, based on misinformation or misguided premises.

In a similar vein, Ike Sugg and Urs Kreuter contend that failed government wildlife regulation, of elephants (ivory) in particular, has led to much social harm in Africa:

> While not all African countries are poor, 29 of the world's 36 poorest countries are situated south of the Sahara, where as many as 325 million people live in conditions of abject poverty, earning annual incomes of less than US $100 (Hanks, 1993a). It is doubtful whether many Westerners can even imagine what it is like to live under the conditions that so many Africans do. Hunger, sickness, misery and early death—human suffering is the primary effect of poverty. While some of its formal causes are complex, poverty in sub-Saharan Africa, as in most of the world, often can be traced directly back to perverse government policies (Eberstadt, 1994)… (Sugg and Kreuter 1994, pp. 18-19).

They point to deficiencies in private property rights allocations as the cause of such tragedies in the Third World:

> As with poverty, habitat destruction is often more a function of a political economy than anything else. A lack of land tenure security—that is, no clearly defined and enforced private property rights—is perhaps one of the greatest problems faced by people in the developing world (Sugg and Kreuter 1994, p. 19).

For instance, Sugg and Kreuter argue that government attempts to define and secure boundaries has been a disaster.

Between 30 and 40 per cent of Kenya's elephants live outside of its parks, and much of its other wildlife roams freely across fenceless park boundaries (Ricciuti, 1993). Not only do parks impose costs on people, but wildlife can eat themselves out of house and home in relatively short order. In Kenya's Amboseli National Park, for example, elephants have destroyed most of the woodlands and half of the park's plants species, and with them have gone giraffe, impala, kudu, and vervet monkeys (Ricciuti, 1993). Elephants became so over-populated in Kenya's Tsavo National Park during the late 1960s that thousands of elephant, lesser kudu, generek, dik dik and giraffe starved to death after a severe drought in the early 1970s, as did twice as many black rhino as exist on the entire continent today (Hall-Martin, 1993) (Sugg and Kreuter 1994, p. 49).

Alternatively Sugg and Kreuter suggest that local market-based regulation is the most tenable solution to the problem. Local people must be given property rights in the wildlife to assure its perpetuation.

Insofar as it is no longer acceptable for governments to protect wildlife *from* the people outside of parks, protecting wildlife *with* the people or *for* the people may not be much better. To ensure its survival, wildlife needs to be protected *by* the people who live with it. The arguments in favour of this position are usually based on economic or ecological concerns, but there are also ethical concerns at stake. To accept truly community-based management is to recognise that people deserve the right to choose their own destiny, to manage their own affairs. People who live with wildlife in developing countries are not 'stakeholders' with interests in a 'global resource'. The resource is theirs. Domestic wildlife laws in most African countries are such that community claims to wildlife resources are rarely recognised as legitimate. Issues of legitimacy notwithstanding, the question remains: Who is best able to manage the resource? (Sugg and Kreuter 1994, pp. 54-55).

Private property holders have a greater incentive to care for their property than do bureaucrats charged with protecting community or state property such as wildlife. Indeed, legislating prohibitions without defining property rights interests creates a policy doomed to failure. As Sugg and Kreuter note:

> Local laws that criminalise the commercialisation of wildlife decrease the chances that wildlife will survive. International trade bans are equally misguided, as they seek to destroy the very value that is most likely to encourage wildlife conservation. Such prohibitive approaches are the hallmarks of preservationism, and are destined to fail without the support of the local people. Without that support, the costs of wildlife protection will remain high—with such support, those costs can be considerably lowered (Bell, personal communication). The most effective way to increase the support of the local people is to make wildlife protection worth their economic while. As soon as this is recognised, conservation will eclipse preservation in Africa and the commercialisation of wildlife will no longer be viewed with the disdain it has been in the past. Commercialisation without proprietorship, however, would be likely to vindicate the detractors of sustainable utilisation. Without the accountability inherent in proprietorship, wildlife declines would be more likely to accelerate than to halt. Ultimately, resource owners will seek to protect their resources from other users, and will allow non-owners to use them only in exchange for sufficient benefits. This will create tangible incentives to ensure that there are no elephants, not fewer. Moreover, this strategy has the

added benefit of not compromising the welfare of Africans in the pursuit of elephant protection. If elephants are to be protected they must be valued and controlled by those who will choose whether they want elephants or not. For these reasons, the CITES [Convention on Trade in Endangered Species] trade ban will prove counterproductive in the end (Sugg and Kreuter 1994, p. 61).

Rhinoceros preservation legislation has likewise led to a dramatic regulatory failure. Part of the problem has been that compassionate people around the world are misinformed about the cultivation of rhinoceros products. They also fail to realize the endless rent seeking activity found in proliferating environmental concerns. As Michael 't Sas-Rolfes argues:

> There are many environmental issues that concern people nowadays, but few that can stir up as much public emotion as the perceived threats to 'endangered species'. Few people want to see *charismatic animals* like elephants, tigers, pandas and whales become extinct. As a result, 'saving endangered species' has become big business; there are countless non-profit organisations claiming to undertake this noble task, and raising considerable amounts of money in so doing. Sadly, the millions raised from well-meaning donors often fail to have much impact. The well-publicised issue of rhinoceros conservation is a typical example of this problem. Most people who know something about rhinos believe that they are being rapidly hunted to extinction by greedy and ruthless poachers, in order to sell rhino horn to Asian people, who use it as an aphrodisiac. They also believe that to 'save the rhino', the trade in rhino horn must be stopped. Then, once again, rhinos could live undisturbed by humans. This view is seriously mistaken and uninformed (Sas-Rolfes 1995, p. 9).

Sas-Rolfes suggests that the best way to prevent rhinoceros eradication is to have well-defined property rights in the rhinoceros:

Possibly the most appropriate approach to rhino conservation policy would be to allow a range of competing institutional models, and to monitor their performance. If strong property rights were defined and recognised, and CITES restrictions on consumptive use of rhino products were eased, the owners of rhino populations would determine an appropriate mix between the demands for consumptive and non-consumptive uses of rhinos. Since rhino owners would have to bear the consequences of their own actions (that is, bear the direct economic costs of any losses), they would have a strong incentive to manage their populations efficiently. As there is undoubtedly a substantial demand for rhinos to be used non-consumptively (most tourists prefer to see live rhinos with their horns intact), some landowners would accommodate this market. Others would supply the product markets, and by doing so would ease some of the pressure on the unharvested populations. The advantage of this arrangement would be that market forces would determine a mixed and balanced approach to rhino conservation. This would be a vast improvement on the current situation, in which those wanting to use rhino products are fighting preservationists in the political arena, and both are likely to end up losing (Sas-Rolfes 1995, p. 50).

Once property rights have been well-defined, trade restrictions and regulation should be lessened in order to enhance the optimal husbandry of the rhinoceros. As Sas-Rolfes states:

As indicated in the previous chapter, it would make little sense to revoke the CITES policy unless certain institutional changes preceded this move. However, if property rights were strengthened, then it would be a logical step to remove the barriers to legal trade in rhino products. With the right incentive structures in place, many conservation agencies and private landowners would decide to harvest horns from live animals selectively, and sell them for a profit. In most instances, these profits would be re-invested in management. With strong property rights, harvesting of animals for other products would take place on a sustainable basis, except in conditions of extreme political instability (there are probably no measures that can effectively protect rhinos under such conditions). As with any other form of animal husbandry, harvesting would be done in a way that ensured the replenishment of stock. Not all rhinos would be husbanded for the horn and products markets. The demands of tourists and environmentalists would ensure that some rhinos remain in natural conditions in protected areas. Although dehorning of animals in national parks and game reserves would probably be used as an initial precautionary measure, some of the animals would eventually be allowed to live with minimal human interference (Sas-Rolfes 1995, p. 53).

Public choice problems intensify regulatory failures

Inadequate allocation of private property rights is not the only reason for regulatory failure. Free market theorists have explained and predicted the failure of government regulation on account of public choice and knowledge problems. These obstacles compound the distortions caused by property rights abridgment.

Thomas McCraw wondered why regulation was a public interest failure (of course it may have been a success from the point of view of rent seekers) before setting out to examine the activities of four famous regulators in the United States.

> Why, I wondered, had regulation so often failed to serve the "public interest," as it had been intended to do? Why, if the commissions had proved so ineffective, did they remain active as apparently permanent parts of the government? Why, if agencies were so often "captured" by interests they were supposed to be regulating, did not other branches of government step in and take away their legislated powers? (McCraw 1984, p. vii)

Bad theory has also contributed to regulatory miscarriages. According to Shughart, many economic models of regulation are not useful because they fail to consider the problems of public choice.

> The failure of the traditional model of economic regulation to consider the motives of the regulators was perhaps its most crucial defect. Economists accepted uncritically the assumption that the goal of regulatory policy was to promote consumer welfare by correcting the allocative inefficiencies associated with decreasing-cost industries. They went about developing elegant theoretical models to derive socially optimal pricing policies for such firms that could be applied by regulatory authorities to minimize lost consumer surplus and simultaneously guarantee the firms' owners a "fair" return on their investment. That regulatory policy does not in fact operate according to the public-interest model was first revealed in a body of research showing that government intervention often failed to achieve its announced goals…Certain groups, whose financial interests are sufficiently concentrated and whose costs of mobilizing political influence

are relatively low, stand to gain more than others from the controls on price and entry imposed by public regulatory agencies. This creates incentives for such coalitions to use the apparatus of public regulation to increase their own wealth at the expense of other groups that confront relatively high costs of acquiring information and of organizing to oppose regulatory wealth redistribution. The regulators, in turn, serve as brokers of these wealth transfers. Their motivation for doing so also has a self-interest basis grounded on the political support offered by the demanders of regulation (Shughart 1990, pp. 43-44).

The study of regulation cannot escape the powerful scrutiny of public choice, as its insights are extended into new areas of research. As Buchanan and Tullock note: "Public choice...has been more concerned with inventing new ideas, or, at least, the discovery of new applications for established methods of analysis" (Buchanan and Tullock 1991, p. 20). Indeed, public choice has revolutionized the way public institutions are analyzed. As Arthur Seldon comments:

A further contribution in 1981 was an essay with Professor Tullock in *The Emerging Consensus*...It proposed a 'leap forward' from the study of markets to constitutional change. The advance was to be to 'the incentives, the rewards, and the penalties' of the politicians and their bureaucrats and the new institutions in which these inducements were more calculated to induce them to work to the general advantage. Conventional orthodox political science offered little solution. It was to be sought rather in recapturing the wisdom of the eighteenth century: its 'scepticism' about the abilities of politics, of government, to handle detailed regulatory tasks, to go beyond the limits of the 'minimal' or 'protection state'. The Buchanan-Tullock espousal of the 'minimal' state opens for liberals the central question of the functions of government. In his eloquent *Hobard Paper* 113, Dr. John Gray argued persuasively that wider function of the 'limited' state. The whole ground has recently been traversed by Professor Joseph Stiglitz in *The Economic Röle of the State,* which favours the wider limited than the narrower minimal röle. And Professor Israel Kirzner in his latest work, *Discovery, Capitalism and Distributive Justice,* envisages a reduced röle for government by the argument, which circumvents John Rawls's on a larger röle and Robert Nozick's on a smaller, that, since new resources and products are not taken from others but are newly discovered and created by individuals, 'social justice' does not require the wide redistributive functions by government envisaged in conventional political science (Seldon 1991, pp. xiv-xv).

Failures in judicial and antitrust regulation

Former Chief Justice Earl Warren was a shrewd judicial activist. He had been the Governor of California and was, without any prior judicial experience, appointed as Chief Justice of the U.S. Supreme Court. Hence, he engineered the unanimous *Brown v. Board of Education* decision (1954) that completely changed proactive policy for education in America. Despite any benefits of that ruling, many grim consequences also emerged. A new and tenacious wave of hatred for black people and for the federal government swept through the South. Moreover, sociologists have demonstrated that desegregation (wrought by the ruling) actually had little or no bearing on improving the educational status of American black people, which was Warren's ostensive intention.

This misguided policy continues to have negative social repercussions. David Armor argues that the contemporary narrowing of the "achievement gap" between black and white students has rather occurred because of non-public institutions: viz., general "improvements in the socioeconomic status of black families" and robust, value-laden training in the home. Accordingly, the success of such judicial activism is disputable (see Armor 1992, p. 80). The judiciary has also been disposed to helping baseball interests deal with antitrust threats, over against other professional sports in the United States. Moreover, Congress has also favored baseball interests. Ellig gives a public choice explanation for why special interests have dominated in protecting baseball club owners from regulators:

> Baseball's lower organizational costs, combined with the sheer size of its minor league system, give it a comparative advantage in lobbying relative to other major sports. When the economics of public decision making are taken into account, congressional acquiescence in baseball's differential treatment under the antitrust laws may not be an anomaly at all (Ellig 1991, p. 143).

In the final analysis, it is unclear that the alleged public interest motivations behind racial or sports regulation has ever been achieved, or that it ever will be achieved. On the contrary, there seem to be rent seeking and perverse incentives lurking behind the scenes that create public policy failures.

Failures in airline industry regulation

Richard Vietor suggests that public choice theory provides a more complete explanation of airline regulation:

> This brief history of the domestic airline industry can tell us something about the economic and political dynamics of regulatory policy. Perhaps we can draw some preliminary conclusions that apply generally to such industries

as trucking and rail transport, telecommunications, natural gas, and commercial banking. First, economic regulation can best and most usefully be understood as a market-structuring process. It shapes virtually all of the market's important characteristics. In this sense, the market, after years of regulation, becomes an artifact of policy that bears little resemblance to any natural economic or technological factors. This process, moreover, does not stop at the boundary of the firm. That is, regulation shapes the organizational resources of the firm, right down to its operational core. This is clear in the case of American Airlines, and would be much the same for firms in other industries undergoing deregulation: AT&T or CSX or El Paso Natural Gas or Bank America. Second, by examining airline regulation from start to finish (more or less), we have an unusual opportunity to generalize on a dynamic theory of political process. This history makes clear that no monocausal explanation—either economic or political—is sufficient. The microeconomic and political circumstances that gave rise to regulation were entirely different from those that forced deregulation. To explain the onset of airline regulation, its workings, and eventual reform, we need to relate several factors. Dramatic changes in basic conditions—especially macroeconomic and ideological circumstances—were key. Economic regulation, in general, was a policy response to the extraordinary failure of markets in the 1930's. Technological developments, which repeatedly undermined the microeconomic characteristics on which regulation was superimposed, were also important. So were new ideas about regulation's failings and alternative approaches. Entrepreneurship in the business and the policy arena helped force the change in policy. And finally, regulation itself contributed by failing to deal effectively with all of these other changes. Third, the sudden impact of deregulation on the incumbent airlines combined with the inherent competitiveness of the industry provide a sharper than usual perspective on the links between regulation, markets, and firms. In the American Airlines case, we see rapid and thoroughgoing adjustment of the firm's business strategy and organizational resources. As an artifact of regulation, American Airlines was ill suited to unrestricted competition. Crandall saw this; he understood the industry's underlying economics, recognized key elements of its emerging value-chain, and hastened to adapt before anyone else. The consequences of this sort of adjustment for market structure were completely unanticipated by economists. Perhaps the profession's tendency to treat firms as data points, operating autonomously within abstract markets, accounts for this. At any rate, the airline story should help us appreciate the extent to which business conduct—especially strategy—is designed to create and capture rents and, thus, to reshape market structure itself. Finally, we can see in the airline story that regulated competition, in contrast to regulated monopoly, is a flawed concept, at least in the U.S. political and legal context. The idea that certain market characteristics could be shaped by the government, without affecting management's other prerogatives reflects a kind of hubris. The boundaries between markets and firms and the economic linkages among market characteristics form a complicated and seamless web. When regulators, no matter how well intentioned, intervene to manage markets, they affect important aspects of the business, directly or indirectly (Vietor 1991, pp. 55-56).

Alternatively, Holcombe argues that market-regulation would work to enhance safety and quality, even in the airline industry.

Thus, lapses in regulation can actually benefit a government regulatory agency because of the knee-jerk reaction to ask the government to do more to take care of us when a government failure becomes apparent. In contrast, if a private sector regulatory agency had the same lapse, its reputation would be damaged, its profits would decline, and it might be forced out of business. If, in place of the government, Aloha Airlines had been regulated by a private company such a lapse in regulation would immediately lower the credibility of any airline regulated by that private company, which would cause other airlines to seek regulatory alternatives. The private regulator would lose business and profits. Thus, it would want to protect its reputation by not allowing a substandard airline to fly using the regulatory logo (Holcombe 1995, pp. 103-104).

Failures in agricultural regulation

Rent seeking and demosclerosis are rampant in food and drug regulation. Indeed, as Coppin and High indicate, early food regulation provided ample opportunity for regressive entrepreneurship.

The triumph of the problem approach in the Department of Agriculture, fed by large appropriations for research, had signaled the end for the old system, in which the Bureau of Chemistry had been the premiere scientific agency. Wiley at first tried to use his bureau's expertise in chemical analysis to combat the new organization. This strategy failed, partly because of mediocre results with sugar production, partly because analytical chemistry was itself a declining profession, and partly because mere technical competence in a scientific field could not stimulate the imagination of the public and politicians sufficiently to create a constituency. The examination of food for adulteration, and the setting of standards for testing and purity, held the possibility of avoiding these causes of strategic failure. Food analysis did not require a knowledge of engineering. Agricultural chemists could adequately examine food and national food law would increase the demand for and restore the prestige of their skill. Finally, ensuring the purity of food was an issue that could excite and attract a constituency. Once Wiley devoted his entrepreneurial abilities to securing passage and administration of a pure food law, his career and his bureau blossomed. He became a nationally respected figure, the "father of pure food" in the United States. Despite the success that followed, it is doubtful that Wiley ever consciously decided to build his bureau around a problem rather than a discipline. As late as 1905, he was still fighting to keep chemical analysis within his division. It was the competitive bureaucratic process that finally led him to crusade for pure food. Changing competitive strategies did not guarantee success. The passage of a national pure food law could insure the continuation of the Bureau of Chemistry as a significant part of the Department of Agriculture, but the establishment of a new bureau to administer such a law should be fatal to the Bureau of Chemistry. In order to prosper, the Bureau of Chemistry would have to administer the act, even if this involved the Bureau in regulatory activities far beyond its chemical expertise. Initially, administrative control by the Bureau of Chemistry was opposed by a significant number of state food officials through the Association of State Dairy and Food Departments. Wiley, through careful planning, maneuvered the organization into supporting his position. Having triumphed in this area, the way was clear to fight for the passage of a national pure food law. In the process, however, he made alliances and public statements that would result in new opposition to the passage and enforcement of a law. Wiley's competitive struggle to succeed within the bureaucracy was far from over (Coppin and High 1991, pp. 117-118).

Failures in electric utility regulation

Finally, Richard Hirsch found public choice related reasons to question the effectiveness of electric utility regulation.

This history of technology and regulation suggests several lessons. First, it teaches that even the well-intended government regulation of industries must be reevaluated frequently to determine whether the original rationale for regulation makes sense. In the utility industry, regulation appeared to bring universal benefits until previous trends in both the business environment and technological progress changed markedly in the 1970s. Reevaluation of the regulatory rationale has led to the industry's restructuring, a move that was aided by the implementation of PURPA [Public Utility Regulatory Policy Act of 1978]. This lesson has already been learned in other industries in the United States. Technological change also played an important role in the restructuring of the long-distance telephone industry, for example. For individuals and corporations involved in the development of technology, the recent experience of the utility industry offers another lesson. Namely, one must constantly monitor and attempt to anticipate the effects of regulatory change on technological strategies. Within the regulatory framework that existed before 1970, manufacturers of power generating equipment pursued R&D on large-scale technologies because their customers—utility companies— benefited from them. But when regulation spurred greater risk aversion and a desire for more modular, incremental capacity additions, manufacturers needed to shift R&D strategies to the production of reliable and efficient gas combustion turbines, cogeneration equipment, and other small scale technologies. While regulation supported one technological strategy for long time, there could be no guarantee that the regulatory environment would always support it. Therefore, R&D managers must remain alert to changes in the regulatory climate. Finally, policy makers should learn from this history, that they must frequently reevaluate policy to assure the original goals of the policy are being achieved. They should also analyze whether the policy has spawned unintended and counterproductive consequences (Hirsch 1991, pp. 175-176).

Hirsch continues:

Overall, the theory of regulation of a natural monopoly in the electric utility industry appeared to apply well for several decades. But regulation depended in part, on the continued integrity of a technological super structure that crumbled in the 1970s. As a new public policy began having its effects, the super structure deteriorated more, and critics called into question the rationale for regulation of the industry in general. They argued (among other things) interdependence between regulation and technology no longer existed, and that a competitive environment for electricity production could now be engineered. Not yet completed, the story of deregulation in the utility industry will revolve around interest-group politics (as usual) and trends in technological developments that further erode the claims of natural monopoly status for utilities (Hirsch 1991, p. 177).

The importance of the public choice critique of regulation

In sum, public choice provides some severe implications for public policy, stemming from its rigorous analysis. As Shughart explains:

One key conclusion of public choice is that changing the identities of the people who hold public office will not produce major changes in policy outcomes. Electing better people will not, by itself, lead to much better government. Adopting the assumption that all individuals, be they voters, politicians, or bureaucrats, are motivated more by self-interest than by public interest evokes a Madisonian perspective on the problems of democratic governance. Like that founding father of the American constitutional republic, public choice recognizes that men are not angels and focuses on the importance of the institutional rules under which people pursue their own objectives. "In framing a government which is to be administered by men over men, the great difficulty lies in this: you must first enable the government to control the governed; and in the next place oblige it to control itself" (*Federalist*, no. 51).

Institutional problems demand institutional solutions. If, for example, democratic governments institutionally are incapable of balancing the public budget, a constitutional rule that limits increases in spending and taxes to no more than the private sector's rate of growth will be more effective in curbing profligacy than "throwing the rascals out." Given the problems endemic to majority-rule voting, public choice also suggests that care must be exercised in establishing the domains of private and collective choice; that it is not necessarily desirable to use the same voting rule for all collective decisions; and that the public's interest can be best protected if exit options are preserved by making collective choices at the lowest feasible level of political authority (Shughart 2008).

References

Armor, David J. (1992), "Why is Black Educational Achievement Rising?," *The Public Interest*, no. 108, Summer, pp. 65-80.

Bailey, Ronald (2002), ed., *Global Warming and other Eco Myths: How the Environmental Movement Uses False*

Science to Scare us to Death, Random House (Prima Lifestyles): New York.

Bast, Joseph L., Peter J. Hill, Richard C. Rue, and Sandra L. Bast [Smits] (1994), *Eco-Sanity: A Common-Sense-Guide to Environmentalism*, Madison Books: Langham, Maryland.

Boudreaux, Donald J. and Ekelund, Robert B., Jr. (1993), "The Cable Television Consumer Protection and Competition Act of 1992: The Triumph of Private Over Public Interest," *Alabama Law Review*, vol. 44, no. 2, winter, pp. 355-391.

Buchanan, James M. (1980), "Rent Seeking and Profit Seeking," in James Buchanan, Robert Tollison, and Gordon Tullock, eds., *Toward a Theory of The Rent-Seeking Society*, Texas A&M University Press: College Station, Texas, pp. 3-15.

Buchanan, James M. and Tullock, Gordon (1991), "An American Perspective: from 'Markets Work to Public Choice'," in James M. Buchanan, *Constitutional Economics*, The Institute of Economic Affairs: London, pp. 17-28.

Coppin, Clayton A. and High, Jack (1991), "Entrepreneurship and Competition in Bureaucracy: Harvey Washington Wiley's Bureau of Chemistry, 1883-1903," in Jack High, ed., *Regulation: Economic Theory and History*, The University of Michigan Press: Ann Arbor, Mich., pp. 95-118.

Edwards, Mike (1994), "Lethal Legacy: Pollution in the Former U.S.S.R.," *National Geographic* (August), pp. 70-99.

Ellig, Jerry (1991), "The Baseball Anomaly and Congressional Intent," in Jack High, ed., *Regulation: Economic Theory and History*, University of Michigan Press: Ann Arbor, Michigan, pp. 119-145.

Hirsch, Richard F. (1991), "Regulation and Technology in the Electric Utility Industry: A Historical Analysis of Interdependence and Change," in Jack High, ed., *Regulation: Economic Theory and History*, University of Michigan Press: Ann Arbor, Michigan, pp. 147-177.

Hirsch, Werner Z. (1988), *Law and Economics: An Introductory Analysis*, Second Edition, Academic Press, Inc.: Boston.

Higgins, Richard S., and Tollison, Robert D. (1988), "Life Among the Triangles and Trapezoids: Notes on the Theory of Rent-Seeking," in Charles Rowley, Robert Tollison, and Gordon Tullock, eds., *The Political Economy of Rent-Seeking*, Kluwer Academic Publishers: Boston, pp. 147-157.

High, Jack C., and Coppin, Clayton A. (1988), "Wiley and the Whiskey Industry: Strategic Behavior in the Passage of the Pure Food Act," *Business History Review*, vol. 62, pp. 286-309.

Holcombe, Randall G. (1995), *Public Policy and the Quality of Life: Market Incentives Versus Government Planning*, Greenwood Press: Westport, Conn.

McChesney, Fred S. (1987), "Rent Extraction and Rent Creation in the Economic Theory of Regulation," *Journal of Legal Studies*, vol. 16, January, pp. 101-118.

McCraw, Thomas K. (1984), *Prophets of Regulation: Charles Francis Adams, Louis D. Brandeis, James M. Landis, Alfred E. Kahn*, The Belknap Press of Harvard University Press: Cambridge, Massachusetts.

Mises, Ludwig von (1996 [1966/1949], *Human Action: A Treatise on Economics*, fourth revised edition, The Foundation for Economic Education: Irvington-on-Hudson, New York (this edition comprises minor editorial changes by Bettina Bien Greaves).

Mitchell, William C., and Simmons, Randy T. (1994), *Beyond Politics: Markets, Welfare, and the Failure of Bureaucracy*, Westview Press: San Francisco, California.

Rauch, Jonathan (1996), "Eternal Life: Why Government Programs Won't Die," *Reason*, vol. 28, no. 4 August–September, pp. 17-21.

Sas-Rolfes, Michael 't (1995), *Rhinos: Conservation, Economics and Trade-Offs*, IEA Studies on the Environment no. 4, The Institute of Economic Affairs: London.

Seldon, Arthur, "Introduction," in James M. Buchanan, *Constitutional Economics*, The Institute of Economic Affairs: London, pp. vii-xvi.

Shughart, William F. (1990), *Antitrust Policy and Interest-Group Politics*, Quorum Books: New York.

Shughart, William F. II (2008), "Public Choice," *The Concise Encyclopedia of Economics* (Library of Economics and Liberty), retrieved on March 4, 2009 from http://www.econlib.org/library/Enc/PublicChoice.html.

Sugg, Ike, and Kreuter, Urs (1994), *Elephants and Ivory: Lessons from the Trade Ban*, IEA Studies on the Environment no. 2, Institute of Economic Affairs: London.

Tollison, Robert D. (1982), "Rent Seeking: a Survey," *Kyklos*, vol. 35, no. 4, pp. 575-602.

Tollison, Robert D., and Wagner, Richard E. (1991), "Romance, Realism, and Economic Reform," *Kyklos*, vol. 44, no. 1, pp. 57-70.

Tullock, Gordon (1993), *Rent Seeking*, The Shaftesbury Papers, 2, Edward Elgar Publ. Co.: Brookfield, Vermont.

Tullock, Gordon (1975), "The Transitional Gains Trap," *The Bell Journal of Economics*, autumn, pp. 671-678.

Vietor, Richard H. K. (1991), "The Hubris of Regulated Competition: Airlines, 1925-88," in Jack High, ed., *Regulation: Economic Theory and History*, University of Michigan Press: Ann Arbor, Michigan, pp. 19-57.

7 Ludwig von Mises: a compendium of his classically liberal thought

His life

Ludwig von Mises was born in 1881 in the Austro-Hungarian city of Lemberg. (His father had been working there with a railroad company.) However, he was raised in the city of Vienna, where he lived for many years, until immigrating to New York City at the age of 59. He died in New York in 1973 at the age of 92. Mises was an erudite scholar in various disciplines of the social sciences and the humanities, an atheist, and a leading economist of the classical liberal tradition.[38]

Mises entered the University of Vienna when he was 19, obtaining his doctorate in law and economics at 27. He studied under a stimulating intellectual environment provided by his mentor Carl Menger, the founder of the Austrian School of economics. Mises also attended the seminar of another giant of this school: Eugen von Böhm-Bawerk.

He served as an army captain in an artillery division during World War I. He worked in the Austrian Chamber of

---

[38] Much of the information in this section, and some of the information in the following sections, was extracted from sources on the website of the Ludwig von Mises Institute (http://www.mises.org/mises.asp) in Auburn, Alabama, USA: (1) "Who Is Ludwig von Mises?" (1998) and (2) Murray N. Rothbard (1980), "The Essential Von Mises."

Commerce (1907-1908) as director of the Austrian Reparations Commission of the League of Nations (1918-1920). He worked as "Extraordinary Professor" at the University of Vienna (1919-1934), a prestigious unsalaried position, along with his position as Consultant and later Chief Consultant in the Chamber of Commerce (1918-1938). In addition, Mises led his own private seminar on alternate Friday evenings in his office (1920-1934). Mises was the founder and Vice President of the Austrian Institute for Business Cycle Research (1927-1938).

However, he was only affiliated with the chamber part time from 1934 to 1938 (after Hitler annexed Austria). At that time, his full time job was in Geneva, Switzerland, as professor of international relations at the Graduate Institute of International Relations (1934-1940). He married Margit (née Herzfeld) Sereny in Geneva on July 6, 1938. In August 1940, he immigrated to the United States.

He was Visiting Professor at New York University from 1945 to 1969, teaching two evening classes (one of which was a seminar). He taught at Mexican universities four times (for periods less than two months each) in 1942, 1946, 1949 and 1958, and gave a seminar about central banking in Peru in 1950, as well as another seminar about diffusing free market ideas in Buenos Aires in 1959. He was visiting professor at the University of Plano, Texas from 1965 until 1971. He was a consultant for the Foundation for Economic Education near New York (1946-1973) until he died in October 1973.

His principal contributions to the field of economics

Government (the central bank) causes the business cycle

After finishing his PhD, Mises wrote *The Theory of Money and Credit* (1912)—his first important treatise. He argued that the purchasing power of money is its price, which is determined by supply and demand (as is the price of any commodity). Moreover, inflation causes the redistribution of wealth from those who save (and earn) money to banks, to government, and to many SIGs that are affiliated with the banking and finance segment of the political process.

Mises held that the business cycle is the most damaging phenomena an economy can face, due to the inflationary booms and busts it causes. When the government inflates, the rate of interest falls to its market level—a function of savings. The artificially low interest rates fool entrepreneurs who make non-viable investments, which in turn create an artificial boom. When the expansion of credit is halted, investment errors become apparent, resulting in inventory reductions, bankruptcies, and unemployment. Consequently, the central bank causes the business cycle.

Money originated in the market, rather than being created by the state or a social contract. Therefore, Mises contended that money should be returned to the market and linked with gold (without placing restrictions on gold trading). Banking must submit to the forces of competition as other industries do. Following his insight, he helped Austria avoid the hyperinflation policy pursued by Germany. In pursuing this line of reasoning, Mises demonstrated how economic theory can powerfully inform public policy. Indeed, monetary policy has been, and continues to be, a key issue for Austrian researchers. We will return to the topics of banking and the business cycle in chapter eleven.

The failure of socialism and the "mixed" economy

Mises argued that the main mission of economics is to refute human errors regarding social action (*Human Action* 1996, p. 93). His selected targets were the errors of socialism and interventionism. He predicted the fall of the communist experiment in his book *Socialism* (1922), which is now praised—or at least is now more widely acclaimed than it was before the fall of communism. He argued that socialism cannot function in an industrial economy since there will be no capital market and, therefore, there would be no price system to calculate gains and losses. Socialism would result in chaos and stagnation. In his book *Bureaucracy*, Mises says that the central office of production in the socialist sate would simply be incapable of resolving many problems. Socialism leads to complete chaos (*Bureaucracy* 1983, p. 83). As Yuri N. Maltsev, an economist in the former Soviet Union, points out: "Mises was right, and Lenin was wrong. That is the great lesson of the twentieth century."[39]

Mises also criticized socialism's drive to transform the relations or roles between the sexes, including marriage and "free love" (*Socialism* 1981, pp. 74-89). Mises did not want to overthrow the fundamental institutions that had evolved over time. In fact, he viewed institutions like the family as purposeful. "The human family is the result of thinking, planning, and acting" (*Human Action*, p. 168).

Mises had thus argued against the sociological policy aspects of socialism, including the abolition of marriage and the family, and social egalitarianism. On the contrary, he affirmed the inequality among human beings and that social cooperation rests in this inequality, that the institutional hierarchies uphold its structures which separate the individual and the state.

Mises rejected the concept of "the mixed economy," which is supposed to have features of the free market mixed with socialism. To Mises, any state intervention in the market that does not deal with defense, justice and the protection of property rights, is merely a form of socialism. A mixed economy, just like socialism, is not able to function in an efficient manner. Taxes, regulations, and public

---

[39] Cited on the Ludwig von Mises Institute website (http://www.mises.org/mises.asp) in the paper "Who Is Ludwig von Mises?" (1998).

expenditures distort prices and thus move resources away from being allocated to their most valuable uses. Accordingly, having a smaller state is always better, *ceteris paribus*. Mises was not an anarchist but he was a liberal (in the classical sense), recommending a severely limited state.

In *Human Action*, Mises points out that "the market economy...and the socialist economy preclude one another. There is no mixture of the two systems possible or thinkable; there is no such thing as a mixed economy" (*Human Action*, p. 258) and "a socialist system with a market and market prices is as self-contradictory as is the notion of a triangular square" (*Human Action*, p. 710). Also, measurements of wealth and income cannot be done or even conceived under such social intervention (*Human Action*, p. 251). Mises affirmed that it would be impossible for a socialist committee to determine values and prices for society. "It is only the market that, in establishing prices for each factor of production, creates the conditions required for economic calculation" (*Human Action*, p. 335).

Planners always lack the ability to perform economic calculation in the public interest. How should production proceed? What procedure would one have to follow? What is the optimal production period for each industry? The committee "cannot calculate from the point of view of his own present value judgments and his own present anticipations of future conditions, whatever they may be" (*Human Action*, p. 700). "He will be like a sailor on the high seas unfamiliar with the methods of navigation, or like a medieval scholar entrusted with the technical operation of a railroad engine" and thus socialism "is just a system of groping around in the dark" (*Human Action*, p. 700). Marxism errs since it says that the ends that men strive for may be known (*Theory and History* 1985, p. 139), but they most certainly cannot be known. We will return to the topic of socialism in chapter eight.

Standing nearly alone in the fight against interventionism

For many years, Mises stood virtually alone as an economist fighting against socialism and interventionism. There were other classically liberal economists, but less strict in their free market perspective—such as Hayek and Milton Friedman—who also fought against these collectivist ideas. Mises did at least have friends and supporters from other disciplines, like Henry Hazlitt, Albert J. Nock, Ayn Rand, and Leonard Read, plus, later in his life, young economists like his former students Rothbard and Kirzner. Nonetheless, Mises was singular in his role as a purely free market economist for most of his life in America.

Mises lambasted interventionist policy. For instance, he contended that the principle of Keynes: "in the long run we shall all be dead" is a crass error when applied to public policy, since policy must consider not only the short term (which is the concern of politicians) but both the short term and the long term (*Human Action*, p. 654). Being against the most popular economists of the period did not produce positive returns for Mises. By and large, his ideas were despised by the majority of economists of his day, and so it has remained to the present—although his relative popularity was raised after of the fall of the Berlin Wall. For this reason, he never had a good reception in the university system, which was controlled by his intellectual adversaries.

Mises criticized the notion of "social engineering". He synthesized in the following manner: "Mankind is to be divided into two classes: the almighty dictator, on the one hand, and the underlings who are to be reduced to the status of mere pawns in his plans and cogs in his machinery, on the other. If this were feasible, then of course the social engineer would not have to bother about understanding other people's actions. He would be free to deal with them as technology deals with lumber and iron" (*Human Action*, p. 113). A social engineer, said Mises:

[P]roposes to deal with men as the breeder deals with his cattle. But the reformers fail to realize that there is no universal principle of alimentation valid for all men. Which one of the various principles one chooses depends entirely on the aims one wants to attain. The cattle breeder does not feed his cows in order to make them happy, but in order to attain the ends which he has assigned to them in his own plans. He may prefer more milk or more meat or something else. What type of men do the man breeders want to rear—athletes or mathematicians? Warriors or factory hands? He who would make man the material of a purposeful system of breeding and feeding would arrogate to himself despotic powers and would use his fellow citizens as means for the attainment of his own ends, which differ from those they themselves are aiming at. (*Human Action*, pp. 242-243)

Mises extended his critique to interventionism in general.

What brought about the decline of the [Roman] empire and the decay of its civilization was the disintegration of this economic interconnectedness, not the barbarian invasions. The alien aggressors merely took advantage of an opportunity which the internal weakness of the empire offered to them…The interference of the authorities upset the adjustment of supply to the rising demand…The marvelous civilization of antiquity perished because it did not adjust its moral code and its legal system to the requirements of the market economy…The Roman Empire crumbled to dust because it lacked the spirit of liberalism and free enterprise. The policy of interventionism and its political corollary, the Führer principle, decomposed the mighty empire as they will by necessity always disintegrate and destroy any social entity. (*Human Action*, pp. 767, 768, 769).

We will return to the topic of interventionism in chapter ten.

The logical method of economics

Mises wrote a lot about economic methodology. He rejected institutionalism (which he says completely denies economics) and positivism (which does not consider the differences between the social sciences and the natural sciences). Mises instead developed his idea of "praxeology," the science of human action, which views each individual as an economic actor with his own goals, purposes, and objectives. Also, he fervently maintained the subjectivity of value and choices —the unexceptional tradition among Austrian economists—clarifying the fact that value is never intrinsic (*Human Action*, p. 96). He pointed out that it is not possible to deal with people as inanimate things, which can be manipulated at will, especially since it would grant power to social engineers to justify their activities. These themes are covered in *The Ultimate Foundation of Economic Science* (1962), *Theory and History* (1957) and *Human Action* (1966) among other works. Above all, *Human Action* is clearly his most important achievement and, although it has been over 40 years since the third edition was published, it still retains importance today as both a valuable and relevant economics resource. The fourth edition was published in 1996 with minor modifications and corrections.

In his book *Theory and History*, Mises acknowledges that history is important and essential. But it is not economics, which is an apodictic science based on the logical method. However, economics (being neutral with respect to judgments of value) informs the historian (who is not neutral to judgments of value) about the economic knowledge, which is essential to the historian's task—lest he err in his interpretations (*Theory and History* 1978, pp. 291, 300, etc.). While each discipline is important, each gives us different knowledge (*Theory and History*, pp. 306-307).

In *Human Action*, Mises bases his methodology in the axiom of human action which says that all human beings act to remove uneasiness and the dissatisfactory elements of life. Indeed, "human action is purposeful behavior...aiming at ends and goals" (*Human Action*, p. 11). "A man perfectly content with the state of his affairs would have no incentive to change things" (*Human Action*, pp. 13, 92). Economics does not deal with the ultimate ends or goals of men, such as "Why act?," but rather the means and the consequences of his action. "It is vain to speculate about ultimate things" (*Theory and History*, p. 73).

"Ultimate ends are ultimately given, they are purely subjective, they differ with various people and with the same people at various moments in their lives." We cannot ponder, he says, about ultimate ends (*Human Action*, pp. 95, 96). In *Theory and History*, Mises says: "Acting man is faced with a definite situation. His action is a response to the challenge offered by his situation; it is his reaction. He appraises the effects the situations may have upon himself, i.e., he tries to establish what it means to him. Then he chooses and acts in order to attain the end chosen" (*Theory and History*, p. 286). He adds in *Human Action*: "Action sorts and grades....Acting man values things as means for the removal of uneasiness...For acting man there exists primarily nothing but various degrees of relevance and urgency with regard to his own well-being" (*Human Action*, p. 119).

From this action axiom, Mises constructs all of economic theory by logical steps. He named his system "praxeology," as the proper word to describe the scientific study of human action (*Human Action*, pp. 12, 14, 21, 28) that does not try to explain a man's ultimate ends or "whether he should preserve or abandon life" (*Human Action*, p. 882).

The logical method of praxeology is not mathematical. Accordingly, Mises rejected the use of the mathematical method in the study of economics. He contended that we cannot gain any new knowledge through the manipulation of mathematical symbols (*Human Action*, p. 108), even though economists can achieve "reverential awe" from onlookers by doing so (*Human Action*, p. 106). The labor of the mathematical economist is futile, Mises contended. "What they are doing is vain playing with mathematical symbols, a pastime not suited to convey any knowledge" and their models "are unreal, self-contradictory and imaginary expedients of thought and nothing else. They are certainly not suitable models for the construction of a living society of acting men" (*Human Action*, pp. 250, 256). Such models err since they fail to deal with "the lapse of time" (*Human Action*, p. 247), an essential element of human action. For Austrian economists, praxeology is the economics of time and ignorance, unlike mathematical models which assume perfect information and focus on a static point in time which is devoid of entrepreneurial action (O'Driscoll and Rizzo, 1996).

Mises argued that "there is no such thing as quantitative economics," since it is not possible to produce economic theory through the mathematical method, or the analysis of historical facts or data (*Human Action*, p. 351). Indeed, "The equations formulated by mathematical economics remain a useless piece of mental gymnastics" (*Human Action*, p. 354). Moreover, Mises blamed mathematical economics for bolstering socialism, since it gives planners some hope that they might be able to succeed by converting economic phenomena into numeric forms (*Human Action*, pp. 702, 713-715).

In his book *The Ultimate Foundation of Economic Science*, Mises points out the difference between the natural sciences and praxeology: "The natural sciences are causality research; the sciences of human action are teleological"

(*The Ultimate Foundation of Economic Science* 1962, p. 7). In *Theory and History*, Mises adds: "In economics there are no constant relations between various magnitudes...The truth is that there are only variables and no constants. It is pointless to talk about variables when there are no invariables." Furthermore, it is absurd to use statistics within the sciences of human action (*Theory and History*, pp. 11-12, 260). "What distinguishes the sciences of human action is that there is no such foreknowledge of the individuals' value judgments" and, therefore, it is not possible to utilize the methods of the natural sciences in economics (*Theory and History*, pp. 306, 305). We will return to the topic of the Austrian method and the fundamentals of the school in chapters eight and ten.

Entrepreneurs

According to Mises, entrepreneurs are the most important or significant individuals in history besides the generators of ideas (see chapter one). They serve consumers and cause the world to advance. "In his capacity as a businessman a man is servant of the consumers, bound to comply with their wishes...he is under the necessity of adjusting his conduct to the demand of the consumers" and "he must, contrary to his own convictions, supply them with such things" as they want (*Human Action*, p. 240). At times in *Human Action*, Mises calls the entrepreneurs "promoters" to emphasize that their role is more special than the typical speculative action undertaken by ordinary businessmen and human beings in general. They are the most important and most capable people in an economy. Mises suggests that the promoter "trusts his own ability to understand future market conditions better than his less gifted fellow men. The entrepreneurial function, the striving of entrepreneurs after profits, is the driving power in the market economy," and he profits when he fulfills the desires of consumers (*Human Action*, p. 299). The static mathematical method of economics has left out the entrepreneur, since its models do not deal with time, dynamism, or rivalry. Yet, the entrepreneur is the most interesting actor in the study of economics. Mises identified this impoverishment and emphasized entrepreneurial activity in his own work. Specifically, the entrepreneur's role in the economy is the "Adjustment of production to the best possible supplying of the consumers with the goods they are asking for most urgently" (*Human Action*, p. 303). His motivation is to gain short term monopoly profits (unless long term ones can be assimilated through using the political process) by means of his extraordinary capabilities. Such people are gifts from God since, according to Mises, it is impossible to obtain their abilities in a business school. Mises remarks that entrepreneurial skill "can neither be taught nor learned" and, in another place he says, "an entrepreneur cannot be trained" (*Human Action*, pp. 585, 314). We will return to the topic of entrepreneurship in chapter nine.

His view of society, idea generators, and the masses

According to Mises in *Human Action*, "man appears on the scene of earthly events as a social being" (*Human Action*, p. 165). Nevertheless, all research pertaining to human action errs which is based on the activities of social groups. Mises says that society is the "total complex of reciprocal relations created by" concerted cooperation, "the combination of individuals for cooperative effort," and "it is division of labor and combination of labor." Moreover, society "is much more than a passing alliance concluded for a definite purpose" (*Human Action*, pp. 143, 158). Furthermore, "Action is always action of individual men" (*Human Ac-*

tion, p. 243) and "it exists nowhere else than in the actions of individual men. It is a delusion to search for it outside the actions of individuals" (*Human Action*, p. 243).

The costs of living in society amount to temporary sacrifices. But the benefits of society include security, peace and the improvement of each individual's own material condition (*Human Action*, pp. 146, 149). "One of the privileges that society affords to the individual is the privilege of living in spite of sickness or physical disability" (*Human Action*, p. 166) while crippled savages or animals without society are enervated and will likely perish. Therefore, persons cooperate because "it best serves their own interests." Hostility is replaced by "partnership and mutuality" and people "tend toward cooperation and association" (*Human Action*, pp. 169, 273, 160). "The fundamental social phenomenon is the division of labor, and its counterpart human cooperation" (*Human Action*, p. 157). The fact is that individuals are able to remove more uneasiness by the division of labor than they can without it (*Human Action*, p. 164).

Mises argues that "society is joint action and cooperation in which each participant sees the other partner's success as a means for the attainment of his own...The idea emerged that every human adversary should be considered as a potential partner in a future cooperation, and that this fact should not be neglected in the conduct of military operations." However, Mises points out:

Society is not merely interaction. There is interaction—reciprocal influence—between all parts of the universe: between the wolf and the sheep he devours; between the germ and the man it kills; between the falling stone and the thing upon which it falls. Society, on the other hand, always involves men acting in cooperation with other men in order to let all participants attain their own ends" (*Human Action*, pp. 169, 170).

To Mises, the popular idea of living in a society without the division of labor is "the outcome of romantic delusions" (*Theory and History*, p. 356). Mankind can never reach a state of perfection (*Theory and History*, p. 363) but is still best served by forming societies based on the division of labor.

Mises says that the idea that there is biological equality between human beings is absurd. Sociologists who idolize the "common man" err since "no new ideas spring from the mythical mind of the masses" (*Theory and History*, p. 263). "Most people are common men. They do not have thoughts of their own; they are only receptive. They do not create new ideas; they repeat what they have heard and imitate what they have seen" (*Theory and History*, p. 191).

According to Mises, "the plight of Western civilization consists precisely in the fact that serious people can resort to such syllogistic artifices without encountering sharp rebuke" (*Human Action*, p. 834). Ideas are important and those who generate them are the most influential people in the world. As some evidence, Mises recounts the three reasons given why capitalism is bad: "poverty, inequality of incomes and wealth, and insecurity" (*Human Action*, p. 835). This notion was generated by supposed experts who were sadly ignorant of economic doctrine and have led the world into many problems. On the contrary, Mises argues that "the masses" are beleaguered by "penury" in many parts of the world because of "the absence of capitalism." Indeed, it was "the abhorrence of capital accumulation that doomed many hundreds of millions of Asiatics to poverty and starvation" (*Human Action*, pp. 836, 843). Within the market, there are means to combat poverty with success—namely the family and private organizations and/or religious charities (*Human Action*, p. 837). On the other hand, interventionism "has caused wars and civil wars, ruthless oppression of the masses by clusters of self-appointed dictators, economic depressions, mass unemployment, capital consumption, [and] famines" (*Human Action*, p. 855).

Consequently, Mises was quick to realize both the importance of public opinion and the indirect power that the idea generators have in influencing the public. In *Theory and History*, Mises suggests:

> There is virtually only one factor that has the power to make people unfree—tyrannical public opinion. The struggle for freedom is ultimately not resistance to autocrats or oligarchs but resistance to the despotism of public opinion. It is not the struggle of the many against the few, but of minorities—sometimes a minority of but one man—against the majority. The worst and most dangerous form of absolutist rule is that of an intolerant majority (*Theory and History*, p. 67).

Conformably, "In the long run even the most despotic governments with all their brutality and cruelty are no match for ideas" (*Theory and History*, p. 372).

According to Mises, the most tragic events in the history of the world have been fostered by philosophical movements that held to the notion that we can know the future stages of humanity. In *Theory and History*, Mises criticizes the main teleological interpretations of history. These include deterministic and authoritarian forms of Christianity (see *Theory and History*, pp. 162 to 169, plus pp. 13, 43, 48-50, 58-59, 61, 73, 83, 149, 175, 373, 155, 37 and 46), Hegelian philosophy, and Marxism, all of which provide frameworks for interpreting the predestined stages of history. That is, they provide a "philosophy of history," where Providence directs the bearing or course of events (*Theory and History*, p. 163). Mises argued that such systems are neither rational nor scientific. "Every system of the philosophy of history is an arbitrary guess which can neither be proved nor disproved. There is no rational means available for either endorsing or rejecting a doctrine suggested by an inner voice" (*Theory and History*, p. 165). Mises preferred to follow the line of Adam Smith, who "did not claim to have guessed the goals which Providence has set for mankind and aims to realize by directing men's actions" (*Theory and History*, p. 167).

His classical liberalism

Mises was a classical liberal *par excellence* on account of the application of his economic understanding. He saw the need to maintain a free market, since it is the mechanism by which the best life possible may be achieved in this world. Mises pointed out that all civilizations are based on private property: "private property is inextricably linked with civilization" (*Human Action*, p. 264) and capitalism, or the economy of the market, is the economic system that emerges naturally in the world (*Human Action*, pp. 264, 267). In an essay entitled "Liberty and Property," Mises argues that, "Private property...is...the means that assigns to the common man, in his capacity as buyer, supremacy in all economic affairs. It is the means to stimulate a nation's most enterprising men to exert themselves to the best of their abilities in the service of all the people" ("Liberty and Property" 1988, p. 39).

Not being an anarchist, Mises admits that "taxes are necessary" but that "progressive taxation" only serves to open the doors to socialism (*Human Action*, p. 807) and to afflict competition (*Human Action*, p. 809). In his view, Marxism is the negation of economics because it denies the role of private property and the fact of scarcity (*Human Action*, pp. 234-237). Thus, it must be eschewed.

Mises warns us about the dangers of having a mixed economy throughout his book *Bureaucracy*. Regulatory bureaus grow perpetually without conferring any net social benefit, due to the fact that they lack the check provided by profit and loss. Along with *Bureaucracy*, his books *Liberalism* and *Human Action* provide a robust defense of a classically liberal order.

For Mises, "collectivism is a doctrine of war, intolerance, and persecution" where the people "become mere soulless pawns in the hands of a monster" (*Theory and History*, p. 61). Christendom has often contributed to the rise of collectivist errors. Mises (in my view mistakenly, see Cobin 2006) thought that the Apostle Paul perceived the state as a collectivist entity that enslaved its subordinates, where human rights which originated from the Creator could be supplanted by "the alleged divine right of the anointed kings." To the collectivist it is clear that "individuals are wretched and refractory; their obstinacy must be curbed by the authority to which God or nature has entrusted the conduct of society's affairs" (*Theory and History*, pp. 324, 58; and cf. *Human Action*, pp. 151ff, 239, 690-691, 879). However, "the characteristic feature of a free society is that it can function in spite of the fact that its members disagree in many judgments of value" (*Theory and History*, p. 61). Mises saw no conflict between a liberal society and any religion. "A genuine conflict of faith and reason does not exist. Natural law and divine law do not disagree" (*Theory and History*, p. 46).

In the first edition of *Liberalism* (1927), Mises supports the position of the old classical liberals, namely, "the philosophers, sociologists, and economists of the eighteenth and the early part of the nineteenth century" (*Liberalism* 1978, p. 1). Mises suggests that "Liberalism...has nothing else in view than the advance of [men's] material welfare and does not concern itself directly with their inner, spiritual and metaphysical needs" (*Liberalism*, p. 4). Moreover, "Liberalism [says that men] ought, in their rightly understood interest, always act intelligently" (*Liberalism*, p. 5). Then, making a link with his economic method, he says that "Liberalism is distinguished from socialism, which likewise professes to strive for the good of all, not by the goal at which it aims, but by the means it chooses to attain that goal" (*Liberalism*, p. 8), where "the means" implies private property and capitalism. In chapter two of *Liberalism*, Mises lists the "foundations of liberal policy,"[40] which include a dozen items:

- property,
- free labor (as opposed to slavery),
- peace,
- equality under the law,
- opposition to schemes that aim to achieve equality of wealth and income,
- a moral duty to preserve private property and institutions that "preserve the social order" (*Liberalism*, p. 34),
- preservation of the state, defined as "the social apparatus of compulsion and coercion that induces people to abide by the rules of life in society" (*Liberalism*, p. 35); as opposed to the anarchist doctrine which holds that if "private property were abolished, then everyone, without exception, would spontaneously observe the rules demanded by social cooperation...is mistaken [and] altogether untenable" (*Liberalism*, p. 36).
- democracy,
- opposition to the right of a minority to use force to seize control of the apparatus of the state (as was necessary in the case of fascism),
- the commitment to having a state that "should not interfere in any questions touching on the individual's mode of life" (*Liberalism*, p. 54),
- intolerance "of every kind of intolerance," and

---

[40] This paragraph on *Liberalism* was developed through several public email comments by Patrick Gunning on May 6, 1999 on the Professors of Liberty email list (home page: http://knight.fcu.edu.tw/~gunning/welcome.htm).

- "The state must be so constituted that the scope of its laws permits the individual a certain amount of latitude within which he can move freely. The citizen must not be so narrowly circumscribed in his activities that, if he thinks differently from those in power, his only choice is either to perish or to destroy the machinery of the state" (*Liberalism*, p. 59).

According to Mises in *Human Action*, liberalism is a political doctrine rather than a scientific theory since it "is not neutral with regard to values and the ultimate ends sought by action" (*Human Action*, p. 154). Mises noted the two fundamental doctrines of liberalism:

First: The [classical] liberals do not assert that men *ought* to strive after the goals mentioned above [life, health, food, wealth, or other higher and nobler drives of humanity]. What they maintain is that the immense majority prefer a life of health and abundance to misery, starvation, and death...Secondly: The [classical] liberals do not disdain the intellectual and spiritual aspirations of man. On the contrary. They are prompted by a passionate ardor for intellectual and moral perfection, for wisdom and for aesthetic excellence" (*Human Action*, p. 154).

Moreover, "liberalism puts no obstacles in the way of a man eager to adjust his personal conduct," including things like his choice of a religion (*Human Action*, p. 157).

Because of his unpopular, yet strongly-held classically liberal opinions, obtaining academic work in the United States posed clear difficulties for Mises. However, through the help of his classically liberal friends Hazlitt and Lawrence Fertig, Mises obtained a position as Visiting Professor in the Graduate School of Business at New York University. The dean there, John Sawhill (who would later become a bureaucrat in the Department of Energy in Washington), lobbied good students to not take Mises's course, since he considered Mises to be a "right wing reactionary." Nevertheless, Mises never became bitter or resentful from this treatment but simply continued the fight for liberty and to promote his vision of economics. He published more than 25 books and 250 articles in academic journals during his life.

His view of the state and government

According to Mises in *Human Action*, the "[s]tate or government is the social apparatus of compulsion and coercion. It has the monopoly of violent action" (*Human Action*, p. 149). When the state pursues its forceful role it does not interfere with the operation of the market. "It employs its power to beat people into submission solely for the prevention of actions destructive to the preservation and the smooth operation of the market economy." Indeed, "the state creates and preserves the environment in which the market economy can safely operate" by protecting "people against violent or fraudulent aggression on the part of anti-social individuals" and the state is the singular means in the world to sustain the public "peace—the absence of perpetual fighting by everyone against everyone" (*Human Action*, pp. 257, 272, 280-281). Thus, the state assures liberty and the market. (Of course, if Mises were living today in the United States or Europe he might have some reservations about this sentiment.) But Mises also reminds us that classical liberals think that the state should be ruled by the best, instead of the masses or the man in the street: "the mean," "the lowbred," or by the "domestic barbarians" (*Human Action*, p. 150).

On the one hand, classical liberalism brings peace and prosperity through democratic processes and persuasion rather than force. It protects "majority rule, tolerance of dissenting views, freedom of thought, speech and the press, equality of all men under the law" (*Human Action*, p. 152). On the other hand, "The modern revival of the idea of collectivism, the main cause of all the agonies and disasters of our day, has succeeded so thoroughly that it has brought into oblivion the essential ideas of liberal social philosophy" (*Human Action*, p. 153).

His confidence in markets

In *Human Action*, Mises says that "the market is a social body; it is the foremost social body...the resultant of each individual's active contribution" (*Human Action*, p. 315). The market brings us the best society that is possible in this world. Regrettably, "those who prefer penury and slavery to material well-being" (*Theory and History*, p. 33) despise the critiques of economists regarding socialism and interventionism, and reject the advances of Western civilization.

Mises contends that it is impossible for consumers to benefit by means of protectionism (*Human Action*, p. 317) or policies guided by nationalism (*Human Action*, p. 326), both of which deny the benefits available through the international division of labor (*Human Action*, p. 325-326). Markets do "not respect political frontiers" (*Human Action*, p. 323) and consumers do not distinguish between internal markets and external ones (*Human Action*, p. 325). Moreover, government should have no role in protecting consumers from deceptive business practices (*Human Action*, pp. 320-322). "The idea that business propaganda can force the consumers to submit to the will of the advertisers is spurious" (*Human Action*, p. 322). Even though the market could be judged to be imperfect—using heaven as a standard—Mises championed the free market as the best means of achieving civilization and prosperity for humanity.

Appendix: Mises and basic economics
Chapter 7 questions

Write short answers to the following questions by utilizing Ludwig von Mises (1996), *Human Action: A Treatise On Economics*, fourth revised edition, Irvington-on-Hudson, New York: The Foundation for Economic Education (this edition comprises minor editorial changes by Bettina Bien Greaves). It is available online if one searches for it. The page numbers reflect where answers may be found in the English version of the book.

1. In what sense is human action always subject to "luck," where each person is a player who speculates or gambles? (pp. 112-113) What is the role of insurance in the market?
2. What does Mises mean when he says, "Every action is speculation. There is in the course of human events no stability and consequently no safety" (p. 113).
3. What does Mises think about the notion that exchange and markets are games, where commerce is a ruse, and many times one person gains at the expense of other participants? (pp. 115-116).
4. Is competition the same as combat? What is the role of cooperation? (pp. 116-117).
5. In what sense "is there strategy in business operations"? (p. 117).
6. To what extent can praxeology predict human action? What constant relations exist in the economic actions of human beings? (pp. 117-118).
7. What does Mises mean when he says that each good's rank is assigned "in the scale of value" (p. 119), which has special meaning when a man must choose between two or more means to obtain them (pp. 120-121).
8. What is the definition of "utility," as given by Mises? (pp. 120-121).

9. Who elaborated the modern theory of value? (p. 121) Why is only the *subjective* value of the marginal satisfaction derived from a good important in economics? (p. 121).

10. What is the law of marginal utility? (pp. 124-125) What examples does Mises give of it? (pp. 125-126).

11. What is the law of returns? (pp. 127-129) and what example does Mises use to demonstrate it? (pp. 129-130).

12. What is work? Why is it not available in abundance? (pp. 131, 136) Why does it have a unique position in our world? (pp. 132-135, 136-137).

13. Why do people work according to Mises? (pp. 131-132, 136-138) and why does the productivity of labor progressively increase by improving and increasing the supply of capital and technology? (p. 133).

14. What is the utility marginal of labor? (pp. 132-133) and What is the disutility of work? (pp. 133, 137-138).

15. Why does Mises consider the creative genius and the entrepreneur to be two special cases of labor? (pp. 134-135, 139-140, 584-585).

16. Does labor become more abundant on account of more efficient methods of production? (pp. 136-137).

17. What is production and what relation does it have with creative activity? (pp.140-141) In what sense are human beings creators? (pp. 141-142).

18. How are imaginary economic models useful? (pp. 236-237).

19. How did Marx view the condition of the bourgeois and that of the proletariat? (p. 268).

20. In what sense are consumers "sovereign" and what character or attitude do they have in the market? (pp. 269-270) What does Mises mean when he says: "on the market no vote is cast in vain"? (p. 271).

21. What is the meaning of competition and catallactic competition? (pp. 273-274, 276).

22. What are the two connotations of "monopoly"? (p. 277).
23. Why is it problematic to talk of "competitive prices"? (p. 278).
24. What problems does Mises mention regarding unions? (pp. 269, 279).
25. What is profit and why is it subjective? (pp. 288-290).
26. What praises does Mises offer for "double-entry book-keeping" and why? (pp. 304-305).
27. What is the "selective process" and how does it function in terms of consumption and labor? (pp. 311-312).
28. Mises argues that "cost accounting is affected" by the increase in quantities of factors expended and goods produced (p. 340). Given that, when should a firm cease production? (p. 340) Should a company lament about its failures or errors in predicting costs (p. 347) or "the fact of unused capacity"? (p. 394).
29. What critique of environmentalism and the "exhaustion" of resources does Mises offer? (p. 386).
30. What are a "market price" and a "price structure"? (p. 393) Why is there "no such thing as prices outside the market"? (p. 395) Does Mises think that it is possible for government to determine prices? (p. 397).
31. What were the factors of production in (a) the classical tradition and (b) in modern theory? (pp. 635-636) What error did the classical economists commit with respect to the classification of land? (pp. 636-638).
32. What is "land" as an economic concept? (pp. 637-638) How is it possible to change its quality? How does it differ from capital goods? (pp. 637-639) What are its three primary uses? (pp. 640-642).
33. What is "the greatest merit of the Ricardian theory of rent"? (p. 636) What are "marginal" and "submarginal" lands and when would acting men value them (p. 640) or be able to assign them positive prices? (pp. 642-644).

34. What is "the myth of the soil" 'and who promotes it? (pp. 644-645).
35. What are the data or "features" of human action in the praxeological sense? (p. 646).
36. What is theory and why is it important in interpreting data? (pp. 647-648) Why is the term "social science" misleading at times? (p. 651).
37. What role have social pressure and ideology had in impelling human action? (pp. 647-648) How does one get market "power"? (p. 649).

Monopoly
38. How do monopoly prices emerge? (pp. 383, 358, 361-362) What do they have to do with entrepreneurial profits? (p. 360).
39. How can a monopolist know the reaction of consumers to an increase in the price of its product? (p. 362).
40. What is an "incomplete monopoly" and what effect does it have on the production of larger firms? (pp. 362-363) As an aside, what quantity would the minor market players choose to sell?
41. Of what order can a monopolized good or service be? (p. 364) When is it impossible to maintain a national cartel? (pp. 365-366) When has it been done? (pp. 386-387) What occurred in the price structure of the German cartels? (p. 367).
42. According to Mises, what happens when a minimum wage is decreed? (pp. 367-368) Why do unions pursue monopolistic positions in the market? What is their bottom line interest? (p. 377).
43. Why are there no social benefits from state intervention to fix world prices for natural resources? (pp. 368-369) What were the consequences of the nationalization and municipalization policies during the time before Mises wrote? (p. 376).

44. What are the four ways that government can create monopoly licenses and privileges? (p. 369).
45. What factors impede people from challenging monopolists? (p. 371) According to Mises, do monopolies always charge monopoly prices? Are monopolies problematic in catallactic terms? (pp. 375, 370-371, 358-359).
46. What are the three kinds of local monopolies and how do they emerge? (pp. 373-375).
47. Why does Mises say that "The buyer must always rely upon the trustworthiness of the seller" (pp. 378-379). What importance is time in the generation of good will? (pp. 379-380) Do higher prices generated by good will correspond to monopoly power? (pp. 380-381) Why does Mises say that a monopolist who sells his products at competitive prices is making gifts to some of his customers? (p. 382)
48. What are the four ways that consumers can react when faced with monopoly prices? (pp. 384-385).
49. What is the only way to maintain the conditions necessary to practice price discrimination? (pp. 390-391).
50. What is the surplus or "the margin" of the consumer? What are the two cases of discrimination that would make this surplus disappear? (p. 388).

References

Anonymous (1998), "Who Is Ludwig von Mises?," Ludwig von Mises Institute: Auburn, Alabama, http://www. mises.org/mises.asp.

Cobin, John M. (2006), *Christian Theology of Public Policy: Highlighting the American Experience*, Alertness Books: Greenville, South Carolina.

Gunning, J. Patrick (2004), "The Goal and Methods of Economic Theory," retrieved from http://knight.fcu.edu.

tw/~gunning/subjecti/mean_sub/gl_meth.pdf on April 22, 2009.

Gunning, J. Patrick (2001), "The Praxeological Concept of Equilibrium," retrieved from http://knight.fcu.edu.tw/~gunning/subjecti/mean_sub/gl_meth.pdf on April 22, 2009.

Mises, Ludwig von (1983/1944), *Bureaucracy*, Libertarian Press: Grove City, Pennsylvania.

Mises, Ludwig von (1996 [1966/1949]), *Human Action: A Treatise on Economics*, fourth revised edition, The Foundation for Economic Education: Irvington-on-Hudson, New York (the edition comprises minor editorial changes by Bettina Bien Greaves). The first edition (1949) is a translation of the German *Nationalökonomie: Theorie des Handelns und Wirtschaftens* (1940), [Economics: Theory of Action and Exchange] with the second English edition 1963, and the third in 1966.

Mises, Ludwig von (1978), *Liberalism: A Socio-Economic Exposition*, Mission, Kansas: Sheed, Andrews & McMeel.

Mises, Ludwig von (1988), "Liberty and Property," in *Two Essays by Ludwig von Mises*, Auburn, Alabama: The Ludwig von Mises Institute.

Mises, Ludwig von (1981/1922) *Socialism: An Economic and Sociological Analysis*, Liberty Classics (Liberty Fund): Indianapolis. The English edition (1936) was translated from the second German edition *Die Gemeinwirtschaft* (1932). In 1951, a new edition was published, enlarged with the small book *Planned Chaos* as its epilogue.

Mises, Ludwig von (1985/1957), *Theory and History: An Interpretation of Social and Economic Evolution*, The Ludwig von Mises Institute: Auburn, Alabama [the original publisher was Arlington House, New Rochelle, New York in 1969, 1976 and 1978].

Mises, Ludwig von (1934), *Theory of Money and Credit*, [translation of the second German edition *Theorie des Geldes und der Umlaufsmittel* (1924)] with a new edition in English in 1953, enlarged with a new essay entitled "Monetary Reconstruction."

Mises, Ludwig von (1962), *The Ultimate Foundation of Economic Science: an Essay on Method*, Sheed, Andrews & McMeel: Mission, Kansas.

O'Driscoll, Gerald P., Jr. and Rizzo, Mario J. (1996), *The Economics of Time and Ignorance* (Foundations of the Market Economy), Routledge Press: New York.

Rothbard, Murray N. (1980), *The Essential Von Mises*, Auburn, Alabama: Ludwig von Mises Institute and Libertarian Press, Inc.: Grove City, Pennsylvania [the book was originally published in 1973 as *Bramble Minibook*, Oakley R. Bramble, Publisher: Lansing, Michigan.]

8 Austrian methodology and the knowledge problem

The Austrian School's research program

The Austrian School of economics is so named because its founder, Carl Menger (1840-1921), and other chief proponents, were of Austrian extraction. Austrian economics is a free market research program, in the sense that markets are viewed as being the best means of allocating scarce resources in society, while socialism is viewed as an unacceptable and impossible means of social organization. Like public choice economists, Austrians do not begin with normative views about how society should be organized and then proceed to find scientific answers to support it. Rather, after conducting scientific analysis of economic issues or policy concerns, they have been led to support market-based institutions.

Austrian scholars do not deny the role that normative views play in any human action. Scholars too color their research choices and interests according to their normative views. On account of personal values and social institutions, it is impossible for scholars to be pure and objective in their academic pursuits. Nevertheless, Austrian and other free market scholarship is not an exercise in finding support for preconceived answers to social problems. It is not so manipulated more than any other social science research program. Austrian economics is a scientific endeavor to explain and predict human behavior.

Austrians have largely remained outside mainstream economic thought since the 1930s, mainly on account of their methodological distinctiveness and strong censure of interventionism. But the collapse of socialism (1989-1995) provided some vindication for the Austrians, and they have begun to have a more significant impact on the economics profession—just as they did before the reign of Keynes (which began in the late 1930s). Many scholars have now come to appreciate some or all of the contributions of the Austrian School, and an increasing number of scholars have been contributing to its revival and extension.

Austrian economists share many similarities with public choice and mainstream economists. However, they have some distinct methods which distinguish them from other economists in their quest to analyze human action. As Boettke remarks:

> The task of the economist, from an Austrian perspective, is twofold: (1) to render economic phenomena intelligible in terms of purposive human action, i.e., to get at the meaning individuals attach to their action, and (2) to trace out the unintended consequences, both desirable and undesirable, of human actions. When analyzing political exchange, the economist's task is not altered (Boettke 1994d, pp. 246-247).

As noted in chapter two, DiLorenzo and High argued that wayward antitrust legislation and other serious policy problems have resulted from overemphasizing static neoclassical models of perfect competition. The implication of their work was that proper advances in economics will come only as economists diminish their reliance on such models. Boettke likewise suggests that economics must free itself from the methodological strictures that bind it in order to make new advances:

> Most practicing scientists uncritically accept the basic premises of the dominant paradigm. Their attention is focused on working out solutions to the problems which the received wisdom throws up at them. Normal science consists of this routine behavior and, during periods of normal science, progress takes place in small incremental steps of improved explanations of the problems which the paradigm allows the scientist to pursue. But an essential tension in the scientific process exists between the necessity to train young scientists in the standard practices and basic principles of the discipline, and the desire to innovate and overturn existing practice and principles (Boettke 1994a, p. 601).

According to Boettke, "What scholars need to do today...is to take one step backward in terms of technique in order to take two steps forward in terms of understanding" (Boettke 1994c, p. 6). The advances in Austrian theory are able to aid this transition. Boettke notes some of the key elements of Austrian economics:

> Rather than maximizing behavior, stable preferences and equilibrium, the core assumptions of Austrian economics are (1) purposive behavior, (2) demonstrated preference, and (3) process analysis. Austrian economists could rework the mainstream results under this alternative set of assumptions (and all that they imply concerning subjectivism, knowledge, expectations, and the passage of real time) and derive different conclusions about market behavior and public policy (Boettke 1994d, p. 604).

Austrian theory can be applied to various areas of scientific inquiry, including economics and public-relevant research. At times, it has provided key insights into human behavior and social theory. Some of the areas deeply affected by Austrian work include the analysis of socialism, entrepreneurship, evolutionary legal systems, and money and banking.

The action axiom

The foremost element of the Austrian School's deductive method is the action axiom. As Mises asserts, "Human action is purposeful behavior" and "Acting man is eager to substitute a more satisfactory state of affairs for a less satisfactory. His mind imagines conditions which suit him better, and his action aims at bringing out this desired state. The incentive that impels a man to act is always some uneasiness" (Mises 1966, pp. 10, 13). From this axiom, the entirety of economic theory can be deduced and, provided that there are no errors in logic and that the axiom itself is true, human action in the market process may be explained and perhaps predicted without error. Like geometry, the study of human action (what Mises calls "praxeology") is axiomatic and tautological.

Because of "uneasiness," people are impelled to act, in spite of imperfect knowledge. Thus, conventional economic models built on comparative statics are both meaningless and unrealistic because knowledge is imperfect. Consequently, these equilibrium models are inadequate because they fail to address the most fundamental component of the economic action of individuals, viz., the process by which uneasiness is assuaged at the least perceived cost.

Kirzner points out that the assumption of perfect knowledge is actually the undoing of these neoclassical static equilibrium models. Given perfect knowledge (a requisite for these models), the market clearing price is the only price conceivable. Hence, the entire equilibrium diagram may be erased entirely, except for the point of intersection.

No other points can exist since they would comprise imperfect knowledge.[41] Therefore, Austrian economic models do not focus on equilibrium but on the market process. Forces are set in motion in a state of ignorance, and individuals do the best they can with imperfect knowledge. Austrians also emphasize the importance of the passage of time in any economic modeling. Entrepreneurs act in time, as do consumers. And thus Austrian economics has been dubbed, as noted in chapter seven, the economics of time and ignorance.

Austrian School's subjective methodology

Subjectivism is the central feature of the Austrian School's research program. As Larry White notes, "Subjectivism has been, in short, the distinctive method of the Austrian School economists" (White 1984, p. 4). White suggests that the Austrian School avoids the emptiness of popular economic methods:

> Such terms as "utility" and "satisfaction" are used by economists in a purely formal way devoid of psychological or hedonic content. "Concrete value judgments and definite human actions," he [Mises] declares, "are not open to further analysis." That is, economics is not concerned with second-guessing the rightness or wrongness of purposes or actions. Mises points out that this neutrality follows from the subjectivist approach of viewing action through the eyes of the actor. Praxeology, according to Mises, is not concerned with why individuals pursue the specific purposes they do, but only with what can be deduced from the axiom of human action, with the aid of

---

[41] This idea was presented at a lecture entitled "The Theory of Market Process" by professor Kirzner at the Foundation for Economic Education, Irvington-on-Hudson, New York, on the afternoon of June 13, 1994 (cf. Kirzner 1985, pp. 155-156).

certain subsidiary assumptions, the praxeologist deduces the entire body of economic theory (White 1984, pp. 15-16).

Hayek viewed men as striving to remove uneasiness under conditions of imperfect information. White remarks about the arduous and perpetual discovery process envisioned by Hayek:

> The market economy for Hayek is an information-gathering process, and this concept springs directly from his subjectivist outlook. In the task of using "available" resources to satisfy "existing" needs, "neither the 'available' resources nor the 'existing' needs are objective facts." Resources and needs "exist for practical purposes only through somebody knowing about them." The fact that each individual's knowledge is limited and specialized means that a "successful solution. . . . must be based on a method of utilizing the knowledge dispersed among all members of society. . . . this is precisely the function which the various 'markets' perform."...To assume perfect information is thus to assume away the very phenomenon supposedly under study, the market process. For the market process, Hayek points out, is a process of discovery unfolding through time (White 1984, p. 23).

Subjectivism is a common motif among Austrian scholars. As Ludwig Lachmann discusses, the inadequacies of modern economic models to deal with reality and human subjectivity have led Austrians to embrace organic methods:

> Austrian economics is perhaps regarded as lending theoretical expression to the features of everyday life in the type of market economy just described. In its essence Austrian economics may be said to provide a voluntaristic theory of action, not a mechanistic one. Austrians cannot but reject a conceptual scheme, such as the neo-

classical, for which man is not a bearer of active thought but a mere bundle of 'dispositions' in the form of a 'comprehensive preference field'. Austrians are thus compelled to look for conceptual schemes informed by a style of thought that is altogether different (Lachman 1991, p. 136).

An aberrant view of subjectivism in the Austrian School

However, in recent years, some Austrians have embraced an extreme view of subjectivism in human action. Hayek's focus on the subjective mental processes of individual economic actors, as well as the market process of social cooperation between them, has led other Austrians to embrace extreme subjectivism. For instance, White notes that Lachmann's focus turned to the disequilibrating tendencies of markets:

> The radical subjectivism of Lachmann has led him to question, even more strongly than Hayek, whether the equilibrating forces in the economy (the transmission of knowledge about economic decisions) will be stronger than the disequilibrating forces (the divergence of expectations); whether the economy can in fact be said to harbor any tendency toward equilibrium. Other Austrian economists have in turn criticized Lachmann for apparently denying the general validity of the concept of spontaneous order, a concept to the development of which Menger and Hayek in particular have made great contributions (White 1984, p. 27).

For the Austrian School, subjectivity is the essential element in a methodology to deduce theory from the action axiom. This has been true ever since Menger founded the Austrian School in the late nineteenth century. White observes:

Individuals and their endeavors, as in Menger's original vision, are seen as the source and the final cause of all that economics studies. But subjectivism is not only the starting point of economic analysis for the Austrians; in his insistence on rendering human action intelligible, Lachmann suggests that economics must also conclude on the subjective level. Here are but two aspects of a single procedure, namely interpretation of economic activity in the terms in which we think because they are the terms in which others think and the other terms in which all of us act (White 1984, p. 28).

Hermeneutics

The extreme subjectivity of Lachmann, and his emphasis on institutions, has led him and a few other Austrian scholars to dabble in hermeneutics.

What strikes the student of hermeneutics when he approaches our subject is not the fact that institutions are ignored in modern orthodox economics, but the fact that, like natural phenomena, they are treated as externally given conditions of human action—whose origin may not be investigated and whose continued existence is taken for granted. *And nobody asks questions about their meaning.* In fact, few economists today possess a vocabulary that would permit them to ask such questions. We thus confront a situation which, while institutions are by no means ignored, most economists do not know what to do with them (Lachman 1991, p. 139) [Emphasis in original].

The emphasis on subjectivity naturally leads to some interest in interpretation and mental processes. The obvious problem with overemphasizing subjective processes is that a denial of objective reality might logically follow. Texts and human actions only have meaning within the perceptions of the individual mind, making objective and external evaluation difficult. Even one's own writing may take on new meaning over time. What is true at one moment in time might be false in the next, in accordance with subjective interpretation. The market process thus becomes a remarkable piece of serendipity which is able to coordinate the unknown and radically subjective, and sometimes tacit or even unknowable, plans of multitudes of economic actors. In order to assist in analyzing such things, hermeneutical Austrians have turned to existential philosophers and evolutionary theorists.

While hermeneutics has not been the foremost interest of modern Austrian theorists, and may not be the most promising aspect of its research program, it is not surprising that some have been attracted to it. It may be that some Austrians will be able to settle the challenges of extreme subjectivism by other means. For instance, an alternative philosophical basis may be derived from theology to provide a basic level of objectiveness in time and space, while still leaving substantial room for micro-evolutionary and subjective processes.

Institutions are important

Austrians like Lachmann, Rizzo, Mises and Hayek have also been led to consider institutions which make purposeful human action more efficient and effective at removing uneasiness. In this endeavor, Austrians form a nexus with public choice theorists and other economists who emphasize the role of institutions. In the Austrian conception, institutions are patterns of life that have evolved over time that permit greater predictability in human action. According to Mario Rizzo, "Institutions are, in an important sense, congealed [i.e., coagulated, condensed] social knowledge"

(Rizzo 1996, p. xiii). Economizing individuals can improve their lives more effectively and efficiently via institutions.

Austrian non-mathematical methodology

Stemming from its axiomatic and subjective method, the Austrian School formalizes its models by logical rather than mathematical techniques. (Of course, logical methodology may easily include game theory—which is also favored by Buchanan and other public choice theorists.) Logic is the basic tool of all science, and the conversion of theory or analysis into mathematical symbols primarily serves to make logical deduction more tractable with less room for error. Doing so presumes, however, that the methods of the natural sciences are useful in either predicting or explaining human action. As we saw in chapters one and seven, Mises had little use for the mathematical method, which he derided in no uncertain terms. Boettke describes the logical approach of the Austrians:

> Austrian economics is 'verbal' and not mathematical. That should not be taken to imply non-formal, for the arguments presented in Austrian works can be quite formal, but they are not mathematical…Austrian economics is really just a set of questions and a basic attitude about the best way to attempt to answer those questions [about economic or social organization] (Boettke 1994a, p. 605).

Many economists, philosophers, and policy researchers have taken an interest in the Austrian School. Moreover, members of the general public have been likewise interested in the Austrian School on account of its ability to produce compelling explanations of human behavior without esoteric mathematical models. Indeed, its compelling logic has drawn many people to embrace some or all of its conclusions. Even the mainstream press has highlighted the

Austrian School in recent years. Writing for London's *Financial Times*, Michael Prowse observes:

In recent decades, mainstream economists—in common with other social scientists—have tried to gain respectability by acquiring the trappings of a "hard" science, such as physics. We are all familiar with the huge computer models used to generate those comically inaccurate economic "forecasts". But, in truth, maths is now central to every aspect of academic economics. Human beings are treated as though they were robot calculators, forever maximizing profits or "utility" subject to known (or at least precisely quantifiable) constraints. Prices are assumed to move rapidly to bring supply and demand into balance so that markets are always at or close to "equilibrium." The upshot is that all the complexities and certainties of a market economy are reduced to a series of neat equations. This makes economics more sophisticated than in the days of Adam Smith (or even John Maynard Keynes). But is the pretension to scientific understanding justified? Can the kind of maths used to describe the natural world really be brought to bear on the decisions of human beings? Is economics really this tractable? Austrians think not. In real science, there are plenty of "constants"—precise relationships confirmed by numerous experiments. After decades of effort, Rothbard points out, economists have not come up with a single "economic constant." All they can ever say is that certain relationships held at certain times in certain places. The crucial difference is that human beings can (and frequently do) alter their behavior—an option not open to planets or atoms (Prowse 1994, p. 19).

Lachmann suggests that Austrians reject mathematical methods as the primary means of scientific inquiry because those methods are antithetical to studying purposeful human action.

But what to Austrians is most objectionable is the neo-classical style of thought, borrowed from classical mechanics, which makes us treat the human mind as a mechanism and its utterances as determined by external circumstances. Action is here confused with mere reaction. There is no choice of ends. Given a 'comprehensive preference field' for each agent, what is there to choose? The outcome of all acts of choice is here predetermined. In response to changing market prices men perform meaningless acts of mental gymnastics by sliding up and down their indifference curves. All this is far removed from meaningful action in our 'life-world' (Lachmann 1991, p. 135).

The Austrians are not the only ones to reject mathematical economics as the primary tool of economic analysis. High remarks that the post-Keynesians, economists with a sharply different vision than the Austrians, have a similar conviction about mathematical models:

As the Post-Keynesians see it, Keynes introduces a new *logical* method of looking at the market. Keynes' contribution lay in discovering that the use of money destabilized the market. If large numbers of people decide to hold more money, unemployment will follow, because no workers are required to produce more money. Only government spending can prevent this unemployment. Thus the Post-Keynesians reject the method of the Revolution, but retain its policy (High 1984, p. 38).[42]

In spite of this methodological affinity, High goes on to note that Austrians are led reject the interventionist side of post-Keynesianism since it produces harmful economic distortions. High continues:

---

[42] Note: to avoid needless distraction, the imbedded page numbers were omitted from the original quotation.

Holding a more critical attitude towards the Revolution are the Austrian economists. They reject both the mathematical method and the Keynesian policy. The Austrians believe that "the attention paid to the formal apparatus has been responsible for failure to appreciate a number of insights crucially important for economic understanding." Austrians look on the market as a *coordinating process*. The trouble with focusing upon a few statistical aggregates, as the Keynesians do, is that it ignores the process of market adjustment. Keynesian policy, by ignoring market complexity, not only fails to stabilize the market, it also *induces* large-scale discoordination. The Austrians believe that the only way to reconstruct economics is to overturn both parts of the revolution. Both the mathematical method and government intrusion into the market should be rejected as unproductive and harmful (High 1984, p. 38).

Austrians do not reject the mathematical approach because it is too difficult, but because it is not be best way to analyze human behavior. Human beings are not lifeless, inanimate objects. They are endowed with sensibilities for thinking, feeling, and acting, as well as the capacity to reflect on the past. They engage in purposeful action to remove uneasiness. Given that action is the essence of life, static models, which of necessity explain only states of rest or inaction, are incapable of explaining or predicting human behavior and the market process. As White summarizes:

> The considered rejection of the mathematical model as sterile, i.e., as incapable of shedding light on the vital questions of economic processes, has been one of the continuing themes of the Austrian School...Weiser raised the objection to the use of calculus in economic theory that economic phenomena are necessarily discon-

tinuous and discrete. The Austrians, with their focus on the way in which agents perceive and act in the real world, have always been careful to formulate their marginalism in terms of discrete units and discontinuous points rather than infinitesimal units of smooth curves (White 1984, p. 11).

While the Austrian School contends that mathematics may have some usefulness in explaining basic economic principles or simple concepts, it is not generally appropriate for advancing praxeological theory. As White notes:

On the one hand, praxeology is like mathematics (and logic) in being an axiomatic or deductive system. On the other hand...praxeology cannot be pursued as if it were a branch of applied mathematics because its starting point (the fact of human goal-seeking), unlike the axioms of Newtonian physics or other mathematical systems, is not arbitrary...Mises did not deny that mathematical techniques could be used to describe equilibrium conditions. But he argued that description of equilibrium conditions was not the ultimate or even main task of economic theory, which aimed at understanding market processes (White 1984, pp. 20-21).

For instance, Hayek criticized the notion of using mathematical methods merely to analyze static points in time. Instead, the task of the economist is to explain, and predict as best he can, the mutable processes of human action. As White comments:

The member of the Austrian School who has produced the most subtle and detailed critique of the notion that the social sciences should ape [imitate] the methods of the physical sciences—an idea he calls "scientism" [in *The Counter-Revolution of Science*]—is F. A. Hayek. The data for the social sciences are of necessity subjective, he writes, for they deal "not with the relations between things, but with the relations between men and things or the relations between man and man"…Hayek has also continued Menger's concentration on the role of information and knowledge in the process of economic decision-making [for instance, in his book *Economics and Knowledge*]. Menger, despite the "exact" nature of economic laws, suggests the impossibility of a "strict regularity of economic phenomena," what we would call equilibrium, due to the fact that economic men are so often "in error about their economic interest, or in ignorance of economic conditions" (White 1984, p. 11).

The knowledge problem

Perhaps the most important contribution of Hayek to the Austrian School, especially for those Austrians engaged in comparative systems and policy-relevant research, is the extension of the theory of dispersed social knowledge. In what would come to be termed *the knowledge problem*, Hayek developed his critique of central planning:

> The economic problem of society is thus not merely a problem of how to allocate "given" resources—if "given" is taken to mean given to a single mind which deliberately solves the problem set by these "data." It is rather a problem of how to secure the best use of resources known to any of the members of society, for ends whose relative importance only these individuals know. Or, to put it briefly, it is a problem of the utilization of knowledge not given to anyone in its totality (Hayek 1945, p. 520).

Social knowledge is dispersed in fragments to individuals. Nevertheless, the market process utilizes it within the price system, coordinating human action amazingly well. Production occurs, wants are satisfied, and uneasiness is removed, despite the fact that no one person has in himself the comprehensive knowledge to accomplish these things. Hayek continues:

> We must look at the price system as such a mechanism for communicating information if we want to understand its real function—a function which, of course, it fulfills less perfectly as prices grow more rigid...The most significant fact about this system is the economy of knowledge with which it operates, or how little the individual participants need to know in order to be able to take the right action (Hayek 1945, pp. 526-527).

The failure of planning

All central planning schemes will end in futility because of the knowledge problem. For Austrian theorists, central planning is always impossible, not only because of the incentive problems discussed in public choice theory, but because no single man or committee of men has enough knowledge to allocate resources or make other economic decisions effectively. Even on a local scale, planning boards face the same knowledge problem that faces larger central planning regimes. Thus, central planning and perhaps most government regulation are simply not possible on account of the knowledge problem.

There is not only an enormous amount of data processing required (a task which may only be slightly alleviated by computers), but "the knowledge needed is a knowledge of *subjective patterns of trade-off that are nowhere articulated,* not even to the individual himself" (Selgin 1988, p. 90—quoting Thomas Sowell). Selgin observes that the major knowledge problem that non-omniscient planners face is knowledge about the future.

The problem of economic resource administration is not, however, merely one of disseminating knowledge of existing conditions. Nor is the solution of this part of the problem the sole contribution of market prices. Economic administration of resources ultimately depends upon correct [present] anticipation of conditions (for example, consumer preferences) of the *future* (Selgin 1988, p. 91).

Dispersed knowledge is translated into price signals via market exchange. Price and profit signals serve as knowledge "surrogates" (rather than mere "communicators" of knowledge) (Selgin 1988, pp. 92, 93). In short, Selgin argues that, "The problem of resource administration is complicated by the fact that the knowledge relevant to its solution is divided among numerous individuals. No single person or bureau can hope to accumulate any significant part of it" (Selgin 1988, p. 90).

Thus, an important aspect of policy-relevant research is manifest. Planning boards, and their plethora of regulations, cannot possibly provide an optimal allocation of resources and will almost certainly be unable to provide betterment in resource allocation. Trying to improve the quality of life with proactive public policy will result in failure.

Government planners encounter insurmountable complications trying to harness the requisite knowledge for any planning endeavor. But under the coordination of the market process, self-interested individuals continually produce requisite knowledge for human action as an unintended consequence of their self-interested pursuits. Holcombe describes this process and the futility of central planning:

> In a market economy, the profit motive gives people an incentive to act on this information [about prices and production efficiency] and change their prices accordingly without consulting anyone. Then, others in the economy can use this information to make their own decisions about resource allocation...To take advantage of all the information like this in a centrally planned economy, everyone would have to be constantly passing in-

formation up the chain of command to the central planners, who then would have to modify the central plan accordingly and pass the information back down to those who need it. The problem with central planning is there is too much information for the central planners to digest and comprehend, and even if they could receive all this information, they would be unable to use it as effectively as the people who originally had it to begin with...How would a central planner decide which potential innovations are worth pursuing? In these areas, where market participants have specific information on the potential value of innovations, markets fare far better than central planning. Hayek's insights on the workings of the market are critical to understanding why central planning failed in socialist countries and why there are perils in trying to use government planning to enhance the quality of life. Every individual has certain specific knowledge that is difficult to share with the central planner and that would be difficult to use even if the information were available (Holcombe 1995, pp. 15-16).

Accordingly, free market theorists combine the insights from public choice and Austrian economic theory into a robust critique of central planning, socialism, and regulation in general. Table 8.1 provides a synopsis:

Table 8.1 The two-pronged critique of regulation

General critique of regulation and planning:
(1) if planners are like angels, or are nearly altruists with hearts of gold and publicly-spirited or good intentions, they will still fail to plan correctly or efficiently on account of the knowledge problem, but
(2) if planners are not like angels, but serve their own self interests (rather than mainly the public interest) like the rest of humanity, they will fail to plan correctly or efficiently on account of public choice problems.

Nexus with property rights theory and the legal order

The Austrian theory of knowledge also impacts policy considerations of property rights. Both Mises and Hayek contended that economic calculation and proper resource allocation require private property rights and a high degree of legal certainty that devolves from useful social institutions. Artificial substitutes for these rights and institutions will fail of necessity and may sometimes lead to totalitarian central planning atrocities (Boettke 1994b, pp. 30, 12). Boettke summarizes this theme:

> The most important component of the Von Mises–Hayek argument was the significance they placed on the institution of private property and the rule of law. Property rights protected by the rule of law provide (1) legal certainty which encourages investment, (2) a motivation for responsible decision-making on behalf of owners, (3) the background for social experimentation which spurs progress, and (4) the basis for economic calculation by expanding the context within which price, and profit and loss, signals can reasonably guide resource use. Moreover, it was precisely because economic life is dynamic and in a constant state of flux, that the clearly defined property rights embedded in the rule of law are fundamental to a sustainable political economy (Boettke 1994b, p. 10).

Indeed, the Austrian theory of knowledge leads to a cogent critique of mechanistic modeling and policies. The market process happens without planning and regulation. It produces the coordinating institutions, market signals, and other things necessary for production, distribution, and resource allocation without central control. As Hayek notes:

> There can be no deliberately planned substitutes for such a self-ordering process for adaptation to the unknown.

Neither his reason nor his innate 'natural goodness' leads man in this way, only the bitter necessity of submitting to rules he does not like in order to maintain himself against competing groups that he had already had begun to expand because they had stumbled on such rules earlier. If we had deliberately built, or were consciously shaping, the structure of human action, we would merely have to ask individuals why they had interacted with any particular structure. Whereas, in fact, specialised students, even after generations of effort, find it exceedingly difficult to explain such matters, and cannot agree on what are the causes or what will be the effects of particular events. The curious task of economics is to demonstrate to men how little they really know about what they imagine they can design (Hayek 1988, p. 76).

Regrettably, economics has done just the opposite at times. Most economists and politicians continue to favor government intervention and regulation. Yet, because of the knowledge problem, many policies turn out to be inefficient and often ineffective. As Rowley notes, the costs stemming from the knowledge problem are manifest in egregious horrors of socialism, resulting from attempts to supersede the market process:

The price system...effectively co-ordinates the separate actions of different individuals in an economy in which knowledge is widely dispersed. Indeed, the real function of the price system is that of a mechanism for communicating information which otherwise could not be communicated. The fatal conceit of the socialist autocracies rests in large part in the denial of this premise (Rowley 1993, p. 26).

Calculation and central planning

From a Hayekian point of view, the idea of central planning is simply preposterous given the knowledge required to perform it. As Hayek states:

Indeed the whole idea of 'central control' is confused. There is not, and never could be, a single directing mind at work; there will always be some counsel or committee charged with designing a plan of action for some enterprise. Though individual members may occasionally, to convince the others, quote particular pieces of information that have influenced their views, the conclusions of the body will generally not be based on common knowledge but on agreement among several views based on different information. Each bit of knowledge contributed by one person will tend to lead some other to recall yet other facts of whose relevance he has become aware only by his being told of yet other circumstances of which he did not know. Such a process thus remains one of making use of dispersed knowledge (and thus simulates trading, although in a highly inefficient way—a way usually lacking competition and diminished in accountability), rather than unifying the knowledge of a number of persons. The members of the group will be able to communicate to one another few of their distinct reasons; they will communicate chiefly conclusions drawn from their respective individual knowledge of the problem in hand. Moreover, only rarely will circumstances really be the same for different persons contemplating the same situation—at least in so far as this concerns some sector of the extended order and merely a more or less self-contained group (Hayek 1988, p. 87).

Nevertheless, many socialist experiments were tried during the twentieth century. A hopeful utopia turned to disarray;

Boettke describes the disastrous consequences of socialism in the early Soviet Union:

The result of this policy of socialist transformation was an economic disaster. "Considered purely as an economic experiment," William Henry Chamberlin commented, "war communism may fairly be considered one of the greatest and most overwhelming failures in history. Every branch of economic life, industry, agriculture, transportation, experienced conspicuous deterioration and fell far below the pre-War levels of output." Economic life completely fell apart. "Never in all history," declared H.G. Wells, "has there been so great a debacle before." As Moshe Lewin points out, "The whole modern sector of urbanized and industrialized Russia suffered a severe setback, as becomes obvious from the population figures....By 1920," he reports, "the number of city dwellers had fallen from 19 percent of the population in 1917 to 15 percent. Moscow lost half its population, Petrograd two-thirds. After only three years of Bolshevik rule, "The country lay in ruins, its national income one-third of the 1913 level, industrial production a fifth (output in some branches being virtually zero), its transportation system shattered and agricultural production so meager that a majority of the population barely subsisted and millions of others failed even that." This debacle is recorded in various memoirs and novels of the time. The burst of productivity expected from the rationalization of economic life was not forthcoming. Instead, economic life and social relations under communist rule merely worsened the condition of the masses of people. If "Lenin was the midwife of socialism," then the "mother's belly had been opened and ransacked and still there was no baby." The socialist project proved unrealizable; utopia became dystopia within three years. The Soviet socialist failure bore full witness to the Mises-Hayek criticism of socialist planning. The economic disorganization of Bolshevik Russia was, as Lancelot Lawton pointed out, a result of the "disregard of economic calculation" (Boettke 1990, pp. 88-89).

The socialist calculation debate

Holcombe provides a synopsis of the twentieth century's *calculation debate* between the Austrians (i.e., Mises and Hayek) and those who were optimistic about central planning. In essence, the critique of Mises and Hayek was discarded in favor of a bold idea to change the course of history. Yet defiant plans for socialist societies were not able to overcome the knowledge problem.

The socialist calculation debate began early in the twentieth century, shortly after the Russian revolution that created the Soviet Union, whose new leaders wanted to establish a centrally planned socialist economy. One problem they faced is that nobody knew how a centrally planned economy should be established or how it would operate. The intellectual foundations leading to the establishment of a socialist country were found in Karl Marx's treatise, *Capital*, but *Capital* was a book about the failings of capitalism and offered little guidance as to how a socialist economy would actually be run. When the socialists in the Soviet Union were searching for answers, economist Ludwig von Mises made the claim that central planning could not work to allocate resources. The problem, as Mises saw it, was that prices and markets are necessary to provide the information about how resources should be allocated. Without prices and markets, there would be no indication about how much of any good should be produced, what production process would be most efficient, how much investment should be undertaken, or where resources used for investment should be allocated. Markets helped the early planned economy in the Soviet Union in two ways, Mises noted. First, some markets did remain in the Soviet Union; second, because most of the world still used markets, central planners could look at world prices as a guide to resource allocation in developing their plans. Prices in world markets would provide central planners in the Soviet Union with good information about how valuable various resources were...If the whole world turned to central planning, Mises argued that there would be no way in which central planners could develop a workable plan. In response to Mises' critique of central planning, Oskar Lange and Fred Taylor wrote a volume in which they explained how central planners could take advantage of the same principles that underlie the market in order to develop a centrally planned economy. In brief, Lange and Taylor argued that central planners could create administered prices and allow plant managers to decide how much of various resources they wanted at those centrally planned prices. The planners would allocate budgets to the managers based upon administered prices for their output. If shortages of some goods developed, that would indicate that the administered prices for those goods should be raised; conversely, surpluses for goods would indicate that those prices should be lowered. Essentially, the central planners in Lange and Taylor's system would duplicate the functions of the market. With this response to Mises' criticisms of socialism, the socialists declared themselves winners in the socialist calculation debate (Holcombe 1995, pp. 13-14).[43]

Hayek's knowledge problem critique was mostly ignored. Unfortunately, even reports of the coming the demise of communism in most of the world did not yield respect for Hayek's theory as it should. Many people in the

---

[43] Mises's critique is cogently presented in his 1922 book *Socialism* (see chapter seven).

West continued to be true believers in the concept. The Austrians were not widely vindicated until the collapse of Eastern European communism late in the twentieth century.

Austrian theory—based on its axiomatic, subjective, and logical (verbal) methodology—was able to both explain and predict the failure of socialism; and it was able to do so much better and earlier than competing theoretical schools. Indeed, the Austrian policy prescription for social organization or regulation, being informed by Austrian theory and verified by history, suggests that maximizing liberty and minimizing the state will provide the best possible social outcome. As Boettke further notes:

> The competitive capitalist process of exchange and production relies on the market system of prices, profit and loss to discover and disseminate the knowledge necessary for the coordination of plans. In advanced capitalist production, that is, a complex economy with higher or more remote stages of production, the coordination between the consumer-goods sector and the producer-goods sector depends crucially upon the ability of the price system to convey knowledge to the various market participants. Economic growth concerns the growth of knowledge in society. It is about the discovery and use of new knowledge of existing or previously unknown opportunities. As Israel Kirzner writes: "The great neglected question in development economics concerns the existence of a social apparatus for ensuring that available opportunities are exploited."…It is a recognition of the knowledge-conveyance role of markets that underlies the case for freedom of exchange and production in economic development. The political and economic institutions of a truly free society are flexible enough to allow for human creativity and innovation, yet at the same time are "rigid" enough to establish the mutually reinforcing sets of expectations necessary for economic coordina-

tion. As F.A. Hayek states: "Liberty is essential in order to leave room for the unforeseeable and unpredictable; we want it because we have learned to expect from it the opportunity of realizing many of our aims. It is because every individual knows so little, and, in particular, because we rarely know which of us knows best that we trust the independent and competitive efforts of many to induce the emergence of what we shall want when we see it" (Boettke 1990, pp. 170-171).

Lessons from failed socialist policy

Surely, the collapse of communism and the vindication of the Austrian School have far-reaching consequences for social theory and public policy. Thus, especially from the Austrian School's perspective, liberty and the free market are necessary policy goals for a well-functioning economy. Otherwise, the world may expect dire consequences. Policy designed to correct or supersede perceived market failures cannot succeed on account of the knowledge problem. As Boettke implies:

> The lesson of the Soviet experience with socialism should teach us more than we are perhaps willing to learn. The failure of the Marxian experiment in social engineering suggests that attempts to supersede market methods of exchange and production are problematic. The utopian aspiration of a fully emancipated world came into conflict with the political and economic reality of the knowledge and totalitarian problems. The result was an atrocity (Boettke 1990, p. 193).

The Soviet Union is not the only example of failed policy that resulted in atrocities. People in the most civilized nations can be misled by utopian or bad policy. As John Flynn showed in *As We Go Marching* (1944), proactive policies can be illusory and harmful.[44] Evidently, people are repeatedly misled by promises of beneficial government intervention via newfangled means. Thus, public policy decisions will continue to benefit from application of the knowledge problem to regulation via policy-relevant research. Indeed, the collapse of socialism and recognition of the knowledge problem provides a means to inform policy-relevant research. Mitchell and Simmons note, "The rediscovery of the market has been enhanced by observation of the clumsy ways by which government regulators and socialist planners attempt to substitute themselves for the market" (Mitchell and Simmons 1994, p. 206). Consequently, Austrian theory can more powerfully instruct public policy about the need for market-based alternatives to regulation and planning.

Austrian insights for policy-relevant research

In his cogent defense of Austrian theory, High distinguishes between the competing realms of the market process and the political process. The former is a coordinating process, based on the voluntary choices and preferences of individuals (High 1984, p. 38—citing Rothbard). The latter is social interaction which results from coercive actions like taxation and money inflation (High 1984, p. 41).

Government intervention, especially by proactive policy (but also with policies of inefficient provision), will not lead to beneficial outcomes according to Austrian theory. Stephen Littlechild suggests that, "the present extent of government intervention cannot be justified if the aim is to encourage an efficient, responsive, and increasingly wealthy economy." For Austrian theorists, a "mixed economy"

---

[44] Flynn demonstrated the incredible similarities and parallels between German fascism, Italian fascism, and Franklin D. Roosevelt's New Deal in the USA. Perhaps President Barak Obama's interventions starting in 2009 may also appropriately be included.

is both unfeasible and unacceptable (see chapter seven). While markets are robust and resilient, a policy of "government intervention has corresponding weaknesses" (Littlechild 1981, pp. 74-75). Therefore, Austrians would recommend severely limiting the role of government to reactive public policy functions. High remarks on the apprehension Austrians have to proactive economic policy:

Strictly speaking, there is no such thing as Austrian economic policy...Austrian economics rejects the army of bureaucrats who regulate and prosecute voluntary production and exchange. Regulation and anti-trust laws have usually been motivated by economic gain (High 1984, p. 40).

As we saw in chapter five, much policy-relevant research has been done to demonstrate the problems of government policy. Moreover, many scholars, including myself, DiLorenzo, Boettke, Ellig, High, Holcombe, Schansberg, and others, have adopted eclectic approaches to policy-relevant research. Thus, Austrian theory can be coupled with public choice theory to create a powerful analytical tool kit. Unlike the mainstream of political science, and even economics, Austrian theorists prefer the unfettered, undirected market process over a "competitive" role for government in either the private sector or on a national level with respect to other nations. Given the recent revitalized interest in markets, contemporary Austrians have an excellent opportunity to advance their theories into the mainstream of policy-relevant research. In this respect, Rizzo notes that Austrians are forward looking:

While the neoclassical mainstream continues to spin its wheels, "Austrians" (meaning the broad subjectivist and market-process school of thought) are asking and answering deep questions at the frontier of social-scientific knowledge. They understand that application of the mechanistic model of nineteenth century physics may well have reached the limits of its useful contributions. They are not afraid to challenge many widely, but passively, accepted beliefs among economists. They know that the twentieth century is almost at an end and that not all of its intellectual developments have been beneficial. They understand that a new century will demand not only "new" techniques (perhaps many of them being old techniques) but also new divisions among academic disciplines (Rizzo 1996, p. xii).

As Prowse points out, the knowledge problem has opened the way for a new critique of welfare economics, a primary area of analysis by Austrians doing policy-relevant research.

Mainstream economists still talk grandly about "maximising social welfare." Hayek's point about the dispersal of knowledge shows that this goal is really nonsensical. Nobody could know enough to measure societies [*sic*] welfare, let alone to maximise it. Hayek's central point is not that market prices convey and summarise already—existing knowledge—something most economists would accept. It is, rather, that the incentives offered by market prices during the dynamic process of competition lead to the discovery and dissemination of *new* knowledge (Prowse 1994, p. 19).

Unlike government regulatory schemes—which are invariably fettered by the knowledge problem—market-regulatory institutions can alleviate imperfect information via robust and rivalrous competition.

The normative idea that government should alleviate imperfect information and negative externalities (many of which may have been fabricated by or involve a government action) is incredulous. On the one hand, the government agent behaves as a coercive ideologue and not as a market participant, resulting in regressive vote or rent seeking behavior, and susceptibility to being captured by special interest groups. On the other hand, such policies errantly presume that government agents have the requisite knowledge to accomplish their objectives.

The only kind of government that might be beneficial is one which is stable and rigorously limited. It would provide a framework to protect private property and individual liberty, as well as to punish predators (particularly on a local level) who assail these rights and institutions (cf. Mises 1966, pp. 280-281). As we saw in chapter seven, Mises suggests that the primary purpose of the state is to create and preserve an "environment in which the market economy can safely operate" (cf. Mises 1966, p. 257). Menger likewise viewed the primary function of public policy as being the protection of private property.

> [I]t becomes necessary for society to protect the various individuals in the possession of goods...against all possible acts of force. In this way, then, we arrive at the economic origin of our present legal order, and especially of the so-called *protection of ownership*, the basis of property (Menger 1994, p. 97).

This sentiment may turn out to be wishful thinking, but it does represent the maximum amount of government that Austrian theorists believe is useful.

Indeed, the state and its interventions might prove to be forever problematic. Selgin notes that economic knowledge in the market is distorted by state interventions, which are "governmentally imposed obstacles to price flexibility" (Selgin 1988, p. 148, drawing from Sowell 1980). At least from an Austrian perspective, any policy with an objective which broadens the role of the state beyond these strict limits will predictably create market distortions and havoc. Hence, only reactive public policy may be beneficial.

Appendix: Mises on socialism, society, and methodology
Chapter 8 questions

Write short answers to the following questions by utilizing Ludwig von Mises (1996), *Human Action: A Treatise On Economics*, fourth revised edition, Irvington-on-Hudson, New York: The Foundation for Economic Education (this edition comprises minor editorial changes by Bettina Bien Greaves).

Action

51. What is Mises pointing out by saying that "human action is purposeful behavior...aiming at ends and goals"? (p. 11) What is "praxeology" and what is its objective? (pp. 11-12, 15, 21-22, 28).
52. What does Mises mean by "Action is not simply giving preference" (p. 12) and "Action is not only doing but no less omitting to do what possibly could be done" (p. 13).
53. What incentive always induces an individual to act? (pp. 13, 92) When does action toward goods occur? (pp. 93-94) [Note: These concepts form the action axiom, which is the basis of economic theory.]
54. Comment on the following idea of Mises (p. 119): "Action sorts and grades...Acting man values things as means for the removal of his uneasiness...For acting man there exists primarily nothing but various degrees of relevance and urgency with regard to his own well-being."
55. What is the only thing certain about an individual's future? Why does it make human action seem inane? (p. 881) Why do human beings struggle to remove uneasiness and what is the role of praxeology in saying whether a man should live or not live? (pp. 882-883).

56. In what sense is economics neutral with respect to value judgments or the philosophical underpinnings of public policy? (pp. 883-885).

Mathematics

57. Why does Mises say that "reverential awe" is generated by using mathematical methods? (p. 106).
58. Why does Mises argue that it is impossible to produce economic theory through mathematical methods and the analysis of historical acts or data? (pp. 350-351) Why is it impossible to use these methods successfully to demonstrate reality or market processes: "The equations formulated by mathematical economics remain a useless piece of mental gymnastics"? (pp. 354, 355-357) What is the only thing that mathematical models can tell us about supply and demand? (pp. 377-378).
59. Why does Mises decry mathematical economics for strengthening the socialist cause and for being impractical in economic science? (pp. 701-702, 713, 714-715).

Other general themes

60. What characteristics are specifically human? (pp. 14, 25).
61. Must human action always be "rational"? (pp. 19ff).
62. Why doesn't economics deal with animals? (pp. 27-28) In what sense is man different than animals? (pp. 16-17).
63. What "irreducible and unanalyzable phenomenon" or "ultimate given" exists in economic science? (p. 17) Does it have a philosophical base that is unusual among sciences or only does it only debilitate economic science? (pp. 17-18).
64. What are the limits of reason and scientific research, and the role of faith? (pp. 25-26) Mises suggests that the person who wants to have "perfect cognition of all things" must "apply to faith" to do what scientific in-

quiry cannot. Yet why are various aspects of oriental religion incompatible with human action? (p. 29).

65. In economics, what is a "means"? How does it relate to praxeology and economics? (p. 92).
66. What is the task of economics? (p. 93).
67. Economic goods also include services (p. 94) plus other things that satisfy people or reduce their uneasiness. Which are the goods of the "first order" and which are of higher orders? (pp. 93-94).
68. What do ethical doctrines and the normative disciplines have to do with praxeology? (p. 95) What are some examples of them?
69. Comment on the following remark by Mises (pp. 94-95): "Ultimate ends are ultimately given, they are purely subjective, they differ with various people and with the same people at various moments in their lives." Mises says that economics cannot ponder ultimate ends (pp. 95-96). What disciplines do so?
70. What is value? (pp. 94-95) Is it intrinsic? (p. 96)
71. What does economics have to do with postulates about what man "should" do? (p. 96).
72. What are the definitions of "action" and "exchange" according to Mises? (p. 97) What are the definitions of profit and of loss? (p. 97).
73. Is human utility cardinal or ordinal? Why? Can we measure or calculate value—especially when it involves interpersonal value judgments? (pp. 96-98).
74. What does Mises mean when he says: "The notion of change implies the notion of temporal sequence...The praxeological system too [like the logical system] is aprioristic and deductive. As a system it is out of time. But change is one of its elements." The difference between the two systems is that praxeology is interested precisely in change: "the notions of sooner and later and of cause and effect"? (p. 99).

75. Toward what time frame or reference is human action always pointed and directed? (p. 100) What are the important aspects about time for praxeology? What is the "real extended present"? (pp. 100-101).
76. Why is it important in economics that a man's "time is scarce"? (p. 101).
77. What critique does Mises make regarding the issue of transitivity? (pp. 102-103).
78. Comment on this idea of Mises: "Acting must be suited to purpose, and purposefulness requires adjustment to changing conditions" (p. 103).
79. Are action and uncertainty about the future independent and unconnected matters? (p. 105).
80. How does Mises avoid the philosophical problem of free will in making praxeological assertions? (p. 105).
81. From which two sources does uncertainty arise? What is apodictic certainty? What is the only possible means to attain it? (pp. 105-106).
82. What is the difference between class probability and case probability? (pp. 107, 110) What does class probability have to do with praxeology?
83. What new knowledge can we gain by transforming our knowledge into mathematical symbols? (pp. 108).
84. What security do probability and statistics render in predicting human action—even when there is a historical trend that favors one result over another? (p. 112).
85. What is society? (pp. 143-144, 158-159, 169-171) What does Mises mean when he says that "society is nothing but the combination of individuals for cooperative effort. It exists nowhere else than in the actions of individual men" (p. 143) and "Man appeared on the scene of earthly events as a social being" (p. 165)?
86. Why are there no real animal societies? (p. 145).
87. What are the costs and benefits of society? (pp. 146, 148-149) Why do people cooperate? (pp. 169, 273) Do we see a social evolution of the human beings in societies?

(p. 160) Why does virtually no one want to return to a more primitive and pristine existence? (pp. 165-166).

88. What does Mises mean when he says that "The fundamental social phenomenon is the division of labor and its counterpart human cooperation"? (p. 157) What are the effects of this phenomenon? (pp. 164-165).

89. What are the three reasons why the division of labor augments production? (p. 158).

90. What is Ricardo's "law of association"—use Mises's example in your answer (pp. 159, 161, 163). How does it deal with protectionism? (pp. 159-162)

91. What is "rational conduct"? (p. 172).

92. What is Benthamite utilitarianism? Why does it advocate egalitarianism under the law? (p. 175).

93. What is the scope of catallactics? Why is there demand for goods? (p. 233) What is the role of "selfishness" in directing human action? (p. 242).

94. Why is Marxism the negation of economics (pp. 234-235) and only serves to mislead us with a "delusive image" of reality? (p. 240).

95. What critique does Mises make about "just" or "fair" prices? (p. 332) Why are profits always abnormal? (p. 350).

96. Would it be possible for a socialist committee to determine values and prices for society? (pp. 334-335).

97. Why do socialists call entrepreneurial profits, land rent, and interest on capital "unearned"? (p. 396) What does Mises say the consequence of socialism is? (p. 397).

98. Why does the long term have greater importance in praxeology? How have economists shown this fact? Why did Keynes err when he said "in the long run we are all dead"? (pp. 652-654).

99. What is an "external cost" and to what type of property rights allocation does it pertain? (p. 656).

100. What are "external economies" or benefits? Do they impede production or plans to produce? (p. 656).

101. Why were various companies not declared guilty for their torts? And why was that trend later modified by government policy? (pp. 655-656) What will happen to taxpayers when government manages a company to avoid external effects from passing to consumers or voters? (pp. 659-660).

102. Why are patents and copyrights important? (p. 661) What is Mises trying to say when he points out that, "If there are neither copyrights nor patents, the inventors and authors are in the position of an entrepreneur"? (p. 661) What counter arguments to policies favoring these two privileges does Mises point out? (pp. 662-663).

103. What is the problem of economic calculation? Why are prices in terms of money indispensable in doing it? (pp. 699, 700, 714-715). What implications does socialism face because of it? What critique have socialists made against it, and Mises of them? (pp. 699-701). According to Mises, how was economic calculation possible in Russia and Germany under socialism? (pp. 702, 849).

104. How does a socialist system work? (pp. 705-706) What do neosocialists argue? (pp. 706-708).

105. Why is central planning impossible and a mixed policy of socialism and capitalism similar to "a triangular square"? (pp. 700-701, 710). What indicators do entrepreneurs have to achieve success and guide their decisions that planners do not have—and which impede their planning efforts? (pp. 704-705). Why can't entrepreneurs be replaced by bureaucratic managers? (pp. 708, 711).

106. According to Mises, what are the six proposed schemes to calculate under a socialist economy? (pp. 703-704).

107. What does Mises say about the feasibility of optimally allocating resources using capitalism? (p. 705).

108. What is interventionism and when is it similar to socialism? (pp. 758-759) Has it been successful in history? How was it justified? (pp. 759-762).

109. What is the "peculiar and unique position" of economics among the sciences and in what way does it differ from economic history? (pp. 862, 867-868).

110. According to Mises, why is public opinion important and what error did "the old liberals" commit? (pp. 863-865). What effect and motives do SIGs have? (pp. 870, 874, 878-879).

111. According to Mises, what are "the primary civic duty" and "the main and proper study of every citizen" and why? (pp. 878-879) What will happen if we fail to recognize the "teachings of economics"? (pp. 884-885).

<u>Other relevant questions from Mises's book The Ultimate Foundation of Economic Science: An Essay on Method</u>

Write short answers to the following questions by utilizing Ludwig von Mises (1962), *The Ultimate Foundation of Economic Science: An Essay on Method*, Sheed, Andrews & McMeel: Mission, Kansas.

A. Why are epistemology and praxeology important? (pp. 1-2).

B. What is the starting point of praxeology? (p. 5).

C. What is the distinction between the natural sciences and praxeology? (p. 7).

D. Why are an understanding of costs and benefits, means and ends, and the capacity to adjust his environment to new conditions, crucial elements in human life? (p. 8).

E. According to Mises, What is "truth"? Is it relative or absolute? (pp. 3, 8-9 and *Human Action* pp. 52-53).

F. How does Mises differentiate the methodological bases for the study of economics, the natural sciences, and economic history? Why are they distinct? (pp. 73-74).

G. Are economists merely thinkers and dreamers while merchants are those who put into practice that which economists investigate? (pp. 77-78).

H. What is the relationship between society and the individual? Why does the individual have greater importance in the study of economics? (pp. 78, 80-81) Why does macroeconomics twist the basis of society? (pp. 82, 83).

I. What is Mises's critique about the concept of "national income"? (p. 85) Why does he say that it is related to Marxism and that it has no value? (pp. 86, 87).

J. Why does Mises say that competition is not a fight but rather cooperation? (p. 88) Is commerce a game? (p. 90).

K. Why does Mises argue that the might of national leaders of any nation ultimately rests in ideas and in public opinion? (pp. 92, 93) What "counts alone" for a modern politician? (p. 94).

L. What is the fundamental means of preserving social cooperation? What is society's main problem? (pp. 97, 98, 100, 101) Why does Mises say that anarchy would be worse than government since human beings are not angelic? (p. 99).

Other relevant questions from *The Methodology of the Austrian School Economists*

Write short answers to the following questions by utilizing Larry White (1984), *The Methodology of the Austrian School Economists*, Revised Edition, The Ludwig von Mises Institute: Auburn, Alabama.

M. What fundamental theme unites the Austrian School? (pp. 4, 19, 23) How does it define capital goods? (p. 8).

N. Why did they reject the mathematical method? (pp. 11, 21) Were the Austrians ignorant of mathematical technique? (p. 9).

O. Is it possible to check economic theory with empirical studies? (pp. 13, 17) What role does empiricism play in Austrian economics? (pp. 14, 18, 24-25).

P. According to White (and Mises), how is the entirety of economic theory derived? (pp. 15-16) At what point does it begin? (p. 17) How did Rothbard differ from Mises in comprehending or conceptualizing it? (p. 30).

Q. What is the doctrine of methodological individualism? (p. 20).

R. Following the thought of Hayek, what does it mean that the market is a *process* of *discovery* in *time*? (p. 23).

S. According to Lachmann, what role do the plans of individual actors play in the market process and why do they tend to elude arriving at equilibrium? (p. 27).

T. According to Kirzner, what are the basic characteristics of entrepreneurs and competition? (p. 29).

References

Boettke, Peter J. (1994a), "Alternative Paths Forward for Austrian Economics," in Peter J. Boettke, ed., *The Elgar Companion to Austrian Economics*, Edward Elgar Publishing: Aldershot, pp. 601-615.

Boettke, Peter J. (1994b), "Hayek's Serfdom Revisited: Government Failure in the Argument Against Socialism," *Economic Research Reports* series compiled by the C.V. Starr Center for Applied Economics, New York University Economics Department: New York, 37 pages.

Boettke, Peter J. (1990), *The Political Economy of Soviet Socialism: The Formative Years, 1918-1928*, Kluwer Academic Publishers: Boston.

Boettke, Peter J. (1994c), "The Political Infrastructure of Economic Development," *Human Systems Management*, vol. 13, pp. 5-16.

Boettke, Peter J. (1994d), "Virginia Political Economy: A View from Vienna," in Peter J. Boettke and David L. Prychitko, eds., *The Market Process: Essays in Contemporary Austrian Economics*, Edgar Elgar: Brookfield, Vermont.

DiLorenzo, Thomas J. and High, Jack C. (1988), "Antitrust and Competition, Historically Considered," *Economic Inquiry*, vol. 36, July, pp. 423-435.

Flynn, John T. (1944), *As We Go Marching*, Doubleday, Doran and Co., Inc.: Garden City, New York.

Hayek, Friedrich A. von (1988), *The Fatal Conceit: The Errors of Socialism*, University of Chicago Press: Chicago.

Hayek, Friedrich A. von (1945), "The Use of Knowledge in Society," *American Economic Review*, vol. 35, no. 4, September, pp. 519-530.

High, Jack C. (1984), "The Case for Austrian Economics," *Intercollegiate Review*, winter, pp. 37-42.

Holcombe, Randall G. (1995), *Public Policy and the Quality of Life: Market Incentives Versus Government Planning*, Greenwood Press: Westport, Connecticut.

Kirzner, Israel M. (1985), *Discovery and the Capitalist Process*, University of Chicago Press: Chicago.

Lachmann, Ludwig M. (1991), "Austrian Economics: A Hermeneutic Approach," in Don Lavoie, ed., *Economics and Hermeneutics*, Routledge: New York.

Littlechild, Stephen C. (1981/1978), *The Fallacy of the Mixed Economy: An "Austrian" Critique of Conventional Economics and Government Policy*, Cato Paper no. 2, The Cato Institute: San Francisco, California [Washington, D.C.].

Menger, Carl, *Principles of Economics* (1994/1871), Translated by James Dingwell and Bert F. Hoselitz, Libertarian Press: Grove City, Pennsylvania.

Mises, Ludwig von (1966/1949), *Human Action: A Treatise on Economics*, Third Revised Edition, Contemporary Books, Inc. (Henry Regnery Co.): Chicago.

Mises, Ludwig von (1981/1922), *Socialism: An Economic and Sociological Analysis*, translated by J. Kahane, second edition, Liberty Classics (Liberty Fund): Indianapolis.

Mitchell, William C., and Simmons, Randy T. (1994), *Beyond Politics: Markets, Welfare, and the Failure of Bureaucracy*, Westview Press: San Francisco, California

O'Driscoll, Jr., Gerald P. and Rizzo, Mario J. (1996), *The Economics of Time and Ignorance*, Routledge: New York.

Prowse, Michael (1996), "Austrian Economics and the Public Mind," *Austrian Economics Newsletter*, vol. 16, no. 1 (spring). Available online from http://mises.org/journals/aen/Aen_sp96.asp.

Prowse, Michael (1994), "'Austrian' recipe for prosperity," *Financial Times*, February 28, p. 19.

Rowley, Charles K. (1993), *Liberty and the State*, The Shaftesbury Papers, 4, Edward Elgar Publishing Co.: Brookfield, Vermont.

Selgin, George A. (1988), *The Theory of Free Banking: Money Supply Under Competitive Note Issue*, Rowman and Littlefield (Cato Institute): Totowa, New Jersey.

Sowell, Thomas (1980), *Knowledge and Decisions*, Basic Books: New York.

White, Lawrence H. (1984), *The Methodology of the Austrian School Economists*, Revised Edition, The Ludwig von Mises Institute: Auburn, Alabama.

9 Entrepreneurship: an Austrian perspective

A suitable environment for entrepreneurship

Both Mises and Hayek contend that the price system is the only efficient means of allocating resources. Austrian theorists, as well as many in the Virginia School of public choice, argue that this claim has been vindicated by the disastrous record of collectivist nations during most of the twentieth century (cf. Rowley 1993, p. 26).

As noted in chapter eight, Hayek says the great economic problem of society is that "the utilization of knowledge is not given to anyone in its totality" (Hayek 1945, p. 520). Moreover, as technology, consumer tastes, resource reserves, and the multitude of other economic variables change, portions of the existing knowledge (distributed and contained in disparate economic actors) become obsolete.

The price system needed for entrepreneurial calculation

Accordingly, "economic problems arise always and only in consequence of change" (Hayek 1945, p. 523). Only the price system, as opposed to central planners, can accurately provide proper and efficient resource allocation. When the government centrally owns the means of production, the one outcome that can be predicted with general certainty is that there will be a misallocation of resources in the capital market, as evinced by the cataclysmic dissolution of centrally-planned economies at the end of the twentieth century. A key reason for this failure is that central planning is precisely the negation of entrepreneurship.

For Austrian theorists, the key role of prices is to permit entrepreneurial calculation, which in turn leads to market coordination. In addition, prices permit consumers to allocate resources to their highest use value, by calculating options within their budget constraint. Prices constrain firms to make optimal investment and production choices. Since knowledge in society is dispersed, and not given to anyone in its totality, the principal role of prices is to communicate knowledge. By knowing relative prices, economizing entrepreneurs, managers, and consumers are led to make optimal economic decisions with resources subject to the constraints they face.

Austrian scholars argue that entrepreneurial action is based on *anticipated* (future) prices. (All prices are either past or anticipated, but none are present.) They are either the data by which consumers and producers base their economic decisions, or a mechanism for entrepreneurs to act on their market strategies. Yet prices are never static equilibrium prices, even if markets tend toward equilibrium. Furthermore, prices are neither just and fair or unjust and unfair. Prices are information derived from monetary phenomena, in large measure resulting from central bank policy, and people use prices to make efficient choices for their lives.

Private property rights needed for entrepreneurship

In addition to the price system, and for similar reasons, private property rights are important in maintaining entrepreneurial activity. Akin to resource allocation, Austrian theorists contend that the complexities of private property can only be adequately managed by markets. As Ellig states:

> Our society needs private property rights because economic activity is too complex to be planned and orchestrated by a dictator, a committee of experts, or even an electronic town hall...private property permits an advanced economy to prosper through a complex division of labor that could not be rationally planned by anyone (Ellig 1994, p. 21).

Private property is necessary for entrepreneurship to thrive. Thus, Hans Sennholz has prudently observed:

> In the private property order and voluntary exchange system, private ownership means full control over the uses and services of property, not merely a legal title while government is holding the power of control. Nothing less than this will ever assure the needed personal stewardship over the limited resources of this planet or the efficient employment of property for the benefit of all (Anderson 1992, p. 44—quoting Sennholz).

Kirzner likewise argues that respect for property rights and a reliable legal system are requisite for robust entrepreneurship.

Thus certain institutional practices in a market economy will tend to encourage a high level of entrepreneurial activity, especially (1) a free and open economy that permits equal access to entrepreneurial opportunities, (2) guarantees of ownership in property legally acquired, and (3) stability of institutional practices that establish points 1 and 2 (Kirzner 1971, p. 55).

Individual self-interest creates a natural tendency to care for property and to optimize the use of property. Social assurances that resource benefits will be secure create the motivation to maintain, improve, and utilize resources over an anticipated period of use. Conversely, the expectation that others will reap the rewards of resource stewardship imposes an external cost on any economic actor, especially the entrepreneur, by creating less motivation to put resources to their most highly valued use. Human action strives to satisfy internal, subjective preferences; and only plenary rights of ownership will impel individuals to use resources optimally. Consequently, these plenary rights are essential to secure the benefits sought by entrepreneurs and to give them the incentive to use their talents in society.

Deficiencies of static models regarding the entrepreneur

Austrian theorists argue that it is impossible to totally quantify human behavior—entrepreneurial behavior in particular.[45] Human action is the result of many unknown or unknowable subjective decisions or impulses. While quantitative models may have some analytic or pedagogical value, ultimately trying to meaningfully measure human behavior through mathematical modeling is as futile as trying to understand the fall of a feather by isolating and measuring the impact of twenty-five particles (out of perhaps a billion) which influence its fall, and then extrapolating to broadly explain or predict its fall.

Moreover, since they do not incorporate the passage of time, changes in human purposes, and imperfect information, static models do not provide a useful—and certainly not a realistic—view of human action or the market process. Although mathematical models can be useful heuristic tools for teaching basic economic concepts, and econometrics may be of some value in evaluating history, these

---

[45] See, for example, High 1984, p. 38; also a more subtle criticism in Hayek 1945, pp. 523-524, 530—in addition to the criticisms by Mises noted in chapters one and seven.

quantitative tools are of little or no value in producing economic theory. That is, they are of little or no value in explaining and predicting the dynamics of human action, the coordinating aspects of the market process, or evolutionary and spontaneous market orders.

Kirzner contends that only models which can accommodate the entrepreneurial function are useful in describing human action and the market process. Competitive static equilibrium models are not of this variety.

> [A] feature common to all these competitive models to which I will be taking exception is their exclusion of the entrepreneurial element from the analysis. We will find that a useful understanding of the market process requires a notion of competition that is analytically inseparable from the exercise of entrepreneurship (Kirzner 1973, p. 9).

The entrepreneur plays no role in static models, as Kirzner points out:

> Thus he cannot contribute to a reallocation of resources or products that will overcome inefficiencies and lack of coordination generated by market ignorance, since no such ignorance and lack of coordination exist in equilibrium (Kirzner 1973, p. 27).

He further argues that entrepreneurial action goes beyond economizing and the confines of static conditions:

> Instead of economizing, I maintain, it will prove extremely helpful to emphasize the broader Misesian notion of *human action*. But the human-action concept, unlike that of allocation and economizing, does not confine the decision-maker (or the economic analysis of his decisions) to a framework of *given* ends and means (Kirzner 1973, p. 33).

For Kirzner, markets are not in equilibrium, although they are constantly moving toward it by entrepreneurial arbitrage:

> The pure entrepreneur, on the other hand, proceeds by his alertness to discover and exploit situations in which he is able to sell for high prices that which he can buy for low prices. Pure entrepreneurial profit is the difference between the two sets of prices (Kirzner 1973, p. 48).

Ignorance or imperfect information—the very thing assumed away in static models—is precisely the object that allows entrepreneurs to profit. Kirzner continues:

> A state of market disequilibrium is characterized by wide-spread ignorance. Market participants are unaware of the real opportunities for beneficial exchange which are available to them in the market. The result of this state of ignorance is that countless opportunities are passed up (Kirzner 1973, p. 69).

Such features are missed in static equilibrium models and thus the most important part of economic theory is left unexplained by them.

The prominent Austrian paradigm of entrepreneurship

Austrian theorists view the market process and the political process as competing realms. The former is a rivalrous, co-ordinating process, based on the voluntary choices and preferences of individuals.[46] The latter is collective action and organization which, especially when democratic processes are involved, will generate public choice problems.

---

[46] See the discussion of this matter at the end of chapter eight (citing High and Rothbard).

Regulation and planning in the political process are fettered by the knowledge problem. However, it may be that policy failures are actually (in a convoluted sense) *successful*—as noted in chapter five. It is possible that rent seeking political entrepreneurs have successfully used the political process to secure profits or status.

Austrians recognize that entrepreneurs can generate profits in either the market process or the political process. In the political process, entrepreneurs can use rent seeking or regulatory capture as political means of acquiring wealth. While the entrepreneur has temporary monopoly gains in the market process, which lead to wider social benefits as a by-product, the political entrepreneur creates narrow transitional gains and wider long term social losses. These benefits are provided narrowly while the costs are dispersed broadly throughout society creating a net social loss.

What is an entrepreneur?

A common, business school definition of the entrepreneur is: the entrepreneur is a businessman who is never hired, who cannot be fired, and is the residual claimant (i.e., he receives the profits or losses of his enterprise). Perhaps this definition is suitable for general application of the term.

However, the Austrian conception extends this simple definition. An entrepreneur is more than just a businessman, and he is more than just an innovator. There are many businessmen who are managers, marketers, and so forth that are not responsible for the creation and exploitation of new opportunities. While they may serve to expand market share of existing product lines, or to make business operations more efficient and effective, they are not entrepreneurs. Likewise, there are many innovators or inventors who do not have the skill to market their products successfully.

From an Austrian perspective, the entrepreneur is the person who can see an opportunity for future profit, correctly predict the demand of consumers, and successfully promote his good or service in the market process. He is a special gift to society. Austrian theorists argue that entrepreneurs are *born* rather than *made* (Mises 1966, p. 585), a view which corroborates mainstream empiricists who witness "only a limited number" of true entrepreneurs in society. He is scarce like the generator of ideas (see chapter 1), and his social influence can be just as prominent.

Table 9.1 Prominent Influencers in Society

The individuals who most influence society are:
(1) Generators of ideas.
(2) Entrepreneurs.

Mises distinguishes speculators (entrepreneurs) and promoters. According to Mises, every economic actor has entrepreneurial aspects because of the speculative nature of the market process.[47] For example, Mises describes the entrepreneur as the engine of the market process:

> The driving force of the market process is provided neither by the consumers nor by the owners of the means of production—land, capital goods, and labor—but by the promoting and speculating entrepreneurs (Mises 1966, p. 328).

Nonpecuniary, unconventional, and status-seeking entrepreneurship

Note that all entrepreneurship is not necessarily pecuniary. The goal of entrepreneurship may be for money, power, or any utility-enhancing goal or bundle of goals. Politicians or bureaucrats might be entrepreneurs, and in some situations rent seekers may be entrepreneurs. In the broadest sense, a

---

[47] In *Human Action*, Mises often uses the term *promoter* to describe what is commonly called an entrepreneur. Nevertheless, most Austrian theorists occupy the common use of the word "entrepreneur," bearing in mind Mises's distinction when reading him.

housewife could conceivably be an entrepreneur, or even a thief could be an entrepreneur (perhaps he has special knowledge to avoid being caught). But these varieties, with the exception of the rent seeking regressive entrepreneur, are not the main focus of economic theory. Entrepreneurial satisfaction might also be viewed as consisting of a combination of money profits and status. Status gains are positive utility additions that come from augmenting power or possibly from peer recognition. At some level of personal wealth, status-seeking may even dominate (as a substitute for) profit-seeking at the margin. In this view, successful entrepreneurship cannot merely be measured by monetary profits of the firm. Instead, case studies would have to be done which demonstrate the relative success of the entrepreneur in obtaining his status or other goals.

The role of the entrepreneur in the market process

Entrepreneurs drive the market process, by creating opportunities for innovative goods and services to reach the marketplace, by closing gaps in the price system via arbitrage, and by exploiting new market openings. Extracting information from prices, entrepreneurs risk their capital (or the capital of others) despite uncertainty. Recognizing its importance, Austrian scholars have done considerable work in building the theory of entrepreneurship. More than any other academic discipline, they grant the entrepreneur an unparalleled preeminence that is that is missing in neoclassical economics. High comments on the centrality of the entrepreneur in Austrian theory:

> Austrian economics accords the entrepreneur a central place in economic theory. The entrepreneur is alert to opportunities for profit; he introduces new goods and new production techniques into the market, and bears the risk of carrying on a business enterprise. In large part,

the market is a process set in motion by entrepreneurs eager to capture profits (High 1984, p. 39).

In short, entrepreneurial action leads to the efficient and effective allocation of resources. The entrepreneur anticipates better than others the future demand of consumers. He notices price discrepancies (or maladjustments) before others do and is able to engage in arbitrage. He makes profits when his judgment of the future is more correct in determining undervalued factors of production than the judgment of others. Thus, in our uncertain world, the *speculative* nature of the entrepreneur is inherent in every one of his actions.

However, higher levels of *alertness* (Kirzner's term) can ameliorate the actual degree of speculation or gamble he faces (Kirzner 1973, pp. 85-86). More alert entrepreneurs will be able to perceive economic conditions and future demand more clearly than others and thus avoid pitfalls and risks that other, less alert people would likely succumb.

Mises's conception of the entrepreneurial mind

Mises contends that entrepreneurs are actually economic agents with extraordinary market prowess:

> The mentality of the promoters, speculators, and entrepreneurs is not different from that of their fellow men. They are merely superior to the masses in mental power and energy. They are the leaders on the way toward material progress (Mises 1966, p. 336).

Mises says that the entrepreneur accomplishes his goals by speculating correctly about the future demand of consumers. His innate forward-looking skills may be honed by, but never learned during, his formal education:

[T]he real entrepreneur is a *speculator*, a man eager to utilize his opinion about the future structure of the market for business operations promising profits. This specific anticipative understanding of the conditions of the uncertain future defies any rules and systemization. It can be neither taught nor learned. If it were different, everybody could embark upon entrepreneurship with the same prospect of success. What distinguishes the successful entrepreneur and promoter from other people is precisely the fact that he does not let himself be guided by what was and is, but arranges his affairs on the ground of his opinion about the future. He sees the past and the present as other people do; but he judges the future in a different way. In his actions he is directed by an opinion about the future which deviates from those held by the crowd (Mises 1966, p. 585).

There is something innately different about the entrepreneur's mind that distinguishes him from common people, according to Mises. The entrepreneur is characterized by his dynamic abilities to react to change, foresee future demand, and subordinate his other interests in order to enhance his capacity to serve consumers. Mises elaborates:

Capitalists and entrepreneurs are never free to relax. As long as they remain in business they are never granted the privilege of quietly enjoying the fruits of their ancestors' and their own achievements and of lapsing into a routine. If they forget their task is to serve the consumers to the best of their abilities, they will very soon forfeit their eminent position and will be thrown back into the ranks of the common man. Their leadership and their funds are continually challenged by newcomers. Every ingenious man is free to start new business projects. He may be poor, his funds may be modest and most of them may be borrowed. But if he fills the wants of customers

279

in the best and cheapest way, he will succeed by means of "excessive" profits. He ploughs back the greater part of his profits into his business, thus making it grow rapidly. It is the activity of such enterprising parvenus [upstarts] that provides the market economy with its "dynamism." These nouveaux [new] riches are the harbingers [heralds] of economic improvement. Their threatening competition forces the old firms and big corporations either to adjust their conduct to the best possible service of the public or to go out of business (Mises 1966, p. 808).

Kirzner's conception of the entrepreneur's mental ability

The essential ingredient of Kirzner's view is his understanding of the entrepreneur's *alertness* to opportunity or "ultimate knowledge," which thrives despite the fact that there is "uncertainty inherent in every action" (Kirzner 1973, pp. 84-85). The entrepreneur engages in deliberate exploitation of perceived opportunities to capture profits. As Littlechild remarks:

Austrian economics takes as its starting point the behavior of people with incomplete knowledge, who have not only to "economize" in the situations in which they find themselves, but also to be on the alert for better opportunities "just around the corner." This alertness, missing from "mainstream" economics, is called entrepreneurship. It leads to the revision of plans and forms the basis of the competitive process, which in many ways epitomizes the Austrian approach. For Austrians, the *changes* over time in prices, production, plans, knowledge, and expectations are more important than prices and output at any one time (Littlechild 1981, p. 74).

The entrepreneur makes profits when his judgment of the future is more correct in determining undervalued factors of production than the judgment of others. Thus, living in time and ignorance, the speculative nature of the entrepreneur is inherent in all his action. As Kirzner notes:

> Mises's way of expressing what I have called entrepreneurial *alertness* is to define entrepreneurship as human action "seen from the aspect of the uncertainty inherent in every action" [in which he is able] "to anticipate better than other people the future demand of the consumers"…The entrepreneur notices this price discrepancy before others do…profits arise from an absence of adjustment between the product market and the factor market; and that successful entrepreneurship consists in noticing such maladjustments before others do…the entrepreneurial function—action seen from its *speculative* aspect—is inherent in *every* action (Kirzner 1973, pp. 85-86).

The opportunity to gain monopoly profits create an incentive for the entrepreneur to engage in his action. As Kirzner states:

> And yet, once his entrepreneurial resource purchase has been made, he is in the position of a producer who is a monopolist by virtue of being a resource owner. It seems, then, that not only may an entrepreneur-producer be a monopolist because he *happens* at the same time to be a monopolist resource owner; he may be a monopolist because he has made himself a monopolist resource owner *in the course of his entrepreneurial activities* (Kirzner 1973, p. 22).

However, these monopoly profits will be short lived in the market process, where new entrants will compete them away. In the political process, monopoly profits found by rent seeking entrepreneurs tend to be permanent and create long term social losses (see the discussion of demosclerosis and the transitional gains trap in chapters one and three). Kirzner's work relies heavily on the economics of entrepreneurial discovery. Therefore, he notes, "it becomes difficult to see the processes of short-run resource allocation as anything but special cases of the more general discovery processes that constitute economic growth" (Kirzner 1973, p. 50). He simplifies Joseph Schumpeter's perspective[48] by earmarking three major types of entrepreneurial activity: "(1) arbitrage activity; (2) speculation activity; and (3) innovative activity" (Kirzner 1973, p. 52).

Kirzner also considers that public policy plays a significant role in the development of entrepreneurial action. The market process is enhanced when entrepreneurs are given wider opportunities to serve consumers by way of fewer policy impositions.

It is simply not useful to treat entrepreneurship in terms of a supply curve. The exercise of specific quantities of entrepreneurship involves no identifiable cost or required amounts. Yet, it is impossible to treat the degree of entrepreneurial discovery prevailing in a society as totally unrelated to public policy. [P]olicy may in principle affect the emergence of entrepreneurial attitudes and character of a population...[if public policy can] stimulate it to be more alert to entrepreneurial opportunities (Kirzner 1973, p. 55).

Kirzner submits that the profit motive is an insufficient motivator for the emergence of entrepreneurial activity. Public policy must also reasonably assure him that he "may keep entrepreneurial profits that he legitimately acquires" (Kirzner 1973, p. 55). As noted earlier, the existence of stable property rights is essential for entrepreneurship to flourish.

---

[48] See the appendix for some details on Schumpeter's perspective.

While Kirzner has reiterated his confidence that entrepreneurship is the central feature of human action, he also emphasizes the element of discovering change in the market process:

> When Mises identified the concept of human action as the essential building block for praxeological economic science, it is now clear to me that this implies far more than simply the importance of purposefulness for the analysis *of decisions made in given situations*. The concept of human action, it is now clear to me, is important in the Misesian system because of its fruitfulness in explaining how *economic agents discover changes that have occurred in their very market situations*, and generate, as a consequence, those systematic market processes which are so central to Misesian economics (Kirzner 1992a, p. 244).

This discovery process is arduous and capricious. Consequently, disequilibrating forces, combined with the need to make decisions in time, make the study of human action far too complex for traditional neoclassical techniques. Such models presume away the most consequential circumstances in which discovery proceeds. Kirzner continues:

> Late twentieth-century Austrian economics has consistently paid at least lip service to the idea that economics is a science of human action. But we have perhaps not paid sufficient attention to what Mises meant by this insight. We can now see, I believe, that human action drives the market in a sense that is quite distinct from any of the implications of the maximizing rationality which governs Robbinsian equilibrium economics. Human action drives the market, more fundamentally, in that it expresses the changes in agents' awareness of their environment and of their visions of the future— changes which are inspired by their "entrepreneurial"

alertness to the dynamic world in which we live. This alertness is motivated by the purposefulness which defines and identifies conscious human action. If we are to understand the world in which we live—the world of disequilibrium as distinct from the analytical-model world of equilibrium—we must recognize how the decisions taken during any given span of time reflect this aspect of human action. It is the systematic market process of mutual discovery so generated, which constitutes the core of Misesian economics (Kirzner 1992a, pp. 247-248).

Consequently, there is diminutive value in entrepreneurial models that cannot accommodate discovery and change over time. As O'Driscoll and Rizzo remark:

Kirzner has analyzed entrepreneurship at the individual level in which the central task is to formulate the "given" means-ends framework. This framework is logically prior to ordinary maximizing behavior. It is the result of a creative insight or relatively condensed activity. This analysis has important implications for the agent's perception of the rapidity of time change. In entrepreneurial or creative activity the preliminary stages in a problem solution are seen as part of the very recent past or, in the limit, as an aspect of the subjective present moment. In contrast, the less creative the activity under study, the more distended those stages become, or, equivalently, the narrower the mnemic [memorable] link between them. Each stage becomes relatively more isolated. Reduction in the degree of creativity is thus associated with a relegation of the stages to the more remote past. Increasing the degree of creativity and the consequent widening of the mnemic link results in a subjective quickening of time. For any given interval of clock time, more is happening *relative to* the less creative state. Thus, the entrepreneur will perceive clock time as passing relatively more quickly (cf. Capek, 1971, p. 200) (O'Driscoll and Rizzo 1996, p. 68).

It may truly be said, from an Austrian perspective, that Entrepreneurs live in a "different world" than other people. They have uncommon gifts and capacities which lead them to impact social life in ways that other people cannot.

Policy considerations pertaining to entrepreneurship

Regressive and progressive entrepreneurship

According to Austrian economic theory, the entrepreneur is the indispensable driving force in an economy. However, he may also serve as a deteriorating force in society by his rent seeking activity. Two distinct categories of entrepreneurship can result from alertness to opportunity. *Progressive* entrepreneurship devolves from entrepreneurial activity in the market process while *regressive* entrepreneurship devolves from entrepreneurial activity in the political process.

On the one hand, progressive entrepreneurship stems from discovering opportunities for arbitrage or bringing innovative products to the market in anticipation of consumer demand. Only a correct prognosis of mutable consumer preferences, capital or resource constraints, and the political process, yields the entrepreneur success and profit.

On the other hand, regressive entrepreneurship stems from finagling opportunities in the political process by rent seeking. Such entrepreneurs enrich themselves and narrow interests, but they add nothing to the productive growth or wealth of an economy. On the contrary, they perfect the craft of inflicting social losses on society. Books like Robert Caro's *The Power Broker: Robert Moses and the Fall of New York* record the harmful effects of this kind of action.

Perhaps, given these two categories, societies in which the majority of entrepreneurs are regressive can be characterized as "rent seeking" or in some cases "socialistic" societies. Conversely, societies which have a minority of regressive entrepreneurs can be characterized as having a relative degree of free markets. Thus, as a seminal definition, a rent seeking society is one in which the majority of its entrepreneurs are regressive entrepreneurs, while relative degrees of free markets exist when regressive entrepreneurs are in the minority. As a hypothesis, this distinction may prove to be useful for policy-relevant research.[49]

Table 9.2 Possible Definition of a "Rent Seeking Society"

A "rent seeking society" may be defined as:
A society in which the majority of its entrepreneurs are regressive entrepreneurs.

Akin to legalized plunder, sophisticated *theft* could well be a form of regressive entrepreneurship since it likewise results in nothing better than a zero-sum game (i.e., one party gains what another party loses). Certainly, there is no social benefit from the activity of thieves. In any voluntary transaction, both sides gain. However, both nonconsensual transactions such as theft, and rent seeking by political entrepreneurs, result in a negative-sum games or zero-sum games.

Given this perspective, the implications for policy-relevant research by free market theorists are obvious. If a criterion for proper public policy were sought to determine what entrepreneurial activities ought to be outlawed, Austrian theorists might suggest that those behaviors which result in zero or negative-sum games should be curtailed.

---

[49] This hypothesis could be partly tested by taking a sample of successful entrepreneurs, and distinguishing them according to whether the majority of their profits come from activity in the market or political process. An alternative test might be to compare GDP with the cumulative number of pages of federal bureaucratic documents over time.

Policy regarding excessive entrepreneurial profits

From an Austrian perspective, it is fruitless to classify certain varieties of progressive entrepreneurship as socially problematic. Proactive policy to restrict the level of entrepreneurial profit would be ludicrous. Mises argues that there is no such thing as "normal" profits (Mises 1966, p. 297). All profit is extraordinary and never normal, and there is no way of measuring what is above normal (or too much) profit.

The existence of short-lived monopoly power by entrepreneurs in the market process is not a sign of market failure. On the contrary, the quest for such power drives the entrepreneurial incentive. Virtually all firms garner some degree of monopoly power (popularly characterized by a downward-sloping demand curve). Thus, short term monopoly power must not be a justification for embarking on antitrust policies (cf. chapter two).

Moreover, even if some progressive entrepreneurs try to profit by disseminating defective information, that fact should not sanction proactive policies of industrial regulation. Deceptive market practices might occur, but the market process has its own means of cleansing away firms that establish a poor reputation.

In an imperfect world, it is impossible—or at least impractical—to alleviate all potential harm to consumers. And proactive polices which aim to do so often result in making the problem worse. Whenever a consumer ventures to buy a new or untested product, he bears the risk of loss, which is incorporated in the price he is willing to pay. Over the long run, the risk of harm to consumers is ameliorated by the market process, since only firms that attend to maintaining their reputation will survive.

Referring to the traditional welfare economics conception of monopoly as a market flop, Mises contends, "Entrepreneurial profit has nothing at all to do with monopoly." It is government policies that make the emergence of long term or permanent monopoly possible. It is government intervention which deals the greatest blow to consumers (Mises 1966, pp. 360-361, 387 and cf. p. 395). If there is a villain to be sought in causing moral decay in society, then the prime suspect ought to be the public policies which permit rent seeking activities, not the free market which facilitates the unchecked "avarice" of entrepreneurs.

Policy aimed at alleged "inside" information

There is little reason to distinguish between progressive entrepreneurs and people who practice "insider trading," designating the former as "good" and the latter as "bad." Surely, any social damage that might be caused by such activity pales by comparison to the deleterious effects of rent seeking by the regressive entrepreneur. Entrepreneurship is not restricted by contrived and arbitrary legal or social maxims. The entrepreneur is someone who is alert to opportunities, wherever and however they might exist.

Consequently, it is perfectly rational and congruent with the theory of self-interest to expect that people will engage in both progressive and regressive entrepreneurship because they see profitable opportunities. Concluding that insider trading is "bad" just because some politicians or bureaucrats decree that it is illegal is a weak and arbitrary premise. Obviously, Hitler's political edict making it illegal to hide Jews did not make the activity of hiding Jews immoral or "bad". Likewise, governmental decrees do not make any activity *immoral*. They simply make such behaviors *illegal*. The morality of any action falls within the sphere of philosophy or theology, not public policy or economics.

Furthermore, progressive entrepreneurs do not cause people to have immoral preferences, and if society wants to

288

change the preferences of consumers then they must look to religious or other institutions that can effectively change consumer tastes and preferences. The entrepreneur's sole function is to discover profitable opportunities and drive and coordinate the market process. As Mises remarks:

> [P]rofits can only be earned by providing the consumers with those things they most urgently want to use...It is not the fault of the entrepreneurs that the consumers...prefer liquor to Bibles and detective stories to serious books (Mises 1966, p. 299).

If there is a bad source of entrepreneurship or arbitrage opportunity, it must stem from the stipulations of the political process. It is only because rent seeking opportunities are permitted to exist that regressive entrepreneurship spawns and thrives. Entrepreneurs are not bad because they are alert and can discover ways to profit that is contrary to proactive public policy.

All entrepreneurial knowledge is "inside information" from an Austrian perspective. The entrepreneur, in both his progressive or regressive forms, has superior knowledge on which he is willing to act. He has special mental abilities or alertness that common men do not have.

Policies resulting from envy over entrepreneurial profits

Successful entrepreneurial action often induces envy, especially when envy is marketed by regressive entrepreneurs who are able to profit by producing and distributing anti-market ideas to sympathetic constituents. As Mises remarks, "Many people are utterly unfit to deal with the phenomenon of entrepreneurial profit without indulging in envious resentment" (Mises 1966, p. 298). "A man is prone to sneer at those who are more prosperous than himself" (Mises 1966, p. 313). As a result, there is a market for envy which regressive entrepreneurs can exploit, utilizing the political process to curtail the profits of progressive entrepreneurs to the overall detriment of society. But such endeavors are misguided from a social welfare perspective.

On the contrary, progressive entrepreneurs provide an immensely valuable service to society. They drive and coordinate the market process, as well as remove uneasiness from consumers. Thus, they are literally worth whatever they can gain. Society simply cannot afford to live without them and their marvelous economic feats.

Austrian theorists argue that progressive entrepreneurs and capitalists do not rule consumers, but serve them (Mises 1966, p. 272). Mises recounts that, rather than dominating consumers in a rigged game, "the entrepreneur is always a speculator...The only source from which an entrepreneur's profits stem is his ability to anticipate better than other people the future demand of the consumers" (Mises 1966, p. 290). Successful entrepreneurs meet the demand of consumers; they do not dominate it (Mises 1966, p. 271).[50] Prowse notes that entrepreneurs promote innovation and growth by "alerting hitherto unwitting market participants to the possibility of pure entrepreneurial profit..." and these discoveries constitute the crucial steps through which markets tend "to achieve...successively better co-ordinated states of society" (Prowse 1994, p. 19–citing the contribution of Kirzner).

In an economy with fragmented and dispersed knowledge, progressive entrepreneurs earn profits because they increase the satisfaction of consumers and coordinate the market process.[51] Most people miss what the entrepreneur sees. As Kirzner remarks, "Market participants have failed

---

[50] As Mises says, "on the market no vote [purchase] is cast in vain" (Mises 1966, p. 271).

[51] Kirzner agrees with Hayek, noting that competition is a process which "digs out what is in fact discovered." Furthermore, market participants are alerted to changes in possible profit by equilibrium prices and, insofar as they are interpreted correctly, from disequilibrium prices (Kirzner 1992b, pp. 150, 151).

to grasp opportunities that *might* have been grasped—if only they had more accurate knowledge concerning what others *might* have been prepared to do." Mutual ignorance and dispersed knowledge invite the entrepreneur to make a profit (Kirzner 1992b, pp. 168, 170). And as a result of the actions of progressive entrepreneurs, uneasiness is alleviated in society. Indeed, rather than generating envious resentment or proactive policies which impede entrepreneurship, entrepreneurial activity ought to generate accolades and approbation.

Entrepreneurial risk aversion and failure

Entrepreneurial risk aversion

The speculative activity of the entrepreneur is not antithetical to risk-averse behavior. People with less alertness or knowledge than the entrepreneur may think he prefers risk. Conversely, the entrepreneur considers his action to be risk averse. His alertness or special knowledge gives him a comparative advantage in both productivity and perception.[52] Thus, he acts on what he considers to be "a sure bet" or at least "a good bet" while others perceive his action as "risky." In short, the entrepreneur is risk averse; he has certain superior knowledge which lessens his *actual* risk. Indeed, it is conceivable that the entrepreneur is in reality more risk averse than most people. The entrepreneur's actions coincide with his assurance of certain knowledge.[53]

The entrepreneur acts when he perceives the riskiness of a proposed action is no greater than the next best alternative action, and when he anticipates that the proposed action will yield a greater increase in utility than the next best al-

---

[52] I am indebted to Ian Runge for this insight.

[53] Cf. the notion of "discovery" in Kirzner 1989, p. 75.

ternative action. Entrepreneurial alertness is consistent with profit maximizing and cost minimizing behavior. Successively higher levels of alertness lessen the severity of a speculative risk, thus leading to cost minimization.

Nevertheless, there seems to be a popular misconception that entrepreneurs are eccentric or even compulsive gamblers. For instance, according to Maryland District Judge Ramsey, "Entrepreneurs by their nature are risk taking individuals."[54] While Judge Ramsay and others perceive the entrepreneurial function to be risky by nature, the entrepreneur has the opposite view. Peter Drucker provides a helpful comment about the entrepreneur's attitude toward risk:

> Entrepreneurship, it is commonly believed, is enormously risky. And indeed, in such highly visible areas of innovation as high tech—microcomputers, for instance, or biogenetics—the casualty rate is high and the chances of success or even of survival seem to be quite low. But why should this be so? Entrepreneurs, by definition, shift resources from areas of low productivity and yield, to areas of higher productivity and yield. Of course, there is a risk they may not succeed. But if they are even moderately successful, the returns should be more than adequate to offset whatever risk there might be. One should thus expect entrepreneurship to be considerably less risky than sources in areas where the proper and profitable course is innovation, that is, where the opportunities for innovation already exist. Theoretically, entrepreneurship should be the least risky rather than the most risky course (Drucker 1985, p. 28).

Congruent with Drucker's conjecture, David McClelland has observed:

---

[54] See *Doe v. Miles* (1987), 675 F. Supp. 1466, abridged case text in Barnes and Stout 1994, p. 139.

[Entrepreneurs] do not work harder than other people at routine tasks or at tasks which are accomplished simply by using the accepted, correct, traditional method. They seek out and work harder at tasks that involve a real challenge, that is, a moderate degree of risk. On the other hand, they avoid gambling situations because even if they win, they get no sense of personal achievement since winning is the result of luck, not skill. They prefer to take *personal responsibility* for their decisions and they want the outcome to depend on their own skill or ability (McClelland 1971, p. 115).[55]

Entrepreneurs do have a comparative advantage in alertness or special knowledge. Yet their relative intelligence amongst themselves (or with the general populace) is of secondary importance and may be inconsequential to their performance.[56] Entrepreneurs prefer to place their efforts where they perceive an opportunity to capture arbitrage or monopoly profits (or status) and demonstrate their abilities.

Entrepreneurial failure

It may be that Austrian theorists need to better address the reasons why entrepreneurs fail. There can be little doubt that the entrepreneur, as marvelous as he is for society, fails at times. However, there are several possible explanations for this phenomenon: (1) failure to anticipate the actions of competitors, (2) failure to anticipate the actions of regulators, (3) failure to anticipate adverse rent seeking activity, or (4) no failure at all, just a case of mistaken identity (i.e., the subject really was not an entrepreneur to begin with).

Mises says that entrepreneurs succeed because they correctly anticipate and provide the goods and services de-

---

[55] Summary of *The Achieving Society* (1961), D. Van Nostrand: Princeton, New Jersey.

[56] This principle does not disclaim the fact that the slopes of entrepreneurs' learning curves vary widely.

manded by consumers. Perhaps entrepreneurs fail because they do not correctly manage or anticipate the rent seeking (or even some market actions) by other entrepreneurs, firms, or by detrimental proactive policy that will coincide with the timing of their activities.

It is certainly plausible that much genuine entrepreneurial failure is due to rent seeking distortions or unanticipated exogenous effects created by competitors in either the market process or the political process. Otherwise, failure is impossible since, by definition, the entrepreneur is the one who *correctly* anticipates the demands of consumers.

Moreover, sometimes the public may mistakenly perceive a person to be an entrepreneur who is in reality only a visionary. Such a person may have capital and may envision many things that consumers would want, but he is nonetheless incapable of providing them on the market. Assuredly, the failure of such visionaries must not be attributed to the failure of entrepreneurs.

Limiting the state to enhance entrepreneurship

As noted earlier, an unfettered price system and private property rights are essential for entrepreneurship to thrive. Mises contends that, "the state creates and preserves the environment in which the market economy can safely operate" (Mises 1966, p. 257). However, he views only a very limited government as beneficial (Mises 1966, p. 280-281). For instance, market processes are harmed by proactive public policies spawning antitrust, labor union or judicial intervention. As Mises notes, "the market economy is still in operation although sabotaged by government and labor union interference" (Mises 1966, p. 279, also cf. pp. 316-317).

Moreover, proactive policies merely produce social engineering distortions, leading Mises to ponder, "What type of men do the man breeders want to rear" (Mises 1966, p. 243)? They do not breed more progressive entrepreneurs. They only foment the rent seeking society. Kirzner likewise has argues, that liberty is an essential feature of a robust market process where progressive entrepreneurship thrives. It is worthy of notice that our deepened understanding of the manner in which human action inspires the market process and identifies the economic aspect of social phenomena affords us a correspondingly deeper appreciation for the role of individual freedom in Misesian economics. Individual freedom, quite apart from its ethical or philosophical appeal, is important, of course, for all schools of microeconomics, as a prerequisite for the beneficial operation of the market system. But for a science of human action this observation means more than the simple insight that free individuals can be relied upon to squeeze maximum benefits from any given situation. For the science of human action, freedom is the circumstance which permits and inspires market participants *to become aware* of beneficial (or other) *changes* in their circumstances. An environment in which human freedom is limited, in which profitably exploited opportunities invoke confiscatory social reactions, is an environment in which beneficial changes may never be noticed in the first place. An understanding of Misesian economics thus permits us to see directly how it points unerringly to the social usefulness of political institutions which guarantee individual liberties and the security of individual rights to life and property (Kirzner 1992a, p. 248).

Austrian theorists argue that the entrepreneurial process of discovery "requires an environment free from special privileges or blockages against new entrants" (Kirzner 1973, p. 57). However, the tortuous political process can be a quagmire, where potentially progressive entrepreneurial effort may be ill-channeled into regressive rent seeking activities (see Saulniers 1986, p. 162).

Table 9.3 The environment in which entrepreneurs flourish

Crucial requirements for entrepreneurs to function well— Under market conditions, it would be imperative to confide in institutions that conserve information and promote productivity:
(1) private property rights,
(2) plenary liberty to advance the development of the human mind, which is the ultimate resource (cf. Julian Simon's *The Ultimate Resource 2*),
(3) a strong and stable legal order, especially with respect to crime, contracts, and property,
(4) a very limited state, mainly dedicated to reactive policy, with few regulations and intervention,
(5) a price system which is unencumbered by government, in order that entrepreneurs may calculate effectively, and
(6) a free market, particularly without restrictions on risk management products provided by futures and insurance markets, which would be relied upon to manage the inevitable risk and uncertainty.

In the final analysis, Austrian theory suggests that an economy cannot grow and remain healthy without (1) progressive entrepreneurs and (2) an environment of freedom and policy predictability. Regressive entrepreneurship is a social bane. Unlike the mainstream of political science, and even economics, Austrian theorists suggest that the unfettered, undirected market process will serve consumers and society better than processes and policies that encourage continued rent seeking or regulatory capture activities.

Appendix: a few notes on Schumpeter and Papanek

Schumpeter, an ethnic Austrian but not an Austrian School advocate, also rejected the neoclassical economic postulate that the entrepreneur is "an abstract figure assumed to be unaffected by the influences external to the rational operation of the firm he directed" (Greenfield and Strickson 1986, p. 5). Conversely, Schumpeter viewed the entrepreneur as "the focal point and key to the dynamic of economic development and growth" (Greenfield and Strickson 1986, p. 5). Yet, despite many similarities with the Austrian School, his understanding is not entirely congruent with it.

Schumpeter distinguishes the entrepreneur from other agents in enterprise in terms of flexibility, mobility, and the creation of new combinations of economic inputs, suggesting that many economic actors may fulfill the entrepreneurial function (Schumpeter 1971, p. 54),[57] regardless of whether they contribute to the "invention" of new products (Schumpeter 1971, p. 65). For Schumpeter the entrepreneur is simply a *disequilibrating innovator*.

Schumpeter provides five general cases where entrepreneurial innovation occurs (Kent 1984, p. 3).[58] Boiled down to its basic elements, by "creating disequilibrium" and that "beyond discovery," the entrepreneur performs "implementation and commercialization" (Kent 1984, p. 3). O'Driscoll and Rizzo remark on the interaction with time within his scheme:

> For Schumpeter entrepreneurial success depends on "the capacity of seeing things in a way which afterwards proves to be true, even though it cannot be established at the moment" (1934, p. 85). A creative leap cannot, by definition, be conclusively "established" because it literally leaps over the requisite logical steps. Through this intuition the entrepreneur may be able to discover better

---

[57] Pages 62-94 of Schumpeter's *The Theory of Economic Development.*

[58] The five general cases he notes are: (1) The introduction of a new good or of a new quality of good, (2) the introduction of a new method of production, (3) the opening of a new market, (4) the conquest of a new source of supply of raw materials, and (5) the carrying out of new organization of any industry.

technologies, new products and new resources (O'Driscoll and Rizzo 1996, p. 68).

Schumpeter's view has generated considerable discussion. For instance, G.F. Papanek differed with Schumpeter somewhat, while maintaining some congruence with Austrian theory. He argued that entrepreneurs are not randomly distributed like Schumpeter suggested, and that some of them may be dissuaded by severe "noneconomic obstacles". They "do not act entirely or even primarily from pecuniary motives," but "must be able to obtain command over resources by obtaining credit or by other means." Furthermore, especially in developing countries, entrepreneurship is not accelerated "by conscious government policy." According to Papanek, religious or ideological imperatives are more important, e.g., as noted in Weber's *The Protestant Ethic*—discussed in chapter three (see Papanek 1971/1962, pp. 317, 318). But Schumpeter remains a significant contributor to the theory of entrepreneurship.

Appendix: Mises and the entrepreneurs
Chapter 9 questions

Write short answers to the following questions by utilizing Ludwig von Mises (1996), *Human Action: A Treatise On Economics*, 4th rev. ed., Irvington-on-Hudson, New York: The Foundation for Economic Education (edition comprises minor editorial changes by Bettina Bien Greaves).

112. According to Mises, in what sense do entrepreneurs serve consumers? (pp. 240, 253-254) Does enterprise have a role or responsibility of compassion?
113. What critique does Mises make regarding the use of static models with respect to time, entrepreneurs, the concept of the society as an anthill, their use of ad-

vanced mathematics, and considering money as a dynamic element? (pp. 244-251, 252, 256).

114. What characteristics do entrepreneurs have and why? (pp. 270-271) What does Mises mean when he says that the entrepreneur "does not rule the consumers, he serves them"? (p. 272).

115. What is the source of entrepreneurial profits and how are they obtained? (p. 290) How long do they last and why? (p. 295).

116. Do entrepreneurs always predict the future correctly? (p. 293) What are the two causes of entrepreneurial failure noted by Mises? (pp. 292-294, 301).

117. What is the "vehicle of economic progress"? (p. 297).

118. Are there "normal" profits? Why? (p. 297) Moreover, according to Mises, why is there envy on account of entrepreneurial profit? (p. 298).

119. In what sense are entrepreneurs different from other men? What culpability do they have for generating present consumer preferences? (pp. 299-300).

120. What is the role and motivation of promoters? How does entrepreneurial action differ from speculative action (which is common to all people)? (pp. 303-309) Is it possible to learn entrepreneurial capacities in a school? (pp. 314, 585).

121. Prices transmit information, although it is always imperfect. Who "takes the lead" in the market? What type of economic actors "drive" the market? (p. 328).

122. What prices do entrepreneurs consider and how do they take advantage of them? Do they tend to move the market toward equilibrium (equalization of prices)? (pp. 329, 336-337) For whom are equilibrium models of supply and demand useful? (p. 333).

123. When is it correct or incorrect to say that "average production costs increase with the increase in the quantity produced" (p. 343) What are the institutional, his-

torical, and geographical factors that entrepreneurs must deal with? (pp. 344-345).

124.   What is the meaning of "competitive prices"? What power do producers (and even entrepreneurs) have in the market, "Except for a privilege derived from government interference with business" (pp. 357-358, 370).

125.   Why does wage and benefit negotiation between managers (or entrepreneurs) and unions not correspond to a market transaction? (pp. 776, 779).

Other general questions

126.   According to Mises, how are prices formed in the market? (p. 327) What "ultimately" causes their formation? (p. 332) Why does Mises say that "The pricing process is a social process" and "What is called a price is always a relationship within an integrated system which is the composite effect of human relations"? (pp. 338, 392).

127.   Mises says that "All the prices we know are past prices" (p. 330). What two basic problems exist when we evaluate past prices, especially when they are compared with another series of prices? (pp. 330-331).

128.   According to Mises, what effect does expropriation have? (pp. 804-805) Who are the objects of it and why? (p. 804).

129.   What does Mises have to say about bribery and rent seeking (although he does not mention "rent seeking" by name of course)? (p. 273).

130.   Why do socialists and interventionists call profits and interest "unearned"? Why does Mises disagree? (p. 300).

131.   What relationship does the market have with individuals? (p. 315) Do consumers benefit from policies protecting producers? (p. 316-317) Would they be benefited by a nationalism which directs that it is best to support national or local industry rather than foreign

industry? (p. 326) Are there benefits from the international division of labor? (pp. 325-326).

132.   Should government protect consumers, since they have imperfect information, due to the fact that firms will deceive them through advertising? (pp. 320-321) What does Mises mean that, "The idea that business propaganda can force the consumers to submit to the will of the advertisers is spurious"? (p. 322).

133.   What does the market have to do with political borders worldwide? (p. 323) Do consumers make a distinction between internal and external markets? (p. 325) Is there exchange between nations as nations? What are the bases of mercantilism? (p. 326).

134.   Why does Mises consider the market to be a process? (p. 257) How does it evolve? (p. 265).

135.   Why are savings important in economics? (p. 260). Cite some examples of capital that are beneficial to an economy (pp. 261-262). Would these benefits exist outside of a market economy? (p. 264).

136.   What have all civilizations been based on and why? (p. 264) What economic system is found naturally? (pp. 264, 266-267).

137.   What is the basis of economic management for all non capitalist systems? (pp. 266-268).

References

Anderson, Robert G. (1992), "The Disintegration of Economic Ownership," in John W. Robbins and Mark Spangler, eds., *A Man of Principle: Essays in Honor of Hans F. Sennholz*, Grove City College Press: Grove City, Pennsylvania, pp. 33-45.

Barnes, David W. and Stout, Lynn A. (1992), *Cases and Materials on Law and Economics*, American Casebook Series, West Publishing Co.: St. Paul, Minnesota.

Caro, Robert (1974), *The Power Broker: Robert Moses and the Fall of New York*, Alfred Knopf: New York.

Drucker, Peter Ferdinand (1985), *Innovation and Entrepreneurship*, Harper & Row Publishers: New York.

Ellig, Jerry (1994), "The Economics of Regulatory Takings," in Roger Clegg, ed., *Regulatory Takings*, National Legal Center for the Public Interest: Washington, D.C., 22 pp. (draft).

Greenfield, Sidney M., and Strickson, Arnold (1986), eds., *Entrepreneurship and Social Change*, University Press of America [Society for Economic Anthropology]: New York, pp. 5ff.

Hayek, Friedrich A. von (1945), "The Use of Knowledge in Society," *American Economic Review*, vol. 35, no. 4, September, pp. 519-530.

High, Jack C. (1984), "The Case for Austrian Economics," *Intercollegiate Review*, winter, pp. 37-42.

Kent, Calvin A., ed. (1984), *The Environment for Entrepreneurship*, Lexington Books [D.C. Heath and Company]: Lexington, Massachusetts.

Kirzner, Israel M. (1973), *Competition and Entrepreneurship*, University of Chicago Press: Chicago.

Kirzner, Israel M. (1989), *Discovery, Capitalism, and Distributive Justice*, Basil Blackwell: New York.

Kirzner, Israel M. (1971), "The Entrepreneurial Process," in Kilby, Peter, ed., *Entrepreneurship and Economic Development*, The Free Press: New York.

Kirzner, Israel M. (1992a), "Human Action, Freedom, and Economic Science," in John W. Robbins and Mark Spangler, eds., *A Man of Principle: Essays in Honor of Hans F. Sennholz*, Grove City College Press: Grove City, Pennsylvania, pp. 241-250.

Kirzner, Israel M. (1992b), *The Meaning of Market Process: Essays in the Development of Modern Austrian Economics*, Routledge: New York.

Littlechild, Stephen C. (1981/1978), *The Fallacy of the Mixed Economy: An "Austrian" Critique of Conventional Economics and Government Policy*, Cato Paper no. 2, The Cato Institute: San Francisco, California [Washington, D.C.].

McClelland, David C. (1971/1961), "The Achievement Motive in Economic Growth," a summary of *The Achieving Society*, D. Van Nostrand: Princeton, New Jersey, in Peter Kilby, ed., *Entrepreneurship and Economic Development*, The Free Press: New York.

Mises, Ludwig von (1966/1949), *Human Action: A Treatise on Economics*, Third Revised Edition, Contemporary Books, Inc. (Henry Regnery Co.): Chicago.

O'Driscoll, Jr., Gerald P. and Rizzo, Mario J. (1996), *The Economics of Time and Ignorance*, Routledge: New York.

Papanek, G. F. (1971/1962), "The Development of Entrepreneurship," *American Economic Review*, Supplement May, pp. 45-58, in Peter Kilby, ed., *Entrepreneurship and Economic Development*, pp. 317-318ff.

Prowse, Michael (1994), "'Austrian' recipe for prosperity," *Financial Times*, February 28, p. 19.

Saulniers, Alfred H. (1986), "Entrepreneurs in Public Enterprises," in Sidney M. Greenfield and Arnold Strickson, eds., *Entrepreneurship and Social Change*, University Press of America [Society for Economic Anthropology]: New York, pp. 162ff.

Schumpeter, Joseph A. (1971), "The Fundamental Phenomenon of Economic Development," in Peter Kilby, ed., *Entrepreneurship and Economic Development*, The Free Press: New York, pp. 62-94.

Simon, Julian (1996), *The Ultimate Resource 2*, Princeton University Press: Princeton, New Jersey.

Vaughn, Karen I. (1994), *Austrian Economics in America: The Migration of a Tradition*, Cambridge University Press: New York.

10 Interventionism: an Austrian critique

Austrian theory proscribes interventionist policies

Austrian economics is notorious for its opposition to government intervention into the economy. Thus, it is perhaps fitting in a book introducing Austrian theory to include a sampling of its criticism of interventionism. Policy-relevant research in economics often entails repetitive motifs or similar critiques of proactive policies over time. Correspondingly, many of the failures explained and predicted by past Austrian theorists often continue to be coddled in their original or some modified form by policymakers.

While this book is about *modern* themes in free market economics, a number of older Austrian themes—from the past fifty years—are still relevant to contemporary policy research. Thus, this chapter provides an overview of some key criticisms from both important past and present Austrian theorists. To begin with, besides the important Austrian themes of subjectivity, fragmented and dispersed social knowledge, and purposeful human action, another two relevant concepts from Austrian theory need to be introduced. These two themes, the concept of catallaxy and *wertfrei* research, allow us to better grasp the Austrian critique of interventionism.

Dangers have evolved from applying neoclassical models

As noted in the preceding chapters, Austrians are critical of static equilibrium models. Such models can neither explain the dynamic rivalry of the market process and entrepreneurship, nor facilitate better understanding of market coordination via dispersed and fragmented social knowledge. In addition, the assumptions they require—e.g., perfect information and perfect competition—are not benign. Those modeling ideals are used to justify much intervention.

Accordingly, Hayek has been critical of the perfect competition model: "competition is by its nature a dynamic process whose essential characteristics are assumed away by the assumptions underlying static analysis" (Hayek 1948, p. 94). Moreover, "[t]he argument in favor of competition does not rest on the conditions that would exist if it were perfect" (Hayek 1948, p. 104). Hayek is concerned that proactive policies not be based on perfect conditions.

The economic problem is a problem of making the best use of what resources we have, and not one of what we should do if the situation were different from what it actually is. There is no sense of talking of a use of resources "as if" a perfect market existed, if this means that the resources would have to be different from what they are, or in discussing what somebody with perfect knowledge would do if our task must be to make the best use of knowledge the existing people have (Hayek 1948, p. 104).

Hayek likewise applies his criticism to proactive policy concerns that devolve from these models.

The practical lesson of all this, I think, is that we should worry much less about whether competition in a given case is perfect and worry much more whether there is competition at all. What our theoretical models of separate industries conceal is that in practice a much bigger gulf divides competition from no competition than perfect from imperfect competition. Yet the current tendency in discussion is to be intolerant about the imperfections and to be silent about the prevention of competition. We can probably still learn more about the real significance of competition by studying the results which regularly occur where competition is deliberately suppressed than by concentrating on the shortcomings of actual competition compared with an ideal which is irrelevant for the given facts (Hayek 1948, p. 105).

The concept of catallaxy

Rather than the term "economy," Austrian theorists prefer to use the term *catallaxy* when describing the coordinating dynamics of the market process. This term and its derivatives are not uniquely used by Austrian theorists,[59] although one might argue that they have their most meaningful home within Austrian theory. A catallaxy is distinguished from an *economy*—which implies a single mind which can optimize resource allocation. It is a social order in which disparate individuals and organizations pursuing their own market ends provide coordination of resources.

Hayek, like all Austrian economists, uses methodological individualism as a basis for his analysis. He contends that the catallaxy is coordinated despite varying subjective market evaluations.

When we deal, however, with a situation in which a number of persons are attempting to work out their separate plans, we can no longer assume that the data are the same for all the planning minds. The problem becomes

---

[59] See, for example, Paul A. Samuelson (1954), "The Pure Theory of Public Expenditure," *Review of Economics and Statistics*, November, p. 389 [using "catallactics"].

one of how the "data" of the different individuals on which they base their plans are adjusted to objective facts of their environment (which includes the actions of other people) (Hayek 1948, p. 93).

According to Mises, "[c]atallactic competition is emulation between people who want to surpass one another" (Mises 1966, p. 274). Thus, the catallaxy contains dynamic rivalry (rather than static rest) that leads to unplanned yet effective coordination of human actions. Indeed, the idea of catallaxy naturally lends itself to a dynamic analysis of public policy possibilities and outcomes.

The commitment to wertfrei *research*

Austrians use the term *wertfrei* to describe their praxeological research program. That is, Austrian theory and analysis is neutral with regard to all judgments of value. Mises contends, "[s]cience does not value, but it provides acting man with all the information he may need with regard to his valuations" (Mises 1966, p. 881). In fact, value neutrality undergirds the praxeological endeavor, as Mises remarks:

> This postulate of *Wertfreiheit* can be easily satisfied in the field of the aprioristic sciences—logic, mathematics, and praxeology—and in the field of the experimental natural sciences. It is logically not difficult to draw a sharp line between a scientific, unbiased treatment of these disciplines and a treatment distorted by superstition, preconceived ideas, and passion. It is much more difficult to comply with the requirement of valuational neutrality in history. For the subject matter of history, the concrete accidental and environmental content of human action, is value judgments and their projection into the reality of change. At every step of his activities the histo-

rian is concerned with value judgments. The value judgments of the men whose actions he reports are the substratum of his investigation (Mises 1966, p. 48).

Policy-relevant research may involve a combination of economics and historical work. Thus, to the extent that policy work entails history, a natural tension is produced between *wertfrei* research and an intrusion by normative postulates into policy recommendations. Austrian theorists realize that it is impossible to be purely objective in choosing areas for policy research but they would also contend that policy-relevant research should be conducted as *wertfrei* as possible. For instance, Rothbard suggests that care must be taken to ensure that such research programs remain as value-free as possible.

> As we have reiterated, economics cannot by itself establish ethical judgments, and it can and should be developed in a *Wertfrei* manner. Yet economics, especially of the modern "welfare" variety, is filled with implicit moralizing—with unanalyzed *ad hoc* ethical statements that are either silently or under elaborate camouflage slipped into the deductive system (Rothbard 1977, pp. 258-259).

Consequently, in terms of policy recommendations, Rothbard suggests:

> Briefly, the *Wertfrei* economist can do two things: (1) he can engage in a praxeological critique of inconsistent and meaningless ethical programs…and (2) he can explicate analytically all the myriad consequences of different political systems and different methods of government intervention (Rothbard 1977, pp. 260-261).

Rothbard further argues that, despite its deductive method, praxeological research can criticize the ethical goals of public policy by pointing out errors in logic and praxeological deficiencies or inadequacies.

Praxeology—economics—provides no ultimate ethical judgments: it simply furnishes the indispensable data necessary to make such judgments. It is a formal but universally valid science based on the existence of human action and on logical deductions from that existence. And yet praxeology may be extended beyond its current sphere, to criticize ethical goals. This does not mean that we abandon the value neutrality of praxeological science. It means merely that even ethical goals must be framed meaningfully and, therefore, that praxeology can criticize (1) existential errors made in the formulation of ethical propositions and (2) the possible existential meaninglessness and inner inconsistency of the goals themselves. If an ethical goal can be shown to be self-contradictory and *conceptually impossible* of fulfillment, then the goal is clearly an absurd one and should be abandoned by all (Rothbard 1977, p. 203).

For instance, Rothbard suggests three propositions which can be evaluated by the praxeologist:

The following are brief summaries of very common criticisms of the free market that can be refuted praxeologically…(1) *The free market causes business cycles and unemployment…*(2) *The free market is likely to bring about monopoly and monopoly pricing…*(3) *The government must do what the people themselves cannot do* (Rothbard 1977, pp. 204-205).

This chapter provides some examples of this kind of critique and explication of interventionist (proactive) policies.

Samples of Austrian criticisms of interventionism

Austrian theorists criticized interventionism long before public choice theory became a dominant force in modern free market research. In fact, so much policy analysis and policy-relevant research has been done by Austrian theorists that a chapter like this can hardly begin to do justice to the theme. However, a few samples can be given to illustrate it. For instance, Austrians have vituperated policies pertaining to failed ideologies, drug prohibition, antitrust legislation, protectionism, and government debt repudiation. Mises states that ideologically-driven policy has been misguided. Indeed, the most significant harm done to social harmony has come from bad *ideas* and bad *ideologies*.

> The mischief done by bad ideologies, surely, is much more pernicious, both for the individual and for the whole society, than that done by narcotic drugs (Mises 1966, p. 734).

Congruent with the findings reported in chapter two, Rothbard is skeptical about the effectiveness and true purpose of antitrust legislation.

> *[A]ntitrust laws* and prosecutions, while seemingly designed to "combat monopoly" and "promote competition," actually do the reverse, for they coercively penalize and repress inefficient forms of market structure and activity (Rothbard 1970, p. 790).

Austrians have also been strict opponents of protectionism, as Mises remarks:

> Many people simply do not realize that the only effect of protection is to divert production from those places in which it could produce more per unit of capital and labor expended to places in which it produces less. It makes people poorer, not more prosperous (Mises 1966, p. 317).

Mises is likewise critical of monetary debasement policies enacted to eliminate government debt.

The simplest and oldest variety of monetary interventionism is debasement of coins or diminution of their weight or size for the sake of debt abatement...Debtors are favored at the expense of creditors. But at the same time future credit transactions are made more onerous for debtors (Mises 1966, p. 783).

Lew Rockwell is one of the leading—and most prolific—Austrian critics of government intervention. His articles appear in various publications, notably *The Free Market* and *Policy Review*, in which he offers witty and provocative vituperations against interventionism. For instance, in typical fashion, he comments, "Every day, our markets are less free, our property less secure, our laws more arbitrary, our officials more corrupt, and our liberty more diluted" (Rockwell 1994). He also proscribes the use of any interventionist policy, regardless of the stated rationale, looking at government policy designed to combat recessions (for which the central bank is ultimately responsible) or terrorism.

There are lessons here. One is to never permit the government to discern the relationship between cause and effect. Government invariably rules out the possibility that the structure of the public sector itself is to blame for the problem, whether that problem is terrorism or recession.

Another lesson is that we need to shut down the machinery that allows government to enact its plans. If there continues to be a slice of the population that gets its kicks from issuing orders and trying to make the world conform to them, these people ought to be given a video-game console to play with. The game can be called Grand Theft Society. The stakes are too high to permit them to play their games using real wealth and real lives. (Rockwell 2008a)

In the introduction to his book *The Left, the Right, and the State* (2008), Rockwell discusses how ideological interventionism is accomplished:

In American political culture, and world political culture too, the divide concerns in what way the state's power should be expanded. The left has a laundry list and the right does too. Both represent a grave threat to the only political position that is truly beneficial to the world and its inhabitants: liberty. What is the state? It is the group within society that claims for itself the exclusive right to rule everyone under a special set of laws that permit it to do to others what everyone else is rightly prohibited from doing, namely aggressing against person and property.

Why would any society permit such a gang to enjoy an unchallenged legal privilege? Here is where ideology comes into play. The reality of the state is that it is a looting and killing machine. So why do so many people cheer for its expansion? Indeed, why do we tolerate its existence at all?...[T]he democratic state in the developed world is more complex [in providing its justification]. It uses a huge range of ideological rationales–parsed out between left and right–that reflect social and cultural priorities of niche groups, even when many of these rationales are contradictory.

The left wants the state to distribute wealth, to bring about equality, to rein in businesses, to give workers a boost, to provide for the poor, to protect the environment...The right, on the other hand, wants the state to punish evildoers, to boost the family, to subsidize upright ways of living, to create security against foreign enemies, to make the culture cohere, and to go to war to give ourselves a sense of national identity...

So how are these competing interests resolved? They logroll and call it democracy. The left and right agree to let each other have their way, provided nothing is done to injure the interests of one or the other. The trick is to keep the balance. Who is in power is really about which way the log is rolling. And there you have the modern state in a nutshell.

While his work tends to be policy analysis rather than policy-relevant research, Rockwell is a notable example of someone who has been deeply influenced by Austrian theorists like Mises and Rothbard. Like his mentors, he has continued to strongly criticize interventionist policies. In addition, O'Rourke certainly embodies one who received considerable influence from free market theorists.

You know, if government were a product, selling it would be illegal. Government is a health hazard. Governments have killed many more people than cigarettes or unbuckled seat belts ever have...And the merest glance at the federal budget is enough to convict the government of perjury, extortion, and fraud...government should be against the law. Term limits aren't enough. We need jail (O'Rourke 1993, p. 38).

Nevertheless, many people love the state. They love it because they are taught to love it in government schools. They believe that the state can improve their quality of life and alleviate market failures, including impeding the plans of greedy capitalists. They love it too because it provides goodies to them through capitalizing on SIGs pressures, rent seeking and capture strategies.

A subjectivist critique of interventionism

The concept of society

One of the principal flaws in the philosophical basis of pro-active policy is its oft-aberrant notion of *society*. It is assumed that groups have preferences, choose and act. Public policy is structured around the idea of doing something in the "public interest" as if the public, or society, had an objectively knowable set of preferences and values.

Austrian theorists reject this notion. Building upon the Misesian understanding of society noted in chapter seven, the Austrian concept of society comprises a common order, a civilization, or a group of objectives held in common by individual economic actors living near each other (or within the same political boundaries) and often with a common language. Policy goals for society are limited to collective action to make a stable legal order and to provide defense from foreign and domestic predators (i.e., reactive policies).

Nevertheless, the Austrian concept of society can be more broadly construed to include any kind of collective action whereby participants believe that they will gain by promoting the welfare of others. As Mises remarks, "[s]ociety is joint action and cooperation in which each participant sees the other partner's success as a means for the attainment of his own" (Mises 1996, p. 169). Indeed, when taken as a whole, the market itself is a *social* process and praxeology is a *social* science. Innumerable individual human actions combine together to make up the catallaxy and facilitate social coordination, although individuals often fail to recognize their role in the market, and end up masochistically using public policy to damage it. As Mises states:

> The market is a social body; it is the foremost social body. The market phenomena are social phenomena. They are the resultant of each individual's active contri-

bution. But they are different from each such contribution. They appear to the individual as something given which he himself cannot alter. He does not always see that he himself is a part, although a small part, of the complex of elements determining each momentary state of the market. Because he fails to realize this fact, he feels himself free, in criticizing the market phenomena, to condemn with regard to his fellow men a mode of conduct which he considers as quite right with regard to himself. He blames the market for its callousness and disregard of persons and asks for social control of the market in order to "humanize" it (Mises 1996, p. 315).

The notion of the public interest

Indeed, social theorists and policy analysts or researchers are prone to make a fatal flaw when they talk about social interests. Statements like: "It is not in the best interest of society to continue with this policy" or "The public interest is not advanced by that policy" are incomprehensible and specious grounds for analysis. As a unit of analysis, "society" has no preferences or feelings; only individuals do. While it may be true that societies are made up of individuals with such preferences and feelings, it is impossible for planners to know them, make interpersonal rankings according to cardinal valuations of them, or aggregate them to produce social preference or welfare functions.

Therefore, proactive policies enacted to make society more "compassionate" or to enhance the public interest (or social preference) are specious. A society has no preferences and does not choose; it cannot act purposefully or compassionately because it is not an individual. *There is no public interest; all interests are private and individual.* Instead, policies to promote the public interest really impose the preferences of a few political actors or special interest groups on the rest of society.

Therefore, from an Austrian perspective, there is no such thing as genuinely beneficial proactive policy. As noted by High earlier, "strictly speaking, there is no such thing as Austrian economic policy" (High 1984, p. 40). Even the most well-intentioned efforts merely serve to coerce one group to conform with (or pay for) the special interests of another group. In a pluralistic world with self-interested actors, only reactive public policy can possibly provide social "benefits" given the premise that all people act purposefully to remove uneasiness and seek to protect themselves from predators. However, even reactive policies must be scrutinized, since they are not guaranteed to be free from rent seeking problems. And reactive policy must be based on the revealed preferences of people to preserve their lives.

The issue of scarcity

Another issue that interventionists sometimes fail to deal with adequately is *scarcity*. They make policy decisions as if they live in a world of plenty. On the contrary, all individuals are forced to economize on scarce resources because we do not live in a world of plenty. In this effort, the price system serves as an invaluable guide for human actors to allocate resources effectively and efficiently.

In order to "provide" goods for social compassion or the so-called public interest, proactive policies of intervention must confiscate scarce resources from one group and give them to another. Legal plunder is justified in the mind of the interventionist because of the resulting social welfare benefits. Yet, according to Mises, the main failure of welfare economics is that it neglects to appreciate the scarcity of capital goods.

The Santa Claus fables of the welfare school are characterized by their complete failure to grasp the problem of capital. It is precisely this defect that makes it imperative to deny them the appellation *welfare economics* with which they describe their doctrines. He who does not take into consideration the scarcity of capital goods available is not an economist, but a fabulist. He does not deal with reality but with a fabulous world of plenty. All the effusions of the contemporary welfare school are, like those of the socialist authors, based on the implicit assumption that there is an abundant supply of capital goods. Then, of course, it seems easy to find a remedy for all ills, to give to everybody "according to his needs" and make everyone perfectly happy (Mises 1966, p. 848).

Fair market value

The importance of methodological individualism leads Austrian theorists to criticize interventionist policies that require valuations of private property. For instance, a "fair market" value for land may be ascertained by the state, and a person may be "compensated" accordingly, when his real property is taken for the public interest via eminent domain. Yet it is impossible for the state to ascertain the value of that property to the individual. All value is *subjective* and the state is wholly incapable of determining such value.

The fact that a person does not sell his property to the highest bidder is evidence of the fact that he values the property more than the money or property which could be exchanged for it at present. Therefore, when a fair market value is assigned by the state, it is usually no better than the second best. The state does not compensate a person based on his subjective value or his opportunity cost criteria.

Fair market valuations can create injustice when judicial activists and social planners fail to recognize subjectivism and the importance of the price system in allocating scarce resources. Accordingly, welfare economics and proactive policies debase praxeological insights in practice. They imply that Benthamite cardinal comparisons may be made such that planners can handle resources more effectively than the catallaxy and the price system. They do so in spite of the compelling argument by Lionel Robbins (stemming from Menger and the other marginalists), that utility rankings are only ordinal, and thus interpersonal comparisons of utility must be rejected (see Rowley 1993, pp. 11, 32, 40, 58). Insofar as Austrian theorists are concerned, any attempt to analyze and alter social phenomenon based on such rationale is specious and dangerous.

Cost-benefit analysis

Another interventionist or policy tool which Austrian theorists have criticized is cost-benefit analysis done by policymakers. At the individual level, everyone uses cost-benefit analysis or economizing behavior to determine whether or not to act in a certain way or invest in a certain market or idea. Austrian theorists understand that individuals undertake this calculus. But cost-benefit analysis is not possible, they say, when a group or society is the focal point of action. In order to improve policy efficiency, planners often resort to such tools. However, these tools do not circumvent or alleviate the problems that will arise from their craft on account of subjectivism. As I have pointed out:

> [W]hile the inclusion of cost-benefit analysis...might help regulators use their time and resources more effectively, by providing an organized analytical methodology, it is not clear that such analysis can really generate any conclusive (or even useful) determinations, particularly because of the knowledge problem. An analytic problem is shared by all public organizations which make decisions about resources that are not owned by individuals, effectively making cost-benefit analysis dubious at best. *There is no way of knowing the actual cost*

of a public decision, and it is likewise impossible to know or measure its benefits. Therefore, cost-benefit methodology can hardly be a justification for supporting government building [or other kind of] regulation. Indeed, it is plausible that all public cost-benefit analysis ultimately falls into one of two categories: (1) it is a sincere, but tenuous or even misguided, effort to be more efficient that will fail because of the knowledge problem, or (2) it is simply a means of rationalizing rent seeking or social policies. In either case its methods do not necessarily make building regulation either scientific or efficient (Cobin 1997, pp. 209-210).

I go on to evince the impossibility of determining the true cost of a public decision.

For instance, if a government allocates $500 million for enforcement of a national building code, it thereby eliminates all other opportunities to use those funds. Consequently, the *cost* of this decision is *not* $500 million, but the value of the highest valued forgone opportunity. Yet who can measure the value of that forgone opportunity? What if the $500 million were given to a group which in turn developed a popular and cheap method of sanitizing homes and office buildings (making Americans 50% more healthy and productive), or what if it were given to an think-tank of inventors who develop a cheap and attractive fireproof siding (which decreases by 40% the number of buildings destroyed by fire), neither of which would occur without the $500 million? Alternatively, what if the $500 million was not taken from taxpayers, so that they had more to spend on home fire prevention (and thus there are 25% less Americans killed by fire)? (Cobin 1997, p. 210—footnote).

Moreover, I conclude that it is impossible to determine the benefits of a public decision as well.

Indeed, there is no way of knowing or measuring the *benefits* of a policy either. Murray Rothbard notes that it is not possible to say that someone benefits from an action if there is no voluntary exchange between individuals[60]...What one person likes, another may detest... Furthermore, there is an incentives difference between public decision-makers, who redistribute resources, and individuals or firms, who allocate their own resources and produce products for *exchange* (Cobin 1997, p. 210).[61]

Rothbard continues this theme:

> The "benefit," then, is simply assumed arbitrarily by government officials. Furthermore, even if the benefit were freely demonstrable, the *benefit principle* would not approach the process of the free market. For, once again, individuals pay a *uniform price* for services on the free market, regardless of the extent of their subjective benefits. The man who would "walk a mile for a Camel" pays no more, ordinarily, than the man who couldn't care less. To tax everyone in accordance with the benefit he receives, then, is diametrically opposed to the market principle. Finally, if everyone's benefit is taxed away, there would be no reason for him to make the exchange or to receive the government service (Rothbard 1970, p. 804).

Because planners lack the requisite knowledge, and because utility is not interpersonally comparable, planners cannot determine whether there is a net social benefit from a public policy. Moreover, an inherent problem with *aggregate* data is that it fails to elucidate costs and benefits to

---

[60] See Rothbard 1956. In his critique of welfare economics and policy, Rothbard advocates using demonstrated preference and the unanimity rule, advocating free markets.

[61] In addition, Henry Hazlitt (1979/1946, pp.72-73, 31ff, 61ff) makes a compelling observation about the shortcomings of full employment and other state planning, with implications for cost-benefit analysis.

individuals. For instance, it is possible to have aggregate or social gains from a policy, where only a small group has had very large positive utility gains, while the vast majority of people have experienced small losses.

We can see that there are social loses in theory by looking at Harberger triangles and Tullock rectangles (see chapter three) and deducing why they are lost or dissipated. But we cannot know the exact cost to any one individual, even if we can measure the benefits accrued to a person or a SIG.

Note that it is conceivable that rent seeking activity might produce positive aggregate gains in a planner's calculus but in reality have deleterious results on the whole. This might occur if there are measurable concentrated benefits while the dispersed costs are obfuscated, non-measurable, or non-pecuniary, and thus remain unnoticed or unaccounted for in the calculus. Indeed, Mises argues that the methods and presumptions of interventionist policymakers contain the seeds of their own undoing.

> The plight of Western civilization consists precisely in the fact that serious people can resort to such syllogistic artifices without encountering sharp rebuke. There are only two explanations open. Either these self-styled welfare economists are themselves not aware of the logical inadmissibility of their procedure, in which case they lack the indispensable power of reasoning; or they have chosen this mode of arguing purposely in order to find shelter for their fallacies behind a word which is intended beforehand to disarm all opponents. In each case their own acts condemn them (Mises 1966, p. 834).

Proactive public policy is simply incapable of improving the quality of life because planners lack the requisite knowledge to act in the interest of others and because they fail to appreciate the illogic of their methods.

Some adverse results of interventionism

Austrian theorists have provided many policy-relevant criticisms of interventionism over the last fifty years. This section provides a sampling of these criticisms. Interventionism is coercion designed to alter catallactic conditions. Rothbard characterizes the state's monopolization of force as contrary to the voluntarism of the market process.

> Intervention is the intrusion of aggressive physical force into society; it means the substitution of coercion for voluntary actions. It must be remembered that, *praxeologically,* it makes no difference what individual or group wields this force; the economic nature and consequences of the action remain the same. Empirically, the vast bulk of interventions are performed by States, since the State is the only organization in society legally equipped to use violence and since it is the only agency that legally derives its revenue from a compulsory levy (Rothbard 1970, p. 766).

As a matter of primary concern, Mises notes that interventionism breeds economic and social chaos. Nevertheless, policymakers continually ignore the warnings of praxeology and blame the market for their own misdeeds.

> The interventionist policies as practiced for many decades by all governments of the capitalistic West have brought about all those effects which economists predicted. There are wars and civil wars, ruthless oppression of the masses by clusters of self-appointed dictators, economic depressions, mass unemployment, capital consumption, and famines. However, it is not these catastrophic events which have led to the crisis of interventionism. The interventionist doctrinaires and their followers explain all these undesired consequences as unavoidable

features of capitalism. As they see it, it is precisely these disasters that clearly demonstrate the necessity of intensifying interventionism. The failures of the interventionist policies do not in the least impair the popularity of the implied doctrine. They are so interpreted as to strengthen, not to lessen, the prestige of these teachings. As a vicious economic theory cannot be simply refuted by historical experience, the interventionist propagandists have been able to go on in spite of all the havoc they have spread (Mises 1966, p. 855).

Public choice and knowledge problems

Mises argues that interest groups benefit from interventionism in ways that are not available in the market process. He is hardly surprised that people practice privilege seeking.

A characteristic feature of the unhampered market society is that it is no respecter of vested interests. Past achievements do not count if they are obstacles to further improvement. The advocates of security are therefore quite correct in blaming capitalism for insecurity. But they distort the facts in implying that the selfish interests of capitalists and entrepreneurs are responsible. What harms the vested interests is the urge of the consumers for the best possible satisfaction of their needs. Not the greed of the wealthy few, but the propensity of everyone to take advantage of any opportunity offered for an improvement of his own well-being makes for producer insecurity (Mises 1966, p. 852).

As a prelude to what would later be popularized as the theory of rent seeking or interest groups, Mises points out that paternalistic policies, subject to the perverse incentives and venality inherent in the political process, will produce harmful social results.

There are hardly any acts of government interference with the market process that, seen from the point of view of the citizens concerned, would not have to be qualified either as confiscations or as gifts. As a rule, one individual or a group of individuals is enriched at the expense of other individuals or groups of individuals. But in many cases, the harm done to some people does not correspond to any advantage for other people. There is no such thing as a just and fair method of exercising the tremendous power that interventionism puts into the hands of the legislature and the executive. The advocates of interventionism pretend to substitute for the—as they assert, "socially" detrimental—effects of private property and vested interests the unlimited discretion of the perfectly wise and disinterested legislator and his conscientious and indefatigable servants, the bureaucrats. In their eyes the common man is a helpless infant, badly in need of a paternal guardian to protect him against the sly tricks of a band of rogues. They reject all traditional notions of law and legality in the name of a "higher and nobler" idea of justice. Whatever they themselves do is always right because it hurts those who selfishly want to retain for themselves what, from the point of view of this higher concept of justice, ought to belong to others. The notions of selfishness and unselfishness as employed in such reasoning are self-contradictory and vain. As has been pointed out, every action aims at the attainment of a state of affairs that suits the actor better than the state that would prevail in the absence of this action. In this sense every action is to be qualified as selfish...The politician is, in this sense, always selfish no matter whether he supports a popular program in order to get an office or whether he firmly clings to his own—unpopular— convictions and thus deprives himself of the benefits he could reap by betraying them...Unfortunately the office-holders and their staffs are not angelic. They learn very soon that their decisions mean for the businessmen either considerable losses or—sometimes—considerable gains. Certainly there are also bureaucrats who do not take bribes; but there are others who are anxious to take advantage of any "safe" opportunity of "sharing" with those whom their decisions favor (Mises 1966, pp. 734-735).

Similarly, Rothbard decries zero or negative-sum games that are inherent in the political process—what would eventually be termed rent seeking losses by public choice economists—while lauding the market process for precluding them.

> In sum, the free market always benefits every participant, and it maximizes social utility *ex ante;* it also tends to do so *ex post,* for it contains an efficient mechanism for speedily converting anticipations into realizations. With intervention, one group gains directly at the expense of another, and therefore social utility is not maximized or even increased; there is no mechanism for speedy translation of anticipation into fruition, but indeed the opposite; and finally, as we shall see, the indirect consequences of intervention will cause many interveners themselves to *lose* utility *ex post* (Rothbard 1970, p. 777). [62]

---

[62] In *Power and Market* (pp. 10-11) he remarks, "One of the most lucid analyses of the distinction between State and market was set forth by Franz Oppenheimer. He pointed out that there are fundamentally two ways of satisfying a person's wants: (1) by production and voluntary exchange with others on the market and (2) by violent expropriation of the wealth of others. The first method Oppenheimer termed "the economic means" for the satisfaction of wants: the second method, "the political means." The State is trenchantly defined as the "organization of the political means." A generic term is needed to designate an individual or group that commits invasive violence in society. We may call *intervener,* or *invader,* one who intervenes violently in free social or market relation. The term applies to any individual or group that initiates violent intervention in the free actions of person and property owners."

In addition, the work of eclectic free market scholars like Holcombe reflects the enduring value of the Austrian critique of intervention, along with public choice insights which produce similar concerns. He remarks that regulators have a perverse incentive to be ineffective.

The government will never lose profits from being a poor regulator; in fact, the opposite is likely to be true. If information that the government is doing a poor job of regulating an industry begins to circulate, typically there is a call for the government to do more regulation, which probably means bigger budgets for the regulatory agency (Holcombe 1995, p. 103).

Holcombe argues that, in addition to public choice problems, the knowledge problem and the subjective nature of value preclude efficient and even effective intervention.

The call for government regulation to solve problems often stems from the idea that something should be done, coupled with the idea that, in theory, it would be possible for someone with a great deal of wisdom, the ability to put the public interest ahead of any personal interests, and the absolute power of dictator to implement the appropriate solution. In practice government-implemented solutions rarely work out as well as their supporters had hoped. Consider why.

First, it is easy to find things in the real world that are not perfect and to say that something should be done to correct the problems. However, for every ten people who see the same problem, there will be ten different ideal solutions. Thus, government action could not possibly solve most problems to the satisfaction of everybody because, while people tend to agree on the problems, they disagree on what would be the appropriate solutions. This is the nature of politics. With collective action, one solution is implemented for everybody, and, whatever that solution is, some people will not like it. Thus, the person who argues that the government should do something to solve a problem must, realistically, be prepared to face the fact that if the government does take action, its action not likely to be the one that individuals would have chosen.

Second, political solutions are necessarily the product of compromise, so in many cases, what course of action the government takes is not determined by choosing one person's solution over another's but, rather, is a compromise that takes bits and pieces of everyone's proposals and combines them. This may be desirable in some instances, but in other cases, compromise cripples policy proposals so that compromise policies work worse than if another option had been taken. In a majority rule system, however, compromise is necessary in order to get the approval of a majority of the voters. The government is not a monolithic benevolent dictator but, rather, a collection of individuals linked together by political institutions where compromise is necessary to implement policies. Thus, in the end, nobody is likely to get the policy he or she really would have liked.

Third, the government does not always know what is the right solution to a problem. It is easier to identify problems than it is to identify ways to successfully deal with those problems, and, perhaps because of some of the reasons just noted, the government does not always find the right solution and often makes matters worse rather than better. That alone is a good reason for taking a close look at ways in which public policies can enhance the quality of life.

Fourth, because of the way that the government is structured, those in the government do not always have the incentive to solve problems. Their personal concerns might override the public interest when they make decisions affecting public policy (Holcombe 1995, pp. 4-5).

Intervention produces perverse incentives, among other public choice problems. As Rothbard points out, public ownership creates a divergent incentive to care for property, and succeeding in the political process requires different action than would be expected in the market process.

Not only does government lack a successful test for picking the proper experts, not only is the voter necessarily more ignorant than the consumer, but government itself has other inherent mechanisms which lead to poorer choices of experts and officials. For one thing, the politician and the government expert receive their revenues, not from service voluntarily purchased on the market, but from a compulsory levy on the inhabitants. These officials, then, wholly lack the direct pecuniary incentive to *care* about servicing the public properly and competently. Furthermore, the relative rise of the "fittest" applies in government as in the market, but the criterion of "fitness" is here very different. In the market, the fittest are those most able to serve the consumers. In government, the fittest are either (1) those most able at wielding coercion or (2) if bureaucratic officials, those best fitted to curry favor with the leading politicians or (3) if politicians, those most adroit at appeals to the voting public (Rothbard 1970, pp. 775-776).

Costly and repetitive failures

While Austrians do not contend that markets produce utopia, they do categorically believe that markets provide the best form of economic and social organization in an imperfect world. Mises derides those theorists and policymakers who rely on obsolete and erroneous economics to justify interventionism because their bad reasoning produces more harm than good.

The objections which the various schools of Sozialpolitik raise against the market economy are based on very bad economics. They repeat again and again all the errors the economists long ago exploded. They blame the market economy for the consequences of the very anticapitalistic policies which they themselves advocate as necessary and beneficial reforms. They fix on the market economy the responsibility for the inevitable failure and frustration of interventionism. These propagandists must finally admit that the market economy is after all not so bad as their "unorthodox" doctrines paint it. It delivers the goods. From day to day it increases the quantity and improves the quality of products. It has brought about unprecedented wealth. But, objects the champion of interventionism, it is deficient from what he calls the social point of view. It has not wiped out poverty and destitution. It is a system that grants privileges to a minority, an upper class of rich people, at the expense of the immense majority. It is an unfair system. The principle of *welfare* must be substituted for that of profits (Mises 1966, p. 833).

But implementing such a system of welfare would not be costless, and such proactive policy has not improved the quality of life. The welfare system envisioned by many to improve on capitalism would require proactive polices of redistribution and restrictions on consumption and other liberties. As Mises comments:

It is a fact that no paternal government, whether ancient or modern, ever shrank from regimenting its subjects' minds, beliefs, and opinions. If one abolishes man's freedom to determine his own consumption, one takes all freedoms away. The naïve advocates of government in-terference with consumption delude themselves when they neglect what they disdainfully call the philosophical aspect of the problem. They unwittingly support the case of censorship, inquisition, religious intolerance, and the persecution of dissenters (Mises 1966, p. 734).

Hazlitt has also criticized policymakers for utilizing bad economics and ignoring economic premises. In stating his famous "Lesson," Hazlitt contends that the principal prob-lem of economic policymakers is that they are myopic and have a narrow view of the consequences of their policies.

In this lies the whole difference between good economics and bad. The bad economist sees only what immediately strikes the eye; the good economist also looks beyond. The bad economist sees only the direct consequences of a proposed course; the good economist looks also at the longer and the indirect consequences. The bad economist sees only what effect of a given policy has been or will be on one particular group; the good economist inquires also what effect of the policy will be on all groups...Yet when we enter the field of public economics, these ele-mentary truths are ignored. There are men regarded to-day as brilliant economists, who deprecate saving and recommend squandering on a national scale as the way of economic salvation; and when anyone points to what the consequences of these policies will be in the long run, they reply flippantly, as might the warning son of a warning father: "In the long run we are all dead." And such shallow wisecracks pass as devastating epigrams and the ripest wisdom. But the tragedy is that, on the contrary, we are already suffering the long-run conse-quences of the policies of the remote or recent past. To-day is already the tomorrow which the bad economist yesterday urged us to ignore. The long-run consequences of some economic policies may become evident in a few months. Others may not become evident for several years. Still others may not become evident for decades. But in every case those long-run consequences are contained in the policy as surely the hen was in the egg, the flower in the seed. From this aspect, therefore, the whole of economics can be reduced to a single lesson, and that lesson can be reduced to a single sentence. *The art of economics consists in looking not merely at the immediate but at the longer effects of any act or policy; it consists in tracing the consequences of that policy not merely for one group but for all groups* (Hazlitt 1979, pp. 16-17). [63]

Reflecting on his previous work, Hazlitt commented in 1978 that his lesson and all the applications he had delineated previously have been ignored by policymakers. And given the interventionist policies of 2009 enacted to combat the worldwide recession, his lesson has still not been learned. Hazlitt had explained and predicted the failures of bad policies in advance. Yet the interventionists would not, and evidently still will not, heed his concerns.

In sum, so far as the politicians are concerned, the lesson that this book tried to instill more than thirty years ago does not seem to have been learned anywhere. If we go through the chapters of this book seriatim [one after another], we find practically no form of government intervention deprecated in the first edition that is not still being pursued, usually with increased obstinacy. Governments everywhere are still trying to cure by public works the unemployment brought about by their own policies. They are imposing heavier and more expropriatory taxes than ever. They still recommend credit expansion. Most

---

[63] Also see Schansberg 1996, pp. 41-45. He gives an excellent applied summary of Hazlitt's Lesson to modern myopic public policy.

of them still make "full employment" their overriding goal. They continue to impose import quotas and protective tariffs. They try to increase exports by depreciating their currencies even further. Farmers are still "striking" for "parity prices." Governments still provide special encouragement to unprofitable industries. They still make efforts to "stabilize" special commodity prices. Governments, pushing up commodity prices by inflating their currencies, continue to blame the higher prices on private producers, sellers, and "profiteers." They impose price ceilings on oil and natural gas, to discourage new exploration precisely when it is in most need of encouragement, or resort to general price and wage fixing or "monitoring." They continue rent control in the face of the obvious devastation it has caused. They not only maintain minimum wage laws but keep increasing their level, in the face of the chronic unemployment they so clearly bring about. They continue to pass laws granting special privileges and immunities to labor unions; to oblige workers to become members; to tolerate mass picketing and other forms of coercion; and to compel employers to "bargain collectively in good faith" with such unions—i.e., to make at least some concessions to their demands. The intention of these measures is to "help labor." But the result is to once more create and prolong unemployment, and to lower total wage payments compared to what they might have been (Hazlitt 1979, pp. 207-208).

In addition to its efforts criticizing interventionism, the Austrian School also provides a solution to interventionist problems. This solution draws from both its deductive theory and economic history studies regarding the collapse of socialism around the world. It is further linked, at least in terms of policy, with the Virginia School of public choice (each of these Schools provide similar prescriptions in their policy-relevant research). Holcombe sums up this policy proposition very candidly:

> The optimal policy for government is to define and enforce the rights of individuals and let market mechanisms operate in order to enhance the quality of life...The collapse of the centrally planned economies in Europe in 1989 and the demise of the Soviet Union in 1991 brought clear evidence that government planning is counterproductive and that it lowers the standard of living and harms the quality of life. The lessons learned so painfully in Europe apply just as forcefully to the United States. The way to improve the quality of life is to rely less on government, not more (Holcombe 1995, p. 180).

An Austrian explication of interventionism

As noted in the previous chapter, Mises poses a puissant question for proactive policymakers: "What type of men do the man breeders want to rear" (Mises 1966, p. 243)? At its core, all proactive economic policy is interventionist, if not Marxist. Conforming to B.F. Skinner's *Walden Two* (1948), the man breeders want to rear men just as a rancher rears cattle; they intend to develop a Brave New World via the proactive policy they enact. Evidently, their fundamental belief is that people are, like children, incapable of looking out for their own best interests and need a big brother to guide them—just as Mises described above.

An interventionist or a Marxist might contend that under capitalism people are perennially duped by clever producers who garner superior bargaining power. In the market process people are opiated by superstitions which prompt them to be placid before their capitalist butchers. But there may still be hope to survive, they claim.

Fortunately, there are a few enlightened intellectuals who are not bogged down like commoners with opiates of superstition. In countering this Worldview, Thomas Sowell calls the former group the "anointed" and the latter group the "benighted" (Sowell 1996). Yet the vision has prevailed. These anointed intellectuals, even if they are at least as clever as the capitalists, do not succumb to the temptation to alienate and ravish their fellow man in order to better themselves. Their intentions may be commendable; they may even have quasi-altruistic motives. They decry nefarious rulers like Adolph Hitler, Joseph Stalin, Mao Tse-tung, Pol Pot, et al, as horrendous interventionist aberrations rather than genuine comrades of intervention, suggesting that pure socialism, Marxism, or interventionism would not result in the barbarous hells that these men fostered.

But barbarism and chaos are precisely what Mises and other Austrians predicted that interventionism would produce. The plain fact of history is that the end of all ideological and egalitarian interventionism is chaos and tyranny. Reflecting on George Orwell's *Animal Farm* (1946), the rent seeking and abusive "pigs" cannot be serenely expunged from the political process once entrenched in it. SIGs become entrenched and demosclerosis sets in (se chapter one). After a course of interventionism is begun it is difficult, if not impossible, to turn back. The mounting benefits gained by rent seekers will be dwarfed by the injurious costs born by the ill-informed, ingenuous and naïve.

As noted in chapters seven and eight, Mises and other Austrian theorists reject the idea of a "mixed economy." The *only* useful realm of government, if there is any useful realm at all, is found in carrying out reactive policies. Intervention may be installed in the form of milder proactive policy agenda or as insidiously as crass totalitarian communism. Yet in either case, or at any point in between the two, the system is an interventionist economy and not a market economy.

Furthermore, the driving force behind any form of man breeding, whether it is called socialism, fascism, or welfare stare interventionism, is *never* altruism. It always rests on the drive for dominance, self-interest, and rent seeking by an individual or a SIG. Government privileges to certain firms or individuals make the emergence of monopoly possible, which deals the greatest blow to consumers (Mises 1996, pp. 360-361, 387, and cf. p. 395). Notions of ethical or value neutrality in policymaking and objective scientism in policy analysis are manifestly spurious, and merely contribute to the disintegration of economic reasoning and further policy failures.[64]

Conversely, the market process serves the consumer and eliminates unreputable firms. Markets, rather than proactive policies and policies of inefficient provision, bring increasing prosperity and improvements to the quality of life. It is proactive policies and the economic distortions they create, rather than capitalists, which are the greatest threat to society. It is interventionist governments, not firms, which misallocate the scarce resources in society to the detriment of consumers. Mises derides the proactive policy facade, highlighting the knowledge problem.

> The welfare propagandist, in whose opinion government control is a synonym for God's providential care that wisely and imperceptibly leads mankind to higher and more perfect stages of an inescapable evolutionary progress, fails to see the intricacy of the problem and its ramifications (Mises 1966, p. 846, cf. Kirzner 1992b, pp. 180-192).

In the final analysis, interventionists cannot allocate or coordinate much of anything. They cannot ameliorate so-

---

[64] See chapters two and three, as well as Nutter 1983, p. 47. Nutter says that they should instead "try to build a good society instead of trying to do good for society," p. 48.

cial ills wholly, and certainly not efficiently. In *The Road To Serfdom* (1944), Hayek warns of the totalitarian perils which devolve from quashing "control of the means of production" which is normally "divided among people acting independently," viz., the interventionist abridgment of private property, in favor of ostensibly altruistic proactive policies (Hayek 1944, p. 104). Surely, history and economic theory manifest the precarious nature and denouement of centralized government coordination policies.

As an alternative to using interventionist policies, catallactic instability and uncertainty may be mitigated by employing policies that promote rule-following behavior and greater reliance on institutions. For instance, people find optimal strategies which economize on knowledge and then repeat them (i.e., routines minimize the amount of cognition required, such as traffic signals).

Moreover, there are certain default rules in society or culture that are often facilitated by reactive public policy, although they may also be generated by other means. Institutionalized laws of just conduct remove uneasiness by backing up contractual arrangements and upholding private property.[65] Austrian economists argue that in an imperfect world, markets are by far more capable of allocating resources in the catallaxy and coordinating the market process. In the final analysis, markets may not bring utopia but they certainly do not bring the mayhem and chaos caused by interventionism.

---

[65] Hayek distinguishes orders from organizations. Orders are abstract rules which facilitate goals in the catallaxy)—like the legal system—that form part of the societal backdrop. The market process embodies a "spontaneous order" without the design of a human planner. While institutions and rules may be questioned at the margin, radical proactive policy changes will cause destabilization, since it is impossible to know how much knowledge is locked up in such institutions and rules.

Appendix: Mises and interventionism
Chapter 10 questions

Write short answers to the following questions by utilizing Ludwig von Mises (1996), *Human Action: A Treatise On Economics*, fourth revised edition, Irvington-on-Hudson, New York: The Foundation for Economic Education (this edition comprises minor editorial changes by Bettina Bien Greaves).

138. What critique does Mises make regarding "social engineering"? (pp. 112-113).
139. Why does Mises say that "there is no means of deriving comparisons other than entirely arbitrary ones between the valuations of various people" (p. 126) What are the implications of this fact for public policy that can be known apodictically?
140. What is the state or government? What critique does Mises make of anarchy? (p. 149) What is the role of the state? (pp. 257, 272-273, 280-282).
141. What relationship exists between theocracies and socialist states? (pp. 150-151) Why does Mises say that both bring conflicts and pathetic attempts at man breeding (p. 166), while classical liberalism brings peace and prosperity through a democratic process and persuasion instead of force? (pp. 151-154) Are there pubic choice problems which are not taken into account by Mises? (pp. 318-319).
142. What are the goals of classical liberalism and what nexus does it have with praxeology? (pp. 153-154), What are the two fundamental doctrines of liberalism? (p. 154) How does liberalism deal with religion? (pp. 155-157).
143. What critique does Mises make regarding welfare economics, man breeding by social engineers (pp. 242-

243), the "mixed" economy (pp. 258-259), and measurements of wealth and income? (p. 251).

144. What is liberty under the free market? (pp. 285-287) When is it impeded or helped by government? (pp. 279-289).

145. Mises says that "The inequity of individuals with regard to wealth and income is an essential feature of the market economy" (p. 287) Why is this fact not gloomy according to Mises?

146. What is a manager and what problems arise due to his incentive structure? (pp. 304-308) What additional problems arise in public administration? (pp. 308-310).

147. How is it possible to eliminate land erosion or forest deterioration? (pp. 656-657) Why does this solution not appear to work well (to some people) in countries that have freer markets? (pp. 657-658).

148. What theoretical reasons support agricultural subsidies and who searches for them? (p. 660) What are the two ways to become exempt from decrees or to obtain legal privileges? (pp. 662-663).

149. What is the essential conflict between economics and interventionism? (p. 761) What should government do to prevent monopoly prices? (pp. 766-767) What caused the decline of the Roman Empire and classical civilization? (pp. 767-769).

150. What is the usual consequence of price fixing intervention? (pp. 762-764) What are two exceptions to this outcome? (pp. 765-766).

151. What results from legislating minimum wages? (pp. 769-770, 778-779) What did Marx and his logical disciples think of such policies? (pp. 771-772) Why does legislation exist which conforms to interventionist philosophy? (pp. 771-772).

152. Why do machines not replace labor? (pp. 773-775) Does assistance granted to the unemployed "dispose of unemployment"? (p. 776).

153. What is the only way that real wage rates can rise in real terms? (p. 775).

154. Why do plans to redistribute land exist, who "foots the bill," and what are the consequences of such reform policies? (pp. 804-806).

155. Who suffers directly and indirectly from the high rates of "confiscatory taxation" and why? (pp. 808-810) How will competition be adversely affected because of it? (pp. 808-809).

156. What critique does Mises make of "progressive taxation" (p. 807) and "death taxes"? (pp. 807-808).

157. According to Mises, what is "the plight of Western civilization" in ideational terms and why? (pp. 834-835) What are the three reasons that some people use as a basis to say that capitalism is bad? (p. 835)

158. Why is there "penury" of the "miserable masses" in some parts of the world? (pp. 836, 842-844).

159. What system exists in the market to combat poverty and for what two "defects" is it criticized? (pp. 837-838).

160. What would happen to the market if there were no income inequalities? Why do people complain about them and struggle for more equality? (pp. 840-842) What do many people think the government can do to combat such inequalities? What problems have theorists encountered with this notion? (pp. 845-846, 850-851).

161. Why do fabulists deny scarcity and, according to Mises, what two things do they fail to comprehend? (pp. 847-848, 850) What have "the harbingers of economic regression" wrought on account of their errors? (p. 854).

162. Does capitalism yield insecurity? Are capitalism's effects on society dreadful? (p. 852). What does Marxism have to do with fostering more certainty? (pp. 871-872) Which two things has capitalism clearly done in

history and during bouts of interventionism? (pp. 854, 859-860, 864-865).

163. What is "interventionism," where does it lead, and why must it disappear? (pp. 855, 858-859, 879-880).

164. According to Mises, what is "the harvest of interventionism? (p. 854).

165. Why "are men and their abilities to work different"? Why does labor itself have a "nonspecific character," yielding different qualities and returns in any vocation, making it impossible to consider labor as a general category? (pp. 134-135).

References

Cobin, John M. (1997), *Building Regulation, Market Alternatives, and Allodial Policy*, Avebury Press: London.

Hayek, Friedrich A. von (1948), "The Meaning of Competition," in Friedrich A. von Hayek, *Individualism and Economic Order*, University of Chicago Press: Chicago, pp. 92-106.

Hayek, Friedrich A. von (1944), *The Road to Serfdom*, University of Chicago Press: Chicago.

Hazlitt, Henry (1979/1946), *Economics in One Lesson*, Crown Publishers: New York.

High, Jack C. (1984), "The Case for Austrian Economics," *Intercollegiate Review*, winter, pp. 37-42.

Holcombe, Randall G. (1995), *Public Policy and the Quality of Life: Market Incentives Versus Government Planning*, Greenwood Press: Westport, Connecticut.

Kirzner, Israel M. (1992), *The Meaning of Market Process: Essays in the Development of Modern Austrian Economics*, Routledge: New York.

Mises, Ludwig von (1966/1949), *Human Action: A Treatise on Economics*, Third Revised Edition, Contemporary Books, Inc. (Henry Regnery Co.): Chicago.

Nutter, G. Warren (1983), *Political Economy and Freedom: A Collection of Essays*, Liberty Press: Indianapolis, Indiana.

O'Rourke, P.J. (1993), "The Liberty Manifesto," *The American Spectator*, July, p. 38.

Orwell, George (1946), *Animal Farm*, Harcourt, Brace and Co.: New York.

Rockwell, Jr., Llewellyn H. (2008a), "Grand Theft Society," *LewRockwell.com*, July 1, retrieved on March 16, 2009.

Rockwell, Jr., Llewellyn H. (2008b), "The Left, the Right, and the State," introduction to his book *The Left, the Right, and the State* (2008), Auburn: Alabama, The Ludwig von Mises Institute, published on *LewRockwell.com*, December 31, retrieved on March 16, 2009.

Rockwell, Jr., Llewellyn H. (1994), "The State of Personal Liberties," *The Washington Times*, Sunday, January 30, section B.

Rothbard, Murray N. (1970/1962), *Man, Economy, and State: A Treatise on Economic Principles*, Nash Publishing: Los Angeles.

Rothbard, Murray N. (1977), *Power and Market: Government and the Economy*, Institute for Humane Studies: Menlo Park, California, 1970 [reprinted by New York University Press, 1977].

Rothbard, Murray N. (1956), "Toward a Reconstruction of Utility and Welfare Economics," in Mary Sennholz, ed., *On Freedom and Free Enterprise: Essays in Honor of Ludwig von Mises*, D. Van Nostrand Company, Princeton, New Jersey, pp. 224-262 [reprinted by the Center for Libertarian Studies, New York, 1977 (occasional paper series no. 3)].

Rowley, Charles K. (1993), *Liberty and the State*, The Shaftesbury Papers, 4, Edward Elgar Publishing Co.: Brookfield, Vermont.

Schansberg, Eric (1996), *Poor Policy: How Government Harms the Poor*, Westview Press: Boulder, Colorado.

Sowell, Thomas (1996), *The Vision of the Anointed Self-Congratulation as a Basis for Social Policy*, Basic Books: New York.

Skinner, Burrhus Frederic (1962), *Walden Two*, Macmillan Co.: New York.

11 The Austrian business cycle and free banking

Money, central banking and the business cycle

As with other forms of interventionism, central bank interventionism has been strongly criticized by Austrian theorists. Austrians have been interested to know how money develops in a catallaxy and how policies which promote government central banking affect both the money supply and the catallaxy. Austrian theorists argue that while money does not manage itself, coordinating institutions will arise in the market process to regulate both money issuance and financial services. Monetary authorities serve merely as a source of destabilization. Thus, Austrians are interested in finding market alternatives to central banking.

The development of money

According to Menger, money is "not an invention of the state" but evolves due to a social need for a more salable or marketable good to facilitate exchange (Menger 1994, pp. 261, 258-259, 268). Apart from state monetary intervention, money will be the commodity which has "preeminent marketability," with its medium of exchange function overriding all other functions (Menger 1994, pp. 271, 280).

As Armen Alchian notes, money is "the intermediary good with the lowest *general* identification costs" (Alchian 1977, p. 120). Thus, a mature and stable monetary system can confer substantial economic benefits in a variety of areas. For instance, Austrians contend that stability in the monetary realm nourishes development by streamlining "roundaboutness" in capital formation. It does so by helping people conserve time (a key component of capital), and by permitting the beneficial "lengthening of the period of production" (Skousen 1990, pp. 136, 139-140, 153, 226).

From an Austrian perspective, money emerges from the workings of an invisible hand, i.e., from an unintended result of human action. It is the emergence of a social convention. In the modern world, people trade their labor services for intrinsically useless pieces of paper or base metal, and these goods thus gain a positive exchange value.[66]

But money did not develop immediately into its modern form. The first money that emerges in any civilization must be *commodity* money. It will be made of an intermediate good that can be used for exchange which is widely saleable. Plus, it will have small costs associated with holding and transporting it. After an appropriate good has been found, there will be catallactic convergence (or a snowballing process) until the good becomes the generally accepted medium of exchange (i.e., money). Eventually, people will begin to realize that it is better to keep an inventory of this good on hand as a medium of exchange. And over time the unit of account (i.e., pound, ounce, etc.) for the money will emerge spontaneously. No public policy action is required.

Over time, the good used as money will undergo further evolution. Its divisibility, durability, uniformity (verifiability), and portability will be improved. For instance, coins

---

[66] Some of this section, and a few other places in the chapter, were adapted from Larry White's two overview lectures on money and banking at the *Austrian Economics Seminar*, June 12th & 14th 1994, at the Foundation for Economic Education, Irvington-on-Hudson, New York.

are a technological advance in the way money is made (rather than just being a useful convention). A coin enhances uniformity, eliminating the need to test for fineness or weight. Markets have provided coinage testing historically, such as when mints coined uniform pieces or coins in gold rush mining areas.

Privately-issued bank notes, which eventually emerge, improve the portability of money (since it is tedious to lug around metal). In addition, banking itself will emerge. Money-changers and goldsmiths have a natural tendency to become deposit banks, especially as they become executors of orders from customers to simply change ownership claims on gold from one account holder to another in satisfaction of some outside private agreement. Modern check-writing does the same thing. Checks are not money, just the claim on someone's bank balance.

The evolution of money is an efficient process. However, problems occur when money issuance is monopolized by government. Bruce Ketler argues that money is a market phenomenon—not a government phenomenon—and monetary regulation via things like legal tender laws will cause economic distortions:

> [L]egal-tender legislation is a form of economic interference. Such legislation directly impairs contracts and interferes with private property rights. Money is not the creation of government. Nor can government guarantee its value. Money is a market phenomenon (Ketler 1992, p. 213).

Other Austrians are even more critical of government-run central banks, especially when they issue paper money without gold backing. In Rockwell's view, monetary policy is simply a means for malevolent government policy:

> Monetary policy is—aside from the war—the primary tool of state aggrandizement. It ensures the growth of

government, finances deficits, rewards special interests, and fixes elections…Our monetary system is not only politically abusive, it also causes inflation and the business cycle (Rockwell 1990, p. 7 of "Introduction" in Rothbard 1990).

Accordingly, White questions the veracity and necessity of central bank monopolization by government:

The most basic question concerning government policy toward money and banking has not changed since the last century's debates over free banking. It is today, as it was then, simply this: Does government have any well-founded reason to play a role in producing money or in regulating private firms that produce money? (White 1992, p. 137)

Central bank monopolization of money and business cycles

In the modern age, the medium of exchange is typically central bank-issued money (what Mises and the Austrians also call "credit," meaning fiduciary media). The central bank controls the money supply, regulates interest rates, and employs hundreds of economists. Unlike Austrian theorists, most economists tend to be less critical of public policies which promote government monopolization and control of the money supply. One of the policy benefits from having a central bank is that it spares the world from having to dig up new gold. However, the public choice problems and costs associated with a central banking system will surely challenge (and likely outweigh) any benefits.

Austrian theorists have been unanimous in their criticism of central banking. For instance, Austrians have blamed monetary and protectionist policies both for causing and perpetuating the Great Depression of the 1930s and the Financial Crisis beginning in 2008. Consider Rockwell's criticism of central banking in the United States:

> The Federal Reserve's stated goal was to provide credit "at rates of interest low enough to stimulate, protect, and prosper all kinds of legitimate business." Even though this expansionist policy did not result in a general rise in prices, it damaged the economy at a deeper level. After the credit expansion ended in 1928, the economy tumbled. But as Johnson notes, "all this was to be expected; it was healthy; it ought to have been welcomed." Recessions and depressions "sorted out the sheep from the goats, liquidated the unhealthy elements in the economy and turned out the parasites." The Austrian explanation of the Great Depression is that this sorting-out process was unnecessarily prolonged. As Rothbard, Lionel Robbins, Benjamin Anderson, and many others have pointed out, the extraordinary interventions in the market by both Hoover and Roosevelt—from cartelizing industry and labor force to erecting trade barriers—transformed what should have been a year-long bust into a decade-long nightmare (Rockwell 1992, p. 75).

According to Austrian theory, the central bank actually causes the business cycle, i.e., periodic "boom and bust" cycles in the economy. Austrians reject any policy which entails having a central bank for this reason. They argue that the central bank is a treacherous means for government to manipulate and debase the currency by inflation, i.e., a means of implicit taxation (often to pay for deficit finance). Moreover, the Austrian theory of the business cycle says that if the central bank lowers interest rates by monetary policy, then people will borrow more at the artificially lower rates. People will be fooled at first, but expectations will adjust if there are repeated monetary manipulations.

Rent seeking political consultants' use of monetary policy

Correspondingly, public choice theory suggests that rent seeking political consultants or regressive entrepreneurs alert to opportunities might arise to aid political actors in selecting the optimal level of monetary policy. Their goal would be to obtain the greatest amount of political benefits through monetary manipulation without adversely altering the expectations of the public.

In the United States, the federal government has been largely successful in attaining this level in the twentieth century. In other nations, especially in South America, the public eye has become more jaded toward monetary policy. In countries like Panama, Ecuador, Bolivia, and Argentina, the preferred currency is the U.S. Dollar, while in other places legal currency substitutes are used.

Chile's Unidad de Fomento (UF)

In Chile, for example, most time sensitive contracts, loans, and savings accounts are denominated in UFs (*Unidades de Fomento*). The mutable value of the UF in pesos is pub-lished daily in the Chilean media, and serves as an effective means of eliminating inflation risk and curbing the political power available through monetary policy. Prices for houses and apartments are often quoted in UFs rather than pesos, as are insurance deductibles and maximum limits for cov-ered charges in policies. Using the UF means that compa-nies do not have to modify contracts to reflect changes in the value of the peso.

Astute political actors in other nations will surely loathe losing power due to such real currency substitutes like the UF. It would come as little surprise to Austrian or public choice theorists if such actors try to ban them by legislation or try to preserve substantial monetary intrusions—but never so much that their policy becomes a public annoy-ance. Otherwise, if these actors do not protect their benefits, opportunities will be created for progressive entrepreneurs to develop currency substitute solutions that remove the uneasiness of people generated by monetary policy (as was the case with the UF in Chile).

How the business cycle is created by the central bank

Consequently, absent any innovation like the UF, if the central bank can inflate in a more or less clandestine manner, then capitalists and entrepreneurs might be fooled into concluding that the abundance of money is a signal of real economic growth. Hence, the benefits from monetary policy may accrue to political actors or rent seekers. The wayward conclusion of the capitalists and entrepreneurs will lead them to build up inventories and expand productive capacity. This phase is called the "boom."

Roger Garrison, an Austrian economics scholar, argues that the interest rate, if it tells the truth, tells how many projects can be completed by genuine savings. However, the central bank can create an artificial boom. A genuine boom comes from people preferring to save more and thus more being invested; it is an expansion of capacity via a lower rate of interest.

Garrison's model of the business cycle

In Garrison's model, as the production possibilities curve shifts out, people prefer to save more (i.e., show that they prefer future over present consumption). Accordingly, the supply of loanable funds increases. Normally, the interest rate disciplines catallactic activity by discouraging or inhibiting overly-ambitious projects. But expansionary monetary policy, which will tend to be popular with vote-seeking politicians, can cause the opposite result.

For instance, vote-seeking politicians have an incentive to create a boom to enhance their probability of reelection. While genuine growth comes from savings, a policy of monetary expansion to create an artificial boom leads to economic detraction. People will save less due to the lower rate of interest and thus consume more. During a depression, the production possibilities frontier actually pulls back since projects are abandoned that can not be completed.[67]

Naturally, if a monetary expansion is determined to be artificial, steps will be taken by firms to reduce inventories and close plants to slow production. The cumulative effect of this reversion generates recessions or depressions, i.e., the "bust." Normally these economic downturns are short-lived and self-correcting. However, damaging public policies, e.g., protectionism, can prolong the downturn by inflicting other harmful or distortive measures in the catallaxy. Such damaging policies were promoted by presidents Franklin D. Roosevelt and Barack Obama.

Public choice enhancements to the Austrian model

Furthermore, the Austrian conception of the business cycle can be broadened by public choice theory. Perhaps political actors have an incentive to foster or perpetuate economic problems in order to accomplish self-interested ends: e.g., to bolster votes, budgets, or legislative power. They may vow to "fix" economic problems—which were likely created by public policies in the first place—to enhance visions of market failure in the public mind (and thus create artificial demand for more government). Economic trouble could also be used to compensate successful rent seeking firms by damaging their struggling or fledgling competitors.

In the market process, economic problems will be expunged by an often painful self-correcting process and then genuine growth will follow—until the next intervention by

---

[67] Part of this paragraph was adapted from Roger Garrison's lecture on the business cycle at the *Austrian Economics Seminar*, June 14th, 1994, at the Foundation for Economic Education, Irvington-on-Hudson, New York.

the central bank triggers another business cycle. But public choice theory suggests that political actors might have a perverse incentive to create and even prolong economic downturns depending on where they are in the election cycle.

For instance, it might be politically expedient for a President to create an economic problem at the beginning of his election cycle, then implement the steps to solve the problem, and finally take credit for solving the problem as his reelection date approaches. This activity can be bolstered in the public mind by finding serious academics (or rent seeking ones) which support the notion that markets cause the business cycle, necessitating public policy to fix market failures and stabilize the economy.

The inherent dangers of having a central bank

For Austrian theorists, giving control of the money supply to government is dangerous. Rockwell contends that Austrians have the correct prescription to mitigate the government-sponsored business cycle:

> The Marxists were wrong: we shouldn't overthrow capitalism to get rid of business cycles. The Keynesians were wrong: the government management only makes things worse. And the Monetarists were wrong: stable prices courtesy of the central bank produce underlying instabilities. The Austrians, however, are right. Business cycles can be eliminated, but only with sweeping reforms. To end business cycles, we must scrap the institutional barriers to a free market in money and banking—bailouts, deposit insurance, and central banking—and establish sound money, market-set interest rates, and a decentralized monetary regime resistant to political meddling. Without central bank intervention, we would have to brace ourselves for a short, painful period of allowing malinvestments to be washed out of the system. Politics

may work against such an approach, but it is the only way to insure that the next recovery starts on a sound foundation (Rockwell 1992, p. 77).

G. Edward Griffin, who writes popular historical accounts germane to public policy, concurs that central banking is the cause of much economic distortion:

It is widely believed that panics, boom-bust cycles, and depressions are caused by unbridled competition between banks; thus the need for government regulation. The truth is just the opposite. These disruptions in the free market are the result of government *prevention* of competition by the granting of monopolistic power to a *central* bank. In the absence of a monopoly, individual banks may operate in a fraudulent manner only to a limited extent and for a short period of time. Inevitably, they will be exposed by their more honest competitors and will be forced out of business. Yes, their depositors will be injured by the bankruptcy, but the damage will be limited to a relatively few and will occur only now and then...But, when a central bank is allowed to protect the fraudulent operators and to force *all* banks to function the same, the forces of the competition can no longer dampen the effect. The expansion becomes universal and gigantic. And, of course, so does the contraction. Except for the bankers and the politicians, *everyone* is injured at the same time; depression is *everywhere*; and recovery is long delayed (Griffin 1994, p. 345).

Within a central banking system, individual banks facing uncertainty will find it difficult to determine if there is a genuine increase in the demand for money because of the decentralized knowledge. An expansion may be genuine or artificial but at a local level the bank can hardly know. When banks perceive a reduction in the turnover of money, they may conclude that the demand for money has increased, leading them to expand loans for the construction of capital goods. Thus, there is a nexus between savings and the supply of loanable funds.

Since the knowledge needed for this process is transmitted from the bottom up, i.e., from the actions of numerous individuals with fragments of social knowledge, the capital structure is created spontaneously via individual choices. Because of the knowledge problem, it is impossible for central bankers to optimally enhance the capital structure in an economy. Hence, the policies of the central bank can lead to intra-system distortions. Alternatively, a free market in note issue, i.e., free banking, can handle the transmission of dispersed knowledge without a central bank.

What is free banking?

Austrians theorists have two divergent views of what should replace the central bank: free banking or 100% reserve banking. Free bankers, led by White and Selgin, argue that in a free market people should be able to contract for banking services *without restriction* (whether of the 100% gold reserves or the fractional reserve variety)—just as they do for other services. White summarizes the system:

> Free banking, generically speaking, denotes a monetary system without a central bank, under which the issuing of currency and deposit money is left to legally unrestricted private banks (White 1995, p. 1).

Under a policy of free banking, no regulation or intervention by the state would be permitted. People would be able to freely choose to accept the risks of depositing their funds into a fractional reserve bank, in exchange for receiving some interest on their deposits. As a result, banking firms will spontaneously emerge to provide typical banking services as well as currency or note issue. There is an endogenous money supply in free banking—meaning that the system is self-regulating. Rivalry between banking firms will serve to enhance note quality. The threat of potential losses from note-redemption "duels" will cause bankers to form organizations to clear each other's notes.

The main feature of note dueling is storing up a competing bank's note and causing havoc at the competing bank (and public concern) by attempting to redeem them all at once, taxing the bank's reserves and making it appear unstable. Since all banks face the same threat, restraint is advisable. Ultimately, banks will cooperate with each other because it is in their best interests to make banking services as convenient as possible for customers.

Table 11.1 Free banking

Free banking is:
"[A] monetary system without a central bank, under which the issuing of currency and deposit money is left to legally unrestricted private banks."—Larry White

Since bank notes are payable to the bearer on demand they are, unlike checks, bounce-proof. Normally, these notes would not be currency or widely-used money since they have nothing to do with other banks. However, if an arrangement were established among a network of banks to accept them at face value, then the notes may serve as currency. Note dueling becomes a very costly activity, because the threat of surprise redemption raids will cause private banks to hold larger reserves. Thus, cooperation will be a natural outcome, along with a clearing mechanism. All banks will have an incentive to cooperate since they want to maximize profits.

Multilateral clearing occurs when all the private banks get together and aggregate their notes and, due to the law of large numbers, they are allowed to hold smaller reserves.

This clearing system is a spontaneous and unintended benefit of competition. Consequently, a banknote clearinghouse represents the institutional embodiment of a spontaneous order, a unified system where specie units are accepted at par. Selgin's work has been instrumental in demonstrating how an efficient and effective system of free banking would evolve in the free market (see Selgin 1988 and 1996). White has also contributed to this research area (see Selgin and White 1987).

The 100% gold reserves vision

In the 100% gold reserves vision, private banks take deposits and retain them in their vaults. They profit by charging for withdrawals and deposits, or for storage. The advocates of 100% reserve banking, led by Rothbard and Joe Salerno, and strongly promoted by policy analysts like Rockwell and Griffin, argue that fractional reserve banking of any kind is fraudulent—including free banking. The fraud occurs, they say, because all depositors cannot regain their money (gold) on demand (since it has been lent to others). Thus, the bank is not behaving like a warehouse as it should.

From this perspective, taking customer deposits is tantamount to theft. The depositors' money has been taken for other uses (some of which may not meet with the approval of the depositors) to enhance the banker's profits. The weakness of this view is that under a system of voluntarism with a free market, people should be able to enter into whatever agreements they wish. For instance, if they wish to permit others to use their money for a fee (i.e., interest), then they assume the risks associated with the fractional reserve system. To support the 100% gold reserves vision one must also support public policy that prohibits voluntary contracting between consenting adults for fractional reserve banking services. Consumers must be protected from the fraudulent and inherently evil system.

In addition, 100% reserve banking advocates are opposed to fractional reserve banking because it has built-in instability, related to the instability caused by the knowledge problem. Rothbard chides fractional reserve banking and warns against free banking as well:

The dire economic effects of fractional bank money will be explored in the next chapter. Here we conclude that, morally, such banking would have no more right to exist in a truly free market than any other form of implicit theft. It is true that the note or deposit does not actually say on its face that the warehouse guarantees to keep a full backing of gold on hand at all times. But the bank does promise to redeem on demand, and so when it issues any fake receipts, it is already committing fraud, since it immediately becomes impossible for the bank to keep its pledge and redeem all of its notes and deposits. Fraud, therefore, is immediately being committed when the act of issuing pseudo-receipts takes place. *Which* particular receipts are fraudulent can only be discovered *after* a run on the bank has occurred (since all the receipts look alike), and the late-coming claimants are left high and dry. If fraud is to be prescribed in a free society, then fractional reserve banking would have to meet the same fate. Suppose, however, that fraud and fractional reserve banking are permitted, with the banks only required to fulfill their obligations to redeem in gold on demand. Any failure to do so would mean instant bankruptcy. Such a system has come to be known as "free banking." Would there then be a heavy fraudulent issue of money substitutes, with resulting artificial creation of new money? Many people have assumed so, and believed that "wildcat banking" would then simply inflate the money supply astronomically. But, on the contrary, "free banking" would lead to a far "harder" monetary system than we have today (Rothbard 1990, pp. 50-51; also see Rothbard 1970, pp. 708-709).

Nevertheless, it is unclear why there is fraud when the fractional reserve aspect of a bank is fully disclosed in the contract and consented to by the customer. Moreover, the 100% gold reserve banking never fully emerged in history, whereas markets have spontaneously generated free banking.

Free banking as a functional policy

In the late twentieth century, the free banking idea received favorable reviews in the mainstream press. Writing for *Forbes*, Peter Brimelow provided a more popular rationale for advocating free banking, citing White, Hayek, and even Milton Friedman as leading proponents of the policy (see Brimelow 1988, pp. 243-250).

Free bankers contend that central banking—like other government regulatory institutions generally—have inherent inadequacies due to the knowledge problem. Moreover, public choice concerns will tend to curtail the effectiveness and efficiency of regulation (see chapter 8). In the British and ante-bellum American banking industries, regulation supposedly designed to reduce instability actually caused more of it. Regulation of banks failed to improve the quality or security it was ordained to provide. As White notes:

> Bank failures should not be expected to occur in droves in the absence of restrictions on adequate bank capitalisation, branch banking, and other means of absorbing or diversifying the risks of banking. Such restrictions were responsible for the instability of the English country banks and the banks in certain American states (White 1995, p. 144).

In a free banking system, reserve losses (i.e., when gold is demanded via the clearinghouse) serve as a signal to the bank that it needs to reduce its liabilities in circulation. When banks create capital adequacy, they make themselves less run-prone and the system more stable along with it. Plus, banks will tend to use legal enhancements: equity, option clause, and solvency assurances, to improve their stability—even with fractional reserves. Karen Vaughn summarizes the development of the free banking idea by White and Selgin:

Lawrence White's work on monetary theory managed to hit mainstream journals (1984a, 1987), although his most interesting work from an Austrian perspective appeared more in specialized publications or in book form (1984b; 1989). His book *Free banking in Britain: theory, experience and debate* (1984b) explored both the history of free banking in England to show that free banking had actually worked well in Scotland in the late eighteenth and nineteenth centuries, and the theory of free banking to show its contemporary relevance to the debate over appropriate financial institutions. White's work had the advantage of being able to tie into contemporary debate over both the positive and normative effects of monetary institutions that did not rely exclusively on Austrian sources. After the inflationary debacle of the 1970s, the design of monetary institutions was an important economic issue. However, White's approach was clearly drawn from the Austrian tradition, which emphasized the role of a central banking system in destabilizing an economy. Further, Hayek's essay "The Denationalization of Money" (1978b) helped to spur Austrian thinking about monetary institutions. The Austrian view on this issue was to argue for non-regulated, free banking as a remedy to the instabilities caused by central banks and regulated fractional reserve banks. By developing an analysis of how a true free banking system could work to the benefit of the economy, White was further developing the Austrian case for the advantages of unregulated competition over managed, central banking. White's student Selgin

(1988; Selgin and White, 1987) took his argument one step further and provided an evolutionary account of how a free banking system could emerge without government direction or regulation to provide all the necessary services that one expects from a banking system. Selgin's analysis was clearly a continuation of Menger's story about the emergence of money from barter, and an illustration of Hayek's claim for the superiority of evolved rather than constructed institutions (Vaughn 1994, pp. 116-117).

Free banking also permits people to economize on gold production (i.e., as with central banking, people might have significantly less need to mine gold). Over time, private banks issuing currency under a free banking system will discover the optimal level of gold reserves to maintain. White suggests that this level might be small and consequently the costs of maintaining bank reserves will be minimized:

Banks are free to hold fractional reserves, allowing society to economise greatly on the use of gold. If banks generally find their optimal reserves of specie to be in the neighbourhood of 2 per cent of demand liabilities, as several Scottish banks did, the annual resource costs of bank reserves fall enormously. We must add to the costs of reserves the costs of the public's holding of coin, if we assume that a free banking system would operate with full-bodied coins (White 1995, p. 148).

Free banking is the most consistently Austrian view

White argues that free banking, rather than the 100% gold reserves alternative, is strongly supported in the Austrian tradition, not only in Hayek's evolutionary thought but also in Mises's support of fractional reserve banking. Moreover, he argues that Mises implicitly supported free banking, rather than a system encumbered with restrictions by government like a 100% gold reserves system.

Ludwig von Mises argued against a legal ban on fractional-reserve banking in the context of a gold standard, primarily on the grounds that such a ban (1) would make the economy more vulnerable to money demand shocks, and (2) would needlessly increase the cost of supplying the economy with the media of exchange. In contrast to the Currency School, he argued that a ban on the future issue of fractional-reserve bank money was not necessary in order to prevent over-expansion by banks. Over-expansion would be most effectively prevented by allowing competitive banking and note-issue, free from any interference that would release banks from their contractual obligations to redeem their liabilities in gold. Free banking would compel banks to behave cautiously, and to limit the volume of their liabilities to the amount demanded by the public at the existing purchasing power of money. Mises concluded that monetary freedom, and not any program of restrictions or privileges, offers the only real remedy for the monetary upheavals the world has known (White 1992, pp. 528-529).

Free banking thus provides the most consistently Austrian idea of banking. In addition, Selgin contends that free banking is the most effective way to deal with the knowledge problem. Central banking mishaps can be particularly distortive because the money supply has such a broad impact on the entire catallaxy, and neither central bankers nor regulators have the requisite knowledge to rectify the distortions caused by their policies.

[T]he existence of competitive markets for all relevant factors used to produce inside money does not significantly lessen the knowledge problem faced by a central bank. Therefore, the risk of incorrect management of the money supply is not limited by its being the only resource in the economy subject to centralized administration. Furthermore, an improperly managed money supply leads to much greater economic discoordination than an incorrect supply of any other good or service. Excess demand or excess supply of money affects spending in numerous other markets, and hence affects the entire system of market price and profit signals (Selgin 1988, p. 95).

Alternatively, under free banking, coordination is maintained automatically. Thus, central banking must, like socialist planning, attempt to find alternate means of obtaining the requisite knowledge for pricing and resource allocation. Selgin continues:

> When the currency supply is monopolized, as it is under central banking, the clearing mechanism ceases to be an effective guide to changing the money supply in accordance with consumer preferences. Creation of excessive currency and deposit credits by a central bank will not cause a short-run increase in its liquidity costs. This means that other knowledge surrogates (including both means for informing money-supply decisions and means for their timely *ex post* evaluation) must be found to replace surrogate knowledge naturally present under free banking. That is why there is need for "monetary policy" and money-supply "guidelines" under centralized issue (Selgin 1988, p. 96).

As a matter of public policy, White argues for adopting free banking in contemporary society. Not only would free banking preclude knowledge and public choice problems associated with interventionism, but it would be compatible with many modern innovations in the development of money. White notes:

In Western Europe and especially the United States, competitive innovations in banking and near-banking designed to overcome regulations have brought the efficacy of banking regulations under scrutiny. Most recently, advances in digital payment technology have begun to foreshadow a world in which central bank currency is obsolete, perhaps replaced by privately issued currency in the form of balances written to 'smart cards' or downloaded to personal computers, and transferred by means of 'electronic wallets' or over the Internet (Browne and Cronin, 1994, Levy, 1994, White, 1995a). Smart-card balances, transferable without bank involvement, may become the 21st-century version of the private bank note. The basic monetary policy question, once debated with reference to the bank notes again arises: Does the government have any well-founded reason to play a role in producing (electronic) money, or in regulating private firms that produce (electronic) money? Specifically, is there any good reason to place legal restrictions on private firms that provide digital payment media or money-transfer services (White 1995, p. 138)?

White, Selgin, and other free bankers do not think so.

Evidence of free banking

Free banking is a theoretically plausible system. Money is not a "public good" (see chapter 12), and other studies of regulation have concluded that the public provision of private goods has been inefficient and perhaps ineffective. Policies of inefficient public provision are unnecessary. Note-issuing services would plausibly be no different than other market-provided goods, leaving little reason to maintain a system of government provision of money. However, central banking might be justified on grounds of imperfect information which leads markets to produce less desirable results than government intervention. The policy question then becomes empirical: "Would free banking truly work?"

The ante-bellum American version of free banking

There is much controversy over the viability of free banking due to the experience in the ante-bellum United States. Yet White argues that much of what is thought of as having been free banking at that time was nothing of the kind. He cautions that banking systems considered to be free have often really been heavily regulated private banking with a free market label. Thus, in the same way that central banking is prone to failures, regulated "free" banking often succumbed to knowledge or public choice problems, resulting in economic debacles. Thus, White argues that free banking period in the United States is not the best or only example of free banking from which we can make policy conclusions.

> Free banking as a monetary régime thus comprises two conceptually distinct elements: (1) unregulated issue of transferable liabilities, and (2) unmanipulated supply of base money or basic cash. Government plays no active role respecting the quantity of money produced inside or outside the banking industry. The experience of Scottish free banking and the arguments of the Free Banking School bear most obviously on the question of deregulation of inside money. But they also shed some light on the potential desirability of an outside money free of central bank control. They are particularly relevant to the question of the desirability of a precious metallic standard, because the most common objections to a specie

standard have been the expense of an exclusively metallic money and the supposed inherent instability of a banking system that economises on specie by introducing fractional reserve inside monies. The Scottish experience indicates that in fact the resource costs of a specie standard can be kept low without instability. An appreciation of the success and stability of Scottish free banking takes on special importance in light of the notoriety of the 19th century American experience with state-regulated banking systems commonly but misleadingly called 'free banking.' Many economists today who favour deregulated free markets for other goods and services, yet fail to extend *laissez-faire* principles to money and banking, apparently believe that unregulated banking proved a failure in the last century. Like the Currency School did, they misleadingly point to American experience as an example of unregulated banking in practice. Unlike the Currency School, which had to try to explain away Scottish experience, today's monetary economists are evidently unaware of a strong counter-example (White 1995, pp. 139-140).

Thus, while the free banking period in the United States is often cited as evidence of the failure of markets to provide banking services, the evidence is not clear. Susan Lee and Peter Passell remark that the failures of free banking in the United States are not as evident as commonly thought:

The "free" in free banking refers to free entry into the banking business, not freedom to conduct business as the banker pleased. Between 1837 and 1860, the majority of states, particularly those in the West, experimented with some form of free banking. Typically, the law allowed anyone to set up a bank, provided they backed their note issue with securities kept on deposit with the state banking authority. If the bank failed to honor its liabilities, the state would sell the securities and compensate depositors and noteholders. Some free banking states, like Louisiana, could boast of perfect success in protecting bank customers. Others—notably Michigan—became refuges for wildcatters. Rockoff pins this partial failure of free banking to the type of security required by the state. Michigan allowed banks to use land mortgages at face value, regardless of their true worth. Thus a wildcatter might deposit a $10,000 mortgage on land which the mortgagee had little chance of repaying, and then issue $10,000 worth of notes to unwary clients. In Minnesota, nearly worthless railroad bonds were accepted as security at 95 percent of their issue value. Much the same thing happened in New Jersey, where the law allowed the use of heavily depreciated bonds issued by other states as security at face value. The fault was thus not in the free banking concept, but in the way it was applied. Actually the case against free banking is even weaker than the preceding paragraphs imply. When free banking did lead to failures, the losses were less spectacular than historians have generally believed. Rockoff's computations show a total *cumulative* loss through 1860 from bank failures to be no more than $1.9 million, and perhaps a great deal less. This redistribution of wealth from noteholder to wildcatter represents less than $1/100^{th}$ of 1 percent of national income during the free banking era. It is true that losses were concentrated in just a few states—Michigan, Indiana, New York—but even so, they hardly represent a significant fraction of wealth. In one sense, the "losses" discussed above weren't losses at all. The $1.9 million was not destroyed; it simply changed owners. But there were true efficiency losses from wildcatting, too. People hold money instead of other assets because of its convenience as a medium of exchange (Lee and Passell 1979, pp. 123-124).

Furthermore, even Rothbard (no fan of free banking) argues that free banking failure in the United States was precipitated by government coercion. It was government failure rather than market failure which led to trouble in the free banking period in the United States:

In the United States, mass suspension of specie payment in times of bank troubles became almost a tradition. It started in the War of 1812. Most of the country's banks were located in New England, a section unsympathetic to America's entry into the war. These banks refused to lend for war purposes, and so the government borrowed from the new banks in the other states. These banks issued new paper money to make the loans. The inflation was so great that calls for redemption flooded into the new banks, especially from the conservative nonexpanding banks of New England, where the government spent most of its money on war goods. As a result, there was a mass "suspension" in 1814, lasting for over two years (well beyond the end of the war); during that time, banks sprouted up, issuing notes with no need to redeem in gold or silver. This suspension set a precedent for succeeding economic crises; 1819, 1837, 1857 and so forth. As a result of this tradition, the banks realized that they need have no fear of bankruptcy after an inflation, and this, of course, stimulated inflation and "wildcat banking." Those writers who point to nineteenth century America as a horrid example of "free banking," fail to realize the importance of this clear dereliction of duty by the states in every financial crisis. The governments and the banks, persuaded the public of the justice of their acts. In fact, anyone trying to get his money back during a crisis was considered "unpatriotic" and a despoiler of his fellowmen, while banks were often commended for patriotically bailing out the community in a time of trouble. Many people, however, were bitter at the entire proceeding and from this sentiment grew the famous "hard money" Jacksonian movement that flourished before the Civil War (Rothbard 1990, pp. 70-71).

Actually, public aversion to government-run central banking extended from the founding of the United States. For instance, Thomas Jefferson vehemently opposed interest groups who sought to centralize banking (see Griffin 1994, pp. 341-342). Andrew Jackson was elected on a platform opposing banking interests, but not without a nasty fight. Griffin remarks about the trouble generated by fraudulent banking in the ante-bellum United States:

The government had encouraged widespread banking fraud during the War of 1812 as an expedient for paying its bills, and this had left the nation in monetary chaos. At the end of the war, instead of allowing the fraudulent banks to fall and letting the free market heal the damage, Congress decided to protect the banks, to organize the fraud, and to perpetuate the losses. It did this by creating the nation's third central bank called the Second Bank of the United States. The new bank was almost an exact carbon copy of the previous one. It was authorized to create money for the federal government and to regulate state banks. It influenced larger amounts of capital and was better organized across states than the old bank. Consequently its policies had a greater impact on the creation and extinguishing of the nation's money supply. For the first time in our history, the effects began to ricochet across the entire country at once instead of being confined to geographical regions. The age of the boom-bust cycle had at last arrived in America. In 1820, public opinion began to swing back in favor of the sound-money principles espoused by Jeffersonian Republicans. But since the Republican party had by then abandoned those principles, a new coalition was formed, headed by Martin Van Buren and Andrew Jackson, called the Democratic Party. One of its primary platforms was the abolishment of the Bank. After Jackson was elected in 1828, he began in full earnest to bring that about (Griffin 1994, pp. 359-360).

Shortly after this time, the free banking era in the United States began. With the political process embroiled over the banking issue, undoubtedly replete with public choice problems, public policy with respect to banking was going to change. Griffin continues:

There was a parallel development at this time [1838-1860] called "free banking." The name is an insult to truth. What was called free banking was merely the conversion of banks from corporations to private associations. Aside from no longer receiving a charter from the state, practically every other aspect of the system remained the same, including a multitude of government controls, regulations, supports, and other blocks against the free market. Selgin reminds us that "permission to set up a bank was usually accompanied by numerous restrictions, including especially required loans to the state." The free banks were no less fraudulent than the chartered banks. The old custom was revived of rushing gold coins from one bank to another just ahead of the bank examiners, and of "putting a ballast of lead, broken glass and (appropriately) ten-penny nails in the box under a thinner covering of gold coins." When one such free bank collapsed in Massachusetts, it was discovered that its bank note circulation of $500,000 was backed by exactly $86.48. Professor Hans Sennholz writes:

Although economists disagree on many things, most see eye to eye on their acceptance of political control.... These economists invariably point at American money and banking before the Civil War which, in their judgment, confirms their belief. In particular, they cite the "Free Banking Era" of 1838-1860 as a frightening example of turbulent banking and, therefore, applaud the legislation that strengthened the role of government. In reality, the instability experienced during the Free Banking Era was not caused by anything inherent in banking, but resulted form extensive political intervention.... "Free banking" acts...did not repeal burdensome statutory provisions and regulatory directives. In fact they added a few.

For banking to have been truly free, the states would have had to do only two things: (1) enforce banking contracts the same as any other contract, and then (2) step out of the picture. By enforcing banking contracts, the executives of any bank which failed to redeem its currency in specie would have been sent to prison, an eventuality which soon would have put a halt to currency over-issue. By stepping out of the picture and dropping the pretense of protecting the public with a barrage of rules, regulations, safety funds, and guarantees, people would have realized that it was *their* responsibility to be cautious and informed. But, instead, the banks continued to enjoy the special privilege of suspending payment without punishment, and the politicians clamored to convince the voters they were taking care of everything. In short, throughout this entire period of bank failures, economic chaos, and fleecing of both investors and taxpayers, America tried everything *except* full redemption by gold and silver. As the name of Andrew Jackson faded into history, so did the dream of honest banking. Not all banks were corrupt, and certainly not all bankers were conspirators against the public. There were many examples of honest men striving to act in an ethical manner in the discharge of their fiduciary responsibilities. But they were severely hampered by the system within which they labored, a system which, as previously illustrated punished prudence and rewarded recklessness. In balance, the prudent banker was pushed aside by the mainstream and became but a footnote to the history of that period (Griffin 1994, pp. 366-368).[68]

Consequently, the so-called free banking era in the United States hardly provides a criticism of genuine free banking. Alternatively, looking beyond the label applied, we find that this era of banking provides a striking example of government failure and the tremendous problems that can result from government intervention.

Chilean free banking

Free banking in Chile has likewise been derided as having devastating results and is used as evidence for the necessity of central banking. However, Selgin points out that, like the experience in ante-bellum America, the Chilean free banking trouble was the result of interventionism and regulation. Thus Chile's free banking failure was a government failure, rather than a market failure. As Selgin notes:

> Free banking did not fail in Chile. Like many other manifestations of economic liberty it was undermined by government intervention before it could prove itself (Selgin 1990, p. 7).

Free banking in Chile had begun well, as Selgin continues:

> The period from 1860 to 1874 was exceptional in that the government refrained from interfering with the free-banking law or with the principle of convertibility. The consequence was an era of remarkable growth and prosperity, free of monetary crises (Selgin 1990, p. 5).

---

[68] The long quotation is from Hans F. Sennholz (1989), "Old Banking Myths," *The Freeman*, May, pp. 175-176.

On the contrary, the banks appear, overall, to have succeeded admirably in preserving their "margin of safety" despite exceptional, legislatively-inspired demands to convert notes and deposits into gold (Selgin 1990, p. 6).

However it ended in a malaise due to bimetallic public policy. Selgin cites government rather than market failure as the cause of the problem, as well as rebuffing Rothbard's contention that free banking is inherently unstable.

Regrettably that era of unadulterated freedom in banking did not last long as unwarranted government interference once again began to take its toll. A banking crisis which began in 1874 culminated in the suspension of specie payments in 1878. Fetter blames this crises and subsequent disorders on the free-banking law of 1860, and Rothbard embraces this interpretation. Yet the facts do not support Fetter's conclusion. They suggest, rather, that the events leading to the suspension of specie payments in 1878 were largely a consequence of Chile's *bimetallic legislation of 1851* fixing the legal rate of exchange silver to gold at 16.39:1 (Selgin 1990, p. 6).

Correspondingly, Pedro Jeftanovic and Rolf Lüders found empirical evidence suggesting that Chilean banks during the free banking era functioned satisfactorily and that prices remained stable (Jeftanovic and Lüders 2006, p. 30).

The Scottish version of free banking

Successful historical examples of a policy can serve to enhance its viability. In contrast to pseudo-free banking in the United States, the Scottish banking system (1800-1845) provides an interesting case of genuine free banking. Acknowledging that the Scottish system had imperfections,

White argued that it was close enough to genuine free banking to warrant the designation.

Scotland, a relatively industrialised nation with highly developed monetary, credit and banking institutions, enjoyed remarkable monetary stability during the eighteenth and early nineteenth centuries. During this time Scotland had no monetary policy, no central bank and very few legal restrictions of the banking industry. Entry was open and the right of note issue universal. If the conjunction of these facts seems curious by today's lights, it is because central banking came to be taken for granted in the twentieth century, while the theory of competitive banking and note issue on a specie standard fell into disrepair (White 1995, p. 21).

In his study, White summarizes some of the important outcomes of the Scottish free banking system, notably that banking-related chaos was held to a minimum. Consequently, he finds reason to support free banking as a market-based policy alternative.

These constitute the lessons, as we see them, taught by free banking theory and Scottish free banking experience...the record of free banking in Scotland indicates, contrary to what otherwise might be plausible, that under free conditions (1) bad bank notes do not drive out good; (2) counterfeiting does not pose a major problem; (3) banks are not inherently prone to over-issue and suspension (4) banks will not hold chronically insufficient or excessive reserves; (5) bank runs are not an endemic problem; (6) there is no clear need for a lender of last resort; (7) no pyramiding of reserves, making credit inherently unstable, takes place; (8) no natural monopoly exists in the production of paper currency; and (9) proliferation of bank-note brands is not a problem (White 1995, p. 147).

Indeed, White concludes that free banking in Scotland, although not perfect, was a success.

The successful record of free banking in Scotland was held up by the Free Banking School as evidence that government has no legitimate reason to intervene in the provision for (non-metallic) money. Scotland's experience remains relevant in re-examining the question today. It still provides useful evidence on the workability of monetary freedom (White 1995, p. 137).

There are many historical examples of free banking successes. As White points out:

Proponents of free banking have traditionally pointed to the relatively unrestricted monetary systems of Scotland (1716–1844), New England (1820–1860), and Canada (1817–1914) as models. Other episodes of the competitive provision of banknotes took place in Sweden, Switzerland, France, Ireland, Spain, parts of China, and Australia. In total, more than sixty episodes of competitive note issue are known, with varying amounts of legal restrictions. In all such episodes, the countries were on a gold or silver standard (except China, which used copper). (White 2008)

Private banks in Scotland, Northern Ireland, and Hong Kong still issue paper currency notes (White 2008).

Conclusion: free banking is the optimal policy

Selgin laments that more people have not recognized the virtues of having a free banking system.

Regrettably, most people are much better at imagining catastrophic banking failures than they are at imagining how such failures might be avoided by an open, diverse, and non-hierarchical banking industry (Selgin 1996, p. 9).

White's thesis about Scotland was criticized by Rothbard, Joseph Salerno, and others which promote a 100% gold reserve banking policy and by those who explain the Scottish experience differently (e.g., it was largely due to the impact of limited liability laws). However, White has answered his detractors and a lively debate continues within and outside the Austrian School.

In terms of practicality, it seems that free banking is an important free market research program and a public policy option that can be arguably demonstrated as a historical success and justified on the basis of knowledge and public choice problems. The 100% gold reserves vision can likewise be justified, but there is little historical evidence to support it as a policy option. Moreover, it may be questioned in terms of its practicality and because it would restrict people from voluntarily contracting into fractional reserve arrangements if they choose to do so. Nevertheless, either Austrian School option would be markedly superior to central banking.

For class discussion

(1) Is there enough gold in the earth's crust to run modern economies? (2) Can a modern economy run as well as it presently does or better without a central bank? (3) Would you prefer to pay a fee and have a 100% gold reserves bank or enter into a contract for interest-bearing account under a fractional reserve but free banking system?

References

Alchian, Armen A. (1977), "Why Money?," in *Economic Forces at Work*, Liberty Press: Indianapolis, Indiana, pp. 111-123.

Brimelow, Peter (1988), "Do You Want to Be Paid in Rockefellers? In Wristons? Or How About a Hayek?," *Forbes*, May 30, pp. 243-250.

Griffin, G. Edward (1994), *The Creature from Jekyll Island: A Second Look at the Federal Reserve*, American Opinion Publishing: Appleton, Wisconsin.

Jeftanovic, Pedro and Rolf Lüders Sch (2006), "La banca libre en Chile," Retrieved on March 18, 2009 from http://www.bcentral.cl/conferencias-seminarios/ seminarios/pdf/luders_jeftanovic.pdf

Ketler, Bruce W. (1992), "The Legal Status of Money," in John W. Robbins and Mark Spangler, eds., *A Man of Principle: Essays in Honor of Hans F. Sennholz*, Grove City College Press: Grove City, Pennsylvania, pp. 213-222.

Lee, Susan Previant and Passell, Peter (1979), *A New Economic View of American History*, W. W. Norton & Co.: New York.

Menger, Carl, *Principles of Economics* (1994/1871), Translated by Dingwell, James and Hoselitz, Bert F., Libertarian Press: Grove City, Pennsylvania.

Rockwell, Jr., Llewellyn H. (1990), "Introduction," in Murray N. Rothbard (1990/1963), *What Has Government Done to Our Money?*, The Ludwig von Mises Institute: Auburn, Alabama.

Rockwell, Jr., Llewellyn H. (1992), "Morning After in America: The Austrian View of the Recession," *Policy Review*, no. 60, spring, pp. 73-77.

Rothbard, Murray N. (1990/1963), *What Has Government Done to Our Money?*, The Ludwig von Mises Institute: Auburn, Alabama.

Skousen, Mark (1990), *The Structure of Production*, New York University Press: New York.

Selgin, George (1996), *Bank Deregulation and Monetary Order*, Routledge: New York.

Selgin, George (1990), "Short-Changed in Chile: The Truth about Free-Banking Episode," *Austrian Economics Newsletter*, Winter/Spring, pp. 5-7.

Selgin, George A. (1988), *The Theory of Free Banking: Money Supply Under Competitive Note Issue*, Rowman and Littlefield: Totowa, New Jersey.

Selgin, George, and White, Lawrence (1987), "The Evolution of a Free Banking System," *Economic Inquiry*, vol. 25, no. 3, July, pp. 439-457.

White, Lawrence H. (2008), "Competing Money Supplies," *The Concise Encyclopedia of Economics* (Library of Economics & Liberty), retrieved March 18, 2009 from http://www.econlib.org/library/Enc/CompetingMoneySupplies.html.

White, Lawrence H. (1992), "Mises on Free Banking and Fractional Reserves," in John W. Robbins and Mark Spangler, eds., *A Man of Principle: Essays in Honor of Hans F. Sennholz*, Grove City College Press: Grove City, Pennsylvania, pp. 517-534.

White, Lawrence H. (1995), *Free Banking in Britain: Theory, Experience, and Debate, 1800-1845*, Second Edition, The Institute of Economic Affairs: London.

Vaughn, Karen I. (1994), *Austrian Economics in America: The Migration of a Tradition*, Cambridge University Press: New York.

12 Market failure fiction

What is market failure?

The theory of market failure has been the key supposition underlying government regulation and intervention. Four types of market failure have been identified and expostulated in welfare economics: monopoly, imperfect information, negative externalities, and public goods. These four types are generally well-known by contemporary students of welfare economics and public policy. A number of summaries of some or all of them have been produced over the last few decades, including those by Stigler and Foldvary (see Stigler 1975, pp. 104-110 and Foldvary 1994, pp. 1-6, 12-15).[69] Foldvary's overview and critique of market failure is especially thorough and compelling. We begin this chapter with a brief overview of the alleged four types of market failure.

Monopoly

One market failure conjecture asserts that monopolies can accidentally form and, in turn, cause consumer and social

---

[69] Foldvary 1994 (chapter 1), the dam example in particular, provides a devastating criticism of market failure theory and a market-based solution to the public goods problem. It should be read by any serious student of market failure theory or welfare economics.

welfare losses. In order to remedy this problem, antitrust legislation has been enacted. However, as noted in chapters two, three, and ten, public choice and Austrian theorists have argued that most monopoly is *intentional* rather than accidental. That is, it is the result of successful rent seeking or the capture of regulators. Only short-lived monopoly can be considered accidental, and that variety of monopoly is beneficial since it gives entrepreneurs an incentive to perform their work (see chapter nine).

Thus, long term monopoly may be considered a government failure rather than a market failure in nearly all cases. Indeed, rather than curtailing monopoly, there is evidence that antitrust legislation has actually perpetuated and extended it (see chapter two). Moreover, short term monopoly is not a failure at all. Austrian theorists argue that successful progressive entrepreneurs receive temporary monopoly profits as a reward for their laudable efforts. Temporary monopoly power is not a market failure but a short-lived market boon or incentive that is essential for the proper functioning of the market process.

Consequently, arguing that monopoly is a market failure is certainly a dubious proposition. On the contrary, its long term form is an example of government failure. Because of the breadth of coverage in earlier chapters, the alleged market failure resulting in intentional monopoly will not be considered further in this chapter.

Imperfect information in exchange

The ignorance of consumers can lead them to make less than optimal choices. Thus, the market allegedly fails to produce socially acceptable results when one firm or person is able to freely deceive another to his hurt (e.g., a consumer may buy something with faults or potentially hazardous ingredients known only to the seller). Likewise, a third party may be injured in his course of action due to a production flaw caused by the actions of others.

Consequently, consumers often demand insurance, grading, certification, and other informational services to guarantee or assure the quality of the products they buy, or to minimize the risks associated with an activity. The theory of market failure contends that the existence of imperfect information implies a market failure that should be partially or wholly alleviated by proactive policy or policies of inefficient provision.

However, there is evidence that firms specializing in information services will develop spontaneously in the market process. They will furnish discipline in the catallaxy which will encourage firms and individuals to build and maintain wholesome reputations. Examples of research that deal with such catallactic provision include books by Foldvary, Holcombe, Selgin, White, Cobin, and others.[70] Therefore, like monopoly, this moot and dubious type of market failure will not be discussed further in this chapter.

Negative externalities

An externality is an effect or unintended consequence to a third party resulting from an economic decision of others. Positive externalities are serendipity or unexpected utility gains generated by others; they are received without paying for the production of the benefits. Examples of positive externalities include seeing someone's beautiful flower garden, watching a parade or fireworks, or hearing a open-air concert, provided that none of these benefits were directly paid for and no added transactions costs were incurred to receive them (i.e., the benefits were received in the course of pursuing some other course of action).

---

[70] See Foldvary 1994, chapter 10; Holcombe 1995, chapters 6-8; Cobin 1997, chapter 3; Selgin 1988; White 1995, chapter 2; and Yilmaz 1998.

Negative externalities are costs or disutility imposed on a person by the actions of others, without receiving any of the benefits from their production. Examples of negative externalities include having clothes on the clothesline soiled by the smoke from a nearby factory, damaged crops as the result of a fire started by sparks from a passing train, second-hand cigarette smoke, noise from jets taking off from a nearby airport, and the obfuscation of a view due to new neighboring construction. Negative externalities are considered market failures since it is presumed that these unfair costs are generated by the market to benefit some at the expense of others (i.e., some of the costs paid to obtain the benefit are unintentionally born by others who do not benefit). Therefore, proactive public policy is called upon to "correct" these failures. Ironically, the government is not normally called upon to force beneficiaries to pay for the positive externalities they receive, except when they are generated by a special class of goods known as public goods.

Table 12.1 Taxonomy of external effects

Motive/Result	Harm	Benefit
Intentional	Crime or Tort	Gift
Unintentional	Negative externality	Positive externality

Public goods

Public goods are goods or services characterized as being non-excludable and non-rival in consumption. The cost is the same to provide them for one or more persons, where consumption by one person does not reduce the amount available for others, and non-payers cannot be prevented from consuming them. Thus, public goods are considered to be a problem—a market failure—because people can free ride on the benefits of goods produced without paying for them. In essence, people can benefit from a positive externality. Some examples of supposed public goods are lighthouses, bees, parks, fire prevention, highways, national defense, law and order, pollution abatement, and flood control.[71] Governments often provide public goods because it is supposed that market provision would otherwise be inadequate. Moreover, free riding is considered to be both unfair and the primary reason for the underproduction of the public good. Foldvary summarizes the market failure hypothesis pertaining to public goods:

> The market-failure proposition is framed as the following hypothesis: *The incentives for personal gain, which induce agents in a market economy to provide private goods, do not in general induce such agents to provide the collective goods that the people in the service domain effectively demand, because even when transaction costs are not an obstacle, there is no way to induce individual users to pay for a portion of the good so that the total amount of the good is paid for* (Foldvary 1994, p. 6) [Italics in original].

Table 12.2 Definition of public goods

What is a "public good"?
"Public goods are goods or services characterized as being non-excludable and non-rival in consumption."

Reactive policies and market failure

Most market failures are addressed by using proactive policies or policies of inefficient provision. In its broadest conception, the need for any government is the result of some market failure. However, stating that "we need government because markets fail" confounds the various kinds of policies used to address problems without considering that the

---

[71] For example, the celebrated dam case in Foldvary 1994, chapter 1.

types of problems have been generated by divergent human needs. Some demand for government services are the result of demand for self-preservation, while others arise from the demand for certain goods and services that enhance the quality of life or one's business practices and results.

Table 12.3 Four alleged types of market failure

The four alleged types of market failure are:
(1) monopoly,
(2) imperfect information of consumers (including transactions costs),
(3) negative externalities, and
(4) public goods.

Indeed, the need for collective goods like defense and criminal justice was initially addressed by the market process. From early feudal arrangements in Europe to circled wagon trains in the early western United States, human actors have always sought out collective means for the preservation of life, liberty, and property from *intentional* aggression. Moreover, at its most essential level, government has been designed to manage this collective action. While defense and justice are considered public goods, they are different than other public goods because they entail reactive policies that are naturally derived in the market process. Government may in fact be the market-mandated means to handle the production of these collective goods and as such they are not examples of market failure.

Other kinds of public policies are the result of people wanting to deal with *unintended* harm—negative externalities—to property (and perhaps life itself), or the desire to obtain certain goods and services that enhance the quality of life. When undesirable by-products of human action occur, or quality-enhancing goods and services are not provided, people might clamor that market provision has failed and seek proactive policies or policies of inefficient provision to remedy the deficiency.

Henceforth, when market failures are considered in this chapter, negative externalities and public goods which are addressed exclusively by proactive policies or policies of inefficient provision will mainly be in view. Reactive public policy deals with an altogether different need for collective action which is probably not a market failure (in the most functional sense of that term). Otherwise, if reactive policy were the consequence of a market failure to provide justice or defense, markets would be considered failing whenever *any* system of governance or public policy is employed. Markets would not merely fail, they would in reality be utterly unable to provide for certain basic human needs (e.g., security). Thus, the state would become an indispensible and necessary feature of human existence. Under such rigor, only in a successful political anarchy would markets be viewed as being free from failure. An alternative view would suggest that reactive policy and government are features of the market process and thus no failure at all. Government could be seen to emerge from the market process in order to provide the only true public good: *protection from predators.* Conformably, in this chapter, reactive policy is presumed to be a beneficial result of market forces rather than a failure of market provision.

The rationale against market failure theory

As discussed in chapter four, there is a tension inherent in the Chicago School's mode of analysis. On the one hand, the virtues of the free market are extolled, but on the other hand markets are often considered to fail—at least compared with perfectly competitive criteria. As Stigler states:

Economists have long had a deeply schizophrenic view of the state. They study an elaborate and remarkably complex private economy, and find that by precise and elegant criteria of optimal behavior a private enterprise system has certain classes of failures. These failures, of which some are highly complex in nature and all are uncertain in magnitude, are proposed for remedial or surrogate performance by the state (Stigler 1975, p. 103).

Stigler goes on to discuss the role of the state in correcting market failures caused by negative externalities, public goods, and imperfect information.

These three types of "market failures" provide the agenda for the state in economic life, according to welfare economics. The externalities, the public goods, and the incompetences of individuals each allow an improvement in economic affairs to be achieved by an intelligent and efficient government. Yet these three classes of actions never developed into even a partial theory of the economic functions of the state. The literature in each area showed an almost perfect immunity to progress in this respect (Stigler 1975, p. 110).

Hence, Stigler is cautious about using government to solve market problems. As with Boettke's story about the Roman Emperor recounted in chapter one, we must not glibly accept public policies because we assume that they can do no worse than the market. Stigler remarks:

We may tell the society to jump out of the market frying pan, but we have no basis for predicting whether it will land in the fire or a luxurious bed (Stigler 1975, p. 113).

As discussed in chapter five, there have been a number of policy-relevant studies which have questioned the validity of designating certain goods and services as public goods. More studies could be cited which support this thesis. For instance, High and Ellig found that education can be provided by markets.

The historical evidence clearly supports the four conclusions stated at the beginning of this paper. Private education was widely demanded in the late eighteenth and nineteenth centuries in Great Britain and America. The private supply of education was highly responsive to that demand, with the consequence that large numbers of children from all classes of society received several years of education. The effect of government intervention in the private educational market was not unambiguously beneficial. Government education displaced, and sometimes stifled, private education. In addition, compulsory-education laws in America forced a kind of education on poor people that they saw as threatening to their ethnic cultures and values. The historical evidence strongly suggests that economists should rethink the view that education is a market failure (High and Ellig 1988, pp. 378-379).

There have been further studies about public goods as well. Coase has perhaps the most famous article of this variety, in which he demonstrates that lighthouses are not public goods (see Coase 1974, p. 376). Foldvary summarized some of the important empirical findings that decimate the public goods argument (Foldvary 1994). By way of review, I made a synopsis of some of these critiques.

Market failures like public goods are cited as the main justification for government intervention. However, the articles in Tyler Cowen's compendium strongly suggest that the theory of market failure as set forth by Samuelson, Bator, and their disciples has theoretical and empirical shortcomings. Kenneth Goldin argues that the case for public goods has been overstated, noting that 'so many [real world] examples have been analyzed, and found wanting.' He suggests that it is misleading to describe some goods and services as 'public' or as externalities. Likewise, Earl Brubaker argues that the free rider problem 'has little empirical scientific basis.' Thus, it is possible that the preponderance of public goods has been exaggerated and identifying true public goods might be more difficult than is often supposed.

For instance, Harold Demsetz concludes that private firms can efficiently produce public goods, which raises questions about the 'public' nature of such goods. Perhaps they are really private goods that are often publicly produced. Charles Tiebout found this to be especially true of local goods considered to be public. They are often provided by government but could be provided by the market as well. For instance, James Buchanan argues that 'clubs' provide an intermediary means of dealing with the vast number of goods between Samuelson's theoretic 'purely public' and 'purely private' extremes. Clubs are 'optimal sharing arrangements,' that determine the membership margin or the optimal level of cost and consumption sharing. Thus, it seems that market provision could be a practicable alternative for most goods and services deemed 'public' (Cobin 1997, p. 90).[72]

This critique also extends to urban concessions, which are abortive privatization attempts that often end in government failure—as Chile's *Costanera Norte* project (Cobin 1999). While few Chileans question the tremendous benefit of having this expressway running through the north side of Santiago, even fewer recognize the enormous cost and inef-

---

[72] The articles cited are from Tyler Cowen, ed. (1988), *The Theory of Market Failure: A Critical Examination*, George Mason University Press: Fairfax, Virginia: Tyler Cowen, "Public Goods and Externalities: Old and New Perspectives," pp. 1ff; Kenneth D. Goldin, "Equal Access vs. Collective Access: A Critique of Public Goods Theory," pp. 69, 90; Earl R. Brubaker, "Free Ride, Free Revelation, or Golden Rule," pp. 93, 109; Harold Demsetz, "The Private Production of Public Goods," pp. 111, 126; Charles M. Tiebout, "A Pure Theory of Local Expenditures," pp. 179, 182, 188-189, 191; and James M. Buchanan, "An Economic Theory of Clubs," pp. 193-194, 207-208.

ficiencies involved with building it—tunneling through several miles near downtown in particular. If Costanera Norte were built without government intervention, even if its location our route were altered, the resulting private roadway—rather than just a twenty year concession—would have been more efficient. As it stands now, the cost to drive Costanera Norte is higher than other expressways in Santiago and the public uproar over its construction has hardly been trivial.

Certain rural activities have also been the focus of important studies. Steven Cheung demonstrated that pollination services are provided to farmers by beekeepers and, thus, bees are not a public good. He concluded that welfare economists have not been supporting their theory from genuine examples of market failure. Instead, they use fanciful stories to make judgments about present circumstances.

> Whether or not Keynes was correct in his claim that policy makers are still "distilling their frenzy from economists," it appears evident that some economists have been distilling their policy implications from fables. In a desire to promote government intervention, they have been prone to advance, without the support of careful investigation, the notion of "market failure" (Cheung 1988, p. 303).

Markets obviously fail when compared to a state of perfection or heaven. Yet, since perfection is unattainable in this world, the only relevant or meaningful sense of market failure comes by comparing how the market stacks up against the accomplishments of proactive policy. That is, "Do markets fail to provide the safety and quality demanded in society that can be provided by government intervention?" The question should never be; "Does the market fail compared to models of perfect competition." One of the themes of this book has been to identify problems caused by using perfect competition models as a basis of judging market phenomena. The abuse of such modeling has led many scholars to embrace what Mark Sagoff has called "the cult of microeconomic efficiency" (Sagoff 1992, p. 212). Correspondingly, Cheung is skeptical of the efficiency criteria used for identifying market failure.

In each case, it is true that costs involved in enforcement of property rights and in the formation of contracts will cause the market to function differently than it would without such costs. And few will deny that government does afford economic advantages. But it is equally true that any government action can be justified on efficiency grounds by the simple expedient of hypothesizing high enough transaction costs in the marketplace and low enough costs for government control. Thus to assume the state of the world to be as one sees fit is not even to compare the ideal with the actual but, rather, to compare the ideal with a fable (Cheung 1988, p. 304).

Logical errors in externality and free rider theory

The critique of market failure theory goes deeper than simply criticizing methodology. The criticism extends to the very core of the idea and its underlying presuppositions. Carl Dahlman contends that externalities, which are arguably the principal problem underlying market failure theory, are themselves a dubious and normative proposition.

It is thus doubtful whether the term "externality" has any meaningful interpretation, except as an indicator of the political beliefs and value judgments of the person who uses (or avoids using) the term (Dahlman 1988, p. 227).

Dahlman goes on to argue that externalities are not the proper focus of welfare economics in the first place. They are merely symptoms underlying transactions costs and the lack of omniscience in market exchange. Transactions costs create the most significant problems in life and those can hardly be mitigated by public policy.

In the final analysis, therefore, externalities and market failures are not what is the matter with the world, nor is it externalities and market failure that prevent us from reestablishing the Garden of Eden here on earth—our sad state of affairs is rather due to positive transaction costs and imperfect information. It is a very strange feature of modern welfare-policy prescriptions that they propose to do away with externalities, which are only one of the symptoms of an imperfect world, rather than with transactions costs, which are at the heart of the matter of what prevents Pareto optimal bliss from ruling sublime. For if we could only eliminate transaction costs, externalities would be of no consequence; and given that there are certain costs of transaction and exchange, it is better to let some side effects remain (Dahlman 1988, p. 233).

Since the free rider problem is related to concerns about positive externalities (i.e., people receiving benefits without paying for them), free riding itself becomes a dubious proposition along with the broader context of externality theory. As Mitchell and Simmons note:

The problem of getting free riders to contribute to providing public goods has caught the attention of and fascinated a great many political scientists, economists, and even sociologists and social psychologists. It is an attention we view as excessive and improperly employed in normative theory and public choice. Far too many analysts have used the free-rider problem as a means of justifying the state and extending its activities. They assume that the market is inadequate to the task of supplying public goods and that therefore, the state must do so. We do not believe that markets and other private institutions are so helpless; as we have seen, it is quite possible to change the nature of alleged public goods as well as to make use of greater private initiatives to supply public goods. Furthermore, political systems face many problems related to the provision of public goods. Demand revelation, for example, is a universal problem whenever political processes are used to determine optimal supplies of goods. But in those instances where the polity must determine supply, society should be able to use better decision rules and obtain different, superior results (Mitchell and Simmons 1994, p. 100).

Consequently, Foldvary argues against the notion that markets fail because free riders can use public goods without paying for them. He contends that market failure theory is spurious because it is theoretically unsound, empirically questionable, and methodologically lame.

Do public goods and services such as streets, parks and dams have to be provided by government? The prevailing view is that they do, because agents (persons and organizations) in a market process normally fail to provide them. According to this view, since people benefit from civic services whether they pay for them or not, many will be 'free riders,' not paying for the services unless they are forced to. For that reason, many economists, as well as much of the public, think that only government or public sector can provide the collective services that people in a community may desire. The theme of this book is that proposition is incorrect. The market failure argument treats persons as atomistic agents living in either [sector] rather than in three-dimensional space and in context of institutions and history. Such an unreal ethereal abstraction, conditional an premises which no real society has ever lived in, produces a theory that may be validly concluded from its premises, but is unsound —incorrect for real-world human existence. Once these real-world factors are introduced into public-goods theory, the market-failure argument not only falls, but is turned on its head: rather than benefiting from the public goods whether or not they pay for them, people must pay private agents for the public goods whether or not these agents provide the goods (Foldvary 1994, p. 1).

Are negative externalities a problem?

The market failure concept is tenuous because it is arbitrary and capricious. For instance, negative externalities, *as special cases*, have a dubious existence. Clearly, every human action produces an externality for someone as a by-product, yielding positive or negative effects, the only exception being the occasional instance of an identical coincidence of preferences. Free market theorists contend that most negative externality problems are spawned by poorly defined property rights or on account of dealing with government-owned property.

Roy Cordato correctly indicates the necessity of having well-defined property rights. He analyzes an idealized institutional setting, and criticizes errant neoclassical positivist attempts to make arbitrary and capricious divisions among externalities, suggesting that "catallactic efficiency" can be improved by government intervention if the externality is "policy relevant." He counters the notion that picking externalities to be ameliorated can be nebulously determined by "philosophy and ethics" which is "informed by economic analysis" and will "provide the normative framework," without prescribing a particular ethical tradition. Such neoclassical positivist ideas are ambiguous, dangerous, and antithetical to the Austrian emphases on subjectivism and methodological individualism (Cordato 1992, pp.

73-81, 86). Special case negative externalities fall under this criticism.

Identifying a negative externality implies that the situation in question could be improved (i.e., someone can perceive a *better* alternative). However, this premise begs the question: "Improved and better for whom?" Planners certainly do not have the requisite knowledge to determine whether society is made better off by a proposed policy change. Indeed, any classification of certain special case negative externalities as particularly bad or woeful is necessarily arbitrary and capricious.

Undeniably, certain negative externalities are viewed as greater problems than others. Social problems are ranked ordinally by politicians or bureaucrats according to their own preferences, vote loss potential, or according to the ideology of some SIG. Subsequently, the drive to expunge negative externalities by government force will naturally lead to public choice problems elicited by rent seekers or SIGs. Accordingly, the alleged "problem" of negative externalities might merely be a justification for rent seeking, and the use of the coercive power of the state to force one group's preferences on another group.

And the theory goes further. Since social pressures or circumstances ostensibly generate a need for interventionist policies, alert regressive entrepreneurs might enhance in their rent seeking activities by *fabricating* negative externalities. It is conceivable that these individuals could specialize in creating artificial demand. By investing capital to create think-tanks that produce economic studies and policy analyses, these institutions may be used to support the regressive entrepreneur's efforts to generate artificial scarcity. In so doing, he can create real profit opportunities through the political process either for his own use or for sale to others.

As previously noted, the term externality can be used to describe either serendipity or unintended disutility (i.e., positive externalities or negative externalities). However, externalities may simply be viewed as characterizations of interpersonal utility comparisons (made between individuals or communities). Surely, no one has an incentive to complain about positive externalities. If a person feels severe moral culpability for receiving unintended serendipity, the benefit might actually become a negative externality to him. In this sense, there is a fine line between negative and positive external effects.

Furthermore, determining whether some unintended consequence is a positive or negative externality is a matter of individual subjectivity. Thus, it is not possible for planners to determine what is a mostly positive or a mostly negative externality to society, and only with great difficulty to one or more individuals in society. Nevertheless, negative externalities exist as legal or academic notion for analyzing social phenomena which are perceived as being undesirable to either the majority of the people or, more likely, to a SIG, a court, a regulatory bureaucracy, or politicians.

Yet a "negative externality" conceived in an aggregate or social sense is always discreditable. The most the term can provide is some descriptive value as a vague indicator of interpersonal friction. An individual and subjectivist definition is more useful: a *negative externality is simply a term used to indicate a difference between competing utility functions which has been observed to cause some contention.* It is an observed conflict in the social process or "community."[73] *In that sense, every difference in interpersonal utility is an externality,* although only expostulated differences are noticed or involve significant economic cost such that people seek to resolve them via public policy.

Furthermore, a negative externality is often linked with the rhetoric of "violation of rights" (usually to property),

---

[73] In addition to Foldvary's use of the term *community*, cf. Paul Heyne, "Free Markets and the Common Good," pp. 186-188, noting his use of this word as well.

for which a demand for a remedy is grounded. If natural law is used as a philosophical basis for human rights, something can only be a *right* if it is received from God as unalienable. In chapter five, these rights were designated as negative rights. All other so-called "rights," e.g., positive rights, are merely degrees of *privilege* assigned by other individuals or by a society that benefit one group at the expense of another. Thus, a violation of private property rights associated with unowned or state property (e.g. smoke transmitted through the air that soils the laundry), would lead people to pursue political solutions by privilege or rent seeking.

In addition, negative externalities may be conceived as always involving some form of "pollution." But pollution is an essentially nebulous word. Paul Heyne is correct in suggesting that pollution refers to "costs imposed on others without their consent" (Heyne 1991, p. 330) that remain irrelevant "until someone objects" (Heyne 1991, p. 331). However, instead of taking this understanding to its logical conclusion by admitting the arbitrary nature of externality theory, Heyne reverts to normative reasoning. For instance, in order to justify the identification and expulsion of arbitrary special case negative externalities, he proposes that (in light of future uncertainties) government should mitigate the speculative aspects of human existence. While this goal seems noble, government can hardly be expected to abate interpersonal conflict or future uncertainties because of the knowledge problem and the subjective nature of value.

For instance, one person might complain to another, "I do not like you building houses" or "I do not like you cutting down trees." That is, this individual considers the other person's action to be a negative externality (or pollution). But so what? A survey of other people might reveal a majority preference in favor of the "offending" party continuing to build houses and cut down trees. The world is a continuum of interpersonal conflict over preferences. Negative externalities and pollution are arbitrary, terms essentially devoid of substance, and often exist in legislation and regulation simply for the promotion of rent seeking.

Indeed, only one person's utility preference prevails when regulators or judges "solve" a pollution or negative externality problem—i.e., when they enforce one person's utility preference over another. In these cases, political actors make value judgments with respect to an interpersonal utility conflict. Evidently, some of these value judgments become so important that politicians, judges, academics, and bureaucrats will decree the maintenance of them to be a "right." In other words, one person or a group of persons becomes entitled by legislation to have his personal preferences trump the preferences of others. Thus, in the rent seeking paradigm, one of the highest achievements of a privilege seeker is to secure such state-mandated rights. Theoritically, artificial scarcity (and profits) will often be maximized at that level.

Heyne cautions that we ought "not suppose we have solved a problem when we've only created a new one to take its place" (Heyne 1991, p. 330). In the modern age, Carlisle may have a new reason to dub economics "the dismal science" (LeFevre 1966, p. 3—quoting Carlisle), if negative externalities merely provide the impetus for empowering rent seeking organizations (e.g., environmental clean-up companies, producers of safety-related products, trial lawyers, feminist groups, politically correct or multi-culturally-sensitive academic departments, etc.). Special case externalities are not a problem that can or should be properly identified or fixed by proactive public policy.

Are free riders a problem?

Likewise, the free-rider problem is actually no *problem* at all. It can be logically dismissed for the same reasons that special case negative externalities can be dismissed.

Every economic decision has beneficial or detrimental external effects to other people. For example, if Joe wants to buy a tie, he will make his choice regardless of the preferences of others. Although he might consult other people because he suffers from imperfect information and has utility gains from pleasing other people, he will ultimately make his own decision based on his own preferences. Even if he prefers to let others buy his ties for him, he remains in control. In that case, Joe simply does not value his judgment as much as the judgment of others, or he simply has too high an opportunity cost to bother. At any rate, Joe ends up controlling the purchase of his tie.

As an unintended result of Joe's action, Tom may benefit from seeing the tie. He receives no great benefit, but some positive benefit nonetheless. However, Mary utterly despises the tie and is afflicted by unintended disutility each time she has the misfortune of seeing it. Joe is not perfectly informed about the preferences of Tom, Mary, and others, and has no idea what effect his action will have on them. Nevertheless, Joe buys the tie according to his preferences and to meet his satisfaction, *regardless* of how his decision impacts others. Therefore, consumers (excepting an imaginary Crusoe) always ignore or internalize in their price the external consequences resulting from their purchase of ties, flower gardens, or any other goods or services. Succinctly, if they choose to engage in trade, they do so despite any unintended external consequences, whether they are realized in Tom's free riding or imposing costs on Mary. Consumers do not refrain from acquiring some good that would benefit them simply because others will free ride, benefitting from it without paying for it.

However, when a person wants a good or service but cannot afford to pay for it, and if an opportunity for successful rent seeking exists, they may choose to fabricate artificial demand or create an abstract social problem that results from supposedly failed market provision. In so doing, a person may be able to compel others to share the cost of a good or service. People may be expected to pursue this kind of rent seeking so long as the cost of rent seeking is less than the cost of pursuing the good or service through community organizations, given that the expected benefits from either means are equivalent.

Further, it is conceivable that people internalize all possible negative externalities, discounting the probability of their occurrence. Every economic actor must deal with unknown future events (e.g., the possibility of an earthquake, an accident, being accosted in the street, eating contaminated food, etc.). For some of these risks he might buy insurance, but for most of them he will prefer to self-insure, depending on his subjective judgment of the probability of occurrence. Accordingly, every individual has some "black-box" factor to cover unknown or unexpected events in his subjective discounting equation.

Nevertheless, if building houses, cutting trees, buying ties, using foul-smelling fertilizers when planting flower gardens, or any of a myriad of other actions are identified by regulators or SIGs as producing special case negative externalities, a catallactic distortion will occur. One group of people will be forced to compensate another. In pollution cases, the regime granting the privilege or right might dictate that an explicit rule, or some social internalization rule, be utilized in order to absorb the alleged pollution cost and thus prevent untrammeled or inconsiderate behavior by others. But this policy is arbitrary and subject to the capricious whims of regulators who face public choice pressures.

Every economic decision has beneficial or detrimental external effects to other people, and it is arbitrary to merely identify some things as special cases. Why should free riding on a new dam or road be prohibited while free riding on ties and flower gardens is considered acceptable? Consumers always internalize (in the price paid) the external effects resulting from their purchase of goods and services, even if they are public goods. That is, just as when they buy ties or flowerbeds, if they choose to trade in public goods, they do so in spite of the external effects.

Note that, given a situation where a person desires but cannot afford to buy a dam or road, the fact that he cannot buy the good does not qualify it as being "public" any more than any other building project. For instance, if the cost of building ten beautiful but very expensive houses (which would disseminate positive benefits on the residents of the neighborhood) exceeds his budget, the new houses do not become public goods simply because he cannot afford them. The principal issue is not the price of the good.

Moreover, the simple fact that a project is socially beneficial does not make it a public good. Capital is likely available to pay for the houses, but they are not built since the individual values his time more than the net benefit gained from building the houses (i.e. netting out the costs of capital and the transactions costs associated with his efforts to obtain financing). Despite the fact that the neighborhood would be improved, and the neighbors by and large elated, the existence of a social benefit does not make the houses in question public goods.

In sum, consumers do not refrain from acquiring some good that would benefit them simply because others will free ride, although they may avail themselves of a rent seeking opportunity by cleverly identifying free-riding as a problem in hope of compelling others to share the cost. Therefore, free-riding is hardly a social problem.

Free-riding is more likely a ruse or a cover for other concerns. These concerns might have to do with:

(1) rent seeking,
(2) a desire by some people to compel others to pay for the goods they desire but cannot (or do not want to) purchase themselves,

(3) an abstract philosophical notion suggesting that, since people do not always know what is in their best interest, compelling them to buy a public good will actually benefit them, or

(4) the benefits received from some big ticket items, like dam or road building, are too large to be ignored like the myriad of other positive externalities in life, and thus potential free riders should be compelled to pay on account of somebody's notion of fairness.

Yet such determinations will always be arbitrary. Indeed, all of these rationales are merely justifications for reallocating the cost of some goods, whereas positive external effects are ignored for most goods.

Therefore, in spite of free riding, markets will be able to provide public goods in the same way that they provide any other good—if consumers demand them. Those who want them will bear their cost, regardless of the overall distribution of benefits or the proliferation of free riding.

In the final analysis, the notion of market failure, along with theories about negative externalities, free riders, and public goods, are dubious propositions. They are mere fiction. In short, the market does not fail by any reasonable standard or compared to proactive policy provision. On the one hand, the free market provides the best social coordination and allocation of resources possible in an imperfect world. On the other hand, government failures tend to exacerbate earthly imperfections and amplify human adversity and uneasiness. The real culprit in perceived social failures is often the state. Accordingly, free market theorists focus on institutions, incentives, and knowledge in developing their policy-relevant research programs. *In doing so, they always ask: "Who benefits?" when a new public policy is being proposed.* They want to find out what SIGs stand to benefit, what institutions are involved, what are the incentives facing the SIGs or political actors, and if the proposed policy is even doable given the knowledge problem.

Table 12.4 Analytical considerations in public policy work

Three crucial elements in the analysis of a public policy:
(1) the *institutions* that would affect it,
(2) the *incentives* that would be generated or that would change, and
(3) the *knowledge* required to perform it.

Communities: a market-based solution

While government failure has often yielded dour circumstances, market-based alternatives can provide both progress and the good life. Foldvary postulates that markets, although they do not generate utopia, are not actually subject to the failure decried by welfare economists. Indeed market-based institutions, what Foldvary calls "communities," would evolve without government intervention to provide public goods more effectively and efficiently than policies of inefficient provision. In the same way economists consider firms to be institutions that reduce transactions costs, and provide efficient collective action, economists should likewise expect communities to provide collective goods in the absence of interventionism. After pointing out the defects in the famous dam and flood control project story due to public choice and knowledge problems, Foldvary provides a community-based solution:

> Suppose, however, that the valley is already settled and not owned by an outside firm. The market-failure scenario assumes that the households are atomistic, each an independent, isolated unit. But human society has always lived in communities, so the premise of atomistic households is anti-historical; if it is meant to apply real-world

civic goods, its ignoring of institutions commits the error of begging the question. The real-world distinction is not community organization versus lack of organization, but what kind of governance or organization an enterprise or a community has, for example consensual governance versus imposed governance (Foldvary 1994, p. 5).

Since communities, like any other human institution, are subject to failure, Foldvary suggests that contractual (i.e., constitutional) constraints must be used to minimize potential problems. In the same way the stockholders and directors find ways to deal with problems in the principal-agent relationship, individuals in communities will find ways to discipline community leaders. Moreover, contracts could be developed to prevent problems that might be caused by strategic behavior, i.e., individual actions to benefit themselves at the expense of the community. Foldvary argues that market-based institutions can effectively and efficiently handle collective goods and overcome the problems associated with government failure:

Hence constitutional safeguards can be built into community organizations, significantly reducing the likelihood of institutional failure. The major safeguard would be the contractual nature of the relationship between a prospective resident and the developer or subsequent community governance—each potential resident or site owner would sign an agreement acknowledging agreement with the rules before joining the community, and know that there are safeguards against the arbitrary confiscation of his site-specific investment. Still, it is possible for a developer or residential association to fail, just as any human individual, organization or institution can fail. The issue of market failure is not whether some collective goods will fail to be produced or be overproduced; such occurrences constitute entrepreneurial rather than systematic market failure and are inevitable in a world of uncertainty, change and imperfect human nature. The market-failure argument is that market or consensual processes must generally fail to provide public or civic goods, and the third story shows how 'the market' need not fail. The issue to be addressed is the feasibility of public-goods provision by private means...The theory presented in the initial chapters shows how collective goods can be provided by agents in a market process, and the case studies described in the in the later chapters demonstrate how real-world communities are in fact providing such goods in accord with the theory. The market-failure hypothesis is thus shown to be unsound in theory and rejected by the evidence. This theory and evidence also contrasts contractual provision with government-imposed provision, showing how government failure can be and is overcome by consensual community arrangements (Foldvary 1994, p. 6).

Policy research cannot ignore public choice and Austrian insights and expect to remain relevant. Alternatively, much policy-relevant research can be done to provide evidence of market provision of social services. From a free market perspective, the primary task of the modern public economist is not to find means for public policies to be more efficient, but to demonstrate how market alternatives to regulation and market provision can replace government regulation and government provision. While admitting that markets will not deliver utopia or perfection, free market theorists contend that they would provide the best resource allocation and coordination possible.

Policymaker analysis to accomplish reactive policy

The previous chapters contain cogent critiques of proactive policies designed to correct market failures. In addition, this chapter and the previous two have argued in favor of markets and community provision of goods and services often mistakenly labeled as "public goods" (and which thus become goals of policies of inefficient provision). Consequently, we are left with the question, "What can and should government do?" According to free market theorists, if there is a role for the state it should be limited to reactive policies.

Of course, this notion raises systemic concerns about what form of government is best and how to transform the present system into that form without devastating costs that might arise from the transitional gains trap, paying off entrenched special interests, and so forth. It is a main task of policy researchers, political scientists, and public finance economists to develop a theory of government that can best facilitate reactive policy while minimizing rent seeking problems and problems related to with dispersed and fragmented social knowledge. In addition, these theorists must develop a way for the state to perform its operations efficiently. So recognizing and demonstrating the need for policy change is only part of the task of free market scholars. They also have the daunting task of developing comprehensive solutions that minimize public choice problems.

Recalling a principal theme from chapter ten, it is impossible to perform meaningful cost-benefit analysis for *public* decisions on account of the subjective nature of value and the knowledge problem. Of course individuals, family leaders, and firms utilize this technique in every decision. But planners cannot possibly calculate or know either the costs or the benefits of public decisions. To show that this premise is incorrect, detractors would have to demonstrate that (1) there is some objective value that a planner can know, (2) that the knowledge problem does not extend to all public decisions because planners at some level can know enough to plan effectively, or (3) in spite of its failings, cost-benefit analysis is the best solution we have for dealing with collective decisions (i.e., we ride the horse even though it is lame and blind). Otherwise, we must accept (4) that cost-benefit analysis is of diminutive value in making public decisions. It may indeed help a planner to think more analytically or help him organize information better, but ultimately it is either a sincere but misguided attempt to consistently make policy substantially more efficient or simply a tool which facilitates rent seeking justification.

Both proactive policies and policies of inefficient provision fall prey to the fourth proposition. It is impossible for planners to know either the costs or the benefits of these actions. Thus, while cost-benefit analysis *might* be better than nothing, there is no assurance that it is—especially when rent seeking activity is probable. Thus, cost-benefit analysis must not be relied on as an optimizer of public decisions. However, with respect to reactive policies, the third option may apply under certain scenarios.

For example, I argued earlier that reactive policy services (i.e., defense and criminal justice) are always in the "public interest" by definition, and are also not responses to genuine market failure. Whether or not these services can be optimally provided purely by non-government agencies remains the task of philosophers, policy researchers, political scientists, and public finance economists who are working on a tenable theory of anarchy. But assuming that reactive policy must be provided by the state, it may be possible for government to provide these services with *net* social benefits. In support of this thesis, consider: (1) collective action for defense is a social and market result and (2) *benefits* may be assumed to exist because nearly all people have *revealed* their preference for the continued maintenance of life, liberty, and property. Sane people do not seek to kill or enslave themselves, nor do they desire to have their property ruined. Moreover, history demonstrates that people have lived in cities, traveled in wagon trains, created mutual assistance plans or clubs, and have developed communities, both with and without help from government, in order to bolster their self-defense and ensure their survival.

Therefore, because benefits are known to be positive from reactive policies, policymakers can perform at least half-baked cost-benefit analysis. On account of the knowledge problem, the method will tend to be lame and blind, although not defunct because it is possible to have net-benefits from a reactive policy to everyone in society. Of course, arriving at the optimal solution will be an arduous task. Policymakers still do not know the opportunity costs of reactive policy. Plus, in a rent seeking society, the capabilities of planners to effectively plan net benefits by means of cost-benefit analysis will also be skewed and distorted because of public choice problems. Therefore, although there can be plenary social benefits from reactive policies, the revealed preferences of consumers or citizens does not automatically lead to efficient or effective provision, or guarantee that there will be social benefits net of social costs.

In order to deal with this calculation problem in generating reactive policy, a political paradigm must be developed that severely restricts government activities to reactive policy and keeps public choice problems in check (perhaps by a constitution). Theoretically, the best system of government would provide defensive services with the least amount of government failure. Therefore, to the extent that government can be so limited, cost-benefit analysis can be of some value. Social benefits can be presumed to be positive in the analysis and cost minimizing solutions for providing the goods may be sought.

As with individual decision makers who buy products but are not able to perfectly measure the opportunity costs, as long as the expected benefits are positive, cost minimization becomes an insurance problem. Consumers often prefer to self-insure against risk when the probability and amount of potential loss is low, but at times they prefer to buy implicit insurance by purchasing products with a higher reputation. Reactive policymakers thus need to provide insurance protection in their policy paradigms that protect against high and unexpected social opportunity costs.

It is conceivable, although certainly difficult, for government agents who face explicit constitutional constraints to choose cost minimizing solutions. Note that opportunity cost can be more closely minimized in this scenario as well, since the only alternative uses for the funds will be how to allocate them among *defense* options. While the money for defense could be retained by taxpayers to achieve other goals (e.g., better home security), this aspect of opportunity cost might be shifted to the taxpayers depending on the type of public finance mechanism used. Voluntary public finance systems might be more conducive to cost minimization than coercive or confiscatory methods, but answering this question must be the present work of public finance economists. A system for analyzing reactive policies would not be perfect but, in an imperfect world, it might be better to do cost-benefit analysis badly than to not do it at all.

Nevertheless, we must realize that any substantial benefits from this method can only be expected when analyzing *reactive* policy decisions. In sum, the techniques of public economics and cost-benefit analysis can be of some use (1) under a political framework in which institutions are construed, constrained, or altered to preclude knowledge and public choice problems as much as possible, (2) where genuine cost minimizing solutions are mandated and practiced, and (3) only when analyzing reactive policy decisions. Ministries of dealing with defense, justice, and public health might thus be able to employ some sort of useful cost-benefit analysis, but the analysis must not be relied upon too heavily. A lame horse may still be a horse, but its usefulness is severely limited.

References

Buchanan, James M. (1988), "An Economic Theory of Clubs," in Tyler Cowen, ed., *The Theory of Market Failure: A Critical Examination*, George Mason University Press/Cato Institute book: Fairfax, Virginia, pp. 193-208.

Cheung, Steven N. S. (1988), "The Fable of the Bees: An Economic Investigation," in Tyler Cowen, ed., *The Theory of Market Failure: A Critical Examination*, George Mason University Press/Cato Inst.: Fairfax, Virginia, pp. 279-304.

Coase, Ronald H. (1974), "The Lighthouse in Economics," *Journal of Law and Economics*, vol. 17, no. 2, October, pp. 357-376.

Cobin, John M. (1997), *Building Regulation, Market Alternatives, and Allodial Policy*, Avebury Press: London.

Cobin, John M. (1999), "Market Provision of Highways: Lessons from Costanera Norte," *Planning and Markets*, vol. 2, no. 1, September, http://www-pam.usc.edu.

Cordato, Roy E. (1992), *Welfare Economics and Externalities in an Open Ended Universe: A Modern Austrian Perspective*, Kluwer Academic Publishers: Boston.

Dahlman, Carl J. (1988), "The Problem of Externality," in Tyler Cowen, ed., *The Theory of Market Failure: A Critical Examination*, George Mason University Press/Cato Institute book: Fairfax, Virginia, pp. 209-234.

Foldvary, Fred (1994), *Public Goods and Private Communities: The Market Provision of Social Services*, Edward Elgar Publishing Co. [Locke Inst.]: Brookfield, Vermont.

Goff, Brian, and Tollison, Robert (1990), "Is National Defense a Pure Public Good?," *Defence Economics*, no. 2, pp. 141-147.

Heyne, Paul (1992), "Free Markets and the Common Good," *Critical Review*, vol. 6, nos. 2-3, spring-summer, pp. 185-209.

Heyne, Paul (1991), "Pollution and Conflicting Rights," chapter 13 of *The Economic Way of Thinking*, sixth edition, Macmillan Publishing Company: New York.

High, Jack C., and Ellig, Jerome (1988), "The Private Supply of Education: Some Historical Evidence," in Tyler Cowen, ed., *The Theory of Market Failure: A Critical Examination*, George Mason University Press/Cato Institute book: Fairfax, Virginia, pp. 361-382.

Holcombe, Randall (1997), "A Theory of the Theory of Public Goods," *Review of Austrian Economics*, vol. 10, no. 1, January, pp. 1-22.

LeFevre, Robert (1966), *The Philosophy of Ownership*, Rampart College (A Pine Tree Publication): Larkspur, Colorado.

Mitchell, William C., and Simmons, Randy T. (1994), *Beyond Politics: Markets, Welfare, and the Failure of Bureaucracy*, Westview Press: San Francisco, California.

Sagoff, Mark (1992), "Free Market versus Libertarian Environmentalism," *Critical Review*, vol. 6, nos. 2-3, spring-summer, pp. 211-230.

Stigler, George J. (1975), *The Citizen and the State: Essays on Regulation*, University of Chicago Press: Chicago.

Yilmaz, Yessim (1998), "Private Regulation: A Real Alternative for Regulatory Reform," *Cato Policy Analysis*, no. 303, April 20, The Cato Institute: Washington, D.C.

13 The economic analysis of law

The foundation of law and economics

Economics is the study of purposeful and rational behavior. That is, economists study the human pursuit of consistent ends by efficient means. Consequently, economics is also a suitable tool for studying law. Judges and lawyers are expected to act rationally, and are subject to criticism if they act irrationally. Moreover, economic models can be useful in explaining law, legislation, and legal institutions.

Law, as a spontaneous order, differs from legislation

Hayek viewed the law as the embodied evolution of useful legal designs which have been adopted by society. In the same way that other technologies have been improved by increases in social knowledge over time (e.g., changing from planting by hand to planting with tools and animals), law continues to undergo a process of evolutionary improvements through marginal changes.

Moreover, law is not the invention of the state. Law arises spontaneously as a result of human action—that is, the drive to find institutions that alleviate uneasiness. But legislation is "law" made by state edict, and should not be confused with antecedent law. As Hayek comments:

Legislation, the deliberate making of law, has justly been described as among all inventions of man the one fraught with the gravest consequences, more far-reaching in its effects even than fire and gun-powder. Unlike law itself, which has never been 'invented' in the same sense, the invention of legislation came relatively late in the history of mankind. It gave into the hands of men an instrument of great power which they needed to achieve some good, but which they have not yet learned so to control that it may not produce great evil. It opened to man wholly new possibilities and gave him a new sense of power over his fate. The discussion about who should possess this power has, however, unduly overshadowed the much more fundamental question of how far this power should extend. It will certainly remain an exceedingly dangerous power so long as we believe that it will do harm only if wielded by bad men. Law in the sense of enforced rules of conduct is undoubtedly coeval with society; only the observance of common rules makes the peaceful existence of individuals in society possible (Hayek 1973, p. 72).

Thus, legislation and law have different origins. For Hayek, law is a means to an end. The legal order is not planned or imposed. It is a *spontaneous order* that gradually evolves by custom. In Austrian economic theory, spontaneous orders are an essential feature of the market process. Institutions that arise without public policy are presumably efficient, cost-minimizing features of civilization. They should be encouraged since they tend to improve the quality of life. The quality of the law is a function of how little it is constrained or reformed by relatively inefficient legislation.

Laws as rules facilitate social interaction, and judges assist in the social acceptance of laws. However, judges are not the *source* of laws any more than legislators are. Hayek sustains that judges play a role in distributing the law:

The efforts of the judge are thus part of that process of adaptation of society to circumstances by which the spontaneous order grows. He assists in the process of selection by upholding those rules which, like those which have worked well in the past, make it more likely that expectations will match and not conflict. He thus becomes an organ of that order. But even when in the performance of this function he creates new rules, he is not creator of a new order but a servant endeavouring to maintain and improve the functioning of an existing order. And the outcome of his efforts will be a characteristic instance of those 'products of human action but not of human design' in which the experience gained by the experimentation of generations embodies more knowledge than was possessed by anyone (Hayek 1973, p. 119).

Rather than being a product of society, law precedes society. It is an error to think that government creates laws, property rights, or individual rights. As Hayek notes:

To appreciate the significance of this it is necessary to free ourselves wholly from the erroneous conception that there can be first a society which then gives itself laws. This erroneous conception is basic to the constructivist rationalism which from Descartes and Hobbes through Rousseau and Bentham down to contemporary legal positivism has blinded students to the true relationship between law and government. It is only as a result of individuals observing certain common rules that a group of men could live together in those orderly relations which we call a society (Hayek 1973, p. 95).

Bruce Benson notes that customary law, rather than legislation, is still used in modern society to facilitate economic actions. Indeed, this kind of law is more powerful than legislation in achieving social order. As Benson states:

Customary law continues to govern a tremendous amount of social interactions, from family relations to commercial exchanges to international relations between governments. It is difficult to visualize this for a number of reasons. First, many customary laws are not adopted and "enacted" by a state authority and are not necessarily written down. Second, customary law "owes its force to the fact that it has found direct expression in the conduct of men toward another." Third, customary law requires voluntary acceptance in recognition of reciprocal benefits, so it is much less likely to be violated than enacted authoritarian law. Customary law, therefore, is less likely to require adjudication, and its role and impact are less likely to be noticed as a consequence. Nonetheless, customary law flourishes and promotes order in many facets of modern society (Benson 1990, p. 230).

In summary, Hayek points out that there is a difference between law and legislation, each of which have distinct origins. Law is the incorporation of useful legal norms in the market process and social cooperation rather than an invention of the state. It includes the customs and traditions that had been settled over time, plus some marginal changes in its ongoing evolution. Judges must be arbiters that make the application of the law more efficient. Accordingly, the law is spontaneous, dynamic, and precedes public policy. Moreover, the state does not create human rights to life, liberty or property, which also emerge spontaneously.

The origin of legislation is far different. It consists of government edicts, basically those of legislators. It is subject to inefficiencies due to lack of knowledge and public choice problems. Thus, legislation is more dangerous than law in that it frequently distorts human life and the market process. Legislation injects inefficient transaction costs into the market process by forcing the ideologies of SIGs on society.

Law reduces information costs, facilitating cooperation

The truly great society results "from human action rather than human design and is a freely grown, spontaneous rather than an imposed, planned society" (Dietze 1976, p. 133). The catallactic environment is enhanced by facilitating the voluntary interaction of individuals responding to the price system and holding private property rights, rather than proactive policies. Rather than succumb to myopic calls for social justice, Hayek supported a strict rule for interpreting contracts and applying the law to property.

> The important thing is that the rule enables us to predict other people's behavior correctly, and this requires that it should apply to all cases—even if in a particular instance we feel it to be unjust (Hayek 1944, p. 80).

Indeed, legal institutions can make the actions of others more predictable when they are consistently applied. Benson sums up the Hayekian vision, and laments the fact that government intrusion into the legal realm has been so extensive:

> Hayek suggested that the rules that emerge from customary law will of necessity possess certain attributes that authoritarian "law invented or designed by a ruler may but need not possess, and are likely to possess only if they are modeled after the kind of rules which spring from the articulation of previously existing practices." The attributes of customary legal systems include an emphasis on individual rights because recognition of legal duty requires voluntary cooperation of individuals through reciprocal arrangements. Such laws and their accompanying enforcement facilitate cooperative interaction by creating strong incentives to avoid violent forms of dispute resolution. Prosecutorial duties fall to the vic-

tim and his reciprocal protection association. Thus, the law provides for restitution to victims arrived at through clearly designed participatory adjudication procedures, in order to both provide incentives to pursue prosecution and to quell victims' desires for revenge. Strong incentives for both offenders and victims to submit to adjudication arise as a consequence of social ostracism or boycott sanctions, and legal change occurs through spontaneous evolution of customs and norms. But nation-states have taken on a substantial role in the creation and enforcement of law (Benson 1990, pp. 35-36).

Hayek's view lends support to liberty-enhancing policies

Gottfried Dietze argues that Hayek's view of law caused him to support liberty-enhancing policies. Hayek wanted freedom under law; he did not just believe in liberty, but in the constitution of liberty (Dietze 1976, p. 140). Ultimately, the law must be subordinate to liberty, since law is merely a means to the procurement and protection of private freedom (Dietze 1976, p. 114). "It economizes intangible freedom into tangible 'properties'...law is a means to an end" (Dietze 1976, p. 115). On the other hand, egalitarian notions of equality compete with freedom (Dietze 1976, p. 127).

This maxim also stands over the social justice notion of John Rawls, who places *justice* as the first virtue of society (see Buchanan 1987, p. 257). "[T]he legal order corresponding to the ideal of the rule of law develops in liberty. It is a spontaneous order. It is not planned...it gradually evolves by custom" (Dietze 1976, p. 121). Conversely, a legislated society will tend to become a rent seeking or a wholly socialist society that precludes liberty. As Dietze remarks:

Therefore, not only was the decline of the rule of law the road to serfdom, serfdom also found its basis in the law by which despots ruled. The traditional emphasis upon private law was replaced by one on public law (Dietze 1976, p. 132).

There is a conflict between those who feel that social justice should occupy the greatest importance in public policy (cf. John Rawls and Buchanan's use of his "veil of ignorance" equity theory) and those who think that human freedom should be preeminent. Hayek says that the most important feature of law is that it provides a means to better predict the actions of others. That is, it reduces transactions costs in society and ameliorates catallactic efficiency. However, planning and social engineering through legislation eventually ruin society, as Hayek laments in much of his work. Therefore, the economic way of thinking can and should play an important role in advising and honing the legal process and the development of the law itself.

The importance of incorporating economic tools into law

In their well known textbook *Law and Economics*, Robert Cooter and Thomas Ulen point out that until recent times law did not make use of economics, except in the areas of antitrust, regulated industries, taxes, and the determination of legal liability settlements (Cooter and Ulen 1997, p. 1). However, a change occurred in the 1970s when its use was extended into the traditional areas of the common law: property, contract, and tort. From that point on, economics has changed the nature of legal scholarship, the common understanding of legal rules and institutions, and even the practice of law (Cooter and Ulen 1997, p. 2)

To economists, legal sanctions seem similar to prices and people respond to them in the same way as they respond to prices. That is, the presumption is that just as people consume fewer goods when their prices rise, they will also develop fewer sanctioned activities when legal penalties are more severe. Therefore, it is possible to predict or even direct human behavior.

In terms of production, companies have two real costs: product safety (i.e., design costs), plus the present value of implicit costs of awards made to clients who will be injured by using their products. Such damages are determined in the judicial process. Consequently, companies compare the expected costs of production with the expected benefits in order to maximize profits. This outcome is attained by the producer adjusting the level of safety until the real cost of additional product safety is equal to the implicit price of the added accidents that will occur by increasing production (and hence consumption too). Thus, economics provides a theory of human behavior which predicts how people will respond to changes in law or legislation. Thus, law and legislation can be utilized to achieve various social goals, and economics can predict the effect of a public policy on efficiency (Cooter and Ulen 1997, p. 3).

Additionally, court rulings pertaining to business practice might make contractual behavior more efficient, by determining which party could have avoided a legal problem, with the least cost (Cooter and Ulen 1997, p. 5). Lawyers thus benefit from studying economics because it serves to make law or legislation more efficient. Economists benefit from studying law because it makes their economic models more realistic (Cooter and Ulen 1997, p. 7). Therefore, according to Cooter and Ulen, economics is a practical tool for studying law, since it is expected that law, lawyers, and judges will behave in a rational manner. (If they behaved otherwise they would be subject to criticism or ostracism.) That is, judges often pursue efficient and coherent ends. This idealistic notion has been challenged, of course, by the seemingly myriad distortive, unfair, and destructive or even

Draconian rulings of overworked family court judges in the United States. The same may be true in other court systems as well, indicating that the economic efficiency and rule-making of judges can be greatly reduced according to the workload he faces. It can also be reduced if public choice problems are present, such as the injection of feminist ideology into family law and practice through the rent seeking or attempted capture activity of SIGs. Nevertheless, effectively ignoring these inefficiencies, the field of law and economics has been widely accepted and formalized in the efficient neoclassical model (witness Miceli 1997).

The law reduces costs by making life more predictable. Cost considerations are central in the field of economics and, therefore, it is very useful to analyze law, legislation, and regulation to see if they are efficient. The law is especially interesting since it is a spontaneous order, which includes some minor marginal changes over time. Economics deals with marginal analysis. The goal of any judicial system should be to make human behavior more predict-table, and this might best be facilitated through strict rules.

Benson points out that the market, traditionally, has been able to carry out many aspects of justice. Voluntary law focuses on individual freedom and contains various features that tend to generate an efficient business environment, where people solve their problems without going to court. These social norms are quite common nowadays, although legislative intrusions and court decrees are growing in importance. Indeed, in some kinds of law, such as family law in the United States, the bias toward favoring women to win is so pronounced—demonstrating the effectiveness of the lobby of feminist SIGs—that it pays opportunistic females to pursue solutions to problems in court rather than by alternative resolution. For that reason, the vast majority of divorce cases in the United

States (especially those involving children) are brought by women (Baskerville 2008, p. 414).

Distortions caused by family courts in the United States

About the only thing that causes family courts to favor men is drug use on the part of the wife. Even proof of severe mental illness: e.g., suicide attempts, auditory hallucinations and psychosis, paranoia, hospitalizations for depression, bipolar disorder (type I or II) , multiple annual driving infractions, etc. will be ignored. For the most part, evidence of a woman's lying, perjury, sexual abuse or promiscuity will be ignored, while the man will be held strictly accountable for such things. A man does not have to be legally married in some states to be subjected to this process on account of "common law marriage" statutes. If a child is involved, the man's life is in jeopardy.

Stephen Baskerville has studied the economic effects of family courts on men and records a number of the dire costs and harm thrust upon men on account of Draconian family court decisions (Baskerville 2007b). In the United States, Baskerville remarks, on account of its feminist-influenced the family court system, marriage is dangerous for men. However, marriage is extremely profitable for rent seeking SIGs, Guardians *ad litem*, psychologists, lawyers and women. For men, marriage may be a one-way ticket to poverty and jail. Baskerville remarks:

> Marriage is a foundation of civilized life. No advanced civilization has ever existed without the married, two-parent family. Those who argue that our civilization needs healthy marriages to survive are not exaggerating.
>
> And yet I cannot, in good conscience, urge young men to marry today. For many men (and some women), marriage has become nothing less than a one-way ticket to jail. Even the *New York Times* has reported on how easily "the divorce court leads to a jail cell," mostly for

men. In fact, if I have one urgent piece of practical advice for young men today it is this: Do not marry and do not have children.

Spreading this message may also, in the long run, be the most effective method of saving marriage as an institution...It is well known that half of all marriages end in divorce. But widespread misconceptions lead many to believe it cannot happen to them. Many conscientious people think they will never be divorced because they do not believe in it. In fact, it is likely to happen to you whether you wish it or not...Under "no-fault" divorce laws, your spouse can divorce you unilaterally without giving any reasons. The judge will then grant the divorce automatically without any questions.

But further, not only does your spouse incur no penalty for breaking faith; she can actually profit enormously. Simply by filing for divorce, your spouse can take everything you have, also without giving any reasons. First, she will almost certainly get automatic and sole custody of your children and exclude you from them, without having to show that you have done anything wrong. Then any unauthorized contact with your children is a crime. Yes, for seeing your own children you will be subject to arrest.

There is no burden of proof on the court to justify why they are seizing control of your children and allowing your spouse to forcibly keep you from them. The burden of proof (and the financial burden) is on you to show why you should be allowed to see your children.

The divorce industry thus makes it very attractive for your spouse to divorce you and take your children. (All this earns money for lawyers whose bar associations control the careers of judges.) While property divisions and spousal support certainly favor women, the largest windfall comes through the children. With custody, she can then demand "child support" that may amount to half, two-thirds, or more of your income. (The amount is set by committees consisting of feminists, lawyers, and enforcement agents – all of whom have a vested interest in setting the payments as high as possible.) She may spend it however she wishes. You pay the taxes on it, but she gets the tax deduction.

You could easily be left with monthly income of a few hundred dollars and be forced to move in with relatives or sleep in your car. Once you have sold everything you own, borrowed from relatives, and maximized your credit cards, they then call you a "deadbeat dad" and take you away in handcuffs. You are told you have "abandoned" your children and [will be] incarcerated without trial. (Baskerville 2007a)

Tragically, the threat of jail, financial punishment, loss of children, and emotional stress can lead men to emigrate or even to engage in acts of violence against judges, lawyers and ex-family members. The current system has reduced social cooperation, increased costs, done irreparable harm to families, and spawned "the growth of [female] single-parent homes and massive increases in fatherless children" (Baskerville 2004) where "a father is forced to finance the filching of his own children" (Baskerville 2008, p. 405, citing Abraham 1999). Family policy in the United States has generated perverse incentives for women, lawyers, judges and bureaucrats which cause dramatic economic distortions, and create immense suffering on the part of fathers which "find themselves inducted into a system of forced labor to satisfy government's growing demand for revenue" (Baskerville 2008, pp. 402, 407, 413, 419).

A more efficient solution to "no fault" divorce cases might be reached if the rule were changed to require the party who gets custody of the children to pay 100% of the costs of raising them, while still mandating visitation rights for the other parent. This scenario would dramatically change the incentives of women to bring no fault divorce actions and economists would expect that SIGs and lawyers would oppose such a rule. In actions for fault, i.e., for adultery, abandonment, habitual drunkenness, etc., the rule could be that the guilty party pays 100% of the costs of raising the children, and visitation rights would depend on the severity of the wrongdoing. That rule would also change spousal behavior. Both rules would likely reduce the case load in family courts, dramatically reduce opportunistic behavior, mitigate public choice problems, encourage men not to be "unwilling...to marry and start families" (Baskerville 2008, p. 418), and make people think twice before they act.

Common law versus civil law

There are two legal traditions that have prevailed over time: the common law tradition (property, contract, and tort) and the civil law tradition. The common law continues in the areas of the former British Empire, while the civil law tradition is more widely accepted, having its origins with Justinian. In the world's two legal systems, one can see the power that judges have to interpret the law. It is clear that lawmakers legislate, but judges have a distinct role. The extent of each political actor's power depends on the legal framework in which he operates. The common law is derived from legislative, judicial, and executive sources, with the judicial branch being the most influential. The legislative branch is dominant under the civil law.

The common law, which is applied in all the countries where English is spoken (Ireland, Great Britain, Canada, the United States, Australia, New Zealand, India and the rest of the countries of Asia and Africa that were colonized by England), was first formally recognized when the royal court in England decided to examine community life in order to find the laws that already existed. These laws were considered to be "laws of nature." In establishing a rule of law, the court created a precedent that future courts had to follow, although all precedents were to be followed flexibly rather than rigidly. Rulings thus become justified through precedent and social norms (Cooter and Ulen 1997, pp. 56-57). When there is no precedent in a dispute, judges must create one, which gives them an opportunity to change the common law (Cooter and Ulen 1997, p. 65).

The civil code exists in most of Europe, Central and South America, Quebec, Louisiana, Puerto Rico and those parts of Asia and Africa not colonized by England. (Note: France too had a common law once, but it was destroyed by the French Revolution).

The civil code is based on the Napoleonic Code, which is derived from the wisdom of ancient scholars and pure reason, rather than more recent legacies. In this system, judges justify their interpretations directly by referring to erudite commentaries. Judges intervene more in these courts than they would under the common law. They even question contestants and lawyers directly in an interrogatory process (Cooter and Ulen 1997, pp. 56-57). Civil law courts seldom have jurors (in France they are used only in murder cases).

Nevertheless, in both systems, the law forms a hierarchy where constitutions take precedence over legislation—which is typically preferred over lower government rules and common law precedents. However, in many countries, judges (whom are often not elected) have power to review legislation in order to ensure that that it conforms to the constitution (Cooter and Ulen 1997, p. 58). At times, judicial review can cause social problems. For instance, as noted in chapter three, Mises argues that many underdeveloped nations are backwards to a large extent due to their legal systems (Mises 1996, pp. 499-502).

Advantages of the common law given public choice caveats

The principles of the common law are codified in its law of torts, and especially in its law of contract and its law of property, which Mises identifies as grandiose examples of Western success. A robust system of contracts and property rights permits the market process and the activities of progressive entrepreneurs to function smoothly, efficiently, and abundantly.

Desirable features of the common law are its mutability at the margin and its adaptability to new social changes. Nevertheless, the common law can become an instrument for rent seekers and judicial planners who claim to be able to improve social welfare with rulings that in actuality cause social harm. Like other political actors, judges are hardly able to make bargaining more efficient and to identify or alleviate special case negative externalities. Thus, on the one hand, the common law is far more spontaneous and flexible than the civil law. That is, the law can be changed locally by a judge and/or jury without having to deal with the wider political process. In this sense, the common law is likely to be most compatible with the Hayekian vision of spontaneous order.

On the other hand, the civil law is more stable. While it can also develop and change according to custom, it often is not as flexible and responsive to catallactic necessity than the common law. However, it may well be more resilient to rent seeking and judicial activism than the common law. Thus, the best system will often depend on the amount of state intervention and other relevant circumstances in each society. But in a free society—given a Hayekian understanding of legal institutions—the common law would arguably be the superior form. Only when public choice distortions become weighty, such as with "family law" in the United States, does the common law become economically inferior to the civil law. At that point, the law tends to push society backwards.

A bad legal system can breed backwardness

Just as rent seeking can retard economic development, so a poor legal system can retard or debilitate catallactic progress. Don Lavoie argues that cultures which are established on private property rights will tend to be more prosperous.

Those cultures that refine their rules in such a way as to define and protect "private property" more effectively find that market relations are thereby enhanced (Lavoie 1985, p. 35).

This was indeed the case in all countries that benefited from the industrial revolution, especially in ones which developed a common law system. Lavoie continues:

Common law principles accompanied the evolution of free markets in Britain, and some form of property rights prevailed in every nation that participated in the rapid economic growth known as the industrial revolution (Lavoie 1985, p. 238).

Mises remarks that exceptional social institutions, especially the legal system, have permitted Western nations to prosper more than other nations:

The start which the peoples of the West have gained over the other peoples consists in the fact that they have long since created the political and institutional conditions required for a smooth and by and large uninterrupted progress of the process of larger-scale saving, capital accumulation, and investment. Thus, by the middle of the nineteenth century, they had already attained a state of well-being which far surpassed that of races and nations less successful in substituting the ideas of acquisitive capitalism for those of predatory militarism. Left alone and aided by foreign capital these backward peoples would have needed much more time to improve their methods of production, transportation, and communication (Mises 1996, p. 497).

Mises notes that Western prosperity is the result of a system of law founded upon reason and good cultural premises:

> [T]he temporal head start gained by the Western nations was conditioned by ideological factors which cannot be reduced simply to the operation of environment. What is called human civilization has up to now [1949] been a progress by cooperation by virtue of hegemonic [dominance or ascendancy] bonds to cooperation by virtue of contractual bonds. But while many races and peoples were arrested at an early stage of this movement, others kept advancing. The eminence of the Western nations consisted in the fact that they succeeded better in checking the spirit of predatory militarism than the rest of mankind and that they thus brought forth the social institutions required for saving and investment on a broader scale...What the East Indies, China, Japan, and the Mohammedan countries lacked were institutions for safeguarding the individual's rights. The arbitrary administration of pashas, kadis, rajahs, mandarins, and daimos was not conducive to large-scale accumulation of capital. The legal guarantees effectively protecting the individual against expropriation and confiscation were the foundations upon which the unprecedented economic progress of the West came into flower. These laws were not the outgrowth of chance, historical accidents, and geographical environment. They were the product of reason (Mises 1996, p. 500).

Those institutions of the West which are fundamentally different than those in the East spring from both religious principles and the legal philosophy which devolves from them (cf. John Locke's use of the Old Testament).[74] Mises

---

[74] The appendix provides samples of social rules supporting private property and ethical behavior in the Bible. Clearly, the Bible is against indolence, squandering, dishonesty, and the diminution or destruction of individual property rights. Therefore, those cul-

claims the West has excelled because of superior reasoning and better cultural framework. Furthermore, Tullock and other public choice theorists would add that nations develop (i.e., mitigate backwardness) as they are able to successfully curtail rent seeking (see chapter 3). Thus, Western culture has been superior because its institutions facilitate the removal of uneasiness better than Oriental culture. Western cultural institutions might, arguably, also serve to better restrain rent seeking tendencies.

The Coase Theorem and judicial activism

Especially in common law countries, special case negative externalities are frequently dealt with by the judiciary. For example, if a woman has her laundry hanging on a line soiled by smoke from a nearby factory, then she ends up paying part of the costs of the factory's production. However, she receives none of the benefits from production, *ceteris paribus*. This special case negative externality has been identified as a violation of her property rights, leaving room for a possible legal remedy which could force the factory to compensate the woman.

For many years, judges were presumed to be able to reduce the level of such pollution by sound judgments. However, in his famous paper "The Problem of Social Cost," Coase presented the rudiments of a theorem that would forever change how civil procedure rulings are evaluated. The *Coase Theorem* essentially says that where the costs of concluding a contract are low, the rule of law will not affect the level of pollution. Coase remarks on one such situation where the rule of law did not affect the outcome of resource allocation when transactions costs were low.

---

tures which have traditionally embraced biblical rules might be expected to champion hard work, saving, equity, and the protection of private property that Mises extols.

Table 13.1 Definition of the "Coase Theorem"

The Coase Theorem says:
"Given free bargaining and low transactions costs, voluntary actions of individuals in the market will allocate property rights to their most highly valued and efficient use. Both parties in a dispute over property rights have an incentive to move to this position. Such allocation occurs automatically without regard to how property rights are initially or legally assigned. Judicial action to allocate them generates a superfluous social cost and is itself a negative externality."
or
"When transactions costs are very low, the efficient solution occurs from free and private bargaining, regardless of how property rights are legally assigned by a court. Under such circumstances, judges cannot expect to alleviate any market failure better than the market itself, which will allocate resources to their most highly valued and efficient use."[75]

It might be thought that it would pay the cattle-raiser to increase his herd above the size that he would wish to maintain once a bargain had been made, in order to induce the farmer to make a larger total payment. And this may be true. It is similar in nature to the action of the farmer (when the cattle-raiser was liable for damage) in cultivating land on which, as a result of an agreement with the cattle-raiser, planting would subsequently be abandoned (including land which would not be cultivated at all in the absence of cattle-raising). But such manoeuvres are preliminaries to an agreement and do not affect the long-run equilibrium position, which is the same whether or not the cattle-raiser is held responsible for the crop damage brought about by his cattle. It is

---

[75] Note: the first part of this definition is very similar to Cooter and Ulen 1997, p. 82. The term used "very low" means "zero or close to it."

necessary to know whether the damaging business is liable or not for damage caused, since without the establishment of this initial delimitation of rights there can be no market transactions to transfer and recombine them. But the ultimate result (which maximizes the value of production) is independent of the legal position if the pricing system is assumed to work without cost (Coase 1960, p. 8).

Thus, when there is free bargaining between the two parties and low transactions costs of doing so, judges will not be able to change the level of negative externality or pollution by the factory since it will be adjusted automatically in the market process. The Coase Theorem says that the individual actions in the market will allocate property rights to their highest valued or most efficient use. Both parties on either side of any property rights dispute have some incentive to move to this position. Thus, efficient allocation occurs automatically, no matter how property rights are initially assigned by a court. The activity of judges in such cases, therefore, merely creates a negative external cost to others, which amounts to a superfluous cost to society in general.

Example of the Coase Theorem

Problem   Consider the following negative externality event: a rancher's cows have been crossing over the property line of his neighbor, a corn farmer, and has been eating the crops. Further consider that damages amount to $100 per year (Cooter and Ulen, p. 80).

Assumptions   The costs of negotiation and conversing are "low" (nearly zero) for the two neighbors involved. It is supposed that no similar problems exist with the rancher's other neighbors, since it would complicate the analysis. The ranch has much more land than the farm does, but the ranch does not surround the farm.

Solution Build a fence. But around which property?

A. Fence the farmer's land (the corn producer):
   1. The cost would be $50 per year to build and maintain it.
   2. Doing so would lower the rancher's profits.
B. Fence the rancher's land (the cattle producer):
   1. The cost would be $75 per year since his land area is larger than the farmer's.
   2. Doing so would also lower the rancher's profits.
C. Given that $50 < $75 < $100:
   1. It would be efficient to build the fence.
   2. It would be efficient to build it around the farmer's land.

The judicial option If the problem were to go to court, the judge would have two alternatives:

D. Rule I: *The farmer is responsible* and should build the fence because:
   1. Doing so would be efficient, and
   2. the farmer would save $50 per year.
E. Rule II: *The rancher is responsible* and he should thus build a fence around his own land. Thus, the rancher:
   1. will save $25 (over what he would have to pay the farmer) and
   2. this rule would give the rancher an incentive to negotiate with the farmer in order to save more.
      (i)   That is, the rancher can build the fence around the farmer's land for only $50 and,
      (ii) therefore, he can save $50 instead of $25,
      (iii) but the farmer will likely know about these circumstances and will thus proceed to negotiate

429

with the rancher in order to capture a portion of the additional savings.

3. Consequently, the rancher will want to build the fence around the farmer's land for $50.

4. But the rancher would be disposed to pay up to $25 more to the farmer for permitting him to build it on his land. (Since the rancher's land does not surround the farmer's but there is still some common boundary, he will have to build at least part of the fence on the farmer's land.) Consequently, for example, the rancher might settle with the farmer by paying him $12.50, saving the other $12.50 for himself.

Outcome Either way, the fence will be built around the farmer's land—regardless of how property rights were assigned by the court (i.e., Rule I or Rule II). Therefore, the Coase Theorem becomes effectual and the market does not fail when negotiations (transactions) costs are very low or, perhaps, when direct dealings are more complex but the cost of using a market-generated arbiter is still relatively low.

Nevertheless, the Coase Theorem provides an important implication: an opportunity to use state courts is generated in negative externality cases where transactions costs are *high*. Since, in reality, transactions and litigation costs probably are high, using the court system may provide a more efficient means of solving property conflicts than may be found in the market process itself.

The Coase Theorem and efficiency economics

The Coase Theorem has changed jurisprudence by providing a reason or a means for judicial activism. However, it is not clear that the judges can arrange resources more efficiently than the market. In fact, transactions costs seem to have risen along with the ascendancy of these judicial efforts.

For example, United States Appellate Court Judge Richard Posner advocates employing legal efficiency. He postulates that jurisprudence can and should determine which disputing party has the lower cost of avoiding a legal problem. Consequently, there are now legal rulings which override contract language and property rights on grounds of social efficiency. Such legal doctrines generate problems within the judicial system and create considerable uncertainty in the law of contract and the law of property.[76]

Posner does not, however, represent all of legal scholarship in the Chicago School where he teaches. Posner's colleague Richard Epstein has produced better theoretical alternatives than Posner, although Epstein still suffers from his reliance on rigid utilitarianism. Nonetheless, Epstein has made solid contributions to the field of law and economics, including his support for the revival of the rule of first possession (cf. John Locke), which could be applied when a problem of assigning property rights occurs. Unfortunately, Posner seems to have assimilated greater influence in the law and economics movement.

The critique of judicial activism by Austrian and public choice theorists rests on the fact that judges, like planners, cannot garner a sufficient amount of knowledge to determine what would be a social betterment. Indeed, no one can know whether a judicial action produces a social benefit or not, given that comparing relative benefits between different people is impossible. There have been many advanced criticisms of the modern law and economics movement by Austrian School and other theorists, as well as some

---

[76] Relatedly, consider, for example, the 1996 Texaco $176.1 million racial discrimination settlement case in the United States District Court, Southern District of New York (White Plains) reported in *Time Daily*, CNN, and in major American newspapers: *Bari-Ellen Roberts, et al v. Texaco, Inc.*, 94 Civ. 2015 (CLB) (S.D.N.Y.), (Also see *New York Law Journal*, vol. 219, no. 63 for application to 18 USC Sec. 1503)—one of many costly cases in recent American legal history designed to improve social efficiency, equity, etc. Roberts and others claimed that Texaco used racially discriminatory employment policies in violation of the Civil Rights Act of 1871, 42 U.S.C. Sec. 1981 (amended 1981) and the Civil Rights Act of 1964, amended 1991, 42 U.S.C. Secs. 2000e, et seq. ("Title VII").

suggested solutions. As Benson has argued, the best legal system to follow might be "voluntary law" and, at the very least, the privatization of civil procedure. Thus, there are market-based alternatives to state judicial power and state provision judicial services that Posner has not grasped.

It is unclear that a government court can correct a failure The alleged market failure in the laundry/factory example does not take into account some crucial elements that are likely to be present. First, the woman might actually be benefiting from the factory's production indirectly. Perhaps her husband is employed there, or perhaps the factory is a major buyer of some product he or she sells. She might at least benefit from her neighbors being employed by (or receiving investment income from) the factory, who in turn become consumers of things that benefit her either directly or indirectly.

Second, if the factory started its production before she rented or purchased her home, the woman would have most likely received implicit compensation in a lower home price. If production began after she rented or purchased her home, then the problem becomes one of insurance and her subjective estimate of the future probability of a negative externality (as noted in chapter twelve).

Nevertheless, static law and economics analysis typically ignores the possible indirect benefits that she might receive from the production. It also often assumes that the factory started its production after she rented or purchased her home and that the ensuing special case negative externality is a market failure. Thus, judges are left an opportunity to fix this alleged failure. Since the woman's property rights have been marred, a legal remedy may be found to mitigate the harm.

The inverse use of the Coase Theorem As noted earlier, the alternate implication of the Coase Theorem is that when transactions costs are high, and/or there are barriers or inhibitions to free market exchange, then the court can indeed make an improvement in property rights allocation. Hence, we can see the reasoning for why the Coase Theorem became the driving force of the law and economics movement. Given that disputes that go to trial, there must be high transactions costs or some market impediment involved—otherwise no one would go to the expense or trouble to litigate them by assumption.

Judges may thus view their mandate to find out the source and the amount of inefficiency from a given special case negative externality, and afterwards to determine what measure should be taken to remedy the situation. *Rather than interpreting and enforcing a strict rule of contract or property rights, judges become guardians of a wider social welfare. In this role, they can abrogate or severely modify the plain meaning of contracts and override property rights.* They may favor whatever they deem is best for society or for the public interest.

The great advancements in common law which began in the thirteenth century have thus been tarnished, if not swept away entirely, by this newfangled view of law. Judges have benefited by promoting the idea that market failure and high transactions costs necessitate the need for judicial resource allocation. From a public choice perspective this behavior is predictable, given the self-interest of judges who want to preserve the level of income, status, and power derived from their profession.

Analytical problems stemming from efficiency models

Posner's hypothesis

Clearly, Richard Posner has been the leading contributor to the modern law and economics school. Although Posner lauds the free market at times, he has also made clear his beliefs that markets fail and that judges can improve social resource allocation. He has done a remarkable job of injecting the "cult of microeconomic efficiency" (Sagoff 1992, p. 212) into the legal process.

In Posner's view, the law is and should be economically efficient (Posner 1992, pp. 10-12). Therefore, courts should assign losses so as to make future contracting more efficient, i.e., assign the loss to the party who can bear it at least cost. Thus, efficiency-minded judges must find which of the disputing parties values the resource most highly and which is the "least cost avoider," given the presumption that the judge can objectively determine costs and benefits to individuals and society. Such a vision has nothing to do with equity and defies subjectivity. Yet Posner is undaunted by these obstacles and the limits of judicial knowledge of the efficiency (or effectiveness) of their rulings:

How is one to know when such [involuntary] transactions [imposed by the legal system] increase, and when they reduce, efficiency? The answer is that one cannot know with anything like the same confidence with which one can adjudge voluntary transactions as efficiency enhancement. One possible if rather sterile response to the problem is complete agnosticism: if the transaction is involuntary, its consequences for efficiency cannot be determined; to attempt to do so would involve an impermissible "interpersonal comparison of utilities" (Posner 1992, p. 11)

Notwithstanding this dismissive sentiment, Posner cannot adequately answer the charge. He could, alternatively, be content with the fact that judicial activism cannot possibly make markets more efficient rather than making such a lame plea of "agnosticism." After all, there is an alternative to the government monopoly on civil procedure: privatization. But this idea is evidently unfathomable to Posner.

Extending Austrian theory, a judge cannot know which party is the least cost avoider. Nevertheless, Posner couples (1) the belief that Chicago-styled efficiency economics is relatively accurate with (2) the reality that most conflicts (especially the ones that make it to court) have substantial transaction costs, in order to create a role for judges in fixing market failures. To do so, judges must, of course, have sufficient training in economic efficiency to determine the most objectively efficient outcome for the disputing parties and society at large. Posner suggests that judges do so in spite of the actual wording of an agreement or issue at common law.

Contemporary courts might refuse to enforce a contract on account of "unconscionability" or because it involves an "efficient breach" or because the *court* perceives that there was no "meeting of the minds." Courts are also interested in applying "efficient remedies." In property law, courts use the efficiency notion to decide who has rights to pollute, to block the sunlight or wind, to cause noise or odors—all running under the dubious notion of special case negative externalities (see Barnes and Stout 1992 for examples).[77] Modern American tort law has become a matter of scorn, if not an unbelievable charade. Under the current system, judges and juries award stifling punitive damages to teach capitalists or producers a lesson. Rent seeking trial lawyers garner incredible fees through contemporary methods of finding people and firms with "deep-pockets" liable for *both* past and even future (potential) damages (see Huber 1988 for examples).

Posner suggests that the common law results from market inefficiencies and high transactions costs. Indeed, the common law developed as a set of standardized rules, a means of encouraging efficiency. Yet, it is constantly un-

---

[77] In addition to these terms, Barnes and Stout list the major cases pertaining to each of the efficiency doctrines.

dergoing change as civilization progresses and encounters new social impediments and technological challenges. In this evolutionary perspective, Posner's view is compatible with Hayek's. However, he divides with Hayek by asserting that judges can reduce inefficiencies and transactions costs by their proactive rulings, and acting as if that those rulings are not always fatally marred by the knowledge problem.

In addition, Posner has been a remarkably effective rent seeker. Public choice theory suggests that all individuals, whether working in the public or private sector, seek to satisfy their own self-interests. Posner is no exception, in either his capacity as a Chicago-area Appellate Court Judge[78] or a scholar. He may indeed provide an ironic but impressive example of regressive entrepreneurship, having been "alert" to opportunities in the political process. Whether or not his rent seeking activity has been conscious and intentional, Posner has bestowed on himself and other judges greater wealth and a reason to glorify his bureaucratic existence. He further provides a strong, logical rationale to continue on the bench. His efforts in promoting the efficiency agenda have yielded him both increased job security and notoriety too.

These concentrated benefits have also spilled over to others in the judicial process, while the social costs that arise from implementing the efficiency premise have been dispersed throughout the unwary populace. Hence, the efficiency premise has inflicted greater uncertainty and higher transactions costs on society—not to mention wider economic distortions and resources misallocations which are caused by bungling judges who lack the requisite knowledge to efficiently allocate resources.

Efficiency-school judges, with Posner and his colleague William Landes at the helm, have taken a course of judicial

---

[78] Seventh Circuit, U.S. Court of Appeals.

activism, or what might correspond with what Roscoe Pound calls legal but forceful control of the "antisocial residuum" (Pound 1942, p. 33, also cf. p. 18). In 1942, Pound feared that individual liberty and natural rights would give way to "regimented activity" in America.[79] After nearly sixty years, his words seem prophetic. Society becomes increasingly unjust as more rent seeking judicial activists—even those with good intentions—interfere with the market process. Moreover, human uneasiness is augmented as knowledge-deficient judges misallocate resources in society.

Pareto optimality

Given the Posnerian efficiency framework, the usefulness of cases must be judged according to whether or not the ruling will enhance social welfare. The efficiency criteria employed has its roots in Jeremy Bentham, who argued that (1) individual well being out to be the end of moral action, (2) each individual counts as one and only one, and (3) the object of social action should be to maximize general utility. This also formed the background for the utilitarianism doctrine of John Stuart Mill and subsequently neoclassical economics.

The Austrian emphasis on subjectivism and methodological individualism, as noted in chapters seven, eight, and ten, discredits any attempt to make a social welfare function. While utility for Bentham was interpersonally comparable and could be measured on a cardinal scale, Robbins and the Austrians showed it is measured on an ordinal scale and is subjective. Nevertheless, social (and subsequently judicial) activists were determined to discover a way to permit planners to enhance resource allocation. The solution ended up being the adoption of the Pareto principle.

---

[79] Also see Barry Warren Poulson (1981), *Economic History of the United States*, Macmillan Publishing Co., Inc.: New York, pp. 654-655.

A Pareto "preferred" move, whether made by judicial ruling or legislative policy, occurs when a ruling or policy makes at least one person better off but no one worse off. Finding a Pareto preferred move is difficult because planners and judges labor under the knowledge problem, public choice pressures, and because the idea of social welfare is tenuous (since it implies that utility can be interpersonally comparable). However, if a quasi-ordering of utility can be found, whereby rulings or policies can be made without making anyone worse off, then such policies or rulings might be feasible.

Hence, building on the work of Guido Calabresi and the other founders of modern law and economics, visionaries like Landes and Posner have successfully merged the Kaldor-Hicks-Scitovsky welfare economics thesis with Chicago-styled efficiency economics and market failure theory. By using the test of "potential compensation" (Kaldor-Hicks-Scitovsky),[80] which says that those who gain from a welfare change can offer something in return to those who lose, and thus yield a welfare improvement, Pareto preferred moves might be possible. In practice, however, there is no way of determining who is better or worse off, despite ill-fated attempts at using cost-benefit analysis. Moreover, rent seeking and interest group pressures begin to distort the effectiveness of efficiency rulings and policies—as is the case with family law in the United States.

Epstein's view

Epstein's understanding of law is far more compatible with fundamental economic principles like subjectivity and methodological individualism than Posner's view. How-ever, according to Rowley and other Virginia School economists, his work has analytical defects that stem from Chicago-style efficiency model premises.

---

[80] See Rowley's comments on (and criticism of) Kaldor-Hicks-Scitovsky in chapter four.

For instance, in tracing his understanding of the law of property, Epstein does a commendable job showing how property rights develop. He suggests that the Lockean rule of first possession be used as a way to determine property rights (Epstein 1986, p. 700ff).[81] Epstein discusses the beneficial outcome of the first possession rule in establishing ownership: "the rule of first possession, though widely ignored historically, offers the best way to establish the priority of rights in external things" (Epstein 1986, p. 668). He argues:

> The first possession rule also has more direct economic virtues for it yields a consistent and exhaustive set of property rights, whereby everything has in principle one, and only one, owner. Vesting ownership in the first possessor makes it highly likely that a person who owns the land will use it efficiently and protect it diligently. At every stage the rule reduces transaction costs (Epstein 1986, p. 670).

Epstein agrees with Hayek that, "A sound system of rights resolves the claims of ownership early in the process to reduce the legal uncertainty in subsequent decisions on investment and consumption" (Epstein 1986, p. 672). He mingles realism into his Lockean view by acknowledging the corrupt (or at least corruptible) state of human nature. Some people "have a systematic bias to take the property of others" and will try to benefit from the system of the rule of law (Epstein 1986, p. 679). Epstein also emphasizes that the rule of property law must uphold inheritance rights.[82]

---

[81] This principle, derived from John Locke, could be an appropriate starting point for a free, intelligent, and morally-concerned society. According to Locke, whoever mixes their labor with the soil of some plot of land first should be considered its owner.

[82] Rothbard apparently concurs with the notion that conquest reallocates real property rights, in order that the system of first possession may be secure. Moreover, he delineates certain practical guidelines for just title under the rule of first possession. "[A]ll existing property titles may be considered just under the homestead principle, provided (a) that there may never be any property in people; (b) that the existing property

Otherwise, rent seeking and distortions of the market process will occur:

A definite system of property rights is preserved across generations. Allowing the present owner to choose the persons who enjoy the property after death reduces the likelihood of wasteful subterfuges designed to minimize the impact of the tax, or for a pattern of immediate consumption, which may be easily approximated by the sale of fixed assets and the purchase of a lifetime annuity, it also cuts down on the premature or hidden transfers of assets to children or other family members (Epstein 1986, p. 697).

Rowley concurs with Epstein's conclusions but rejects his use of neoclassical efficiency notions to make his case. Epstein's analysis is defective since "[e]verything is made to rest on transaction costs" (Rowley 1986, p. 773), his assumptions are "unashamedly utilitarian" (Rowley 1986, p. 772), and he clings to a romantic view of government despite the insights of public choice theory. As Rowley notes:

Epstein...does not rely upon higher-level consensus between the transacting parties as evidence of an efficient outcome. Statutory interventions via a special-interest-ridden, pluralist machine of government do not necessarily reflect a calculus of consent. Transaction-cost differentials, which fuel Epstein's explanation, are asserted without any evidence. More importantly, Epstein does not rely upon a theoretical structure such as that advanced by Williamson, to predict transaction-cost differentials qualitatively, given the difficulty of quantitative analysis. In the event, with neither consensus nor evidence, his commentary rests uneasily

---

owner did not himself steal the property; and particularly (c) that any identifiable just owner (the original victim of theft or his heir) must be accorded his property" (Rothbard 1974, pp. 120-121).

on repetitive assertion. Libertarian rights and corrective justice are overridden by this uneasy utilitarian imperative, and administrative innovations praised as cost effective may be no more than constrained lower level responses to coercive government intervention... Whether or not Epstein believes that Congress really would toll the statutes in this meticulous fashion is unclear. Recent evidence of legislative behavior with respect to the tax treatment of the pensions of federal employees, suggests that senators and congressman, at least, would receive privileged treatment. Public choice does not predict that fine-tuning would operate elsewhere in accordance with Epstein's benevolent hand. Epstein presents no convin-cing theory of benevolent government to explain effici-ency in the tolling of statutes by the political process (Rowley 1986, p. 771).[83]

Consequently, much work is left for scholars in the Virginia School and Austrian School to incorporate their knowledge into the field of law and economics. Until such knowledge becomes widely understood in the discipline, public policy will continue to suffer from the defects and distortions found in other proactive attempts to improve the quality of life (e.g., drug prohibition, antitrust, or smog reduction).

Appendix: Biblical texts on law and economics themes

The Bible has profoundly affected the history of Western culture. While many scholars dispute Max Weber's thesis in *The Protestant Ethic and the Spirit of Capitalism* (1958),

---

[83] Rowley contends that a solution to legal problems must be sought outside of the utilitarian paradigm. "It is possible that judges may view good economics as bad law and lash themselves hand and foot to the strict constructionist mast as they pass between the sirens of liberty and utility. In order to determine whether this is so, someone sooner or later is going to have to dirty his hands and find some numbers concerning the relative transaction costs of alternative legal systems" (Rowley 1986, p. 774).

it is manifest that historically Protestant countries[84] have emerged as economic leaders (also see chapter three).[85] Historic Protestantism is strongly tied to a literal application of the Bible. This tie emerged spontaneously and led to much social efficiency in promoting productive activity.

Hayek suggests that social knowledge evolves over time, retaining only the best means and methods of production. In addition to its place as a religious book, parts of the Bible might be seen as transmitting optimal social knowledge pertaining to law and economics issues. Consider the following biblical dictates about property rights, business ethics, economic gains, and economic principles.

Protection of private property rights

"You shall not steal." (Exodus 20:15; cf. Deuteronomy 5:19, 23:24; Zechariah 5:3; Matthew 19:18; Romans 2:21, 13:9; Ephesians 4:28; I Peter 4:15) "Do not remove the ancient landmark which your fathers have set." (Proverbs 22:28) "Do not remove the ancient landmark..." (Proverbs 23:10a) "A false balance is an abomination to the Lord, but a just weight is His delight." (Proverbs 11:1) "Diverse weights and diverse measures, they are both alike, an abomination to the Lord." (Proverbs 20:10) "Diverse weights are an abomination to the Lord, and a false balance is not good." (Proverbs 20:23)

Business ethics

"Wealth gained by dishonesty will be diminished, but he who gathers by labor will increase." (Proverbs 13:11)

---

[84] E.g., Great Britain, Germany, Holland, Switzerland, Denmark, Sweden, the United States, Canada, Australia, New Zealand, South Africa and, more recently, South Korea.

[85] The only major exception to this rule is Japan, which has a transcendent work ethic, where work itself seems to be the touchstone of religious sentiment—perhaps even an ultimate end rather than just a means.

"Getting treasures by a lying tongue is the fleeting fantasy of those who seek death." (Proverbs 21:6) "He who loves pleasure will be a poor man; he who loves wine and oil will not be rich." (Proverbs 21:17) "One who increases his possessions by usury and extortion gathers it for him who will pity the poor." (Proverbs 28:8) "For the *love* of money is a root of all kinds of evil, for which some have strayed from the faith in their greediness, and pierced themselves through with many sorrows." (I Timothy 6:10) "He who is greedy for gain troubles his own house, but he who hates bribes will live." (Proverbs 15:27)

The necessity of maintaining a good reputation

"The refining pot is for silver and the furnace for gold, and a man is valued by what others say of him." (Proverbs 27:21) "A good name is better than precious ointment, and the day of death than the day of one's birth." (Ecclesiastes 7:1) "Dead flies putrefy the perfumer's ointment, and cause it to give off a foul odor; so does a little folly to one respected for wisdom and honor." (Ecclesiastes 10:1)

Riches are not to be despised but rather are God's blessing

"Abram was very rich..." (Genesis 13:2) "The Lord makes poor and makes rich..." (I Samuel 2:7a) "Both riches and honor come from You..." (I Chronicles 29:12)

Hard work and responsibility commended

"But if anyone does not provide for his own, and especially for those of his household, he has denied the faith and is worse than an unbeliever." (I Timothy 5:8) "The plans of the diligent lead surely to plenty, but those of everyone who is hasty, surely to poverty." (Proverbs 21:5) "He who tills his land will be satisfied with bread, but he who follows frivolity is devoid of understanding." (Proverbs 12:11) "The slothful man does not roast what he took in hunting, but diligence is man's precious possession." (Proverbs 12:27) "The soul of a lazy man desires, and has nothing; but the soul of the diligent shall be made rich... There is one who makes himself rich, yet has nothing; and one who makes himself poor, yet has great riches. The ransom of a man's life is his riches, but the poor does not hear rebuke." (Proverbs 13:4, 7-8) "In all labor there is profit, but idle chatter leads only to poverty." (Proverbs 14:23) "Laziness casts one into a deep sleep, and an idle person will suffer hunger." (Proverbs 19:15) "She [the virtuous woman] considers a field and buys it; from her profits she plants a vineyard." (Proverbs 31:16) "Whatever your hand finds to do, do it with your might; for there is no work or device or knowledge or wisdom in the grave where you are going." (Ecclesiastes 9:10) "And whatever you do, do it heartily, as to the Lord and not to men..." (Colossians 3:23).

Personal planning and stewardship

"Cast your bread upon the waters, for you will find it after many days." (Ecclesiastes 11:1) "Houses and riches are an inheritance from fathers..." (Proverbs 19:14a) "A good man leaves an inheritance to his children's children..." (Proverbs 13:22a) "Be diligent to know the state of your flocks, and attend to your herds; for riches are not forever, nor does a crown endure to all generations." (Proverbs 27:23-24)

The Bible contains wisdom from many economics principles too, such as:

Economic costs

"The sleep of a laboring man is sweet, whether he eats little or much; but the abundance of the rich will not permit him to sleep." (Ecclesiastes 5:12)

Public Choice economics and regulatory studies

"If you see the oppression of the poor, and the violent perversion of justice and righteousness in a province, do not marvel at the matter; for high official watches over high official, and higher officials are over them." (Ecclesiastes 5:8) "A feast is made for laughter, and wine makes merry; but money answers everything." (Ecclesiastes 10:19) "For wisdom is a defense as money is a defense, but the excellency of knowledge is that wisdom gives life to those who have it." (Ecclesiastes 7:12)

Nonsatiation

"Hell and destruction are never full; so the eyes of man are never satisfied." (Proverbs 27:20)

Bureaucracy

"Because of the transgression of a land, many are its princes; but by a man of understanding and knowledge, right will be prolonged." (Proverbs 28:2)

On the basis for socialism (or regressive entrepreneurship)

"Again, I saw that for all toil and every skillful work a man is envied by his neighbor. This also is vanity and grasping for the wind." (Ecclesiastes 4:4)

Sorrow over scientific knowledge about social problems

"What is crooked cannot be made straight, and what is lacking cannot be numbered...For in much wisdom is much grief, and he who increases knowledge increases sorrow." (Ecclesiastes 1:15, 18)

References

Abraham, Jed (1999), *From Courtship to Courtroom: What Divorce Law Is Doing to Marriage*, New York: Bloch.

Anonymous (1996), "Texaco to Pay Historic Settlement," *Time Daily*, 1 p.

Barnes, David W. and Stout, Lynn A. (1992), *Cases and Materials on Law and Economics*, American Casebook Series, West Publishing Co.: St. Paul, Minnesota.

Baskerville, Stephen (2007a), "Be Careful Who You Marry," November 11, NewsWithViews.com.

Baskerville, Stephen (2004), "Divorce as Revolution," July 22, NewsWithViews.com.

Baskerville, Stephen (2008), "From Welfare State to Police State," *The Independent Review*, vol. 12, no. 3 (winter), pp. 401-422.

Baskerville, Stephen (2007b), *Taken into Custody: The War against Fatherhood, Marriage, and the Family*, Cumberland House Publishing: Nashville, Tennessee.

Benson, Bruce L. (1990), *The Enterprise of Law: Justice Without the State*, Pacific Research Institute: San Francisco.

Buchanan, James M. (1987), *Economics: Between Predictive Science and Moral Philosophy*, Texas A&M University Press: College Station, Texas.

Coase, Ronald (1960), "The Problem of Social Cost," *Journal of Law and Economics*, vol. 3, pp. 1-44.

Cooter, Robert and Ulen, Thomas (1997), *Law and Economics*, second edition, Addison-Wesley, chapters 1 and 3: Reading, Massachusetts.

Dietze, Gottfried (1976), "Hayek on the Rule of Law," in Fritz Machlup, ed., *Essays on Hayek*, New York University Press: New York, pp. 107-146.

Epstein, Richard A. (1986), "Past and Future: The Temporal Dimension in the Law of Property," *Washington University Law Quarterly*, vol. 64, no. 3, pp. 667-722.

Hayek, Friedrich A. von (1973), *Law, Legislation and Liberty*, University of Chicago Press: Chicago.

Hayek, Friedrich A. von (1944), *The Road to Serfdom*, University of Chicago Press: Chicago.

Huber, Peter W. (1988), *Liability: The Legal Revolution and Its Consequences*, Basic Books: New York.

Lavoie, Don (1985), *National Economic Planning: What Is Left?*, Ballinger Publishing Co.: Cambridge, Mass. [Harper & Row Publishers: New York.]

Miceli, Thomas, J. (1997), *Economics of the Law: Torts, Contracts, Property, Litigation*, Oxford University Press: New York.

Mises, Ludwig von (1996 [1966/1949]), *Human Action: A Treatise on Economics*, fourth revised edition, The Foundation for Economic Education: Irvington-on-Hudson, New York (with minor editorial changes by Bettina Bien Greaves).

Posner, Richard (1992), *Economic Analysis of the Law*, Little Brown and Company: Boston.

Pound, Roscoe (1942), *Social Control Through Law*, Yale University Press: New Haven, Connecticut

Rowley, Charles K. (1986), "The Law of Property in Virginia School Perspective," *Washington University Law Quarterly*, vol. 64, no. 3, pp. 759-774.

Rothbard, Murray N. (1974), "Justice and Property Rights," in Samuel L. Blumenfeld, ed., *Property in a Humane Economy: A Selection of Essays Compiled by the Institute for Humane Studies*, Open Court: LaSalle, Illinois, pp. 101-122.

Sagoff, Mark (1992), "Free Market Versus Libertarian Environmentalism," *Critical Review*, vol. 6, nos. 2-3, spring-summer, pp. 211-230.

14 Cases and criticisms in law and economics with a focus on property rights

Catallactic adversity caused by "efficient" rulings

Socially adverse rulings pertaining to contracts

The idea of injecting economic efficiency into law is seductive and, at first glance, compelling. As University of Chicago-bred economist David Friedman notes:

> Economics, whose subject, at the most fundamental level, is not money or the economy but the implications of rational choice, is an essential tool for figuring out the effects of legal rules. Knowing what effects rules will have is central both to understanding the rules we have and to deciding what rules we should have.
>
> The fundamental assumption of the economics approach, to law and everything else, is that people are rational. A mugger is a mugger for the same reason I am an economist: Given his tastes, opportunities, and abilities, it is the most attractive position open to him. What laws are passed, how they are interpreted and enforced, ultimately depend on what behavior is in the rational interest of legislators, judges, and police. (Friedman 2001, p. 1)

However, there have been many contract law rulings in the United States that have undermined the common law as an institution that provides catallactic stability. Consider some examples. First, in *Peevyhouse v. Garland Coal & Mining Co.* (1962), a stated contractual payment of $29,000 to restore land after a mining operation was reduced to $300 arbitrarily by the Supreme Court of Oklahoma. It said that the latter figure was socially efficient since the value of Peevyhouse's farm would only be increased by $300 if the $29,000 worth of repairs were made. It made no difference that the contract specifically stated $29,000 for damages.

Second, in *Jacob & Youngs v. Kent* (1921), a contractual requirement specifying the use of only "Reading" brand pipe in the construction of a man's summer home was overridden by the court. In using another brand, the contractor showed "substantial performance" toward fulfilling the agreement. It would be inefficient for the relatively poorer builder to purchase and replace the pipe after the job was completed. The contractual wording became irrelevant.

Third, in *Eastern Steamship Lines, Inc. v. United States* (1953), the $4 million specified reimbursement for repair of a ship was cut in half by the court. (The merchant ship had been borrowed by the government during World War II.) The value of the repaired ship would be less than the cost of the repairs and thus abiding by the contract's exact wording would be socially inefficient.

Fourth, in *Lake River Corp. v. Carborundum Co.* (1985), Posner snubbed what he considered to be an inefficient contractual provision. It imposed a "penalty" in excess of a reasonable effort to estimate damages. The fact that both parties agreed to the provision initially made no difference; Posner was concerned with a higher objective, viz., what he thought was a proper social allocation of resources.

Finally, in *Williams v. Walker-Thomas Furniture Co.* (1964-1965), the court voided an agreement, calling it an "unconscionable" contract. The court protected Williams despite the fact that she defaulted on her obligation. The ruling was considered socially efficient since the business was deemed to have superior contracting capacity compared to the poor woman (who was a welfare recipient with seven children).[86] As a result, what certainty is there now that contracts will be upheld in the United States?

Socially adverse rulings pertaining to tort

Likewise, the law of tort has been adversely influenced by efficiency jurisprudence. In *Liability: The Legal Revolution and Its Consequences* (1988), Peter Huber records some of the more detestable rulings of government-run civil procedure in the United States. Consider the following example:

> Lilly Gray bought a new Ford Pinto in November 1971. Six months later she set out on a drive to Barstow, California, accompanied by thirteen-year-old Richard Grimshaw. While going up the freeway exit ramp, the car stalled; moments later another car slammed into its rear, driving the gas tank forward and impaling it on a bolt. The passenger compartment was engulfed in flames. Mrs. Gray was killed, and Richard suffered permanently disfiguring burns over his face and body. He sued Ford. The placement of the Pinto's gas tank behind the rear axle, his lawyer argued, made it unsafe in rear-end collisions. Inexpensive changes would have protected against the danger. Ford responded that the car had a reasonably safe overall design and met federal standards for crash-

---

[86] The case citations for these decisions are: *Peevyhouse v. Garland Coal & Mining Company* (1962), Supreme Court of Oklahoma, 382 P.2d 109; *Jacob & Youngs v. Kent* (1921), Court of Appeals of New York, 230 N.Y. 239, 129 N.E. 889; *Eastern Steamship Lines, Inc. v. United States* (1953), United States Court of Claims, 112 F.Supp. 167, 125 Ct.Cl. 422; *Lake River Corporation v. Carborundum Company* (1985), U.S. Court of Appeals, Seventh Circuit, 769 F.2d 1284; and *Williams v. Walker-Thomas Furniture Company I* (1964), District of Columbia Court of Appeals, 198 A.2d 914 [not overturned] plus *Williams v. Walker-Thomas Furniture Company II* (1965), United States Court of Appeals District of Columbia Circuit, 350 F.2d 445, 121 U.S.App.D.C. 315.

worthiness in effect at the time. A jury awarded Richard $2.5 million in compensation for his injuries, much of it for the pain he had suffered, and a further stunning $125 million in punitive damages against Ford, which the trial judge cut to $3.5 million. Ford did not bother to contest the award for Richard's pain but it did appeal the punitive award, insisting that it had no evil motive. In 1981, a full nine years after the accident, the court of appeals conceded as much but sustained the jury award anyway. California law, it declared, allows punitive damages even if the defendant had no "actual intent to harm the plaintiff or others." All that is necessary is "conscious disregard" for the safety of such persons. "Punitive damages," the court explained "provide a motive for private individuals to enforce rules of law and enable them to recoup the expenses of doing so." So Ford paid Richard $6 million, most of which went to cover intangible distress, on the one hand, and corporate iniquity, on the other (Huber 1988, pp. 115-116).

While modern jurisprudence in the United States might be considered efficient from a rent seeker's point of view, it is not clear that it is efficient for society. Efficiency rulings and "hard cases" tend to augment uncertainties which exacerbate human uneasiness rather than establishing a means to alleviate it. As Huber reminds us, civil procedure is creating much uncertainty, especially in the area of tort law (e.g., product liability).

One might wonder whether it would be less costly for large firms based in the United States today to move their main operations to a politically less stable developing country. Perhaps they could purchase thousands of acres inexpensively in a Third World nation and then build a "complex" to facilitate their production and security. It might include factories, a shipping port, an airfield, a paramilitia, a communications center, etc., along with a division of payola specialists to administer the optimal bribing of local officials.

While such an extravagance may seem farfetched, given the uncertainties faced by American firms today due to product liability, it is entirely plausible that taking such extreme steps would be less costly than retaining a base of operations in the United States. In the starkest terms, doing business in America entails paying for (1) the high costs of regulation, (2) the potential punitive damages from product liability, and (3) the potential abrogation of contracts or property rights by judicial (public interest) determinations based on the efficiency criteria. Upcoming stable countries like Chile might be able to capitalize on this American crisis in law. Furthermore, it is worthwhile to consider in more depth how modern property law theory has contributed to rulings that further exacerbate these social adversities.

Rights in property

One can see how the common law evolves through two important tort cases that relate to the use of property (Cooter and Ulen 1997, pp. 63-67). Property is often involved in causing economic damages, and the courts have been the traditional means of determining responsibility. When there is an accident involving private property, courts have to decide which contestant has the responsibility of avoiding risks—and thus who must pay damages.

In the case of *Butterfield v. Forrester* (1809), the court decided that the plaintiffs could not obtain the compensation they sought if their own negligence had *contributed* in causing the harm—even though the defendant was also negligent (Cooter and Ulen 1997, pp. 65). But later on, in a similar case *Davies v. Mann* (1842), the judges modified this common law precedent (the lawyers had understandably argued using the *Butterfield* case). The court invented the "last clear chance doctrine," which says that if both parties in an accident were negligent, the one which had the last clear chance to avoid it will be liable to pay for any losses (Cooter and Ulen 1997, p. 67). The common law thus evolved.

The law of property supplies a legal framework for allocating resources and distributing wealth (Cooter and Ulen 1997, pp. 69). It is concerned with how property rights are established or acquired, what types of things can be owned, how negative externalities are to be dealt with, how regulation restricts property rights, and what legal remedies are provided against illegal entrance into property. Accordingly, Cooter and Ulen identify four fundamental questions that make up the categories of the law of property: (a) How are property rights established? (b) What things can be privately owned? (c) What may owners do with their property? (d) What remedies are there when property rights are violated? (Cooter and Ulen 1997, p. 71) Cooter and Ulen also use the common, yet dubious, concept of property as "a bundle of rights" (see chapter fifteen), which describe in what way property is owned (Cooter and Ulen 1997, p. 72).

Public policy also plays an important role in the use and enjoyment of property. For instance, there are theoretical reasons why property rights in land are defended through reactive policies. Given that rational people allocate resources to defense such that the marginal cost of defending land is equivalent to the marginal benefit of doing so, then, at the margin, the value of resources used for military ends (the marginal cost) is the same as when they are used for productive ends (the marginal benefit). A practical example may be seen in the production of agricultural products and livestock (marginal opportunity cost), where owners must decide how much labor to allocate to defense of the land and how much to cultivation (Cooter and Ulen 1997, pp. 75-76). Likewise, the optimal amount of reactive policy used to defend and real property is a function of the marginal benefit received from it. And one would expect that more resources would be expended for real property in Manhattan than in remote areas of Alaska or Nevada.

A constitutional order reduces costs and increases security

It might be that landowners create government to defend themselves and to protect their property rights, because they can do so at a lower cost per person than each individual would have to pay for self-defense. Thus, savings might result from scale economies in having a large army for a region or a society that can defend everyone, rather than having many tiny privately-owned armies. That is, government could be granted a natural monopoly of force (cf. Mises 1966, pp. 238, 397, 419, 431). Consequently, men can move from the "state of nature" (the absence of civil government) to a "social contract," which dictates the terms of common defense and coexistence (Cooter and Ulen 1997, p. 76). For example, cooperation can permit people to dedicate more resources to cultivating and less to defense. As a result, everyone can produce more and thus generate a social surplus. Therefore, the law of property enhances the incentives structure to prevent theft by means of democratic reactive policy (Cooter and Ulen 1997, p. 78).

The terms of exchange are more pleasing and efficient when people agree on them—instead of being forced to comply by government. Thus, legislation is not necessarily desirable where exchange and negotiation are operative, although it might be where those things fail (Cooter and Ulen 1997, pp. 79). The latter represents the inverse case of the Coase Theorem: when transactions costs are sufficiently high to impede exchange, the efficient allocation of resources could well depend on how property rights are assigned in the political process (Cooter and Ulen 1997, p. 82).

Accordingly, policies might be designed in such a way to optimize the benefits of private property. Because the law of property evolves and engenders catallactic stability and predictability, it becomes one of the most important aspects of law and economics analysis. Policies can be enacted to classify or define property. For instance, property has been characterized as a "set of privileges and responsibilities" or a "bundle of rights."[87] As Werner Hirsch states:

> The concept of property rights relates to the set of privileges and responsibilities accorded to a person in relation to the owning of property in general and real property in particular. These rights are determined by a long history of property laws, whether common laws or statutory laws. The right to property is the power to exclude others from or give them access to a benefit or use of the particular object (Hirsch 1988, pp. 24-25).

The concept of property rights is evolutionary in some sense, especially since the nature of property is dynamic. Sometimes technology emerges that create artificial property, as in the case of intellectual property (e.g., patents, trademarks, copyright). What exactly is ownership in property? LeFevre says that "the act of ownership is the assumption of sovereign control over property, to the exclusion of the rest of the world" (LeFevre 1966, p. 34). In the modern world, ownership rights may be natural or a function of public policy. In the former case, the constitution would be ordained to protect the rights that precede the state. In the latter case, legislation is use to create and maintain them.

Should the state control or define property rights?

Sanctioning proactive policy to control or define property rights is troublesome. According to free market theorists,

---

[87] For instance, one may see the modern use of "bundle of rights" by the U.S. Supreme Court in *Florence Dolan v. City of Tigard*, 114 S.Ct. 2309, 129 L.Ed.2d. 304, 321.

the attenuation of property rights by the state leads to economic distortions. Indeed, when government centrally owns the means of production, the one outcome that can usually be predicted with some certainty is that there will be a misallocation of resources, as evinced by the cataclysmic dissolution of formerly communist economies in Europe. Furthermore, in Hayek's view, losing control of productive property to the state destroys liberty:

> [I]n transferring all property in the means of production to the state, they put the state in a position whereby its action must in effect decide all other incomes (Hayek 1944, p. 103).

Hayek continues:

> It is only because the control of the means of production is divided among people acting independently that nobody has complete power over us, that we as individuals can decide what to do with ourselves. If all the means of production were vested in a single hand, whether it be nominally that of 'society' as a whole or that of a dictator, whoever exercises this control has complete power over us (Hayek 1944, p. 104).[88]

Thus, Hayek sees a grave danger in allowing the state to define or control property rights. Congruently, Mises remarks that private property is an essential catallactic institution, and should be guarded jealously above all freedoms.

> Private property of the material factors of production is not a restriction of the freedom of all other people to

---

[88] Hayek also comments here: "It is pathetic, yet at the same time encouraging, to find as prominent an old communist as Max Eastman rediscovering this truth: 'It seems obvious to me now—though I have been slow, I must say, in coming to the conclusion—that the institution of private property is one of the main things that have given man that limited amount of free and equalness that Marx hoped to render infinite by abolishing this institution. Strangely enough Marx was the first to see this'."

choose what suits them best. It is, on the contrary, the means that assigns to the common man, in his capacity as a buyer, supremacy in all economic affairs. It is the means to stimulate a nation's most enterprising men to exert themselves to the best of their abilities in the service of all of the people (Mises 1988, p. 39).

Rowley adds:

The natural right to property is simply another name for the freedom to act according to one's own choices, defining allowable acts of transformation of the material world (Rowley 1993, p. 73).

Individual self-interest creates a natural tendency to care for property and to optimize the use of property. Social assurances that resource benefits will be secure, create the motivation to maintain, improve, and utilize resources over an anticipated period of use. Conversely, the expectation that others will reap the rewards of resource stewardship reduces the incentive to care for and put resources to their most highly valued use.[89] Therefore, great caution should be taken before enacting any public policy which grants power to the state to define or regulate private property.

---

[89] The important of private property free of state intrusion is a common theme among free market economists. Buchanan states that private ownership of property is "necessary for efficiency in the production of economic value" and it protects personal liberty by "providing viable exit from, or avoidance of entry into, potentially exploitative economic relationships" (Buchanan 1993, pp. 55, 32). Robert Anderson contends: "Without the institution of private property in the ownership of productive economic resources and a legal framework securing contractual agreements in the transfer of economic resources, an advanced world market economy would never have developed" (Anderson 1992, p. 33). Mises remarks that, "private property is inextricably linked with civilization" (Mises 1996, p. 264). Vaughn sums up the need for private property: "Without private property, there can be no market prices to reflect the consensus of individual valuations. Without market prices, there can be no rational economic calculation. Without private resource markets (which of course would be impossible without private resource ownership) there would be no way for any central authority to decide whether in making a resource decision, it was sacrificing a less valued opportunity for a more highly valued one, or using a valued resource in the production of a less valued product" (Vaughn 1994, pp. 42-43).

Unlike personal property rights, *real property* rights have infrequently been *absolute*. Real property means land and things attached to the land. Since real property comprises the most basic and essential means of production, private ownership of it is essential for the operation of a market economy. Yet government often retains some of the rights from the "bundle" of real property ownership claims. Thus, besides criticizing government monopolization of money and suggesting free banking as a policy alternative (chapter eleven), free market theorists have also criticized government intervention and controls on real property. Due to real property's unique place in the structure of production, regulating it can adversely affect social resource allocation.

In *Building Regulation, Market Alternatives, and Allodial Policy* (1997), I argue that the contemporary real property system (in the United States in particular) is essentially *feudal*. Conformably, Sylvester Petro and other scholars have correlated modern real property policy with feudalism.

The antithesis of feudalism, or current real property policy, is *allodialism*. As policy, allodialism would mandate *absolute* ownership of real property. According to *The Oxford English Dictionary*, allodial real property ownership means: "An estate held in absolute ownership without service or acknowledgment of any superior, as among the early Teutonic peoples; opposed to feudum or feud." Allodial real property is owned absolutely without being subject to any rent, service, or right of superior or lord, including the state. In order to understand and classify the important legal elements of real property law, I have summarized and contrasted each of these real property policies as follows:

Allodialism is a system or policy where real property is held in absolute ownership without service or acknowledgment of any superior, as opposed to a *feud*. It is an estate held by absolute ownership, without recognizing any superior to whom any duty is due on account thereof. *Feudalism* is a system or policy where real property is held of a superior or lord. The superior exacts fees (taxes) from his tenants and has the power to regulate the use of his real property. *Manorialism* is a system where the rights of a lord to demand personal services from his tenants (serfs) is maintained. It was associated with real property and feudalism but essentially referred to the duties performed by the serf rather than a structural system or policy of real property (like feudalism) (Cobin 1997, p. 116).

Land is a higher-order capital good, although topsoil, crops, timber, etc. are capital goods of a somewhat lower order (the land supports these goods). Allodial rights include all of these capital goods plus man-made structures attached to the land, along with contractual improvements or benefits (e.g., restrictive covenants). Under plenary allodialism, real property could not be taxed or regulated.

Interestingly, a *quasi-allodial* policy is also feasible—as was manifest in the ante-bellum United States—where only trifling and occasional taxes or regulations were imposed on real property. Under this policy, real property would not be held in allodium technically, but it would be closer to allodialism than feudalism to warrant distinction.

Why are allodial or quasi-allodial policies important to discuss in the field of law and economics? From a free market perspective, allodial policy is an important means of solving government failures that is wholly compatible with an evolutionary system of law and market-based regulation. In the Hayekian sense, legal rules for property develop to recognize, establish, and defend property and its boundaries, as well as to foster catallactic activity and coordination. Allodial or quasi-allodial policies provide a model or paradigm in which the state's influence is removed from real property policy and the effects of human action with respect to real property can be analyzed apart from public choice or knowledge problems. Moreover, such policy contributes to individual liberty, which provides other beneficial results. Indeed, such policy affects the principal basis for law, being congruent with the human desire to be free that affects all of human action. As Dietze reminds us:

[L]iberty is not just one value among others, a maxim of morality on a par with all other maxims, but the source of, and necessary condition for, all other individual values (Dietze 1976, p. 111).

[M]aterial subordination of the law to liberty. For law is merely a means which has the protection of freedom as its end...the general rules of law were intended to protect the private sphere (Dietze 1976, p. 114).

Laws supporting allodial policy conform to this premise. Conversely, for non-allodial lands, legal rules for real property must be developed to restrict the use of real property resources, to regulate occupancy, and to determine the degree of control a possessor has over his "fee."[90] Allodial policy is a banner example of how the main theories covered in this book—public choice theory, Austrian economics, and law and economics—can be applied to public policy research and practice. As such, allodial policy will be considered in depth in the final chapter.

Problems in the law and economics movement

John Robson and Owen Lippert suggest that governments function as rule creators and administrators of services that

---

[90] The feudal term "fee" (which is still used in property law today) is a "freehold estate in lands, held of a superior lord, as a reward for services, and on condition of rendering some service in return for it." See *Black's Law Dictionary*, fourth edition, p. 741.

help people resolve disputes under such rules. They must make good rules and assure that disputes, the majority of which refer to civil cases (usually pertaining to contract), are resolved in an efficient and fair manner. Civil courts thus form a necessary, desirable, and integral part of a market economy (Robson and Lippert 1998, p. 3). Robson and Lippert argue that equilibrium must be found between expediting legitimate suits and impeding unjustified ones.

Contract rules and dispute resolution must be adapted to that useful end. In particular, the dispute resolution process should attempt to assure all the legitimate rights that it possibly can, without transforming itself into a complex system that consumes so much time that winners end up wasting the biggest part of what they recoup on legal expenses (Robson and Lippert 1998, p. 4).

Robson and Lippert contend that, so far, the traditional common law system (in Canada), has functioned well. The law has permitted reasonable adults to contract in whatever way they choose, and the courts have applied a useful definition of "reasonable person" within the dispute resolution process. However, there has been a proliferation of new rules concerning regulation and tort law, along with many socially adverse efficiency rulings in general, that have negatively affected the judicial system in recent decades (Robson and Lippert 1998, p. 4).

One major catallactic problem arises when the risks and responsibilities are distributed unfairly. In such cases, nobody is going to contract. Also, if the dispute resolution process is too slow, too expensive, or arbitrary, the benefits that would normally be attainable by contracting will not be sought after (Robson and Lippert 1998, p. 4). It is of paramount policy importance to determine how the legal system influences and possibly damages the market economy. As we have seen, there is evidence from the United States that the contracting process and various rulings have been meddlesome and injurious. Procedures for litigating suits and jury selection also seem to have wrought in stilted effects. At least many Canadians are concerned (for good reason) that the problems in the United States will appear in Canada also (e.g., absurd liability cases and ruinous family court decisions). Perhaps people in other common law countries should be worried as well (Robson and Lippert 1998, p. 5).

Courts in the United States used to evaluate contracts according to a few clear and fundamental common law rules. But now the judicial branch must increasingly determine whether completing the contract under dispute will fulfill the requirements of various regulations and obscure legislation. Judges and jurors already lack the information necessary to judge correctly in terms of the public interest. It might be that the current legal system has turned into what Hayek forecast-ted: an over complexity of rules creates uncertainty for all that both erodes the common law and damages the free market (Robson and Lippert 1998, p. 9). Several proposi-tions can be identified as contributing to this predicament.

Transactions costs in relation to property

Transactions costs involve three elements: (a) search and information costs, (b) bargaining costs (including hostility problems at times, and communication problems), and (c) enforcement costs (Cooter and Ulen 1997, pp. 84-86). Recall that transactions costs do not have to be zero in order for the Coase Theorem to be applicable (as implied in Cooter and Ulen 1997, p. 87). They must merely be lower than the cost of litigation.

In contrast to what free market theorists would suggest as the best policy to reduce transactions costs, Cooter and Ulen ignore public choice and knowledge issues and suggest that property rights can be assigned through judicial intervention. Like Posner and Landes, they incorrectly imagine that judges can resolve problems that arise as consequence of high transactions costs (Cooter and Ulen 1997, p. 88). They justify such judicial activism on specious philosophical theorems: the normative Coase theorem and the normative Hobbes theorem.

Coase: positive and normative theorems

Cooter and Ulen give us two philosophical theorems to aid judges in applying the law. The first one is the normative Coase theorem. It says that the law should be structured such that impediments to contracting or private negotiation are eliminated. Then, with the resulting increase in private exchange, the economy will become more efficient (Cooter and Ulen 1997, p. 89). The second one is the normative Hobbes theorem. It says that the law should be structured such that damages caused by negotiating or contracting failures are minimized. To put these ideas into effect, the law should assign property rights to the party that considers them most valuable. Along with the Coase theorem, these two theorems form the rationale for the economic analysis of the law of property, and provide further justification for efficiency rulings (Cooter and Ulen 1997, p. 90).

Clearly, when transactions costs are greater than the consumer surplus in an exchange, the net benefits from private trading would be negative (i.e., at least one person will lose by trading). In such cases, exchange will not occur between rational human beings. However, when the net benefit is positive, both parties will gain and trading will likely occur (Cooter and Ulen 1997, p. 91). Therefore, under the perspective disseminated by Cooter and Ulen, legislators and judges might be able to allocate resources efficiently if they can grant them to the party who considers them most valuable.

However, free market theorists contend that judges do not always (if ever) know who considers them to be most valuable. Such information is impossible to determine. However, Cooter and Ulen rightly recognize that legislators and judges face a trade-off between transactions costs and information. By strictly following precedent, courts avoid the information costs associated with determining who considers a right more valuable, and leaves with the parties any transactions costs that exist. To determine who considers a right most valuable, it frees both sides from the transactions costs of exchanging legal rights, but incurs the costs of information to determine who considers a right to be most valuable. Efficiency requires that the contestants do what is cheapest (Cooter and Ulen 1997, p. 92). Nevertheless, a consideration of knowledge and public choice problems would require that strictly following precedent is the best policy.

Doctrinal errors of the law and economics movement

In sum, an overall critique of the law and economics movement can be made based on the key themes developed in this book. The ideas presented by Posner, Landes, Cooter, Ulen, and other efficiency school idealists fail to adequately consider or take seriously five key issues: (a) the knowledge problem judges and legislators face, (b) that value is subjective and nobody can assign it objectively, (c) the impossibility of making interpersonal utility comparisons, (d) that government-directed or judge-directed resource and property rights allocation causes greater uncertainty, thus impeding catallactic efficiency, (e) and that judges, bureaucrats, and legislators involved in administering the common law—along with various legislative or regulatory activities—are susceptible to public choice problems. Furthermore, it stands to reason that the social costs that arise from these five problems will exceed the social benefits provided by efficiency judges, bureaucrats, and legislators. In short, the public interest is likely not served by the ideals presented in the law and economics movement.

Inefficiency in the law of contracts

Given this five-fold critique (especially the first, fourth, and fifth critiques), efficiency notions in the law of contract are replete with defects and dangers that will lead to government (judicial) failure. Contract law must be transparent and clearly minimize transactions costs in order to be effective in the market process. As Cooter and Ulen hope to facilitate: *"economic efficiency requires enforcing a promise if the promisor and promisee both wanted enforceability when it was made"* (Cooter and Ulen 1997, p. 167).

This criterion would be fine if it were strictly enforced. Judges, bureaucrats, and legislators would then have the objective of enabling people to cooperate by converting bargaining games from having uncooperative solutions to cooperative ones (Cooter and Ulen 1997, p. 171). However, in many rulings, judges are using efficiency and other normative criteria to justify the nonenforcement of agreements, thus turning this potentially beneficial criterion on its head and amplify social inefficiency by impairing contracts. Under the guise of improving social efficiency with economic theory, many judges are making business less predictable.

Inefficiency in the law of the tort

The five-fold critique also applies to the law of tort. Cooter and Ulen say that the law should "induce injurers to *internalize*" the external costs they impose on others. Thus, victims may be compensated and social efficiency will thus be enhanced. When those who cause harm must internalize the respective costs, they have incentives to invest in an efficient level of safety and precaution. Therefore, "the economic essence of tort law is its use of liability to internalize externalities created by high transactions costs" (Cooter and Ulen 1997, p. 262), as well as to promote incentives that yield "efficient precaution" (Cooter and Ulen 1997, p. 274).

They further contend that even *"small random errors in the legal standard imposed by a negligence rule causes the injurer to increase precaution"* (Cooter and Ulen 1997, p. 287). In economic models where judges and planners have perfect knowledge and are benign or benevolent executors or vicars of the public interest, such hypothesizing might make sense. But such fancies wither in light of the five-fold critique above.

Impact of the legal system on the free market

From the perspective of free market theorists, it is imperative to have a strong legal system in a free market. It is important to have institutions that establish or enhance social certainty too. Contrariwise, activist legislators and judges foment various distortions and raise social costs by applying efficiency and normative philosophy that thwart bargaining activity and property rights. A summary of many important cases is contained in the appendix which exemplify the influence that such activism has had on the law. In most of these cases, the difficulties generated by the efficiency theory of the law, along with evidence of the five-fold critique mentioned above, are evinced.

This book does not provide the first or the only critique of the modern law and economics movement. Other erudite scholars in law and economics, such as David Friedman in *Law's Order: What Economics Has to Do with Law and Why It Matters* (2001), have criticized the ideas of Posner, Landes and others who teach the doctrine of legal efficiency. The law has an enormous impact on the market process, and abusing the law will likely produce profound implications. Such was the impact of the 1995 United States Supreme Court *Sweet Home v. United States*, and again in *Kelo v. City of New London* (2005) where property rights were restricted and, conversely, in that court's 1994 *Dolan v. Tigard* decision, where property rights were exalted.

Thus, the impact of the efficiency school has been and will continue to be far-reaching. Yet, from a free market point of view, the efficiency school has generated more problems than it has resolved. Incentives, institutions, certainty, subjectivity, and knowledge are not trivial elements in economic theory. Catallactic success depends on public policy that minimizes state-sponsored distortions and which places confidence in those institutions and institutional arrangements that permit the market process to run smoothly.

Summary of criticisms, advances and solutions

Free market theorists, as advocates of the principle of subjectivity and the idea of catallaxy, have little use for modern notions of legal efficiency. The efficiency doctrine of Posner, et al, implies that a single intelligence is able to harness the requisite knowledge for a correct allocation of resources. From there, judges can issue a decree which makes the market more efficient, according to the Paretian principle. Correspondingly, if judges use an objective and unbiased ordinal ordering of utility they can decree Pareto preferred (or superior) moves for society. Thus, the logical conclusion is that judges may make economizing decisions on behalf of society that are socially efficient. Free market theorists reject this notion.

Subjective value theory precludes using judical activism

Because all value is subjective, Austrians argue that it is impossible to aggregate individual utility preferences or to make a decision on behalf of (or in the best interests of) society. Societies neither choose nor have preferences. Only individuals do. A judge cannot have the requisite knowledge to see a disequilibrating problem and correct it via decree.

Moreover, Posner, et al, cannot possibly know who is the least cost avoider, or what the social costs and the aggregate benefits are in any reallocation of resources. He can hardly know the value of an action to the relatively small group of people in his courtroom, let alone society. The Posnerian approach to social welfare is pernicious because the judge's notion of "fairness" is imposed upon others who may not share his preferences or value determination, and market distortions and greater uneasiness become dominant as a result.

Money awards do not accurately substitute for utility losses

Furthermore, efficiency theorists err by presuming they can use money as a proxy for general utility when comparing litigants' costs and benefits which would result from judicial decisions. Money is not a valid substitute for utility, just as the fair market value of property paid in cash is not a valid substitute for property (as noted in chapter ten). Efficiency judges blunder if they assume that people are indifferent between having their property or the fair market value of it in cash.

Market failure is not cured by judicial activism

Moreover, since the market does not fail—at least relative to what the state can do—there can hardly be any catallactic improvements made by judges who try to allocate resources efficiently. Indeed, for them to identify—and then try to fix—a special case negative externality is simply arbitrary and capricious (as noted in chapter twelve). Therefore, methodological individualism and subjectivity provide a strong basis to criticize Posnerian law and economics, just as it does other manifestations of social welfare philosophies which make use of the Paretian principle.

Accordingly, Austrian advances in the field of law and economics have been extensions of the subjectivity of value and the use of the individual as the focus of analysis. As Vaughn summarizes:

Law and economics, mercifully free of arcane mathematics and less hostage to formal modeling than other subdisciplines within economics, became an area congenial to new Austrians. For instance, new Austrians discussed the question of whether the common law is efficient from a Hayekian perspective (O'Driscoll, 1980b: Rizzo, 1980a). Rizzo was especially successful in carving out a niche in mainstream law journals for an economic approach to liability and tort law that reflected Austrian assumptions and methods of argumentation (1980c, 1981, 1982, 1987; Rizzo and Arnold, 1980). In particular, Rizzo criticized the Landes and Posner approach to law and economics that recommends that judges use efficiency as a criterion for rendering decisions (1980b). Rizzo argued that to use efficiency as a criterion for deciding tort cases, one had to be able to define wealth and to calculate appropriate shadow prices for objects subject to litigation. Both were necessary to make it possible to know what decision would increase rather than decrease wealth (643): yet, given the limits of our knowledge, it is impossible to do either. Wealth is a subjective concept that includes many nonmeasurable elements such as moral valuations that defy objective definition (646). Further, even if it were possible to define wealth, the calculation of correct shadow prices to measure wealth is impossible outside of equilibrium (647). The theory of the second best tells us that existing market prices are not necessarily good proxies for equilibrium prices, and hence judicial decisions that use market prices as shadow prices in settling disputes may make decisions that increase inefficiency (652). Rizzo's arguments reflected Austrian themes of limitations on knowledge, subjectivity of value, and the empirical irrelevance of general equilibrium. As an alternative to using efficiency standards to make judicial decisions, Rizzo advocated a rule of strict liability that requires only the establishment of causation. This, too, demonstrates an Austrian approach, given its congruence with Hayek's preference for rules over discretion in the legal framework (Hayek, 1973) (Vaughn 1994, p. 116).

According to Hayek, a social order should simply "facilitate the achievement of the projects and plans of its citizens" and "create a climate for peaceful, cooperative interaction among all the various actors in the order." However, judicial activism necessarily ravishes individual liberty and the enjoyment of private property (Vaughn 1994, p. 123).

Legal institutions are hamstrung by efficiency ideas

Menger, Hayek, Mises, Rizzo, and other Austrian scholars focus on the *institutional* legal framework of society. They know that resource allocation and prices will work themselves out. Proactive policy by legislative or judicial intervention to "improve" society will only harm the wider market and people in the long run (cf. Hazlitt's Lesson in *Economics in One Lesson*). For Hayek, the common law embodies the aggregation of social knowledge over time, and such knowledge should not be lightly regarded or shunned as it is with efficiency-school theorists. If Hayek's insights are to be taken seriously, then newfangled ideas about efficiency and social welfare rulings must be looked upon with suspicion.

Judicial activism is a harmful form of interventionism

Mises likewise maintained a critical view of social welfare ideas (see chapters seven and ten). The "babble" of interventionists, whom Mises called "the harbingers of economic retrogression, preaching a philosophy of decay and social disintegration," must be disregarded. A nation may avoid becoming "a society of progressing poverty for all its members" by jettisoning the "vicious economic theory" of interventionism (Mises 1966, pp. 854-855). Mises remarks that interventionism "cannot lead to a permanent system of organization" but only "directly lead toward socialism" and "the traditional caste system" that it purports to abhor (Mises 1966, pp. 858-859, 840-841).

Sowell has also been critical of judicial activism. With tremendous insightfulness, he laments over the uncertainties and economic misallocations it causes:

> In their zeal for particular kinds of decisions to be made, those with the vision of the anointed seldom consider the nature of the *process* [italics in original] by which decisions are made. Often what they propose amounts to third party decision making by people who pay no cost for being wrong—surely one of the least promising ways of reaching decisions satisfactory to those that must live with the consequences. It is not that the anointed advocate such processes, as such, but that their preoccupation with goals often neglects the whole question of process characteristics. The very standards by which social "problems" are defined tend likewise to be third party standards. Thus "waste," "quality," and "real needs" are terms blithely thrown around, as if some third party can define them for other people. Government actions to enforce these third party preemptions are often advocated in the form of bureaucracies to replace the systemic processes of the marketplace. Such practices as **judicial activism** [emphasis added], intended to produce socially more beneficial results than a strict adherence to legal rules and traditions might produce, look very different within the framework of systemic causation. To derange

a whole process, evolved from the experiences of millions of people over centuries of legal development, on the basis of the beliefs or feelings of a particular judge or set of judges about a particular issue before them, risks raising up humanity in one place and pulling it down in another, to use Homes' analogy. "Hard cases make bad law" is another way the tragic vision has been expressed. To help some hard-pressed individual or group whose case is before them, judges may bend the law to arrive at a more benign verdict in that particular case—but at what cost of damaging the whole consistency and predictability of the law, on which millions of other people depend, and on which ultimately the freedom and safety of a whole society depend. There cannot be a law abiding society if no one knows in advance what law they are to abide by, but must wait for judges to create *ex post facto* legal rulings based on "evolving standards" rather than known rules. An expanding penumbra of uncertainty surrounding laws creates incentives for a growing volume of litigation, as well as for a black-mailing of law abiding individuals and organizations into out-of-court settlements because they cannot be sure how some speculative charge against them will be viewed by judges operating under "evolving standards" (Sowell 1995, pp. 129-130).

Huber likewise deplores the debasement of tort law in the United States, suggesting that further derogation of rights and the reduction of freedom lie ahead.

I shall conclude by paraphrasing Grant Gilmore, whose words have rich meaning for those sincerely dismayed, as I am, by the recent, hasty, and ill-considered transformation of tort law. Law reflects but in no sense determines the moral worth of a society. The better the society, the less law there will be. In heaven there will be no law, and the lion will lie down with the lamb. The worse the society, the more law there will be. In hell there will be nothing but law, and due process will be meticulously observed (Huber 1988, p. 232).

Protecting property from visionary policies

The uncertainties and government failures generated by efficiency jurisprudence are only part of the problem. The destabilization of private property rights also has a devastating effect on catallactic conditions. Perhaps with Mises in mind, Petro reminds us that private property rights are a necessity for advancing human action:

> Men act. Action means deliberate movement from a less satisfactory to a more satisfactory state of affairs. Satisfaction is subjective. If it is to be striven for effectively and broadly, universal personal freedom is the necessary condition. But freedom without broad, coherent property rights is a contradictory concept; the two are not separate and integrating concepts; they are the same idea analyzed with different ratiocinative [reasoning] techniques. I am not a free man unless I am in broad control of my person, unless I have a full property right in myself, and, of course, in that which I acquire without infringing upon the equal right of others. When action is hampered by arbitrary controls, when acquisitions are subjected non-consensually to fragmented proprietary dominions, freedom is diminished and society characterized by conflict and contradiction (Petro 1974, p. 178).

Robert Anderson contends that the damage done to private property has adversely affected economic calculation:

> Both consumers and producers have felt the heavy hand of interventionism through regulations and edicts that have caused a disintegration of economic control of their

property. The consequential destruction of both economic resources and human creativity has been devastating (Anderson 1992, p. 35).

Along with Austrian and public choice theorists, Anderson argues that stable property and contract rules are necessary for economic development.

This historical accomplishment has resulted from a rule of law that eventually secured both private claims to property and the freedom to contract. Without the institution of private property in the ownership of productive economic resources and a legal framework securing contractual agreements in the transfer of economic resources, and advanced world market economy would never have developed (Anderson 1992, p. 33).

Accordingly, William F. Buckley is wary of purported liberty-enhancing policies that in reality ravage social welfare.

That passion for freedom that catapulted us [Americans] two hundred years ago into national independence and into the most exciting attempt in history at the incorporation of human freedom into a federal constitution, had by and large been reduced to a velleity [a casual wish] for some kinds of freedom, though a complicated libertarian vocabulary was constructed, the purpose of which was to demonstrate that freedom is in fact enhanced, rather than diminished, when we assign to the government control over our lives (Buckley 1976, p. 97).

Posner and the efficiency school purport that they can improve social welfare by applying their newfangled approach to law. For free market theorists, this claim is incredulous at best, and the results of the proactive policies that are engendered by efficiency ideals are always destructive.

Voluntary law: an institution facilitating human action

The contemporary trend in law and economics differs significantly from the Austrian paradigm, being established on a static and anti-subjectivist method. Furthermore, its intimate nexus with the state and proactive policy poses incompatibilities with the Virginia School of public choice.

However, a mechanism exists to facilitate a reliable legal institution and development of civil procedure that is suitable for the Austrian and Virginia Schools. From the perspective of these schools, the law is a voluntary enterprise. Law consists both of rules of conduct and the mechanism or process for applying those rules. It subjects human conduct to the governance of law, and it directs purposeful human action. Individuals must have incentives to recognize rules of conduct or they will become irrelevant and institutions of enforcement would become necessary.

There are basically two ways that laws (or legislation) emerge: by coercion (i.e., imposed or involuntary law) or voluntarily (i.e., from customs and practices). Imposed law usually results from a powerful interest group who persuades government to enforce widespread acceptance. Alternatively, voluntary law garners widespread acceptance naturally. Such a customary law would tend to be followed as people recognized the attractive benefits that result from behaving according to the expectations of others. Thus, voluntary or customary law is reciprocity driven, i.e., reciprocities are the basic source both of the basic duty to obey and enforcement of the law.

Three conditions allow the reciprocity premise to work: (1) the relationship of reciprocity must evolve from voluntary agreement of immediately affected parties, (2) the reciprocal performance of the parties in some sense must be equally valued, and (3) relationships must be sufficiently fluid so that the same duty you owe me today I may owe you tomorrow (principle of reversibility), like accident insurance. Offenses would be treated as torts (private wrongs) rather than as crimes. Since there is no such thing as a victimless tort, this type of law would not rise voluntarily—leaving room for reactive policy.

The major source of legal change in a voluntary system is dispute resolution. Participants would be obligated to aid other members in a valid dispute, with reciprocal loyalty, with non-violent dispute resolution. Of course, obliging them to do so would be a form of reactive policy. The power of arbitrators would be limited to persuading everyone that his ruling is beneficial to both groups. The typical punishment for the guilty would tend to be economic restitution in the form of a fine or an indemnity to the plaintiff.[91]

A market-based (private) legal system

From an Austrian and Virginia School point of view, a private system of civil procedure would be most appealing. There is no compelling theoretical reason for maintaining government-monopolized civil procedure. Especially in the United States, where the present scheme fosters much rent seeking behavior, market distortions, and misallocations of resources on account of judicial activism.

If all civil procedure were conducted by the market process, rather than by government monopoly, the knowledge problem would not be a factor. The appropriate level of coordinating knowledge would be managed in the catallaxy automatically. Moreover, social losses from rent seeking would be diminished substantially, as would a commensurate number of lawyers and law schools, correcting distortions in both the labor and education markets. Benson remarks on how a private system would work:

---

[91] Portions of these two paragraphs were derived from notes from Charles Rowley's class lectures on Law and Economics at George Mason University, spring 1994.

Private contractual arrangements can create a strong demand for clear, well-founded, impartial decisions—the types of decisions that serve as precedents whether that is their intent or not. In effect, given the contracts and agreements between diverse groups and protection firms, the benefits of precedents would be internalized. Internalization arises because of the reciprocal cooperation and competition between numerous identifiable groups rather than by merger of those groups into a single political party entity (government) (Benson 1990, p. 365).

He further contends that a private system would eliminate public choice problems and generate efficiency gains:

The misallocation of resources due to interest group demands and nonprice rationing could be far more significant than misallocation due to bureaucratic production inefficiencies. Thus, the major shortcoming of contracting out is that it can only overcome a few of the problems that arise from government failure: "in reality, the factors which militate against efficient production in the public sector also militate against getting highest-quality results from contracts." Of course, gains in the production efficiency are better than no gains at all (Benson 1990, p. 196).

Benson goes on to argue that the negative externalities generated by government failure are far more worrisome than the imperfections to be expected in a market-based system:

Once again, such negative externalities imply government produces *too much* law. Thus, even if the private sector would produce too little law, as is implied by the public good externality argument for government provision of law, it does not follow that the public sector does a better job. Neither system is likely to be perfect. The question is: Which creates the most significant imperfections? This discussion implies that private sector failures have been substantially exaggerated by government law advocates while significant government failure arguments have been overlooked (Benson 1990, p. 286).

Buchanan likewise remarks that market alternatives may not be perfect, especially when they are afflicted by public choice problems and judicial activism, but they are still the best option for obtaining the highest level of social welfare:

> Market forces may not be trusted for several reasons, including the lack of understanding of how these forces work. But, also, markets may be recognized to be vulnerable to interference by politicians. *Laissez-faire*, as a policy stance, may be trusted more than its opposite. And individuals who feel too dependent on markets may seek greater protections for their residual liberties through structures of property ownership. But with modern jurisprudence on the legitimacy of governmental takings of privately-owned assets such security may be impossible to achieve (Buchanan 1993, p. 57).

Benson continues his discussion, pointing out that government-generated negative externalities are (not coincidentally) an often-overlooked issue in the public provision of law and legal services:

> Those who advocate government production are quick to point out the externalities associated with markets but, as Tullock pointed out, the externalities generated by the government process are often ignored. The argument presented here is that public production of law and order produces negative externalities. Police are inefficiently used to produce services that do not warrant the costs, too many laws are passed, and too many court cases are

brought. The private-public issue is not simply one of detailing the potential inefficiency of private law and order and opting for public provision. When the commons problem of public law enforcement services is combined with bureaucratic tendencies to over-produce and inefficiently produce the resulting output, it becomes obvious that the public production of law and order is not an efficient substitute for market production. Bureaucratic over-enforcement precludes political efficiency which, if it were achieved, would not translate into economic (or allocative) efficiency because of the commons problem. Beyond that, it *must* be remembered that government institutions of law have a different purpose than the institutions of customary law. Customary law and its institutions facilitate voluntary interaction; government law and its institutions facilitate involuntary transfers (Benson 1990, p. 101).

Private law enforcement

The reality is that market-based solutions have a solid track record of success and would likely prove to be an excellent policy option for the future. Not surprisingly, therefore, private services have been a growing element in the legal enterprise already. As Benson remarks:

Privatization of many aspects of the enterprise of law are occurring, the benefits of privatization are substantial, and historical examples of successful customary law systems abound. Furthermore, the arguments for government production of law and order are generally false. Major resistance to privatization arises from the self-interest motives of those in government or those who gain transfers through the legal system, and government failure in providing law and order is significant. Finally, private arrangements for law production and enforcement can be visualized. Thus, government production of internal order is unnecessary, and there is justification for as much privatization as can be developed. If excuses for expanding government involvement in the enterprise of law are recognized as invalid, perhaps resistance to government growth will be a little stronger. Perhaps the trend can even be reversed. The fact that government may be inevitable for one society as long as an aggressive government exists some place else is certainly no reason to accept the level of government involvement we have today or to discourage or prevent any of the privatization that is currently underway (Benson 1990, p. 374).

Indeed, private law enforcement services have been theoretical and empirical successes. As Benson notes:

Using economic theory, then, it can be convincingly demonstrated that private-sector (i.e., market or voluntary) institutions are capable of establishing strong incentives that lead to effective law making and law enforcement. The resulting legal constraints facilitate interaction and support social order by inducing cooperation and reducing violent confrontation. It can also be shown that public-sector institutions create incentives that can lead to substantial inefficiencies in the provision of these same functions. In fact, our modern reliance on government to make law and establish order is not the historical norm. Public police forces were not imposed on the populace until the middle of the nineteenth century in the United States and Great Britain, for instance, and then only in the face of considerable citizen resistance. Crime victims played the prosecutors' role in England until almost the turn of the century, and they did not yield to public prosecution without a struggle. The foundation of commercial law was developed by the European merchant community and enforced through merchant courts.

To this day, international trade is "governed" to a large extent by merchants, as they make, arbitrate, and enforce their own law; and in the United States, at least 75 percent of commercial disputes are settled through private arbitration or mediation with decisions based on business custom and practice (customary commercial law) (Benson 1990, p. 2).

As a result, Benson concludes that great benefits would be derived from plenary privatization of the legal system, even though one might expect considerable resistance from SIGs to such a change. A vigorous free market perspective would be to concur with Benson—at least with the privatization of civil procedure—and to reject entirely the wayward judicial efficiency conjectures of Posner, et al. The role of the state would thus be reduced to reactive policies for criminal justice, a role wholly congruent with the thinking of Mises, Hayek, Buchanan, Tullock, and the majority of free market theorists.

Appendix: Important cases in law and economics

Property law

1. ***Boomer v. Atlantic Cement Co.*** (1978, Court of Appeals of New York). Negative externalities (air and land): limit damages to promote social efficiency. A cement plant near Albany, New York, was causing a nuisance by emitting dirt, smoke, and vibration. The plant cost more than $45 million. The company had been paying damages for claims. Nonetheless, the court wanted to avoid the plant being closed on account of never-ending fines and potential lawsuits. Therefore, the court awarded what it called "permanent damages," which were designed to spur the owners to incur research costs to eliminate the nuisances. The company would then be able to continue

operating, and the permanent damages would be a one time compensation for all past and future property losses (precluding any future recovery actions). Thus, neither side emerged completely victorious in the suit. The dissenting judge said that it was wrong to apply such a rule which would not enjoin the firm's operations. The decision was unfair and dangerous, he said, since pollution causes continual damages. Thus, he concluded, the decision promotes the interest of the company rather than the public interest.

2. *Spur Industries Inc. v. Del E. Webb Development Co.* (1972, Supreme Court of Arizona). <u>Negative externalities (air): judges decide the efficient allocation according to his determination of the preferences involved</u>. Ranch land was purchased to start developing the community of Sun City, Arizona. The stench from the nearby stables (which had been there first) was very strong and affected value of Webb's new housing development. Flies due to the operation also provoked a considerable nuisance. Consequently, Webb was not able to sell his building lots and sued for relief. The court ruled that the annoyances were as much private as they were public and thus decided to enjoin the cattle operation. However, the court did not blame Spur Industries for the negative externality. The expanding city had simply sprang up against its land. Consequently, Webb was ordered to pay Spur's costs to discontinue operations and to move it to a new location.

3. *Carpenter v. Double R Cattle Co.* (1983, Court of Appeals of Idaho). <u>Negative externalities (air): judges decide the efficient allocation according to their wish to fix the market and improve the quality of life (and thus augment social value)</u>. Like Spur Industries, this appeal also involved a noxious and offensive stench from a feedlot. The lower court permitted the operation to continue. A homeowner's group (Carpenter) tried to overturn the lower court decision by alleging a techni-

cality, viz., that the instructions to the jurors to consider the "social value" and "the interests of the community as a whole" by keeping the feedlot running were improper —making the first decision invalid. The court held that issues like community or firm size and social value were irrelevant. However, it sided with the homeowners in order to fix the market failure, saying that "without compensation, our market system does not reflect the true cost of products or services provided by the enterprise" and that "externalities distort the price signals." The judges argued that the ruling was necessary to defend efficiency and distributive justice.

4. ***Orchard View v. Martin Marietta*** (1980, Federal District Court, Oregon). <u>Negative externalities (air): it is socially efficient for companies to be liable for damages that result from their airborne activities</u>. This case dealt with negative externalities caused by aircraft fly-overs which caused pollution emission and damage to the property of the landowners below. The court ruled that the company had and has a social obligation to pay the external costs.

5. ***Fountainbleau Hotel v. Forty-Five Twenty-Five*** (1959, Court of Appeals, District of Florida). <u>Negative externalities (sunlight): blocking the rays of the sun is *not* a problem</u>. Fountainbleau was going add a fourteen-story addition to its building. Doing so would shade a substantial portion of the neighboring hotel, and so Fountainbleau's neighbor sued for relief. A temporary restraining order was put on Fountainbleau. But the court held that while the proposed property would damage his neighbor, it was not a violation of rights. No one has a right to the air or sunlight. The order that had favored Forty-Five Twenty-Five was rescinded.

6. ***Prah v. Maretti*** (1982, Supreme Court of Wisconsin). <u>Negative externalities (sunlight): blocking the rays of the sun is a problem</u>. The defendant's new house was blocking the plaintiff's solar panels, so he sued for injunctive relief.

In handing down its ruling, the court ignored nineteenth century precedents which it considered obsolete. It said that relief will be due if the objectionable conduct is found to be "unreasonable." So it was in this case. Modern technology and the necessity of developing new energy resources were given as reasons to ignore the precedents. The court held that no one may block the sunlight when it is being used to generate electricity (akin to social efficiency ideals).

7. *Moore v. Regents of the University of California* (1988, Court of Appeals of the second division of California). <u>Positive externalities (health): it is efficient in property law that the individual rather than society retain owner-ship of his body</u>. A patient was diagnosed with hairy-cell leukemia at the UCLA medical center. Moore's spleen was removed. Without his consent, cells from his spleen were used to create a pharmaceutical product that generated sales of three billion dollars. The court ruled that Moore must retain the profits from this drug. His right to decide whether his spleen can be used or not must be maintained. A dissenting judge argued that some societal values are more important than wealth.

8. *Doe v. Miles Laboratories* (1987, District Court of the United States in Maryland). <u>Negative externalities (health): efficiency mandates that all firms be liable, even when dealing with an indispensable social function</u>. A woman ("Jane Doe") contracted AIDS from a blood transfusion administered after doctors dealt with a case of vaginal bleeding. The court said that markets are only partially efficient since there are externalities. There are indirect and hidden costs not included in the price of a good. Therefore, giving a strict liability rule will alter precautionary costs of manufacturing firms, which it said could set new prices for its goods. The court thought it was generating a mechanism for a "rational allocation of resources." The court also rejected the notion that social

policy should exempt the firm from such a lawsuit since blood producers "promote the general welfare." The court said that they are liable.

9. ***United States v. City of Niagara Falls*** (1989, Federal District Court, Eastern New York). <u>Negative externalities (governmental): social efficiency mandates that consumers should pay considerably higher prices in order to achieve an environmental social goal.</u> The city was dumping ill-treated sewage in the Niagara River. The Clean Water Act of 1974 said that the level of "toxic pollutants" in the river was too high. The city repaired its sewage system in 1978 (using federal grants) but the carbon system failed and so the city continued to discharge untreated sewage into the river. The city claimed that there was no efficient means of rediverting the water back through the treatment plant. Nonetheless, when the city failed to redivert it, federal workers sued and demanded that the contamination be halted. The court said that despite the fact that diverting the sewage would be a heavy financial burden on the city and its consumers, it was necessary to do it anyway.

10. ***Ploof v. Putnam*** (1908, Supreme Court of Vermont). <u>The necessity to trespass on real property: in extreme cases it is permissible to negate property rights temporarily.</u> Ploof moored his sloop to Putnam's dock to avert catastrophe on account of a violent storm. Putnam untied the rope, claiming his right of ejectment and the sloop and its contents were destroyed on the rocks, with Ploof being injured. The court ruled in favor of Ploof, saying that "entrance into the land of another person is permissible when it is justified by necessity."

11. ***Vincent v. Lake Erie Transport Co.*** (1910, Supreme Court of Minnesota). <u>The necessity to trespass on real property: rights to the use of property may be violated in extreme cases, but payment must be rendered for any damage.</u> In another boating decision related to a violent

storm, the court ruled that it would not have been wise to unmoor the defendant's boat and either leave it adrift or let someone to try to navigate it. The court said that "The ordinary rules regulating property rights were suspended by forces beyond human control." However, the court directed that compensation be paid when property used in such circumstances had been taken or used, such as the broken dock cables in this case. The dissenting judge said that there would not have been a problem if Vincent had used stronger cables to begin with and he blamed him for poor planning.

Contract law

12. **Williams v. Walker-Thomas Furniture Co.** (1964, Court of Appeals of D.C. and 1965, United States Court of Appeals for D.C.). Contract breached on account of socially inefficient "unconscionability." Williams had purchased furniture from 1957-1962 under contract but then defaulted. She was an uneducated single mother of seven children. The firm tried to repossess all the furniture she bought, just as the contract provided. The lower court felt badly, but sided with the merchant. It also said that Congress should protect people from such "exploitive" contracts, since they are contrary to the public interest. However, citing Uniform Commercial Code 2-302, the appeals court rebuked the merchant for being an exploiter and annulled its contract with Williams. The store's dealings were "unconscionable" and the court needed to make an "efficient" allocation of the bargaining costs of determining which party is most competent. In this case, the merchant could have avoided the problem with the least cost (and was thus the "least cost avoider").

13. **Lake River Corp. v. Carborundum Co.** (1985, Seventh Court of Appeals of the United States, Judge **Posner**). Contractual damages recalculated to improve

efficiency. Carborundum did not fulfill its contractual promise to deliver a good "Ferro Carbo" to Lake River, because of a change in market conditions which had made their provision impractical. (It delivered only 12,000 tons of the 22,500 tons it had guaranteed). Consequently, the expected income of Lake River dropped substantially, and they sued to recuperate the loss. Carborundum argued that the remedy formula of the contract imposed a "penalty" and, therefore, the clause was invalid. Posner ruled that a single sum for all and any breaches is "not a reasonable effort to estimate damages" and thus consti-tuted a penalty. Nevertheless, the court gave Lake River the contractually stated default amount of $241,000 less the variable costs saved from the lower amount of production—determined by an efficient formula.

14. ***Jacobs & Young*** v. *Kent* (1921, Court of Appeals of New York, Judge **Cardozo**). <u>Enforcement of a contract according to its terms: provision repudiated to improve efficiency or justice</u>. Judge Cardozo determined that the contractual obligation that had specified using "Reading" brand pipe in the construction of a rich man's summer home could be disregarded and left undone. The contract was abrogated by the court based on the contractor's "substantial performance" of his obligation, even though he installed another brand of pipe. It would have been very inefficient for the poor contractor to spend his time and money to take out and then reinstall the pipe. Furthermore, this case was a precursor to the thinking of Posner, Landes and the rest of the law and economics efficiency school. And, much like his successors, Judge Cardozo became notorious for his radical decisions.

15. *Eastern Steamship Lines* v. *U.S.* (1953, United States Court of Claims). <u>Enforcement of a contract according to it terms: provision repudiated to improve efficiency</u>. The government of the United States guaranteed the

repair of a ship that it "borrowed" during the Second World War. Then, after of the war, the cost of repairing it was estimated to be four million dollars. However, Eastern Steamship, being rational, would never carry out the repairs since the value of the repaired ship would be only half of the cost of repairs. Consequently, the court breached that clause of the contract and reduced the obligation of the government to an amount equivalent to the value that the ship would have if repaired. This ruling was based on the notion of social efficiency.

16. *Peevyhouse v.* **Garland Coal and Mining Co.** (1962, Supreme Court of Oklahoma). Enforcement of a contract according to its terms: provision repudiated to improve efficiency. A contract specified that $29,000 would be paid to Peevyhouse to compensate him for the mineral exploitation of his land. Nevertheless, this amount was reduced arbitrarily by the court to only $300. The court said that the amount was not socially efficient. The improvements planned to remedy Peevyhouse's land would increase its value by only $300. (Thus, if Peevyhouse were rational, he would not have spent the proceeds to improve the land). Therefore the court breached the contract. A dissenting justice said that the breach was intentional and not in good faith. It is always the case in contracting that one cannot correctly anticipate future conditions. In this case, Garland got his benefits but Peevyhouse is denied them.

17. *Transatlantic Financing Corp. v.* **United States** (1966, United States Court of Appeals for D.C.). Disputes over lack of a contractual provision: efficiency mandates making the most informed party responsible to avoid an unspecified problem. The court denied the relief sought by Transatlantic for additional payment due to the costs it incurred while delivering wheat to Iran. The company had to change its transport route on account of an unexpected Middle Eastern war that resulted in the

closure of the Suez Canal. The contract did not specify a route—only a destination. There is a three-fold test for altering a contract due to changed circumstances (if the change was (a) unexpected, (b) unagreed to, or (c) would make performance impractical). However, in this case, the court ruled that Transatlantic should have bought insurance, since it was the party that could have avoided the problem at least cost. Moreover, it had the better information about possible regional risks. The court ruled that Transatlantic had to pay the added costs.

18. *Wilkins v. **First Source Bank*** (1990, Court of Appeals of Indiana). <u>Positive externalities (on account of imperfect information): efficiency mandates that the seller retains rights in unknown items in a sale</u>. In this case, the court ignored a contractual clause, using a rationale founded on efficiency. It said there was no "meeting of the minds" when the contract was signed. Serendipity was not included in the original consent. Mutual assent means that the parties share common assumptions. Both thought the stuff in the house was "junk, stuff, or trash" and did not know that among that clutter were valuable paintings. There was, thus, an unbargained for gain and unbargained for loss. The court thought that each side did not act rationally or efficiently in their agreement.

Tort law

19. *Sturm, Ruger & Co. v. **Day*** (1979, Supreme Court of Alaska). <u>Negative externalities (injuries) and liability: efficiency mandates that the manufacturer pay for accidents</u>. Day bought a new .41 caliber Ruger. He dropped the gun while cleaning it inside his pickup truck and it went off (note: it is surprising that Day was cleaning a loaded gun). His leg was seriously injured. The jurors decided for Day due to the alleged defective design. Damages were set at $137,750 plus $2,895,000 in puni-

tive damages. The lower court had ruled that punitive damages required malice and reckless indifference to the rights of others, since they are used to punish and deter wrongdoers like Sturm, Ruger & Co. But the Supreme Court of Alaska did not agree, ruling that the punitive damages were excessive, and remanded the case for a new trial with respect to the punitive damages. A dissenting judge wrote that he thought the damages were reasonable given the profits from the sale of 1,500,000 guns of this model. To him, the jury did not seem to be prejudiced. The cost of repairing each gun would have been $1.93. So the damage calculation $1,500,000 \times US\$1.93 = \$2,895,000$ was within the realm of reason.

20. ***Escola v. Coca Cola Bottling Co.*** (1944, Supreme Court of California). <u>Negative externalities (injuries) and efficient liability: efficient mandates that firms be liable for their defective products</u>. A waitress was injured when a bottle of Coca Cola broke in her hand due to excessive pressure inside it. The court ruled that Coca Cola was negligent, and the circumstances were similar to the *Greenman* case below (#21). Public policy demands that liability be fixed wherever hazards to life and health are reduced most effectively and efficiently. Given that the public cannot possibly insure itself against such risks as well as manufacturers can, damages should be used to discourage the marketing of potentially troublesome products. Liability is determined according to what is "normal and proper use" and in this case the waitress should be compensated. The judges thought that by their decision consumers would be able to use products with more confidence, instead of approaching them warily.

21. ***Greenman v. Yuba Power Products*** (1962, Supreme Court of California). <u>Negative externalities (injuries) and efficient liability: manufacturers must pay damages in order to internalize harm caused by defects</u>. Greenman

was injured when a chunk of wood was flung out of a "shopsmith" lathe. The accident was due to "negligent construction" since the grip of the set screws was loosened by the vibration. The court ruled that "the manufacturer is strictly liable in tort when an article he places on the market, knowing that it is to be used without inspection for defects, proves to have a defect that causes injury to a human being." The manufacturer was fully liable due to the fact that Greenman had studied and followed the instructions for use that were included with the product. Moreover, the company could have made the product better. Yuba Power Products was ordered to pay $65,000 in damages.

22. *Williams v. **Brown Manufacturing Co.*** (1970, Supreme Court of Illinois). <u>Negative externalities (injuries) and efficient liability: consumers must pay, especially when they become informed about product dangers.</u> Williams was injured by trenching equipment produced by Brown. He sued, alleging that the product had an "unreasonably dangerous design," and claimed that the company should be liable to pay damages. The unit had jumped up after hitting a pipe and then ran Williams over. Nevertheless, the court ruled that Williams "assumed all risk in relation to use and operation" of the equipment. Perhaps the machine did need a "throw out clutch" as Williams claimed. But the court said that Williams had read the manual and was contributorily negligent. He was simply not behaving as a reasonable person by continuing to use the unit. Williams was an experienced worker who voluntarily accepted the danger of using the machine and so the judges reversed the lower court's decision, remanding the case for a new trial.

23. ***Cryts** v. Ford Motor Co.* (1978, Missouri Court of Appeals, St. Louis District, Division #3). <u>Negative externalities (injuries) and efficient liability: producer must always pay for defects, even when a product had confor-</u>

med to the best safety standards at the time of manufacture. A two-car crash resulted in the paralysis of Cryts, who was thrown up against a hard plastic, pointed and thus "defective" arm rest of a 1957 Thunderbird. The court applied the "second collision doctrine," since Cryts hit the arm rest *after* the cars themselves crashed. Ford argued that the collision "was not an anticipated use" for the car it made. However, the court disagreed and said that "misuse of a product may be reasonably foreseeable." It added that the fact that Ford had used the safest technology available in 1957 when designing its car simply did not matter.

24. *Daniell v.* **Ford Motor Co**. (1984, United States District Court, New Mexico). Negative externalities (injuries) and efficient liability: producers do not have to pay for design defects if a consumer used a product abnormally and unreasonably. Daniell was locked in the trunk of her Ford LTD for nine days. (She was attempting to commit suicide.) Nevertheless, she sued Ford alleging defective design because there was no interior lever to open the trunk. The court found for Ford, saying that Daniell was responsible for the "dreadful circumstances" of her attempted suicide. The court defined a "design defect" as something that is "unreasonably dangerous to the user or consumer." The court added that unreasonable use is not necessarily foreseen. (Note the 1981 case *Grimshaw v. Ford Motor Co.*, Court of Appeals of California, noted earlier in this chapter and in Huber 1988, pp. 115-116. In this case, $2,500,000 in damages were awarded to the burned survivor of a tragic accident where the Ford Pinto's gas tank exploded on impact. Plus, the lower court originally awarded compensation for an incredible $125,000,000 for pain and suffering, which was subsequently reduced on appeal. This case shows how juries can be moved strongly against manufacturers and create decisions that can result in tremendous distortions in the

economy and production. Companies like Ford face perpetual uncertainty as to whether in any given year they will be faced with a favorable or unfavorable decision seemingly according to arbitrary and capricious rationale.)

25. *Drake v. **Lerner Shops of Colorado*** (1960, Supreme Court of Colorado). <u>Negative externalities (sunlight) and efficient liability: companies are not liable in cases where the reflection of sunlight eclipses warning signs</u>. Drake fell on stairs while she was leaving Lerner's shop. The door had a sign that said: "Step down," but the brightly shining sun made the sign difficult to read. The lower court ruled that the incident was extraordinary and that Lerner's duty of "ordinary care for safe conditions" was met." The state Supreme Court agreed, saying that there was no unreasonable risk of harm to her as an invitee. Lerner did not have to prevent the reflection of the sun. The shop had complied with common care secu-rity requirements and no unreasonable risk of harm exist-ed.

26. *Winn Dixie Stores, Inc. v. **Benton*** (1991, District Court of Appeals, Florida, Fourth District). <u>Negative externalities (injuries) and efficient liability: companies are liable if they do not correct a problem immediately</u>. Spilt milk in a Winn Dixie supermarket caused Benton to fall. The court said that the supermarket was guilty and liable, since the milk was not cleaned up for a long time, and awarded her damages. The circumstances had persisted, in the view of the jurors, for a long enough time for employees to realize the potential danger.

27. ***Scott** v. Alpha Beta Co.* (1980, Supreme Court of Illinois). <u>Negative externalities (injuries) and efficient liability: companies are partly liable for injuries since they have a duty to wipe up a wet floor immediately</u>. Scott fell in the supermarket after slipping on the wet floor, causing a permanent injury to her knee. She sued for damages of $200,000. (It was raining a lot that day

and the floor was wet.) She was described as having a "trick knee" and for her noticeable "obesity." Plus, she had entered the store wearing "pink furry house slippers". However, the court decided that both parties were contributorily negligent. Scott was 40% responsible for the accident by not noticing the water on the floor, while the supermarket was 60% responsible by leaving the floor wet. Scott won $120,000 as a result.

References

Anderson, Robert G. (1992), "The Disintegration of Economic Ownership," in John W. Robbins, and Mark Spangler, eds., *A Man of Principle: Essays in Honor of Hans F. Sennholz*, Grove City College Press: Grove City, Pennsylvania, pp. 33-45.

Barnes, David W. and Stout, Lynn A. (1992), *Cases and Materials on Law and Economics*, American Casebook Series, West Publishing Co.: St. Paul, Minnesota.

Buchanan, James M. (1993), *Property as a Guarantor of Liberty*, Edward Elgar Publishing Co.: Brookfield, Vermont.

Buckley, William F. (1976), "The Road to Serfdom: The Intellectuals and Socialism," in Fritz Machlup, ed., *Essays on Hayek*, New York University Press: New York, pp. 95-106.

Cobin, John M. (1997), *Building Regulation, Market Alternatives, and Allodial Policy*, Avebury Press: London.

Cooter, Robert and Ulen, Thomas (1997), *Law and Economics*, second edition, Addison-Wesley: Reading, Massachusetts, chapter 4.

Dietze, Gottfried (1976), "Hayek on the Rule of Law," in Fritz Machlup, ed., *Essays on Hayek*, New York University Press: New York, pp. 107-146.

Friedman, David (2001), *Law's Order: What Economics Has to Do with Law and Why It Matters*, Princeton University Press: Princeton, New Jersey.

Hayek, Friedrich A. von (1944), *The Road to Serfdom*, University of Chicago Press: Chicago.

Hirsch, Werner Z. (1988), *Law and Economics: An Introductory Analysis*, Second Edition, Academic Press, Inc.: Boston.

Huber, Peter W. (1988), *Liability: The Legal Revolution and Its Consequences*, Basic Books: New York.

LeFevre, Robert (1966), *The Philosophy of Ownership*, Rampart College (A Pine Tree Publication): Larkspur, Colorado.

Menger, Carl, *Principles of Economics* (1994/1871), Translated by James Dingwell and Bert F. Hoselitz, Libertarian Press: Grove City, Pennsylvania.

Mises, Ludwig von (1966/1949), *Human Action: A Treatise on Economics*, Third Revised Edition, Contemporary Books, Inc. (Henry Regnery Co.): Chicago.

Mises, Ludwig von (1988), "Liberty and Property," in *Two Essays by Ludwig von Mises*, The Ludwig von Mises Institute: Auburn, Alabama.

Petro, Sylvester (1974), "Feudalism, Property, and Praxeology," in Samuel L. Blumenfeld, ed., *Property in a Humane Economy: A Selection of Essays Compiled by the Institute for Humane Studies*, Open Court: LaSalle, Illinois, pp. 161-180.

Robson, John and Lippert, Owen (1998), "Introduction: Law and Markets," chapter 1 in John Robson and Owen Lippert, eds., *Law and Markets: Is Canada Inheriting America's Litigious Legacy?*, The Fraser Institute: Vancouver, British Columbia, pp. 3-10.

Rowley, Charles K. (1993), *Liberty and the State*, The Shaftesbury Papers, 4, Edward Elgar Publishing Co.: Brookfield, Vermont.

Sowell, Thomas (1995), *The Vision of the Anointed: Self Congratulations as a Basis for Social Policy*, Basic Books: New York.

Vaughn, Karen I. (1994), *Austrian Economics in America: The Migration of a Tradition*, Cambridge University Press: New York.

15 Allodialism as economic policy

Introduction

This chapter presents a revolutionary contribution to free market thought with respect to real property policy. Since policy changes are often met with public resistance, and often involve significant costs, radical change is rare and often only comes when accompanied by a revolution. In the academic and public policy worlds, leaders often view change as threatening or even harmful in an institutional sense. Yet, many scientific advances have only been feasible through such radical change. In the field of economics, we have observed how radical change can have either a very bad or very good effect. For instance, consider the horrors of Marxist theory applied to public policy during the twentieth century, versus the economic advances gained from the marginalist revolution. Radical policy change may not always be good, but it certainly can be good.

Academics and politicians, perhaps ironically, are often at the forefront of those who resist policy changes. There are some theoretical reasons for this fact. Public choice theory suggests that self-interested academics, especially in research institutions that rely on state funding, might resist change if it threatens their research programs. Likewise, self-interested political actors might resist change if it would threaten their employment, budget, potential number of votes, or political power. Thus, we find that new ideas tend to be opposed by many mainstream economists, policy analysts, and regulators.

For instance, both the public choice and Austrian schools of economics once faced strong resistance. For years, these groups fought on the fringe of the mainstream to have their ideas accepted. Public choice founders Buchanan and Tullock once suffered much scorn by their fellows, and their revolutionary ideas were consigned to oblivion for many years. However, public choice has now achieved considerable notoriety in fields such as economics, political science, and public policy. Likewise, many twentieth century Austrian scholars, such as Mises and Hayek, lived in virtual obscurity for much of their academic careers. Nevertheless, since the fall of the Berlin wall and the other events following 1989, Mises (posthumously), Hayek, and the Austrian School have been exonerated. Their old suggestion that planners do not have sufficient social knowledge to effectively and efficiently plan an economy are now being taken seriously by a wide variety of academicians in disciplines that deal with planning, development, and regulation.

At present, there has been some debate about real property regulation, and newer theories might expect to meet with similar rejection or ridicule that public choice and Austrian economics once faced. This reaction might arise if such theories predicate a substantial change in public policy that may be regarded as threatening to certain academicians and regulators.

In recent decades, scholarly thought pertaining to real property policy has also undergone considerable revision. The widely reported failures of real property regulation, including Jane Jacob's scathing critique of urban planning and regulation (Jacobs 1961), the costly distortions caused by environmental and historic site legislation (Moore

1992), the costly and arbitrary aesthetic restrictions on land use (Pollock 1994), and the costly planning failures from unsuccessful attempts to create socialist utopias (Myers 1994), can often be explained by either public choice and/or Austrian knowledge theories.[92] Yet neither of these theories has yet to provide a cogent economics-based solution to solve the problems in real property regulation which they have identified and explained (unless, perhaps, one accepts political anarchy as a solution). Thus, free market theorists would like to see further change occur in the area of real property policy.

Accordingly, useful policy change could come from alternative concepts of real property rights and ownership. If augmenting individual liberty and the use of competitive market forces would ameliorate the quality of life for most people, as the Austrian and public choice schools contend, then policy solutions should be sought to facilitate such objectives. A real property policy that eliminates or dramatically reduces public choice and knowledge problems could be very beneficial.

Therefore, this chapter presents *allodialism* as a revitalized public policy paradigm for real property policy and regulation which harmonizes with many of the themes found in public choice and Austrian economic theories.[93] Allodialism is an old concept of real property policy, having strong roots in America and Europe. But, in spite of its antiquity, its revival will be of special interest to research in economics, public policy, legal studies, and regulation. A modern system of allodialism could ameliorate real property regulation and provide ample basis for using market alternatives such as private grading and certification services (Cobin 1997a, 1997b), restrictive covenants (Siegan

---

[92] The first appendix gives examples of government failure in real property regulation.

[93] The second appendix provides support for a congruent nexus between allodialism and Austrian and public choice economics.

1993/1972, 1990 and Cobin 1997a, 1997b), allowing market incentives to regulate land use (Siegan 1993/1972, 1990), and private contractual "communities" (Foldvary 1994), instead of commonly used planning methods.

A modern definition and understanding of allodialism

Allodialism is a legal philosophy and absolute system of real property ownership that is, more or less, the antithesis of feudalism. It is a system where real property is held absolutely by persons, without being subject to property taxation or regulation by a superior.[94] In order to define and understand allodialism further, we must first clarify the meanings of "ownership," "real property," and "feudalism."

Ownership of real property

Ownership means having a legal or rightful title to *all* the rights to property, i.e., to enjoy, to sell, to transfer, to change the form of, to control, to destroy, to possess, or to otherwise use it as one wishes. Of course, under an established social order, ownership would have to be conducted

---

[94] There are a number of other words related to allodialism that should be defined and clarified. *Allodium* is the condition of real property when its ownership is absolute, and no recognition is given to a superior or overlord with respect to it. An *allodiary* is a person who owns real property in allodium. *Allodial* and *allodian* are adjectives which designate that the noun it is coupled with is related to, affected by, or otherwise shares the characteristics of allodium (e.g., allodial real property, allodian lands, allodial system, allodial policy, etc.). The adverb *allodially* has similar significance. *Allodification* (also *allodify*) is the process of making non-allodial (or feudal) real property allodial. Conversely, *infeudation* is the process of making a real property feudal; i.e., making allodial real property subject to a superior whereby it becomes subject to payment of fees or taxes and regulatory obligations, typically by force. An *allodialist* is someone who favorably researches in, supports, or promotes allodial policy. The term might also possibly be used to describe a person (also called an *allodiary*) who owns, or at least claims to own, his real property in allodium. Interestingly, allodialism is etymologically derived from the Greek phrase αλλ δε Διος, meaning "but from God." This phrase apparently signifies that there is no earthly ruler or superior who can claim a higher right over real property held in allodium, since God is the direct lord of it and has entrusted it to the allodiary.

without violating the negative (or natural) rights of others, under penalty of law.

Real property (or *realty*) is land and things attached to the land, usually with well-defined spatial boundaries. Personal property (or *personalty*) is everything that is not real property. In addition, in antiquity, real property was called *immovables*, and personal property *movables* (Kinsella 1994, p. 1265), which probably reflected the technological limitations of the time, where most of humanity was confined to land and generally low structures.

Defining "real property" in economics terms can be somewhat daunting, especially because the vernacular use of the term connotes primarily residential real estate (e.g., a building lot and a house, or a farm and the farmhouse). But real property is more than just a house and surrounding land. Ideally, real property rights could extend from the core of the earth to the top of the atmosphere (or higher),[95] but this conception is not a restrictive or even a defining characteristic of allodialism. Indeed, arbitrary distances below and above the surface of any given point of the earth could be assigned without detriment to an allodial system. Perhaps the most complete system of allodialism, at least in terms of dealing with real property policy and negative externalities or market failure theory, would include points above and below the surface of the earth in which human activity takes place or potentially could take place.

Accordingly, real property can take different physical forms. For instance, the sea and other bodies of water with land under them, as well as air over the land, and even satellites and satellite orbits could be conceived of as real property. In this sense, real property and its policy become primarily spatial issues, although in terms of practical real-

---

[95] Of course, land below the crust of the earth is remote. The present range of useable real property would only extend from the crust to low orbits and trajectory windows.

ity, real property is confined to space that contains matter (liquid, gaseous, or solid) from the core of the earth to the top of the atmosphere.[96]

Feudalism

Feudalism is a system where one person (such as a king or the state) is the sole allodiary who owns, possesses, and ultimately controls all the rights to real property in a political jurisdiction. In the modern age, this position is held by force. Indeed, coercion is a major factor in feudal policy, both because none but the sole allodiary are able to obtain allodial rights and because all subjects must comply with regulations and pay taxes on real property. These constraints are more or less unilaterally established by the sole allodiary and may not be agreeable to his tenants. This process commences when a political jurisdiction is conquered by a ruler who in turn becomes the sole allodiary, or when a democratic election or other political means empowers a sole allodiary like the state. Therefore, a basic feature of feudalism is that the sole allodiary retains his unique rights by forcing others to accept his legislated or tacit unilateral contracts. Since the "contract" is forced upon others, and is thus involuntary, it is likewise mutable according to the caprice of the sole allodiary.

This ruler may subsequently allot "estates" in real property to another group of persons, who in turn nobly provide or manage the unilateral contractual arrangements with other people to use and possess real property. Thus, under a feudal policy, only one person (or entity) is the absolute owner of real property, and perhaps some favored individuals could have quasi-plenary ownership privileges (i.e., they were and would be "rights" for most practical pur-

---

[96] Such an extension of real property, would probably preclude using the terminology immovable and movable in the modern age, except in terms of spatial boundaries.

poses), while the rest of the people are forced into accepting merely contractual privileges to use and possess real property.

Another key feature of feudalism is that it is typically *involuntary*. While it is likely that feudalism was, at its inception during the middle ages, a result of the market process —an expression of people's desire for self-defense (Cobin 1997a, p. 125-126)—it evolved relatively quickly into a system of coercion where ownership rights in real property were prohibited to nearly everyone. Thus, the market in allodial real property under feudalism simply does not exist (at least not in any practical sense), or it is in some convoluted sense collectivized. Moreover, there are several pertinent points about feudalism that must be emphasized.

- *Compulsion exists* The fact that individuals did not voluntarily accept the terms of the contractual arrangement for the real property they use and possess is irrelevant in terms of the vigorous practical application of feudal public policy. Under feudalism, political and regulatory forces will compel all subjects to comply.

- *Privileges can be lost* Non-owners must meet the obligations of the unilateral contractual commitment: to pay real property taxes (fees) and to abide by the rules and regulations mandated by the owners. If not, they will likely lose their privileges to possess and use the real property granted by the allodial owner.

- *Property management structure is mutable* It is also important to note that the noble middlemen between the sole allodial owner of real property and the contractual users and possessors of real property are not essential to the functioning of feudalism. The owner could choose to manage his real property holdings directly.

- *The allodial nature of real property always abides* Feudalism is not mutually exclusive from allodialism, since a sole allodiary always exists. In this sense, allodialism always exists in theory and can never be wholly abolished in practice. It is important to comprehend that feudal policy does not eliminate the underlying allodial nature of real property. In its pure form, feudalism can only restrict the number of allodial owners to one person within a political realm, and prohibit market activity for allodial rights. There is no trading of real property within a realm where one person owns all the real property and no others are permitted to hold such rights.

The notion of modern feudalism might be problematic when viewed from an abstract macro perspective. For instance, there are presently some 182 nations in the world and each of them could likely be classified as a feudal realm (in terms of real property). The legitimacy of their dominance might be questioned because they maintain their local allodial monopoly by forcibly precluding others from obtaining similar rights. Yet each of these realms does indeed have one sole allodiary, viz., the state, meaning that there are perhaps 182 allodiaries in the world.

Thus, from a macro perspective the infeudated modern world might be broadly considered allodial. However, since public policy decisions for real property normally only affect the micro side, that is the persons and land within a realm, policy-relevant research will naturally be directed toward the micro side of analysis. There is no known sovereign world power that dictates real property rules across political boundaries, and no useful way to explain, alter, or suggest improvements to public policy on a macro scale. And no binding international public policy exists. Hence, this chapter only deals with real property policy within national boundaries where feudalism plainly exists.

Allodialism

Allodialism is not a novel concept in public policy. American founders Thomas Jefferson and John Adams discussed it, along with many of their contemporaries. For them, allodialism was an important policy issue (Cobin 1997a, pp. 149-151, Alexander 1991). Subsequently, ante-bellum America had adopted a quasi-allodial policy (Cobin 1997a, chapter 4), but its post-bellum and present real property policy has been feudal in theory and at least quasi-feudal in practice. Public policy for real property in places like modern Chile is likewise quasi-feudal or feudal (Cobin 1997b, pp. 1-2, 20-22), although in rural areas of Chile property taxes can be zero or negligible, with considerably less regulation—making for a quasi-allodial policy. In the modern world, the *state* has become the allodial owner of real property over a feudal realm (Cobin 1997a). However, rather than using middlemen between allodial owners and the contractual users and possessors of real property, the state manages its real property holdings directly. In the United States, it accomplishes this through an agency system of localities, which function as modern-day nobility. And the system is certainly not allodial.

Under allodialism, real property would not be subjugated to any political jurisdiction. Thus, in theory, a policy of aver-allodialism (true or pure allodialism) for all cannot co-exist with a policy of feudalism. Moreover, under aver-allodialism, political actors could not lawfully renounce allodial rights by coercive measures except, perhaps, for punishment of a crime. Thus, a key feature of the truly allodial system is that it has a *free* market in real property and *voluntary* regulation, exchange, and contracting with respect to it. That is, allodial policy would permit a level of freedom that is neither obtainable nor sustainable under feudal policy.

Unlike with feudal policy, there would be no coercive political force which holds rights to real property and prohibits others from obtaining those rights under allodial policy. Indeed, there would be a wholly free market in real property under allodialism without political barriers to enter the market, or to use or exchange it. In order to avoid misunderstanding the concept, several other characteristics and policy implications of allodialism should be considered.

- *Contracts affecting real property would still be possible* It is still possible to have contractual arrangements for the use and possession of real property under allodialism. Perhaps some persons will not prefer to own real property absolutely, but would still like to benefit from its use and possession. Such arrangements would not be precluded of necessity, since allodial policy would not require persons to be allodiaries. People could opt to spend their entire lives contracting for the use and possession privileges from allodiaries instead of owning real property. The real property system and market would be wholly free, constrained only by the law of property. Note that while feudalism might be considered a system of contracts, and thus somewhat similar to what might arise under allodialism, it differs in that feudalism typically involves conquest or coercion by a sole allodiary, without a free market in allodial rights, where people (or "serfs") are essentially compelled to agree to contracts of adhesion.
- *Subdividing would be possible* Allodialism does not preclude subdividing or leasing. Under allodialism, it would be possible to sell portions of absolute real property holdings, e.g., to sell allodial ground-level or cross-sectional segments (even laterally), as well as on, below, or above the surface of the earth. For example, an allodiary could sell his land that goes from the center of the earth to 100 feet below the surface, or all the rights 200 feet above the surface to the top of the atmosphere.
- *Particular rights cannot be split in the same property* Like ownership rights in all other things, it is possible for individuals to own real property jointly with other

individuals, or for firms, corporations, or trusts to own it. However, under allodialism, there cannot be multiple persons owning different rights on the *same* real property. There must be one allodiary who owns *all* the rights to each parcel of real property (this person could be an individual, a corporation, a partnership, a trust, etc.). Hence, the rights can be held in common or jointly, but they may not be split. Allodial lands themselves could be subdivided, but all the rights must be sold along with each parcel. While subdivisions can be multidimensional, there may not be strings attached to the rights, by either the seller or a government agency, when they are transferred. Of course, contracts may be used to sell privileges to use or possess certain rights (e.g., mineral rights) in an allodial tract of land.

- *Distinction between realty and personalty lessened* In effect, allodialism would make the absolute nature of owning real property the same as the absolute nature for owning most personal property, and hence the distinctions between "real" and "personal" property would become less important (other than as a means of categorizing types of property or for clarifying public policy objectives).

- *Allodial policy does not affect taxes on personalty* Accordingly, because allodialism is not a system of personal property, it is possible for allodialism to exist while there are taxes or regulations on personal property or persons (e.g., manorial duties, sales or income taxes, slavery, import tariffs, etc.) that might make personal property ownership less than absolute.

- *Absolute ownership does not grant immunity from committing crimes* As with all property, holding absolute rights of ownership, including absolute rights of use and possession, does not imply a justification for persons to commit crimes with their property against the negative rights of others. Furthermore, allodial policy does not require that real property may *not* be confiscated as a penalty for crimes committed of any kind, whether denounced by law or legislation (cf. Hayek 1973, pp. 72, 95, 119 and Benson 1990, p. 230). Allodialism would not make real property activities "above the law." Correspondingly, as a legal philosophy and absolute system of real property ownership, allodialism does not create or change the legal environment in which it operates. In sum, while allodiaries would be able to do anything they wish with their real property, they may not be inclined to do just anything, on account of legal, environmental, religious, cultural, or human limitations. For instance, they may not want to randomly launch missiles from their allodial land, just because they can do so as an allodiary, any more than they would choose to use a firearm to launch bullets at random just because they absolutely own the gun.

No legislation needs to be enacted to make real property rights absolute. Allodial rights are natural or spontaneous,[97] just as are rights of absolute ownership in all kinds of property. Conversely, feudal policies abridge allodial rights, confining them to one person or entity. Feudalism must be enacted by state decree or legislation. All taxation and regulation of real property under feudalism is a function of legislation and the ability to successfully coerce persons to give up absolute real property rights, or to keep them from obtaining such absolute rights. Thus, feudalism becomes at length a function of legislation itself, rather than a natural outcome in the market process.

Allodial policy is not merely about eliminating real property taxes and regulation. It is policy directed at returning real property to its pre-legislation absolute nature. On ac-

---

[97] Some philosophers might be more content with describing allodial policy as a "Schelling point." See David D. Friedman (1994), 'A Positive Account of Property Rights', *Social Philosophy and Policy*, vol. 11, no. 2, summer.

count of this transformation, there would be no taxation or regulation (the latter being just as—or more—important than the former). In effect, allodialism would affect the way externalities are handled, allow the Coase theorem to be broadly applied, expand the realm of markets, reduce the dilapidation of "unowned" or public real property, and dramatically alter public finance, land use planning, and building regulation. Indeed, allodification would likely affect virtually every human production process on earth, since all production ultimately has something to do with land and the costs of using it.

Theoretical issues in allodial and feudal real property

Only allodial real property can be properly *owned* by persons. Non-allodial real property "ownership" is simply euphemistic parlance for contractual privileges to use or possess real property. These contractual privileges permit the use of the real property in limited ways for a certain period of time—or in the case of modern fee simple titles an indefinite period. From a public choice perspective, it might be most efficient for governments to offer perpetual contractible privileges and promote such euphemistic parlance, in order to reduce transactions costs and to encourage long term development of government allodial real property by their contracting tenants. If people believe they truly own their real property they will have a greater incentive to care for it. Moreover, some academic parlance and policy ideas likewise would probably garner little economic value under allodial policy.

The bundle of rights concept Under allodialism, it is superfluous to characterize real property as a "bundle of rights" —a common phrase used in law and economics research. Since the real property holding is plenary and absolute by definition, the owner always has all the rights. Dividing up the "rights" (i.e., privileges) might make some sense under feudalism, but even then is not very useful since the allodiary (i.e., the state) still retains all the ownership rights in real property. Phrases suggesting that contract holders have a portion of the allodial rights are specious and misleading. While both allodiaries and unilateral contract holders enjoy some protected status under the law, the former are protected by the law of property and the later by the law of contract (insofar as contract law pertains to unilateral contracts). Fundamentally, the contract holder does not have rights in real property as the allodiary does. Consequently, with application to both allodialism and feudalism, it would make more sense to identify the privileges of use and possession granted by the allodiary to a contract holder as a "bundle of privileges."

Nevertheless, the bundle of privileges notion could be most useful for arranging the institutions of feudalism. It might aid political authorities to define a scaling method or a means of distributing and accounting for possessionary or use interests in real property. Indeed, it seems plausible that the state would distribute as many privileges of use and possession as possible, in order to tax away (and thus roundaboutly benefit from) a portion of the productivity gains made by tenants. A paradigm that makes such distribution more efficient would be beneficial to the sole allodial owner.

Mutable privileges The allodiary, as the true owner, can relieve the possessor or user of real property from his "ownership" privileges when the taxes (fees) are not paid, or when a regulation—even a mutable one—is violated. If drug labs were legal and there were no contractual prohibition of them by the allodiary yesterday, real property users could have installed them licitly. Yet with arbitrary coercion, the rules could be modified tomorrow, even to the point of justifying reversion of the real property on account of a regulatory "violation." When a contract is unilateral, it is virtually impossible for the contractee to compel the contractor to abide by the terms without the contractor's consent. Moreover, the contractor can easily insert a clause into the contract permitting him to change the terms at any time at will—if such a provision were not already obvious. Modern contractual changes to real property rules are arbitrary and capricious, and are effected through public policy.

Incentives and public property Accessible real property that is declared to be "public" by the sole allodiary under feudalism will be prone to dilapidation, especially outside of enforced "wilderness" areas. The owner will not be able to properly care for vast real property holdings and will likely find that principal-agent and bureaucratic problems will further obfuscate his capacity to do so. Alternatively, incentives could be created to make tenants increase their level of care by granting perpetual privileges, since tenants would have greater incentive to care for that which they believe will be used and possessed perpetually. But public property, which has no tenants, and may or may not be looked after by bureaucrats, will likely be subject to the tragedy of the commons or other forms of dilapidation. Consequently, it seems plausible that the sole allodiary (i.e., the state) would tend to allocate most infeudated real property to users via long term contracts, in order to enhance the incentives for private individuals to care for it.

Value estimates The value of feudal real property to the contract holder or tenant is equal to the discounted stream of utility that can be derived over the expected duration of the privileges (either in terms of the length of the contract or expectations about when regulation might change). It is analogous to valuing a lease, trademark, or other artificial commodity created by a legal process. The satisfaction thus received by tenants is real, akin to the satisfaction garnered from leasing an automobile, but it is not the same utility gained from plenary and absolute ownership of something (which might be greater or lesser depending on individual preferences). Therefore, real property values would change in a policy transition from feudalism to allodialism.

Inspectors, graders, and certifiers of non-allodial real property interests provide different services than inspectors, graders, and certifiers of allodial real property. For the sole allodial owner, these estimates serve to apprise him of the value added to his real property by tenants (and to modify taxation levels), as well as to assure the sole allodiary that his tenants have been complying with his regulations. However, given that allodiaries today (i.e., states) demonstrate a revealed preference not to transfer allodial interests (at least to others within their realms), estimates of market value will be of diminutive use to them, other than for purposes of setting the level of taxation. Under feudalism, improvements usually increase tax revenues. Thus, the person who improves the real property where he has contractual privileges will also increase his tax burden, and the sole allodiary receives a dual benefit. Conversely, under allodialism, all improvements would be internalized in the market value of the real property, and this added value would accrue to the allodial owner without any tax increase.

Nonetheless, inspectors, graders, and certifiers could provide useful market value and quality estimates to those who only hold contractual privileges. These estimates can take into account the value of the expected benefits that remain in a contractual privilege, less the taxes or fees paid to the allodiary and the risk of regulatory change. Such valuations could generate practicable present value estimates of future utility flows (cf. Menger 1994/1871, p. 167), even when based on historical transactions. Thus, they may facilitate transferring or collateralizing contractual privileges for real property.

Defense Allodial policy would grant greater opportunities and control to individuals, i.e., lessen state control, but it would also require greater responsibility from allodiaries. While costs from taxes and regulation would be eliminated, transactions costs would likely rise—especially considering the extensive knowledge that real property ownership and transference would involve. In order to protect their property, allodiaries might have to step up its defense. If the state were not the sole allodial owner, it would presumably have less incentive to care for the allodial real property of others, at least until negative consequences are realized by vote-seekers (and depending on constitutional arrangements for national defense).[98]

Thus, the level of defense services would likely be less. And, consequently, the tendency of people to economize on scarce resources would likely generate an optimal provision of defense services. Indeed, Tibor Machan argues that such a spontaneous system of defense could occur without coercive taxation or intervention, operating much like other insurance agreements (Machan 1982, pp. 201, 204, 206-207). Conformably, Holcombe contends that government-run defense services primarily serve to enhance the private interests of those who run the government, suggesting that permitting some level of private provision to arise via allodiaries would provide betterment to defense services and the public interest (Holcombe 1997).

Possible policy hybrids of feudalism and allodialism While allodialism itself is an absolute system, public policy for real property need not be. It is possible to have degrees of feudalism or allodialism—in the sense of mixing legal ideas or practices—so that public policy is not clearly or wholly feudal or allodial (aver-allodial) in a practical sense.

---

[98] Carl Menger calls defense the principal legitimate function of collective action: "it becomes necessary for society to protect the various individuals in the possession of goods...against all possible acts of force" (Menger 1994/1871, p. 97).

Thus, on a continuum of points between the two extremes, it is conceivable to have policies of quasi-feudalism or quasi-allodialism which will tend to be mutable over time (Cobin 1997a, pp. 117-118).

On the one hand, the extent of privileges and provisions in the unilateral feudal contract could be optimized to engender the greatest possible sense of freedom and security of benefits to the contract holder. Such a policy might be considered "quasi-feudal" because the true feudal nature of real property is concealed. On the other hand, a close-but-not-pure-to-allodial system is also possible. Even the most minor tax or regulatory encumbrance removes real property from the purely allodial realm. However, when these impositions are relatively diminutive, rare, or sporadic, the policy should warrant some distinction, such as "quasi-allodial." For instance, if the sole allodial owner in a feudal realm chooses to tax real property only four times a century, and to eliminate nearly all regulation of it, contractual privileges will not be very distinct from aver-allodialism in practice.

Moreover, both types of hybrid policies are mutable since changes in the political process with respect to the level of taxing and regulating of real property could make real property policy vary widely from quasi-feudal to quasi-allodial, although quasi-allodial policy in history has been rare. For instance, in the United States, many constitutions, court cases, and legal authorities claim that real property is allodial. But this affirmation is not correct given the various levels of taxes and regulation that were present at the time of the court ruling or writing of the law. As such, real property policy in the ante-bellum United States was quasi-allodial. Moreover, current United States real property policy is purely feudal in theory and no better than quasi-feudal in practice (Cobin 1997a, chapter 4).

Present real property policies

There are variations of feudal policy being developed today which seek to reform present feudal policy to a more benign position. Common policy alternatives in real property regulation include (1) direct government provision and control and (2) schemes of semi-privatization. Traditional direct government provision and control mandates reliance on the political process to provide "public goods" and leaves bureaucrats with the task of selecting, planning, financing, and constructing projects, with the goal of promoting the public interest. Governments (taxpayers) bear the risks associated with cost overruns or non-completion of projects. Semi-privatization schemes, whether through contracting or franchising arrangements, are generally no different than direct government provision and control except that the financing and provision of the public goods is performed by the private sector, and that such franchise or concession schemes do expand the feasible set of fundable projects. For example, a new highway might be built and operated for twenty years by a private concessionaire that earns its returns by toll collection during that period. Afterwards, the highway reverts back to the state. Since the state never relinquishes its allodial position, semi-privatization options more or less fall within the feudal paradigm.

Alternatively, especially when taking public choice and Austrian knowledge theories into account, allodialism could provide a better policy option. Allodialism would mandate complete reliance on contracting and the private sector to select, plan, finance, construct, and promote urban and rural real property projects, or pertinent market-based regulation. And there would never be any reversion of the good produced to the state. Accordingly, pressures from the political process and government failure would not be factors under allodial policy.

Allodial policy prohibits any government action directed at real property, except for a commitment (constitutionally or otherwise) to leave real property as it is naturally, with no taxes, regulation, or other restrictions. A policy of *no* real property policy is basically an allodial policy. All other policies are abridgments of it, and are, in effect, feudal, or in certain cases quasi-allodial or quasi-feudal in a practical sense. Allodial policy would still provide a means for delivering services normally associated with real property.

There can be spontaneous market-based enhancements that facilitate ease of transfer and holding of allodial real property, such as title issuance and insurance, plus expanded legal features like endorsement, adjudication, and enforcement of rights. Accordingly, allodial policy requires complete reliance on market-based mechanisms for regulation. All other policies that tax or regulate real property, whether they are designated as socialist, for the "public interest," Georgist, or otherwise, are more or less feudal policies that abridge natural or spontaneous allodial rights.

Moreover, there would be no special inalienability provision under allodialism. Real property rights would be absolute, just as rights are with most personal property. For instance, if one owns a bicycle, there is usually nothing that prevents him from making contracts to rent it (entirely or in parts) for some period of time. Yet, the absolute nature of the bicycle's ownership is unaffected by the contract. Indeed, if the right to make contracts concerning bicycles or real property were restricted (e.g., exchanging some use or possession of it for money over a term), then the "rights" over them are less than absolute. Such a restriction would surely create a market disincentive, since most prospective allodiaries would presumably only hold portfolios of real property (beyond their homesteads) to secure benefits by means of both tenancy or other contracts and industrial production and marketing.

Of course, a buyer of allodial real property would be bound by private contracts that apply to it, and any restrictions would be internalized in its price. These contracts might include restrictive covenants or private contacts with the seller (or others) to use or possess the real property over a period of time. Contract holders would be subject to paying the rent due and to the regulations imposed by the allodiary. As noted previously, contracts could also be renewable perpetually, if the allodiary chooses to so encumber his real property. The allodiary can buy back such contractual rights once granted, provided that the (likely) buyout clause is included in the contract granting use and possession. But even without such a clause, the price system would tend to allocate the real property to its highest valued use through normal, dynamic market pricing to eliminate, alter, or retransfer contractual rights. Indeed, it is plausible that speculators and arbitrageurs would constantly serve to close inefficiencies in real property contracts and thus keep prices for contract revision or changes relatively low.

Advantages (and transitional issues) of allodial policy

The advantages of allodial public policy include its historical precedent in America (Cobin 1997a, pp. 136-152) and Europe (Smith 1937/1776, p. 387; et al), its simplicity, its use of market-based regulation and alternatives (including contracting and market incentives to direct land use), which leads to increased efficiency and fewer social losses, and its single-issue focus, uncomplicated by ancillary policy problems. These pragmatic aspects are important in a democracy or a republic where it is necessary to persuade politicians (via a wide pool of voters) to accept such a dramatic change in policy.

Allodialism would be attractive to those who advocate lower taxes (e.g., classical liberals and American conservatives), to those who want relief for the elderly with fixed incomes that must pay rising real property taxes, and to those who want more freedom in utilizing airspace, telecommunications, radio and television, and land and water resources for construction, transportation, conservation, agriculture, mining, fishing and hunting.

Therefore, it would be inappropriate to link the idea of allodialism to party politics, especially right-wing politics (economically speaking). While it has a nexus with public policy, and thus indirectly tied to politics, it is non-factional policy-relevant research. Indeed, allodialism has found support in all the major political factions. Perhaps libertarians like it the best, although non-allodial views like neo-Georgism have also been defended by a strong minority of libertarians (e.g., Foldvary). Similar interest exists among the ranks of many American conservatives—liberals elsewhere around the world—where many (if not most) would opt for allodialism. Plus, there even exists partial support for allodialism among American liberals. Many in that group, but surely not all, think that regulations and especially rising real property taxation on the elderly are both unjust and inefficient (Hale 1985, pp. 382, 399). Consequently, there might be some support for allodialism by leftists (at least with respect to real property tax relief). Consequently, allodial policy must not be identified with a particular party or platform. Allodialists can be found in all political factions: right, left, and center, to some extent.

Dealing with negative externalities and real property risks

Allodial policy would rely on markets to resolve externality problems. Externalities are *unintended* consequences to third parties as the result of some production or agreement between others. For instance, consider the famous example of a factory smokestack that soils a housewife's laundry. The factory does not bear the cost of soiling the laundry (or intend to harm the woman), and the woman who incurs this cost of the factory's production gets no direct benefit from it. The housewife is thus affected by a negative externality. Conversely, if the same housewife plants a beautiful flower garden in the front yard to please herself and her family, she does not intend to gratify those who pass by. Yet, the passers-by pay nothing for the production of the flower garden and thus are beneficiaries of a positive externality.

However, when a person *intentionally* damages property or imposes costs on another person (e.g., dumping trash on another's real property), he has committed a crime rather than created a negative externality. Similarly, if someone gives property or some true benefit to another person intentionally, he has given a gift (or shown generosity) rather than created a positive externality.

Of course, gifts are not a public policy problem. Crimes fall outside of the scope of allodialism since they would continue to be handled under the legal process. Allodial policy would not alter *laws* established to protect private property from predators, it would only eradicate real property legislation. There might be a constitutional provision permitting the taking of the life, liberty, and even the allodial real property of a convicted criminal, depending on the social or legal order, but such considerations are beyond the scope of allodialism itself. As noted earlier, allodial policy would not make real property use above the law; it would only make it "above" legislation pertaining to real property.

Restrictive covenants Employing restrictive covenants would likely be a key means of dealing with negative externality problems under allodial policy. It is possible that restrictive covenants would raise the value of allodial real property for many people who have similar tastes regarding what is considered a real property "bad." Likewise, a restrictive covenant might reduce the value of allodial property by excluding too many goods or permitting too many bads.

On the one hand, consider a one million acre parcel that has a restrictive covenant prohibiting the construction of drug laboratories, nuclear reactors, airports, prostitution houses, casinos, etc. In this case, the restriction benefits might be positively internalized in the price of the real property because the restriction for many people would be considered a good. On the other hand, consider ten thousand acres restricted by covenant to exclude every activity *except* the aforementioned things. While confining users to the production of widely considered bads, which might ordinarily debase the value of the real property, in this case they might not if demand for such services exists and the available supply is small.

Restrictive covenants, like other valuable goods and services, will be priced according to the tastes and preferences they reflect. In general, restrictions on goods would likely reduce the opportunities available from real property and thus also reduce its market value. However, if questionable business activities are widely prohibited, and real property permitting them is quite scarce, then such restrictions on real property might cause its price to rise.

Allodial policy would likely create opportunities for large scale developers to discover and employ optimal restrictive covenants for each local market (to control goods and bads), thus mitigating the search costs to individuals in locating sectors with the optimal level of restrictions for them. In the same way that tract homes are developed today, which are often desirable to search and information cost-minimizers, allodial policy would facilitate a market mechanism to deal with contracting costs, externalities, and risks associated with real property (Cobin 1997b, pp. 20-21).

Subjective values and prices would also depend on the location of each parcel within the restricted area. Assuming negative externalities are a genuine problem (but cf. Dahlman 1988), parcels in the middle of a restricted land area would likely become more valuable and expensive since they have the greatest buffer from potential negative externalities generated in areas without (or with less limiting) restrictive covenants. Parcels closer to the edges would involve considerably more risk, which would likely be reflected in lower values and prices. However, these parcels would also provide a speculative aspect that might be preferred by the less risk averse. For instance, an edge buyer would be able to self-insure by paying a lower price. The premium for more central parcels effectively represents the price of insuring against negative externalities. If an undesirable element is eventually built near the edge buyer, then he will bear the loss in a lower market price, without recourse to the government for relief. But if the adjoining parcels adopt a similar or stricter restrictive covenant, then he will receive a windfall in the market price of his real property. Thus, it is reasonable to believe that the price system (the market process) will automatically deal with negative externalities and land use planning via restrictive covenants, especially as land speculators absorb market risk.

Pollution A complication might arise if "common space," which fosters a "tragedy of the commons," were permitted under allodial policy. Even if all spatial rights were assigned, liquid and gaseous matter would be able to flow between spaces. Note that, to a lesser extent, land can also be moved into other spaces (other than by controllable human design) by earthquakes, floods, tornadoes, volcanoes, etc. In any case, the movement of these natural resources could cause externalities. Under allodial policy, private insurance markets could develop products to help resolve such externality problems. Indeed, insurance is used to protect persons from a variety of natural disasters already. Like land speculators, provision of insurance would be an integral and essential result of allodial policy.

Nevertheless, the movement of physical matter over allodian space, such as polluted air, would indeed cause complicated policy problems. If all land were allodial, then one would have to track down the cause of pollution and demand from the originator some market rate for spewing out the bad. Then, if nearby allodiaries refuse to accept polluted air, a legal demand may be made to halt its production, or at least its distribution. However, if contentions become widespread, there will be an opportunity for alert allodiaries to offer restrictive covenants that permit pollution-generating production and demand a higher price for the underlying real property. The price system would thus engender an incentive for firms to develop technologies that reduce or prevent the pollution caused by its production.

In some sense, pollution is similar to wildlife. The deer is precious to the hunter but a nuisance to the gardener, and thus a good or a bad depending on one's preferences. Pollution is dear to its producer in that it is an integral by-product of his profit-making activity. Even if it is a bad to him otherwise, the potential benefits foregone by ceasing production exceed the expected negative utility from the pollution. Others might also be content with pollution if they were paid to take it. As a solution, perhaps large tracts of cheap allodian lands could be bought to facilitate pollution dispersion at a level where the allodiary (who need not live on that land) finds it profitable. At any rate, a market for pollution privileges would result from allodial policy.

Even if some negative externality could be created secretly (e.g., invisible yet harmful fumes from a drug lab), there would be legal remedies available and firms would likely arise in the market to detect, patrol, and root out such clandestine tactics. In sum, the market process would allocate real property resources to their highest valued use and would, since rent seeking pertaining to real property would be precluded, successfully work to mitigate such negative externalities.

Benefits of allodialism The fact that allodiaries would be free to use and enjoy their real property as they wish (excepting restrictions imposed by voluntary restrictive covenants) should *not* be a cause for concern. There are many market incentives: financial, contractual, religious, or the drive to maintain social status, friends, and a good reputation that automatically work to curtail negative externalities. Moreover, there is evidence that most expostulated negative externalities result from government failure, i.e., public choice problems and poorly defined real property rights. Allodial policy would preclude such problems. Alternatively, it would facilitate private communities, market-based regulatory alternatives (e.g., standards-setting institutions), and greater reliance on market incentives and restrictive covenants to alleviate negative externalities. Plus, the price system would serve to improve resource allocation, and opportunities would be created for trading real property risks on the market (perhaps through derivatives and insurance products), generating more flexibility in real property markets (Cobin 1997b, pp. 20-21).

Of course, since urban areas already exist, the transition to allodialism would be costly. It might take many years to accomplish. But it would become feasible as market incentives and advances in production methods facilitated moving to optimal venues. Therefore, allodial policy would likely be a superior policy alternative to modern feudal policy in the long run because public choice costs and economic distortions caused by the knowledge problem are so huge. The evident feasibility of quasi-allodialism in antebellum America illustrates the potential of at least quasi-allodial policy, so long as contracts—mainly restrictive covenants—are strictly enforced.

The Coase Theorem

As noted in chapter thirteen, the Coase Theorem says: when transactions costs are low and there is free bargaining, the market (individual actions) will allocate real property rights to their highest valued or most efficient use. This allocation will occur automatically, no matter how property rights are initially allocated. In other words, the Coase Theorem implies that costly actions by civil law judges (i.e., public policymakers) are inefficient and perhaps ineffective when there are low transactions costs (Coase 1960).

Applying the Coase Theorem to real property problems, such as solving conflicts caused by negative externalities, produces powerful implications because it is often the most efficient and effective means of conflict resolution. However, when feudal real property regulations are present, it is possible that Coasean solutions are undermined or even eradicated through the regulatory impositions. Alternatively, since allodial policy would require complete reliance on market mechanisms, the application of the Coase Theorem would be fully vitalized.

The flip side of the Coase theorem implies that when transactions costs are significant, a court's ruling might have a positive impact on efficiency. The danger in this scenario is that courts might presume that transactions costs are high by virtue of the fact that one or both sides have been willing to incur significant court costs to litigate a dispute (Scott and Leslie 1993, pp. 90-95; Posner 1988). When this happens, what the judge determines to be the socially efficient solution can override the plain language of a contract or the legal title to property, and thus violate individual or natural rights.

For example, as noted in chapters thirteen and fourteen, modern American courts might refuse to enforce a contract on grounds of "unconscionability," or because it necessitates an "efficient breach," or because the *court* perceives that there was no "meeting of the minds." Modern courts are also interested in applying "efficient remedies" to real property problems. With respect to allocating privileges for using real property and negative externalities, courts use the efficiency notion to decide who has rights to pollute, to block the sunlight or wind, and to cause noise or odors (see chapter fourteen for cases). Rather than interpreting and enforcing the letter of the contract, judges become guardians of social welfare, and do in fact abrogate or severely modify the plain meaning of contracts in favor of what *they* deem is best for "society."

Nevertheless, the idea of social welfare (especially in policy decisions) is dubious since it is not possible to objectively know the aggregated subjective valuations of individuals. Thus, the court has no assurance that social welfare will be improved or optimized by efficiency criteria. On the other hand, "efficiently" breaching a contract has certainly increased social uncertainty in contracting and property rights, has raised the costs to individuals and firms to prevent such outcomes (as well as the risks of participating in the market), and has violated the rights of one or more individuals in favor of *society's* rights. Roscoe Pound argues that this sort of judicial activism, what he calls the legal, forceful control of the "antisocial residuum," debases individual liberty and natural rights, and merely expands what he calls "regimented activity" (Pound 1942, p. 33).

Allodialism would exclude judicial experimentation and participation in modifying real property rights, or contracts pertaining to real property, in order to improve what judges deem to be socially efficient. They would be powerless to "fix" negative externalities by reallocating resources or rights. Instead, markets would be relied on to produce restrictive covenants, pressure (e.g., from community outrage), private grading and certification services (Cobin 1997a, chapter 3), market incentives to guide resource allocation (Siegan 1993/1972, 1990), and private insurance against potential negative externalities.

In a purely allodial world, where all property is owned and all real property rights are assigned, there would likely be fewer long-unresolved negative externalities or environmental concerns (assuming a robust legal framework and low transactions costs so that the Coase Theorem applies). Government and social agendas are precluded from the real property arena.

It is entirely plausible that groups of individuals with similar preferences would eventually end up as neighbors. For example, people with little tolerance for the possibility of fires set by neighbors might tend to move to other (perhaps more expensive) areas populated by people with similar tolerances.[99] Otherwise, people may simply reach efficient compromise solutions by contracting activity with others, until each neighborhood's inhabitants are satisfied with the living conditions. When a person's felt uneasiness about his community circumstances is considerable, he will tend to make arrangements with his neighbors to alleviate it (e.g., by contract, social pressure via churches or community groups, etc.), up to the point at which the cost of the new arrangement equals the benefit of greater ease. Otherwise, he will have an increasing incentive to relocate. Moreover, since bureaucratic interference would be precluded under allodialism, most of these arrangements would likely be made quickly. In short, a suitable environment and satisfactory living arrangements could be obtained without feudal mandates, especially when transactions costs are low. Consequently, the transition to allodialism would invigorate Coase Theorem benefits, making social life more efficient.

Property abuse problems

Clearly, there are some individuals who choose to abuse their property, a tendency which is amplified when state regulation reduces its value. It is rare to find someone will-

---

[99] However, there are so many dimensions of "similarity" that the commonalties may not noticeably preclude conflicts in all cases.

ing to burn a $100 bill, but it does happen. However, we would expect to find many more people who are willing to burn a $1 bill, because it is less valuable. Yet, eighty years ago, fewer people would have been willing to burn that dollar bill because a dollar was worth more in terms of other goods compared to the dollar of today which has been debased by gradual inflation. Accordingly, under allodial policy the world would not be perfect. There would still be a few allodiaries who would be willing to abuse their real property, especially property that is relatively less valuable.

Problems with zoning and building regulation

Likewise, public policy pertaining to feudal real property can also cause dilapidation and debasement of real property. When real property values or returns are diminished by feudal policy (taxes or regulations), the incentive to care for property declines and real property dilapidation becomes more pronounced. People purchase real property given the current information available to them and would naturally expect those rights in real property to remain unchanged forever, except that feudal policy creates uncertainties and complications. Both zoning and building regulation are coercive feudal mechanisms that demonstrate state ownership, and the state's ultimate control over real property—which can lead to a vast variety of predictable distortions predicted by public choice and Austrian economic theories.

Conceptually, all non-zoned land must be equally privileged, in that it may be used for any lawful purpose. Zoning policies can either artificially enhance or diminish the value of real property. However, zoning cannot magically increase the value of non-productive or waste lands. Zoning can merely reduce the uses of land, it cannot expand them.

Zoning which prohibits certain activities, such as industrial manufacturing, decreases a tract of real property's value since it is left with fewer uses. Apropos to Tullock's "transitional gains trap" (Tullock 1975, pp. 671-675, see chapter three), zoning restrictions cause future real property purchasers of nearby land to rely on zoning as a sort of public insurance policy against undesirable neighborhood activities leading to a decline in market values. Subsequently, development occurs on that basis, such that any loosening of restrictions in the future would cause considerable losses to current real property or contract holders. For instance, if zoning regulations are arbitrarily changed to permit industrial use, then real property might become more valuable in the sector, while the value of existing improvements and intangible benefits (like desirable location) might decline. Likewise, the value of a parcel of land would decline if it were not possible to obtain a building permit.

Thus, on the one hand, the removal of zoning restrictions and building regulations that would result from enacting allodial policy would cause painful repercussions to some people in the period of transition. Increased rent seeking and vote seeking activities would be expected to prevent the change. On the other hand, the benefits that would accrue to a large majority of people would be substantial and would perhaps (likely) outweigh any costs they might bear.

Expansion of markets

Under allodial policy, the market would provide a wide variety of real property alternatives to satisfy a wide range of consumer risk preferences, just as it does with other goods and services (Cobin 1997b, p. 21). "Allodial policy would permit the market process to function vibrantly; indeed there would be no other option" (Cobin 1997a, p. 205). Incentives to use real property for commercial and industrial purposes would be driven by the desire to maximize profits and minimize costs. Since causing negative externalities erodes goodwill, and augments the costs of repairing reputation, an incentive would emerge to avoid locating businesses where consumers might complain. As Bernard Siegan concludes, "[E]conomic forces tend to make for a separation of uses even without zoning" (Siegan 1993/1972, pp. 36, 62, 75, 97, 116, 144; Cobin 1997b, p. 17).

Consequently, allodial policy would vastly expand the role of markets. The entirety of real property regulation would be replaced by market-based alternatives, including industries to produce restrictive covenants (and standardized forms), to grade and certify the safety and quality of real property (Cobin 1997a), to insure against negative externality risks, to create a variety of contracts for the use and possession of real property, and to properly transfer allodial rights from one person to another.

Furthermore, an allodial world would provide more efficient intergenerational transfers of real property. Indeed, a definite system of property rights is preserved across generations. Allowing the present owner to choose the persons who will enjoy his real property after he dies, as is the case under allodial policy, reduces the likelihood of wasteful subterfuges designed to minimize the impact of taxes, suboptimal patterns of immediate consumption by a "spendthrift wife," and premature or disguised transfers to children or other family members (Epstein 1986, p. 697).

In sum, allodial policy would promote individual liberty, demand greater individual responsibility, and extend reliance on contracts and private communities for roads, dams, sewer and water service, and other public works. Allodial policy would also create an environment to optimally use and care for real property resources without knowledge problems or public choice problems. These benefits would begin accruing immediately during the transition to allodialism. There would be, no doubt, difficulties in adjustment to new norms, depending also upon the cultural climate in which the policy is enacted. But, as with all positive changes, transition costs can be reasonably expected to be less than the long term benefits.

Public finance and urban planning issues

Two probable objections to allodification of real property would arise from concerns about public finance. First, tax revenues from real property would be eliminated, reducing government revenues. No politician or bureaucrat will like that fact. Second, public choice theory suggests that allodification would face difficulties unless a favorable incentive can be found to compensate or motivate self-interested and vote seeking political actors who benefit from the current system of public finance, and whom would effectively lose power or money from the reduction in tax revenue.

However, it is possible to have tax reform that would shift needed tax revenues to other sources and/or to reduce the level of taxes needed by implementing more privatization. Allodial policy would not preclude a tax shift to other sources, and certainly would not discourage privatization measures to eliminate the need for those taxes. As noted previously, eliminating property taxes could gain wide popular support (which would be of interest to vote seeking politicians) from both the right and the left.

Allodification might also generate positive externalities to those who presently have use and possession privileges since they would become allodial owners without cost. Those who thought they had merely purchased privileges to use real property would receive a windfall, and might increase their level of support or loyalty to the vote seeking politicians who mandated the policy change. Others who might have been deluded into believing they had become genuine owners of real property already would tend to be less influenced by the policy change, which they might perceive as being merely semantic.

Furthermore, allodial policy might increase tax revenues indirectly by bolstering economic growth (assuming there are other taxes present to capture a portion of the growth). Indeed, even partial allodification in a political realm might be a useful development tool, particularly in sparsely populated regions of developing countries, since it would probably create a greater incentive to buy and develop real property in those regions (Cobin 1997b, p. 22). For instance, Chile has many remote regions with sparse population. To encourage settlement, allodial policy could be installed in those regions to attract domestic and international immigrants or businesses. Thus, over the long run, public finance might be augmented by allodial policy. In the short run, governments could implement tax shift policies, user fees, and more privatization to ease the transition.

Urban planning would also be dramatically reduced, since it would be impossible to arbitrarily condemn real property under eminent domain and take it for public works planning, and because allodial policy would preclude any interventionism with respect to real property. Of course, all bureaus directed to tax and regulate real property would be eliminated. These reductions would result in substantial cost savings for governments. Therefore, with careful planning to accomplish appropriate tax shifting and privatization, the transition to allodialism could arguably produce benefits in excess of transitional costs.

Production of all things

Land is one of the few components of production that is not created by human effort. Producers tend to acquire and defend as much land as possible to secure their enterprises, making land and all real property a rather special commodity in the market process. "[L]and is an essential input into any economic activity" (Stahl 1987, p. 759). Consequently, allodialism is a public policy that would positively affect every production process in the world, particularly as cost reductions are favorably reflected in consumer prices.

All human production ultimately has something to do with real property. Moreover, real property affects more than just living or working space. All food basic higher-order goods—paper, wood, metals, energy, and other mining products—come from land. These basic higher order goods are a function of every production process at some level (Menger 1994/1871). Indeed, all human action (and thus all labor in production) is predicated on the existence of a food supply, which is closely related to real property for farming and grazing. Thus, nearly all economic production of lower order goods is conducted on land.

Even production of internet or cyberspace capacity has some relationship to real property. Computer systems that allocate cyberspace were created on real property, using minerals from the earth, by designers who live and work on real property. Such systems are always (up to the present) housed on real property. The same is true with radio bands which must use some frequency of the electromagnetic spectrum, which is a type of economic land (i.e., natural resource space). Accordingly, even the production of ethereal goods is a function of real property.

In sum, every process, at least in some small way, is affected by real property. Thus, any distortions caused by real property regulation will be far-reaching while liberating real property from its feudal moorings by allodial policy would preclude such distortions. When a feudal regime (i.e., the state) is the sole allodiary or, to use contemporary legal terminology, the "lord paramount" or the "lord of the soil" (Cobin 1997a, pp. 145-146, 176), public choice and Austrian knowledge theories suggest that the inefficiencies, distortive effects and misallocations of resources will be considerable. Given the existence of competition, the reduction in production costs due to the elimination of real property regulation and taxation by the transition to allodialism, would likely grant increasing benefits for consumers. Of course, the few producers who currently have artificial monopoly privileges or cost savings due to rent seeking and regulatory capture successes would be harmed by the transition and should be expected to vigorously resist the change.

Constitutions, allodial monopolies, and coercion

As noted earlier, an essential feature of modern feudalism is coercion. The problem of coercion means that it might be possible to revert to feudalism after the implementation of allodial policy, just as some European allodial lands were infeudated during the middle ages (Hughes 1991/1977, pp. 5, 12; Noyes 1937; Cobin 1997a; Strayer, 1965, p. 173). In order to prevent such a reversion, public choice and constitutional theory may be applied to design a constitutional amendment that prevents it. After all, the goal of basic constitutional theory is to find the optimal level of government to produce defense and justice with a minimum amount of coercion and harm to individual liberty.[100]

In an extreme case where all people but one freely prefer to contract for real property privileges rather than have allodial rights, the single allodiary would try to act as a monopolist. The only market discipline he would face would be revolt, or at least demands for constitutional reform (cf. Smith 1937/1776, p. 388), in reaction to his attempt to change the contracts and impose harsher restrictions or higher rental rates. Since land is an essential part of human life and all production, self-interested human actors might ignore the rule of law and even confiscate real property from the threatening monopolist, in spite of his attempts to use court and public actions to stop them. While his monop-

---

[100] Maybe under political anarchy it would be easier to preclude coercion, but that is a separate philosophical issue with wide application to other policy considerations.

oly power would theoretically provide extraordinary profits, particularly because the good is real property, the basic need for real property by the tenantry would likely lead them into delinquencies such as arson, refusing to pay rent in mass, etc., in order to avoid economic slavery.

However, such monopolization is probably an unlikely scenario in a free market for real property. A monopoly situation would hardly be achievable (or at least not sustainable) without legislative barriers to entry. It is unlikely that all previous owners but one would abandon their allodial rights. While a contraction leading a much smaller number of allodiaries is possible, it would seem to be very unlikely for the number of allodiaries to decline to one (without coercion), because real property is an essential part of life and production. Any problems would thus be curtailed by competition. If a case could be made that monopolization would be more than a mere possibility under allodial policy, then the problem might be resolved by a constitutional provision mandating a minimum number of allodiaries in a nation.

The key issue is that, under allodial policy, no allodialist would be able to coerce people into contractual servitude and thus retain a sort of permanent monopoly or regulatory power through force (or conquest). While in some abstract sense it may be argued that property law forces others to respect allodial rights and thus there is an element of force used to retain both allodialist and feudalist claims, allodialism differs greatly in that the law of property is a function of tradition, custom, and, in short, the market process. Feudal lords rely on the force of legislation and police power to maintain their status and to resolve real property policy problems. Alternatively, allodiaries must derive any benefits they receive under the forces of competition, and problem solving must come through decentralized real estate (and related) markets, because government power would be precluded from affecting real property rights by allodial policy.

Since all humans need to live and produce on real property, feudal coercion leads to distortive consequences. Allodial policy would eliminate the negative aspects of modern feudalism like costly environmental legislation (as it pertains to real property at least), "takings," drug-related confiscations, capture of regulators leading to non-production (often through zoning or building codes), special legislation that raises costs (e.g., the Americans with Disabilities Act requirements), expropriation for public projects "to promote the general welfare," and deal making in which politicians trade building permits for commitments to install public parks, libraries, greenways, bike paths, and other public projects (that benefit vote seekers).

Such deal making results in an additional cost to the person granted the permit, and this cost is subsequently passed along to the consumer as an indirect and hidden tax.[101] A similar public choice problem was seen in the famous U.S. Supreme Court case, *Dolan v. Tigard*. Florence Dolan was instructed by planners in Tigard, Oregon that she could only receive permission to improve her real property if she first "dedicated" a portion of it for environmental purposes.[102]

The ultimate insurance against the threat of coercion would be to become an allodiary. Then, so long as the rule of law and perhaps the constitution were maintained, no one would be able to dictate the terms of life and production with respect to real property. Hence, being an allodiary becomes a market-based form of coercion insurance. We see that even in today's infeudated world, individual state allodiaries enjoy a degree of autonomy and are usually left uncoerced by more powerful allodiaries. Nevertheless, less risk-averse individuals might still prefer to take their

---

[101] E.g., A permit problem that occurred in Ventura, California (MacGregor 1997, p. B1).

[102] *Florence Dolan v. City of Tigard*, 114 S.Ct. 2309, 129 L.Ed.2d. 304, 318, 62 USLW 4576, 38 ERC 1769, June 24, 1994 [5-4, U.S. Supreme Court, Justices Stevens, Blackmun, Ginsburg, and Souter dissenting]; cf. *Kelo v. City of New London* (2005).

chances that competition (and perhaps a constitution) would protect their rights under multilateral contracts. Yet, both options would be available under allodial policy, creating a wider choice for individuals.

Other transitional issues

Assignment of real property rights One important practical matter is how feudal privileges should be converted into allodial rights. After the Revolution in the United States, a policy change in favor of allodialism was apparently attempted and partially succeeded in that at least quasi-allodialism was produced. But that largely agrarian civilization with relatively small populations and densities (especially in cities) during that era, make it difficult to draw transitional lessons for today. Nevertheless, there are four obvious means of reallocating real property rights, including both the privileges that are currently assigned to a feudal tenant and those which are not assigned to anyone. As transitional policy, any one or combination of the following alternatives may be utilized.

The first alternative would be to hold an auction where all real property in a political realm is sold to the highest bidder, with the stipulation that the current contract holders will be permitted to retain their privileges, at least for some guaranteed amount of time. The proceeds of the auction would go to the government, as the current allodiary. It seems plausible that both rich persons and firms would bid for the real property in earnest. It also seems plausible that mutual funds or other entities would form to help small investors buy allodial rights. These organizations might even have special provisions by which allodial rights to parcels may be divided for each small investor.

A second alternative would be to hold a lottery and assign allodial rights at random to all whom voluntary wish to participate. If the lottery is free of corruption, it is plausible that the likelihood of a special class or interest group dominating allodial rights would be reduced dramatically. Of course, such amelioration would be less effective if the lottery tickets were sold at a low or zero price and wealthy people could buy more of them (although in a relative sense the wealthy will always be able to buy more than the poor). The price of a lottery ticket will also determine how much revenue the government would receive from the transfer.

A third alternative would be to convert all feudal privileges into allodial rights. If the rights to, say the center of the earth to most of the earth's crust, or from just above the earth's crust to the top of the atmosphere, are not included in these current privileges, they may be either given to the contract holder as well or auctioned or assigned as noted in the first and second alternatives. Such a conversion would obviously entail a considerable wealth transfer from the government to the feudal contract holders; a redistributive measure which could certainly cause dramatic external and political effects. However, the sweeping notion that contract holders would all receive *positive* benefits assumes that they value allodial rights more than feudal privileges, which may not be true in all cases given the subjective nature of value.

Finally, the Lockean rule of first possession could be applied so that the first person to mix his labor with the "soil" with some degree of permanency would attain the allodial rights (including "unowned" or public bodies of water, airspace, and the remote regions of the inner earth). Such a mechanism would require that more or less arbitrary spatial boundaries be assigned for the current holders of feudal privileges, unless they can make a compelling case why the boundaries should be different (at their own expense). Like in the third alternative above, most current contract holders would receive a nearly automatic and immediate conversion of their privileges into allodial rights, especially for their homesteads.

Those contract holders who hold privileges on undeveloped tracts of land where they have not mixed their labor with the soil, but are waiting for development or simply enjoy preserving scenery, might be required to in some way improve this land within a specified period of time, or to prove that the land is indeed being used is some significant economic way. While proving the case might be easy for mining interests, environmental groups, and hunting clubs, it might not be so easy for others, possibly raising the transactions costs for some persons.

Redistribution or transfer of wealth As noted above, assuming that allodial real property interests are typically more valuable than feudal privileges, allodial policy would cause an immediate transfer of wealth (and presumably power) from the state to the new allodiaries whenever current contractual privileges are simply *converted* to allodial rights (as in the third alternative above). This would be especially true for contract holders with large scale or high-rise buildings located in densely populated and highly developed urban areas. Under the other options, there would still be a transfer of wealth and power but it must be purchased in some indirect way paid for, making it little different than power or wealth benefits currently available on the market. Thus, state power or control might be reduced as its allodial interests are converted to cash. Market forces and decentralization automatically confer benefits to everyone, especially those who do not receive direct or indirect privileges and transfers from the state.

Nevertheless, if the conversion alternative is selected, non-contract holders will be relatively deprived, especially where feudal constraints are fairly rigorous. The wealth status of those who do not have contractual privileges will remain unchanged, except in the sense of future benefits they will receive in lower consumer prices and bureaucratic costs savings, while the real wealth of the contract holders turned allodiaries will rise. It is difficult to know the full extent of this relative wealth difference but, if it is expected to be too high, these costs might be reason to select one of the other transitional alternatives.

Transactions costs Policy changes are rarely costless, and we can plausibly expect that a policy change to allodialism will require considerable utilization of legal research, court costs, scientific studies, improvement costs, and other resources. However, the ultimate concern in any public policy decision is not whether there will be costs but whether the expected public benefits from the change will likely exceed those costs. The previous pages have outlined a number of probable benefits, not the least of which are increased individual liberty and alleviating public choice and knowledge problems which lead to costly government failures. In addition, many predictable transactions costs might be mitigated by careful and thoughtful transitional arrangements before the change is enacted.

Several industries that might face high transactions costs include aerospace, mining, and transportation. Airlines which currently use regulated airspace would no longer be able to do so without trespassing. Thus, they will have to go through the costly process of reaching agreements with all allodiaries that would permit them to fly-over. But the market will tend to mitigate many potential problems.

For instance, many smaller allodiaries will not likely receive a large benefit from the fly-over payments from airlines. Thus, it will be in their interest to sell these rights, or contract the privileges to them, to firms that specialize in buying and managing such interests. Accordingly, the transactions and bargaining costs would likely be diminished by such spontaneous collective action. There is no compelling reason to believe that the opportunity cost of most small allodiaries would be so small that they would have little incentive to contract or sell certain rights to private industry. Where sporadic recalcitrance does arise, firms would simply avoid the affected parcels.

Similar arrangements would also be feasible for mining firms wanting to expand their operations, although in cases where the potential gains are very high, the allodiaries might indeed want more than a lump sum payment; perhaps a percentage guaranteed by contract. But those provisions can also be made by firms specializing in such services.

Moreover, such shifting arrangements would be especially evident in transportation services industries. Provision of railways, highways, and other kinds of roads would not have the benefit of eminent domain. Indeed, it is possible that a coalition of allodiaries could block a transportation route by refusing to sell the needed lands. However, especially when the number of allodiaries is large, it is plausible that the price system will allocate the needed resources for transportation. At some price, one or more of the allodiaries will likely sell. At times, the road or railway may take an odd or crooked route under allodial policy, but it will be efficient and the costs of construction will be internalized in the price consumers have to pay. If the railway or roadway is not profitable (or if the quantity demanded is very low because the toll or fee is too high), it will simply not be built or if it is built the mistaken firm will suffer bankruptcy.

Therefore, markets would work to resolve potential land allocation problems. It might be feasible for a transportation firm to solicit various allodiaries to sell out at the same time and ask at what price they would sell. Moreover, in order to heighten competitive pressure, this firm might also tell each allodiary that his neighbors are being each asked to come to terms at the same time by other representatives. When the chance of collusion is small (given large numbers of allodiaries) it is likely that the price will be bid down and the transportation route built efficiently, using only the spontaneous tools of the market process. There will certainly be transactions costs of such acquisitions, but there would also be offsetting benefits by avoiding dealing with bureaucrats.

Indeed, allodialism would spawn a new set of transactions costs. Nevertheless, it must be noted that, despite these costs, the long term benefits secured by these and other affected industries would be substantial. Instead of facing the instability of changeable government regulation, and fighting of the rent seeking and regulatory capture activities of other firms, they will have predictable and enforceable contractual security or certainty, plus cost savings due to the reduction of rent seeking or anti-rent seeking personnel. Furthermore, for many firms, staff reductions could likely be made in compliance departments that deal with zoning rules, building codes, occupational safety standards, environmental mandates, hazardous waste edicts, and other regulations that relate directly to real property activities. Of course, such freedom also carries added responsibility. For instance, a firm that buries hazardous waste on its land will be subject to strong legal reprisals if the pollutants are transmitted to other allodian lands, creating an incentive for firms to utilize clean-up companies who specialize in disposing of hazardous materials and which bear most or all of the legal risks.

Legislative changes Allodial policy would automatically abrogate much legislation, including zoning rules, building codes, environmental edicts, and all other forms of legislation directly or indirectly related to real property. For instance, not only could real property itself not be taxed, but the *titles* to real property would be similarly immune to prevent any indirect abridgment of allodial rights. (Such requirements and policy changes might be empowered by a constitutional amendment.)

Table 15.1 Advantages of allodial policy

Even if implementing allodial policy would be complicated by transitional issues, it would bring various advantages:
(1) it would provide an improved means to deal with negative externalities and real property risks,
(2) it would extend the use of restrictive covenants,
(3) it would improve pollution problems by changing incentives and improving institutional arrangements,
(4) it would provide benefits from the use of market regulatory alternatives which would extend individual liberty, alleviate negative externalities, and contribute to making a successful environment for a free market to operate in (see chapter 9, Table 9.3),
(5) it would facilitate an expanded use of the Coase Theorem, along with its resulting efficiencies, which would be revitalized due to the fact that there would not be any real property policy or judicial "efficiency" rulings,
(6) it would create greater incentives for individuals to care for real property,
(7) it would extend the role of markets and secure the benefits of efficiency and effective provision that they bring, as well as eliminate much coercion of individuals by the state,
(8) it would eliminate most urban planning and the costs related to it,
(9) it would reduce the costs of consumers in general by augmenting efficiency in the production of all things, which is always a function of real property to some extent, and
(10) it would eliminate knowledge and public choice problems related to real property, and would likely have the effect of reducing them elsewhere as well.

Certainly, the change would be painful for entrenched special interests groups and firms that benefit from such legislation via concentrating benefits and dispersing costs. It would also be painful for the bureaucrats who work in these areas and the political actors who benefit from favor-brokering. But as public choice distortions are eliminated, the broader public interest will likely be well served as the dispersed costs of such activities are retained by consumers and firms who do not enjoy net benefits from real property taxes and regulation.

Reversion (escheat) policy The feudal system has a clear answer for what happens when an individual with feudal privileges dies without heirs. His privileges simply revert to the allodial owner, viz., the state. Under allodialism, a constitutional mandate would probably have to be adopted to determine the status of allodial real property when no heirs have been designated. One option is to simply use an auction to reassign the real property with the proceeds going to the state for, perhaps, defense services.

Another option is to reassign the property randomly by means of a privately run lottery with near zero-price tickets. A final option would be to open the real property for homesteading and permit the Lockean rule of first possession to prevail. At any rate, this is a matter of relatively minor importance and a reasonable solution could likely be found.

Concluding remarks

Allodialism is not a new idea. Besides its European roots, similar policy seems to have (partly) existed in ancient Israel.[103] Moreover, it has at times been discussed by academ-

---

[103] Under the Israelite theocracy of the Old Testament era, God was the Lord of the land. He permitted rural lands and village real property to be leased but perpetual ownership could not be transferred from the tribe or family to which it was assigned allodially. This created a special form of inalienability. In the year of jubilee, all such real property reverted to the original tribe or family to whom it was assigned. Thus, the lease price was determined according to how many years remained before the year of jubilee. However, in the "walled cities," real property could be held perpetually and transferred in absolute form. The only exception to this rule was in the cities of the Levites (the priestly tribe that was not given an allocation of rural land). The urban land of these walled cities was treated the same way as if it were rural land. An es-

ics (especially over the last two hundred years), and in American court cases and debates on political philosophy. But the fact that an idea is old and somewhat obscure (and maybe widely forgotten) does not mean it is insignificant. It is hardly unusual for ideas to gain or lose importance as public policy changes over time. Thus, allodialism, as a historically-practical and logical public policy alternative, may prove insightful in applied economics and public policy.

In an age where public choice and Austrian theories have made widely recognized criticisms of regulation and the political process, allodial policy is a positive market-based solution to alleviate social problems. The Austrian and public choice schools can inform public policy by endogenizing the actions of government into their theories, in order to explain and predict economic phenomena. Government institutions are not benign external elements that have little effect on economics. They are an integral part of human action, individual incentives, and social institutions.

Allodialism is a practicable policy alternative which, when coupled with its inherent market-based corollaries, would provide significant benefits without public choice and knowledge problems. Pervasive rent seeking problems would be highly unlikely under allodial policy since land use, building regulation, and other real property regulation would not be subsumed in the political process. The transition costs of changing to allodial policy might be high for some people, but the wider savings and long term benefits generated by its implementation could be far greater.

This chapter has presented a practical theory of allodialism, having identified potential transitional problems in public policy that might arise during and after its implementation and how they would be dealt with. Thus, allodialism should be of special interest to planners and aca-

---

cheat policy also existed. If a man died without heirs, his property reverted to God, meaning to the religious establishment of the day. See Leviticus 25:15-16, 23-33, 27:17-24; Numbers 36:4; Jeremiah 32:7-16, 25, 44; and Ezekiel 46:18.

demics who work in areas of urban and agricultural regulation, architecture, law and economics, public choice, Austrian economics, and political science. Thus, in comparing regulatory alternatives, allodialism should be included as one model or paradigm along with the popular varieties of feudalism—including direct government provision and control or schemes of semi-privatization.

Finally, allodialism raises interesting questions for further applied research in political science and philosophy. For instance, if a government were constitutionally prohibited from owning land allodially, it would be forced to contract for it. Hence, some interesting policy implications might develop. The uncertainty of renewing a lease or not abiding by the rules of the private and free allodiary would create an additional check on government power, and allodiaries might compete away inefficiencies in the leaseholds being offered to government. Consequently, the side effects of allodialism could provide indirect benefits and costs that should be analyzed further. Philosophers might also refine and extend the legal framework of allodialism, especially in terms of the meaning of absoluteness in ownership, its transitional problems like arbitrary assignment of spatial boundaries, its ethics and even morality, as well as the logic of social welfare and real property redistribution issues in general. In the final analysis, an allodial world would be considerably different than the world in which we currently live. The spillover and ancillary effects of allodification are intriguing and thought-provoking, and the direct positive effects on efficiency and liberty would be substantial.

Appendix A: Disturbing accounts of USA real property policy—cases for class discussion

There have been numerous real-life "horror stories"—outrageous incidents in the western United States in the

1990s—which led to considerable public outcry pertaining to real property policy. Consider a dozen examples.

- Alan and Bonny Riggs who live near Kingston, Washington were compelled to give up 30% of their five acres, without compensation, because an eagle was living in a neighbor's tree (K. George 1995; Foreman 1995).

- Kathleen Hedlund's property in Buckley, Washington was declared a wetland by the City, although there is development on adjoining land around it. Consequently, her land has become nearly worthless, while she has not been compensated for the loss. But she has been nearly bankrupted by the high property taxes she has to pay on the unsaleable land (Foreman 1995).

- Lois Jemtegaard was not compensated when her property in Clark County, Washington (along the Columbia River) was declared a national scenic area. Unable to sell a portion of her property, she recently logged the trees on her land in order to finance the replacement of her crumbling home (Pryne 1995).

- Bill Devine owns land near Maple Falls, Washington. Beavers were damming up some of his culverts and causing water to flow on to the highway (producing dangerous driving conditions). So Bill corrected the problem by building his own dams in front of the culverts. The Washington Department of Fish and Wildlife was unhappy that they were not consulted and filed criminal charges against Bill for changing "the natural flow or bed of state waters without written approval." The area below Bill's stream was considered a "salmon habitat" and it did not matter that Bill had removed a dangerous road hazard. The jury acquitted Bill, but not before the Department tried to make an out of court settlement where Bill would "convert his property into a salmon enhancement project to be henceforth managed as salmon habitat!" Obviously a lot of time and money were wasted on this new twist to partial regulatory takings (Moats 1995).

- Jim Watts from Deschutes County, Oregon was denied a building permit to build a home on his land, since it had been zoned for exclusive forest use only, in spite of the fact that the state department of forestry has certified that his soil is not suitable for forestry and probably never had trees on it. Now he can't even sell his parcels (for which he pays taxes). The Senior Planner told him to just learn to live with the law (Oregonians in Action—Education Center 1995).

- Dan Dority wanted to build a home on his land near Wilsonville, Oregon. He was denied permission since the land was only to be used for farming, in spite of the fact that another concern certified it as worthless for farming. It was zoned for exclusive farm use, and a home could not be built there. He had to fight for a reduction in taxes. After a long legal battle, the Oregon Supreme Court denied him relief, curiously noting that a "reasonable farmer 100 years from now" might be able to make a profit on that land (Oregonians in Action—Education Center 1995).

- Joe Mallin was forbidden to build on his 14 acres of land in eastern Oregon, which had been re-zoned as exclusive farm use *after* he bought it. In order to have a shot at relief he would have to take aerial photographs and provide an incredible amount of survey and impact report information first, at a cost far beyond the value of the land (Oregonians in Action—Education Center 1995).

- Rex Barber, Jr., who works on his family farm in rural Oregon, was prohibited from building a second home on a rocky outcrop on the property (one-third of his family's land is unusable desert). He was told to either commute fifteen miles to work or wait until his parents die and then take their home. To alleviate this problem sooner, he would first have to divide the farm into separate tax lots and map all their roads (Oregonians in Action—Education Center 1995).

- Oregon's Land Conservation and Development Commission has been responsible for mis-zoning millions of acres of marginal or useless Oregon land as exclusive farm or forest use—rocky land with sagebrush which is not suited to any crops or grazing. There is no longer any local input. Many small communities in Oregon, such as Alsea (near Corvallis), stagnate under stricture that prevents industrial expansion in their communities (Oregonians in Action—Education Center 1995).

- Dwight Hammond is a rancher who owns water and grazing rights in Diamond, Oregon (south of Burns). However, the U.S. Fish and Wildlife Service disputed his rights. During a *peaceful* confrontation over a historic waterhole, Hammond was arrested by "special agents" of the Service for "forcibly impeding and interfering with a federal officer" and dragged through four days of jail, chains, and Oregon courtrooms from Bend to Portland. After pleading not guilty, the charges against Hammond and his son were reduced, but his legal expenses and personal deprivation have been enormous (Stewards of the Range 1995).

- Wayne Hage is a rancher in Nevada. On account of a property rights dispute, his cattle were confiscated by 30 Forest Service agents, many armed with semi-automatic rifles and wearing bullet-proof vests. Wayne has since filed a takings suit (Stewards of the Range 1995).

- Margaret Rector lives in Texas. Because of regulation pertaining to protection of the Golden Warbler bird, her property once worth $900,000 is now worth only $30,000 (Stewards of the Range 1995).

- Bonnie Agins owns a small parcel in the Bay Area city of Tiburon, California. She hoped to build a home there and raise her children. However, the city wanted her property too, but instead of paying for it they simply zoned it "open space." After *twenty-seven years* of persistent legal efforts, the city finally granted her application to build, but only after she and her attorneys threatened a constitutional challenge (Stewards of the Range 1995).

These are not isolated cases but representative of wider problems in United States real property policy. Why have these problems occurred? Opinions vary, but criticisms of government regulation and intrusion into private property are growing. Carl Henry blames communism and sundry western "political adjustments" for blunting Western convictions about private property, which "now staggers under problems, compromises, and uncertainties." He takes a holistic approach to property, wherein the whole social system around it plays an integral role and property rights "cannot long be preserved apart from other social ingredients" (Henry 1974, p. 23). The larger problem which Henry did not see is feudalism and feudal real property policy.

John White says that land ownership is now merely a lever for extracting tribute (i.e., feudal ground rent) via police power. The state collects its fee (property tax) because it knows people would die without the land and must use it. White emphasizes that feudalism is strongly supported by the legal establishment, and that it "claims first consideration in our fundamental law of property" under the guise of "vested interests" (White 1935, pp. 45, 54, 222-223).

Russell Kirk adds that there is a danger when the state controls private property, which could lead to the foregoing problems. Indeed, the endangering of liberty by long-term feudalism is a serious problem.

[C]onservatives *are persuaded that freedom and property are closely linked.* Separate property from private possession, and Leviathan becomes master of all. Upon the foundation of private property, great civilizations are built. The more widespread is the possession of private property, the more stable and productive is a commonwealth. Economic leveling, conservatives maintain, is not economic progress [emphasis his] (Kirk 1993, p. 21).

In the absence of private property, civilization dwindles.

Appendix B: Allodial roots in economic theory & history

Allodialism can be grounded in reasonable economic theory. This appendix demonstrates this basis, especially with the literature on public choice and Austrian knowledge theories and the powerful conclusions that emanate from them. Since the problems addressed by these schools are exacerbated by feudal policy, allodialism becomes a viable policy solution for such problems.

Feudal policy has far-reaching effects, especially due to real property's physical characteristics. Epstein remarks:

Temporal issues arise with evident urgency in the law of real property. Land itself lasts forever, and the improvements upon it can last for a very long time. The durability of the asset means that no one person can consume it in a lifetime, so that any legal relations with respect to land will of necessity involve a large number of persons over a long period of time (Epstein 1986, p. 669).

Epstein agrees with Hayek that, "A sound system of rights resolves the claims of ownership early in the process to reduce the legal uncertainty in subsequent decisions on investment and consumption" (p. 672). But feudal policy has eroded these ends.[104]

---

[104] Perhaps Walter Williams is justified in commenting on the erosion of private property rights: "Through numerous successful attacks, private property and free enterprise are mere skeletons of their past. Jefferson anticipated this when he said, 'The natural progress of things is for government to gain ground and for liberty to yield.'" Feudalism is manifest in present real property policy since "taxes represent government claims on private property" (Williams 1993, pp. 4, 11, 19).

Economic historians, political scientists, and legal theorists have found the continuance of feudal policy perplexing. Jonathan Hughes argues that American "land tenure" is still as feudal as it was in 1650. "A modern conveyor of real estate is still 'seised with the fee,' even though neither he nor his lawyer is likely to know beyond boiler-plate repetition what those words actually mean (Hughes 1991/1977, p. 3; also Cobin 1997a). Accordingly, Dennis Hale argues that western nations are still under feudal policy, and the real property tax is just "a legal facade" that conceals its real medieval nature (Hale 1985, pp. 382, 384, 398-401). Hughes contends that the state is the real (or allodial) owner of American land, and the system of real property ownership is clearly feudal. Real property "owners" merely hold quasi-perpetual contractual privileges of use and possession while the state is the true owner (Hughes 1991/1977, pp. 22, 25; also Cobin 1997a). The great American jurist James Kent likewise concludes that real property policy is feudal, with the state being the only allodiary, since the state can reenter real property for nonpayment of taxes; "failure to pay taxes still allows the 'donor' to step in and realize his prior right by selling the land for taxes alone. The donor is not now the Crown, or a feudal lord, but he still exists—he is the state government" (cited in Hughes 1991/1977, p. 25, cf. p. 28). John White comments:

> "Freedom" has but partly been achieved. The tyranny of feudalism has been modified greatly, but has not been destroyed...it struggles with tireless energy and great capacity to recover powers it has lost. In this struggle it is ably assisted by the prejudices and customs that still have control in much of our legal procedure...feudal power... [is] passed from hand to hand in customary

transactions of the market, for it is concealed in legal forms that secure possession and control of property (White 1935, p. 12, cf. p. 223).

Instead of having truly private real property, Robert Le-Fevre states that the city, county, or state "collects a fee for the use of the land. The governing body has a prior lien upon any property where the fee (tax) has not been collected. In this sense, all 'privately' owned land in the United States is fundamentally owned by the collective. This practice, aided by the customs of eminent domain, central planning, and zoning, emphasizes that we still pay tribute to the primitive system of collective land ownership" (LeFevre 1966, pp. 7, 47). Sylvester Petro argues that the main difference between old feudal tenures and modern ones is the conceptual changes in the ideas alienability and heritability. In other respects, feudalism remains intact: a fee is still paid to the lord. Nonpayment results in foreclosure or what was previously known as distress (Petro 1974, p. 168).

Allodial policy extends Austrian and public choice theories

Land economics and property rights have been important themes for Austrian economists, although the themes have not been well-developed. Hence, rather than being orthogonal or perpendicular to the Austrian research program, allodialism is a theoretical advance which will prove useful for Austrian policy-relevant investigation. High says that "there is no such thing as Austrian policy" strictly speaking (High 1984, p. 40) and, fittingly, to have allodialism is (practically speaking) to have no real property policy. Yet, Austrians can inform public policy by commending paradigms like allodialism.

Austrian economics Austrians are interested in the role of institutions in simplifying life (reducing thinking costs and experimental requirements), and allodialism does this because it is far less complicated than the exigencies of feudal policy. Plus, it eliminates all the costly distortions associated with regulation, condemnation, construction, transference, and "takings." Further, there is no need to have divinely ordained boundaries to implement the policy. Allodialism could be established by lottery, reassigning current rights, or any number of allocative inventions. Austrians might simply suggest to allodify current real property privileges, except for government-owned land, which could be distributed by lottery or auctioned (e.g., perhaps as part of a policy to retire government debt).

Consequently, allodialism is pertinent to Austrian economics and, indeed, derives much theoretical force from Austrian theories about knowledge, interventionism and private property. It may well extend a dormant theme touched on by Austrians which has not been adequately developed. Consider the following relevant quotations from important Austrian economists that allude to a natural nexus between allodialism and Austrian themes, some of which are also similar to public choice themes like rent seeking. Mises argues:

> Not shepherds, but sophisticated aristocrats and city-dwellers were the authors of bucolic poetry. Daphnis and Chloe are creations of fancies far removed from earthly concerns. No less removed from the soil is the modern political myth of the soil. It did not blossom from the moss of the forests and the loam of the fields, but from the pavements of the cities and the carpets of the salons. The farmers make use of it because they find a practical means of obtaining political privileges which raise the prices of their products and of their farms (Mises 1966/ 1949, "myth of the soil" section, pp. 644-645, cf. p. 81).

Political regimes serve to preclude natural allodial benefits by the enactment and enforcement of coercive real property legislation. But such policies are hazardous to economic development. Robert Anderson comments:

> Without the institution of private property in the ownership of productive economic resources and a legal framework securing contractual agreements in the transfer of economic resources, an advanced world market economy would never have developed (Anderson 1992, p. 33).

Mises corroborates:

> In the ages of caste privileges and trade barriers there were revenues not dependent on the market. Princes and lords lived at the expense of the humble slaves and serfs who owed them tithes, statute labor, and tributes. Ownership of land could only be acquired either by conquest or by largesse on the part of the conqueror. Even later, when the lords and their liegemen began to sell their surpluses on the market, they could not be ousted by the competition of more efficient people. Competition was free only within very narrow limits. The acquisition of manorial estates was reserved for the nobility, that of urban real property to the citizens of the township, that of farm land to the peasants... (Mises 1966/1949, p. 312; cf. Mises 1988/1958).

As noted previously, research on modern real property policy has shown that we still live in the feudal age more or less (Hughes 1991/1977, pp. 5, 22; Cobin 1997a, chapter 4), making allodialism an important issue for Austrians who might have errantly assumed that feudal policy had ended. Mises also considered time and expectations with respect to land use, as well as privilege seeking activities, that proceed from the indestructible nature of the "powers of land" (Mises 1966/1949, pp. 638-639).[105] Carl Menger, the founder of the Austrian School, likewise recognized the preeminence and "powers" of land in the structure of production.

Land and the services of land, in the concrete forms in which we observe them, are objects of our value appraisement like all other goods. Like other goods, they attain value only to the extent that we depend on command of them for the satisfaction of our needs...A deeper understanding of the differences in their value, therefore, also only be attained by approaching land and the services of land from the general points of view of our science and, insofar as they are goods of a higher order, relating them to the corresponding goods of lower order and especially to their complimentary goods...it also follows that whenever I refer to the services of land I mean the services, measured over time, of pieces of land as we actually find them in the economy of men, and not the use of the "original powers" of land...When a farmer rents a piece of land for one or several years, he cares little whether its soil derives its fertility from capital investments of all kinds or was fertile from the very beginning. These circumstances have no influence on the price he pays for the use of the soil. A buyer of a piece of land attempts to reckon the "future" but never the "past" of the land he is purchasing (Menger 1994/1871, pp. 168, 166-167, cf. pp. 85-86).

Allodialism affects both expectations on land use and transactions costs of buying or using land optimally. It also affects the theory of value, as well as the production of all lower-ordered goods, since land is always a higher order

---

[105] Of course, topsoil can be destroyed so it is not clear that Mises is correct completely in this assertion, unless we make a distinction between land and topsoil. Mises further discusses the uses and prices of land in relation to economic theory. See Mises 1966/1949, pp. 642-644.

good somewhere in the structure of all production. As Mark Skousen notes:

> Land and labor, the two original factors of production, are applied at each stage of product transformation, and can therefore, like capital goods, be classified according to their role in the production architecture. If land is used for the production of lower-order consumer goods, then it is a first-order good. If the land consists of minerals and other natural resources, then it is a higher order good ...Jevons divides landowners into six "classifications of trade" in his principles textbook, which he describes as "the principal orders of industry, or ranks of traders, as it were, who successively contribute some operation to the complete production of a commodity" (Skousen 1990, p. 165).

Allodialism stresses the importance of land in production, perhaps even more emphatically than Skousen does. Likewise, Rothbard has perhaps the most complete Austrian treatise on real property within the Austrian School, although he does not provide as comprehensive market-based solution as the allodial paradigm does. Karen Vaughn correctly notes the importance on land economics in Rothbard's work, where he combines it with natural rights theory.

> [Rothbard] criticized even Mises' use of the notion of consumer sovereignty for its possible implication that the producer did not have the right to do with his property what he wished. Markets were based on "individual sovereignty," not consumer sovereignty, except in the most formal sense. Property itself was a completely unproblematic institution. Property rights were derivable from a Lockean process of mixing one's labor with unowned resources, which then led to a property right over those re-

sources in perpetuity. None of even John Locke's caveats and qualifications entered into Rothbard's schema. And virtually all policy could be related to the question of property rights. Externalities problems, for example, were simply failures to enforce property rights, as if they were all clearly and unambiguously defined and as if there were no problems of transactions costs in doing so (Vaughn 1994, pp. 98-99, cf. 42-43).

Allodialism is well suited to such considerations. In some sense, it is Rothbard's missing link in solving the problems of real property policy. In *Man, Economy, and State*, Rothbard discusses real property theory and policy at considerable length, manifesting his conviction that land economics and real property are eminent and crucial themes in economic theory (Rothbard 1970/1962, pp. 8, 147-152, 282, 292, 312-314, 347, 410-417, 421-424, 457, 462, 479-481, 502-528, 551, 609-611, 813-814, 888, 894, 929-931, 933). Rothbard has also delineated certain guidelines for just title under the Lockean rule of first possession (Rothbard 1974, pp. 120-121).[106] Such a system would avoid rent seeking and distortions in the market process.

Since allodial real property would be wholly *private*, unlike feudal real property privileges, allodialism would positively affect key economic issues that Austrians point out, like valuation and entrepreneurial calculation. Conforming to other Austrian scholars, Sennholz remarks:

In the private property order and voluntary exchange system, private ownership means full control over the uses and services of property, not merely a legal title while

---

[106] Rothbard contends, "[A]ll existing property titles may be considered just under the homestead principle, provided (a) that there may never be any property in people; (b) that the existing property owner did not himself steal the property; and particularly (c) that any identifiable just owner (the original victim of theft or his heir) must be accorded his property" (p. 120-121).

government is holding the power of control. Nothing less than this will ever assure the needed personal stewardship over the limited resources of this planet or the efficient employment of property for the benefit of all (cited in Anderson 1992, p. 44).

In his famous work, *The Road to Serfdom*, Hayek warns of the perils of collectivism and, by implication, the infeudation of land. He notes that the transfer of property that is used in the means of production to the state (and surely real property was of paramount concern), elevates the state to the precarious position where its action will decide all other incomes (Hayek 1944, p. 103).

It is only because the control of the means of production is divided among people acting independently that nobody has complete power over us, that we as individuals can decide what to do with ourselves. If all the means of production were vested in a single hand, whether it be nominally that of "society" as a whole or that of a dictator, whoever exercises this control has complete power over us (p. 104).

Austrian critique of Georgism Mises has suggested that the primary purpose of the state is to create and preserve an "environment in which the market economy can safely operate" (Mises 1966, p. 257). Allodial policy would help accomplish what Mises suggests. Dabbling in the policy arena as well, Hayek commented that, at present, Georgist policy is: "the theoretically most defensible of all socialist proposals and impractical only because of the de facto impossibility of distinguishing between the original and permanent powers of the soil and the different kinds of improvements" (Hayek 1994, p. 63; cf. a similar statement in Hayek 1960, Chapter 22 Housing, Section 5, pp. 352-353). Note that Hayek is clear that Georgism is still a *socialist* policy. Rothbard also offers an extensive and grating critique of Georgism (Rothbard 1970/1962, pp. 148-149, 512-513, 813-814, 888, 930). Georgism is not a free market position and it will not eliminate public choice problems.

Henry George said, "This thing is absolutely certain: Private property in land blocks the way of advancing civilization" (H. George 1930/1881, p. 104).[107] Neo-Georgists have modified his sentiment to suggest that private ownership of rents, not real property, is the problem, and some say that neo-Georgism might be reconcilable with Austrian economics (Foldvary 1996). But this is certainly an aberrant suggestion among Austrians. Georgism gives a "superior" (e.g., the state) control of real property by debasing real property rights (or at least by confiscating land rents). Thus, the prevailing Austrian view from Mises, Hayek, and Rothbard, as well as quasi-Austrians like Herbert Davenport, seems to be that Georgism is based on erroneous economics and is most certainly anti-Austrian School (at least in the area of real property rights and public finance). Indeed, Georgism and neo-Georgism are feudal.

Public choice The Virginia School of public choice, whose founders were largely indebted to Mises and Hayek, as well as Frank Knight of the University of Chicago, share a similar concern for real property policy as the Austrian School. Tullock says he was influenced greatly by Mises (Tullock 1988, pp. 1-2), and the Austrian influence on Buchanan is evidenced in his book *Cost and Choice* (Buchanan 1969). Thus, public choice economics has a natural interest in allodialism for the same reasons that Austrians do, facilitating a nexus between the two schools.

---

[107] Henry George (1831-1897) was a nineteenth century economist and land reformer, famous for his "single tax" view (viz., the state should tax away all rent but abolish all other forms of taxation). He saw only "anarchy and bloodshed" in the wake of private property rights. Some of the more important recent works on neo-Georgism include: Nicolaus Tideman, ed. (1994), *Land and Taxation*, Shepheard-Walwyn: London (this has several chapters by different authors, including Foldvary); Fred Harrison (1983), *The Power in the Land*, Universe Books: New York; and Richard Noyes, ed. (1991), *Now the Synthesis*, Shepheard-Walwyn: London.

Valuation issues in real property policy form a key link between the Austrian and Virginia public choice schools. A key Austrian insight since the work of Menger (e.g., Menger 1994/1871, p. 168) and the early writings of Mises, is that property has no intrinsic or objective value. It must be given a value by acting men, and, therefore, value is purely *subjective*. Furthermore, every object is valued differently by every individual. "The result is a subjective judgment of value, colored by the individual's personality. Different people and the same people at different times value the same objective facts in a different way" (Mises 1962/1949, p. 430 and Menger 1994/1871, p.76).

Much of this link comes by the matter of valuation. Buchanan notes: "the value of the property right in one's own person, as expressed in the liberty to choose among alternative buyers is measured by the full amount of the goods (purchasing power) received in exchange" (Buchanan 1993, p. 28). Private property protects personal liberty by "providing viable exit from, or avoidance of entry into, potentially exploitative economic relationships" (p. 32) by providing economic mobility "out of the network of exchange-market interdependence and towards the valued position of self-sufficiency" (p. 35). Buchanan and other public choice theorists stress liberty in choice as an essential feature of a private (real) property order. Allodialism would help facilitate such liberty.

Rowley talks about both the importance of protecting property rights and the limited power constitutions have had in doing so (Rowley 1993, pp. 52, 54). He also notes, "The natural right to property is simply another name for the freedom to act according to one's own choices, defining allowable acts for transformation of the material world" (p. 72). Rowley argues that government regulation of land provides no benefits to anyone beyond the bureaucracy. He also criticizes Epstein for failing to present a "convincing theory of benevolent government to explain efficiency in the tolling [enactment] of statutes by the political process" (Rowley 1986, pp. 772-773). Such a defect would not be present under allodial policy, creating a natural inclination towards it from a public choice perspective.

Allodialism in these theories

Since allodialism maximizes market alternatives to regulation, and maximizes the opportunity set and choices an individual has over real property, it serves as a natural extension of these theories. The theory of real property has been of importance to Austrian and public choice scholars in terms of externalities, subjective valuation, wider consumer choice, efficient production, ownership without adverse influence from the political process, time in the structure of production, and regulation. Allodialism provides a legal and historical paradigm to apply such theories (as they pertain to real property) and to evaluate public policies. Indeed, allodialism is a useful or even necessary research program within Austrian and public choice schools.

Allodialism is a practical policy alternative that would alleviate public choice problems and many policy concerns of Austrians. The new feudalism has failed to raise the quality of life (Cobin 1997a, 1997b; cf. Holcombe 1995), concurring with the warnings and predictions of public choice and Austrian theory. Congruent with the implications of Austrian theory, the best policy solution is not to make an improved feudal system or constitution, but to scrap feudalism and replace it with allodialism, permitting markets to handle problems. As Austrians have shown in their critique of central planning, markets may not be perfect, but they are surely better than the distortions and misallocations of central planning and, by implication, regulation in general.

Mises rightly suggests that individuals perform effective cost-benefit calculations in order to ensure an action is in their best interest. They allocate their resources (i.e., time and property) according to their subjective preferences of the germane costs and benefits. Private property of the material factors of production is *not* a restriction of the freedom of all other people to choose what suits them best. It is, on the contrary, the means that assigns to the common man, in his capacity as a buyer, supremacy in all economic affairs. It is the means to stimulate the best enterprising men to exert themselves to the best of their abilities in the service of all of the people (Mises 1988/1958, p. 39). Thus, economic progress can only be obtained via the establishment and protection of private property. As Mises contends, "private property is inextricably linked with civilization" (Mises 1966/1949, p. 264). In spite of the changing market and their own ignorance, "acting men" in the "social system" comply with "an incessant urge toward improvement" (p. 542). Unlike allodial policy, which would facilitate such human action, feudal policy distorts the calculations and actions of individuals, and leads to resource misallocations and costly government failures.

References

Alexander, Gregory S. (1991), "Time and Property in the American Republican Legal Culture," *New York University Law Review*, vol. 66, May, pp. 273-352.

Anderson, Robert G. (1992), "The Disintegration of Economic Ownership," in John W. Robbins, and Mark Spangler, eds., *A Man of Principle: Essays in Honor of Hans F. Sennholz*, Grove City College Press: Grove City, Penn., pp. 33-45.

Benson, Bruce L. (1990), *The Enterprise of Law: Justice Without the State*, Pacific Research Institute: San Francisco.

Buchanan, James M. (1969), *Cost and Choice: An Inquiry in Economic Theory*, University of Chicago Press: Chicago.

Buchanan, James M. (1993), *Property as a Guarantor of Liberty*, Edward Elgar Publishing Co.: Brookfield, Vermont.

Coase, Ronald (1960), "The Problem of Social Cost," *Journal of Law and Economics*, vol. 3, October, pp. 1-44.

Cobin, John M. (1997), *Building Regulation, Market Alternatives, and Allodial Policy*, Avebury Press: London.

Cobin, John M. (1999), "Siegan Brought Up-To-Date: A Critical View of the Expansion of Zoning in Santiago, Chile" (working paper), forthcoming in *Estudios Públicos*, also at http://www.mises.org/scholar_interests.asp.

Dahlman, Carl J. (1988), "The Problem of Externality," in Tyler Cowen, ed., *The Theory of Market Failure: A Critical Examination*, George Mason University Press/ Cato Institute book: Fairfax, Virginia, pp. 209-234.

Epstein, Richard A. (1986), "Past and Future: The Temporal Dimension in the Law of Property," *Washington University Law Quarterly*, vol. 64, no. 3, pp. 667-722.

Foldvary, Fred (1996), "Is there an Austrian Theory of Public Finance?," presented at the Austrian Scholars Conference, Auburn University, January 26.

Foldvary, Fred (1994), *Public Goods and Private Communities: The Market Provision of Social Services*, Edward Elgar Publishing Co. [The Locke Institute]: Brookfield, Vermont.

Foreman, Rep. Dale (1995), "Property Rights Initiative," *Seattle-Post Intelligencer*, Sunday, June 25.

George, Henry (1930/1881), *The Land Question: Property in Land—the Condition of Labor*, Doubleday, Doran & Co.: Garden City, New York.

George, Kathy (1995), "Celebrity case for property rights: But Kingston couple's story isn't typical, regulators say," *Seattle-Post Intelligencer*, Thursday, August 17.

Hale, Dennis (1985), "The Evolution of the Property Tax," *Journal of Politics*, vol. 47, no. 2, May, pp. 382-404.

Hayek, Friedrich A. von (1960), *The Constitution of Liberty*, Gateway Editions: South Bend, Indiana.

Hayek, Friedrich A. von (1994), *Hayek on Hayek: An Autobiographical Dialogue*, edited by Stephen Kresge and Leif Wenar, University of Chicago Press: Chicago.

Hayek, Friedrich A. von (1973), *Law, Legislation and Liberty*, University of Chicago Press: Chicago.

Hayek, Friedrich A. von (1944), *The Road to Serfdom*, University of Chicago Press: Chicago.

Henry, Carl F. H. (1974), "Christian Perspective on Private Property," in Samuel L. Blumenfeld, ed., *Property in a Humane Economy: A Selection of Essays Compiled by the Institute for Humane Studies*, Open Court: LaSalle, Illinois, pp. 23-45.

High, Jack C. (1984), "The Case for Austrian Economics," *Intercollegiate Review*, winter, pp. 38-42.

Holcombe, Randall G. (1997), "A Theory of the Theory of Public Goods," *Review of Austrian Economics*, vol. 10, no. 1, January, pp. 1-22 (manuscript version).

Holcombe, Randall G. (1995), *Public Policy and the Quality of Life: Market Incentives Versus Government Planning*, Greenwood Press: Westport, Conn.

Hughes, Jonathan R. T. (1991/1977), *The Governmental Habit Redux: Economic Controls from Colonial Times to the Present*, Second Edition, Princeton University Press: Princeton, New Jersey.

Jacobs, Jane (1961), *The Death and Life of Great American Cities*, Vintage Books (Random House): New York.

Kinsella, N. Stephan (1994), "A Civil Law to Common Law Dictionary," *Louisiana Law Review*, vol. 54, pp. 1265ff.

Kirk, Russell (1993), *The Politics of Prudence*, Intercollegiate Studies Institute: Bryn Mawr, Pennsylvania.

LeFevre, Robert (1966), *The Philosophy of Ownership*, Rampart College (A Pine Tree Publication): Larkspur, Colorado.

Machan, Tibor R. (1982), "Dissolving the Problems of Public Goods: Financing Government without Coercive Measures," in Tibor R. Machan, ed., *The Libertarian Reader*, Rowman and Littlefield: Lanham, Maryland.

MacGregor, Hillary E. (1997), "City Process for Granting Permits Due for Overhaul Development: Many Say Winning the Right to Build Houses in Ventura Is Based On Politics and Deal-Making Rather than Good Planning," *Los Angeles Times*, Ventura County Edition, Tuesday, January 21, p. B1 (Metro).

Menger, Carl (1994/1871), *Principles of Economics*, Translated by James Dingwell and Bert F. Hoselitz, Libertarian Press: Grove City, Penn.

Mises, Ludwig von (1988/1958), "Liberty and Property," in *Two Essays by Ludwig von Mises*, The Ludwig von Mises Institute: Auburn, Alabama.

Mises, Ludwig von (1966/1949), *Human Action: A Treatise on Economics*, Third Revised Edition, Contemporary Books, Inc. (Henry Regnery Co.): Chicago.

Moats, Ed (1995), "Leave It to Beavers: Takings by Prosecution," *National Review*, vol. 47, no. 17, September 11, p. 6 (West).

Moore, Lisa J. (1992), "When Landowners Clash with the Law: Regulations May Crimp Your Plans to Build," *U.S. News & World Report*, April 6, pp. 80-81.

Myers, Garth A. (1994), "Making the Socialist City of Zanzibar," *Geographical Review*, vol. 84, October 1, pp. 451ff.

Noyes, C. Reinold (1936), *The Institution of Property: A Study of the Development, Substance and arrangement of the System of Property in Modern Anglo-American Law*, Longmans, Green and Co.: New York.

Oregonians in Action—Education Center (1995), "Oregon's Land Use System: A Betrayal of Trust," videocassette, *Oregonians in Action*, Tigard, Oregon, telephone +1-503-620-0258.

Petro, Sylvester (1974), "Feudalism, Property, and Praxeology," in Samuel L. Blumenfeld, ed., *Property in a Humane Economy: A Selection of Essays Compiled by the Institute for Humane Studies*, Open Court: LaSalle, Illinois, pp. 161-180.

Pollock, Robert (1994), "Architectural Correctness: Property Owners Challenge Aesthetic Restrictions on Land Use," *Reason*, vol. 26, October 1, p. 16.

Posner, Richard A. (1988), *The Economic Analysis of Law*, third edition, Little, Brown, and Co.: Boston.

Pound, Roscoe (1942), *Social Control Through Law*, Yale University Press: New Haven, Connecticut.

Pryne, Eric (1995), "Private Land, PUBLIC FIGHT," *The Seattle Times*, Sunday, March 19, pp. A16ff.

Rothbard, Murray N. (1974), "Justice and Property Rights," in Samuel L. Blumenfeld, ed., *Property in a Humane Economy: A Selection of Essays Compiled by the Institute for Humane Studies*, Open Court: LaSalle, Illinois, pp. 101-122.

Rothbard, Murray N. (1970/1962), *Man, Economy, and State: A Treatise on Economic Principles*, Nash Publishing: Los Angeles.

Rowley, Charles K. (1986), "The Law of Property in Virginia School Perspective," *Washington University Law Quarterly*, vol. 64, no. 3, pp. 759-774.

Rowley, Charles K. (1993), *Liberty and the State*, The Shaftesbury Papers, 4, Edward Elgar Publishing Co.: Brookfield, Vermont.

Scott, Robert E., and Leslie, Douglas L. (1993), *Contract Law and Theory*, second edition, The Michie Company Law Publishers: Charlottesville, Virginia.

Siegan, Bernard H. (1990), "Land Use Regulations Should Preserve Only Vital Pressing Government Interests," *CATO Journal*, vol. 10, spring/summer.

Siegan, Bernard H. (1993/1972), *Land Use* without *Zoning*, Bartholdi & Lazarus: Houston, Texas [originally published by Lexington Books, D.C. Heath and Company].

Skousen, Mark (1990), *The Structure of Production*, New York University Press: New York.

Smith, Adam (1937/1776), *An Inquiry into the Nature and Causes of the Wealth of Nations*, The Modern Library: New York.

Stewards of the Range (1995), various policy studies on the Hammond, Hage, Rector, and Agins cases, *Stewards of the Range*, Mark Pallot, Director (author of *Grand Theft and Petit Larceny*), Boise: Idaho, phone +1-208-336-5922.

Stahl, Konrad (1987), "Theories of Business Location," in E.S. Mills, ed., *Handbook of Regional and Urban Economics*, vol. 11, Elsevier/North-Holland: Oxford, pp. 759-820.

Strayer, Joseph Reese (1965), *Feudalism*, Von Nostrand: New York.

Tullock, Gordon (1975), "The Transitional Gains Trap," *The Bell Journal of Economics*, autumn, pp. 671-678.

Tullock, Gordon (1988), *Wealth, Poverty, and Politics*, Basil Blackwell: New York.

Vaughn, Karen I. (1994), *Austrian Economics in America: The Migration of a Tradition*, Cambridge University Press: New York.

White, John Z. (1935), *Public and Private Property: With Reference to Several Decisions by the Supreme Court of the United States*, The Beaver Press: Greenville, Pennsylvania.

Williams, Walter E. (1993), *The Legitimate Role of Government in a Free Economy*, The American University: Bryn Mawr, Pennsylvania.

Index

100% gold reserves, 356, 358,
360-361, 375

A

abandonment, 422
abundance, 218, 222, 350, 445
academics, ix, 3, 5, 7-8, 79, 120,
134, 165, 218, 228, 238, 256,
394, 396, 498, 499
accidents, automobile, 82
action axiom, 208, 231, 234, 258
activity, creative, 222, 284, 298
adultery, 422
advertising, 301
aggregate data, problems with, 321
aggregation, 89, 108, 316, 321,
355, 394, 468
agricultural products, 454
agriculture, 249, 519
air conditioning (policy), 122
air pollution, 175-176, 395, 442,
523
airbags, 82
airline, 189, 191-192
airport, 381
Alaska, 455
Alchian, Armen, 3, 345, 376
alcohol, 142
alertness (entrepreneurial), 167,
195, 274, 277-278, 280, 282,
284-285, 288-289, 291-293,
349, 393, 437, 523
Alexander, Gregory, 506

allocation, of resources, 30, 57,
59, 185, 244, 246, 262, 273,
278, 400, 428-429, 434, 450,
455, 465, 468, 483, 485, 487,
525, 541, 545
allodialism, 459-461, 500-525,
527, 529-546, 551-558, 561-
563
definition, 501
production, 532
quasi, 460, 506, 515, 517, 524,
537
allodification, 546
altruism, 119-120, 336
America, 133, 560
anarchy, 114, 123, 204, 215, 217,
265, 338, 384, 405, 500, 534,
560
Anderson, Gary, 138, 160
Anderson, Robert, 302, 458, 474,
495, 555, 563
Animal Farm (Orwell), 335, 342
anointed, the, 335
anticompetitive, 44
antisocial residuum, 438, 526
antitrust, 18-19, 29, 31, 33, 36, 39,
40-46, 76, 99, 105, 111-112,
169, 188-189, 229, 287, 294,
311, 379, 416
Apostles, 2
Araujo, Karen, 71
arbitrage, 274, 277-278, 282, 289,
293
arbitrary, 111, 146, 214, 241, 288,
312, 338, 392-393, 395, 398-

B

M

P

Panama, 349
paperwork contests, 61, 64, 166
parasite, the state as a, 102-103,
    348
Pareto optimality, 106, 438
    preferred move, 439, 468
    principle, 438
pariahs, of the economics
    profession, 1, 10
parties, political, 98
passports, 49-50
patents, 456
*Peevyhouse v. Garland Coal and
    Mining Co.*, 489
perfection, 388, 403
perjury, 419
permanent legal framework, 153
persecution, 216, 331
perverse incentives, 16, 88, 104,
    174, 189, 329, 421
Petro, Sylvester, 459, 474, 496,
    553, 567
philosophy of history, 214
physics, 238, 241, 256
    Newtonian, 241
Pipes, Richard, 72
Plagues and Peoples (McNeill),
    102
planners, 175, 245, 337, 405
    central, 245, 251, 269
planning, 32, 193, 203, 243-246,
    250-251, 254, 263, 270, 275,
    307, 334, 362, 416, 445, 487,
    499, 501, 510, 516, 522, 531-
    532, 543, 563
    central, 242-246, 248, 250, 263,
    553, 563
plenty, world of, 317
Ploof v. Putnam, 486
police, 449
policies, failed policies replete with
    atrocities, 246, 253
policies, fair and efficient, 137
policies, interventionist, 25, 310,
    314, 318, 323, 393
policies, paternalistic, 324

policies, perverse, 180
policy, alimony, 129
policy, allodial, 460-461, 498,
    500-501, 506-509, 516-525,
    529-530, 532-535, 537, 539,
    541, 543, 545, 562-563
    advantages, 519-522, 524, 529,
    531, 543
    for defense, 514
    hybrid types, 514
    legislative changes, 542
    reallocation of property rights in
    transition to, 537
    redistribution or wealth transfer
    in transition to, 539
    reversion policy, 544-545
    transaction costs of transition to,
    540
policy, ancillary problems, 518
policy, antitrust, 18-19, 29, 31, 33,
    39, 40-46, 76, 99, 105, 111-
    112, 169, 188-189, 229, 287,
    294, 311, 379, 416, 442
policy, Austrian, 252, 553
policy, big brother, 126
policy, central bank, 270
policy, changes, 404, 498
policy, child support, 129
policy, dam, 401
policy, defense, 384, 408
policy, defensive, 123
policy, designed, 136
policy, divorce, 420-421
policy, driving, 419
policy, drug, 145, 419, 442
policy, economic, 12, 13, 255,
    317, 331, 334, 498
policy, education, 129
policy, educational grants, 130
policy, environmental, 126, 179-
    180
policy, family, 421
policy, farm, 129
policy, feminist, 419
policy, feudal, 515, 550
policy, food stamps, 129
policy, foreign, 143
policy, housing, 126, 129

property, management of, 504
property, private, 73, 152-153, 179, 180, 185, 215, 217, 246, 257, 270-271, 318, 325, 337, 346, 414, 425, 426, 443, 453, 455, 457-458, 471, 474-475, 520, 550-552, 554-555, 559-560, 563
property, productive, 457
property, public, 512
property, real, 318, 440, 456, 459, 460-461, 486, 499-537, 539, 542-547, 551-555, 557-562
prostitution, 141-142, 167, 521
protection, 38, 49, 68, 149, 177, 182, 187, 203, 257, 311, 415, 427, 461, 478, 549, 563
protectionism, 40-41, 78, 80, 125, 146, 150, 220, 262, 311, 347, 351
Protestant Ethic, The (Weber), 69, 442
Protestantism, 443
Providence, 214
Prowse, Michael, 238, 256, 268, 290, 303
psychosis, 419
public choice, vii-viii, 1, 5-6, 8-15, 20-26, 29-32, 34, 38, 41, 47, 49, 52, 54-56, 62, 80, 86, 89, 91, 93, 95, 102-107, 112, 114, 119-121, 127, 131-133, 135-141, 143-145, 148, 150, 154-155, 163-166, 170, 174-175, 178, 185-187, 189, 194-196, 228-229, 243, 245, 255, 269, 274, 311, 326-327, 329, 347, 349, 351, 358, 363-364, 369, 375, 379, 390, 393, 398, 401, 403-404, 406-407, 413, 418, 422-424, 427, 432, 434, 439, 441, 461, 463, 465, 475-476, 478, 479, 499-500, 510, 516, 524, 528, 530-531, 533, 534, 536, 540, 543-546, 551, 553-554, 560-562
    problems, 413, 418, 422, 461, 500, 560

does not impugn motives or character of planners, 174
public emotion, 183
public enterprises, 123, 124
public finance, 404-405, 407, 510, 531-532, 560
public goods, 124, 128, 384, 399
public interest, 5, 13, 17, 21, 31-33, 35, 39, 43-44, 76, 83, 88, 92, 121-122, 127, 131, 135, 165, 169, 171-172, 177, 186, 189, 196, 204, 245, 315-318, 327, 329, 405, 434, 453, 463, 465, 483, 487, 514, 516-517, 544
public opinion, 165, 214, 264-265, 368
public policy, viii, x, 1, 5, 6, 32, 39, 46, 70-71, 74, 76, 82, 119-123, 131-138, 145, 150-151, 154-155, 164, 174, 176-178, 189, 195, 202, 205, 230, 244, 253-255, 257-259, 282, 286, 288, 289, 294, 308, 310, 315, 317, 321, 328, 337-338, 345, 347, 351, 353, 356, 361, 362, 369, 372, 375, 378, 383-385, 395-396, 401, 403, 411, 413, 416-417, 442, 456, 458, 461, 468, 498-500, 504-505, 508, 514, 518-520, 525, 533, 540, 545-546, 554, 562
public policy, 88, 505, 528
    primary purpose, 136
    romantic and quixotic vision, 14
public provision, 5, 140, 363, 479, 480
public sector, 57, 61, 391, 478
public treasury, 154
pyramid, intellectual of society, 6, 135

Q

quality of life, 140, 171, 245, 328, 334, 383, 483, 500, 562
quotas, 109, 146-147, 333

R

Rule of First Possession (Locke), 544
rule of law, 72
rulers, political, 117
rules, 196
   legal, 449
   real property, 512
rulings, Draconian, 418

S

Salerno, Joseph, 375
Sas-Rolfes, Michael, 183-185, 199
savings, 202, 301, 349-350, 354, 431, 455, 532, 534, 540, 542, 545
scarcity, 7, 23, 62, 65, 79, 139, 155, 215, 228, 261, 317-318, 336, 340, 514, 521
Schansberg, Eric, 136, 138, 141-145, 162, 255, 332, 342
scholars and politicians, non-economists, iii-iv, x, 15-18, 21, 24-25, 27-28, 30-31, 35, 46, 50, 54-56, 65, 69, 76, 78-81, 83-84, 88, 91, 94-97, 100-101, 106-107, 111, 117, 137-139, 143-158, 160-162, 164, 169-170, 173, 180-183, 188, 192-193, 197-199, 205, 218, 238, 253-254, 256, 267-268, 290, 292-293, 302-303, 312, 314, 331-335, 341-343, 346-348, 352-353, 356, 358, 368-370, 376, 386-387, 390-391, 396, 408-409, 412, 414-417, 423, 426, 428-429, 432, 436, 438-442, 447-448, 451-456, 459, 461-466, 471, 473-474, 493, 495-496, 500, 502, 505, 514, 527, 530, 534, 550-553, 556, 558, 560, 562, 564-568
schools, government, 126, 314
Schumpeter, Joseph, 282, 297, 298, 304
science, 237
Scotland, 374
Scott v. Alpha Beta Co., 494

self interest, 13-14, 22, 26, 32, 35, 39, 41, 47, 76, 92, 119-120, 131, 164-165, 169, 172, 196, 245, 514
   does not impugn motives or character of planners, 174
   natural goodness, 247
self-defense, 123, 406, 504
selfishness, 120, 262, 325
Selgin, George, x, 4, 243-244, 257, 268, 354, 356, 359-363, 369, 371-372, 374-375, 377, 380
sellers, 37, 48, 225, 379, 490, 508, 518
Senators, 41
Sennholz, Hans, 26, 83, 271, 302-303, 342, 369, 371, 376-377, 495, 559, 564
Shortt, Bruce, 126
Shughart, William, 18, 19, 28, 34, 43-44, 46, 50, 103, 117, 169, 186-187, 195, 199
Siegan, Bernard, 500, 527, 530, 564, 568
Sierra Club, 126
silver, 374
Simmons, Randy, 15-18, 21, 24, 27, 28, 30-31, 35, 46, 50, 65, 78-81, 84, 88, 91, 94-95, 100-102, 106-107, 117, 137, 139, 161, 164, 169-170, 173, 198, 254, 268, 390-391, 409
Simon, Julian, 3, 179, 296
Skinner, Burrhus Frederic, 334, 343
Skousen, Mark, 345, 377, 557, 568
slavery, 26
smart cards, 363
Smith, Adam, 14, 25, 106, 215, 238, 518, 534, 568
Smith, Vernon, 2
smog, 176, 178, 442
smoke, 395, 520
social benefits, 399, 406
social cooperation, 152, 203, 217, 234, 265, 413
social coordination, 41, 315, 400

W

Y

Yates, Steven, 132

Z

zero-sum games, 166, 286
zoning, 171-172, 174, 528-530,
536, 542, 553

About the Author

 Dr. John Cobin is Professor of Economics and Public Policy at the Universidad Andrés Bello and the Universidad Austral in Chile. Plus, he often lectures in other cities in Europe and Latin America (e.g., Belgrade, Prague, Lima, Buenos Aires, etc.). He serves as Director of the MBA program in Santiago for Universidad Andrés Bello. In addition, he does financial planning and business consulting.

He was the libertarian candidate for U.S. Congress from South Carolina's 4th district in 2006. He was the host of *Christian Worldview with Dr. John Cobin*, a weekday morning radio talk show (2004 to 2005). He wrote a weekly column for *The Times Examiner* and *Free Market News* for several years.

Dr. Cobin taught part time in American universities from 2001 to 2008. And he retains his status as Visiting Professor of Economics and Public Policy at Universidad Francisco Marroquín, Guatemala. He worked at Universidad Finis Terrae in Santiago as Professor of Economics and Public Policy from 1996 to 2000, he occasionally taught at other universities in Chile too, including Universidad Católica in Santiago, the International MBA program at Universidad Adolfo Ibañez, Viña del Mar, plus the MBA program at Universidad del Desarrollo in Santiago and in Concepción.

Dr. Cobin received his ARE from Reformed Bible College (1984), his BA in Business Economics from California State University, Long Beach (1985), his MA in Business Economics from University of California, Santa Barbara (1987), and both his MA in Economics (1995) and his PhD in Public Policy (1996) from George Mason University in Fairfax, Virginia.

Dr. Cobin's research has focused on evaluating urban public policies such as zoning, building and fire safety regulation, and highway construction, as well as theoretical ways to reduce economic problems associated with them (e.g., his book *Building Regulation, Market Alternatives, and Allodial Policy*, Avebury 1997). He published this book in English (*A Primer on Modern Themes in Free Market Economics and Policy*, Universal Publishers 2009) along with its Spanish translation *Ensayos sobre Temas Modernos de la Economía y las Politicas de Mercado*, Universidad Andrés Bello 2009. Dr. Cobin's provocative books *Bible and Government: Public Policy from a Christian Perspective* (Alertness Books, 2003) and *Christian Theology of Public Policy: Highlighting the American Experience* (Alertness Books, 2006) deal with the nature of the state and the interrelation between Christian faith or action and public policy. He authored *Life in Chile: A Former American's Guide for Newcomers* (2009), published in both English and Spanish (*¿Por qué Vivir en Chile? Experiencias de un gringo que se convirtió en un chileno más*).

In addition to his academic work, Dr. Cobin has been a successful entrepreneur and consultant, having started and operated several small businesses. He helped homeschool six of his seven children. http://www.PolicyOfLiberty.net contains his papers, columns, and information about his books, as well as a number of popular pages for free market links, quotations for liberty, and more. He runs a popular blogsite http://www.escapeamericanow.blogspot.com geared toward prospective expatriates considering Chile.

Lightning Source UK Ltd.
Milton Keynes UK
UKOW06f1907280415

250516UK00007B/293/P